*Introduction to*

# EXCEPTIONAL
# CHILDREN

*Introduction to*

# EXCEPTIONAL CHILDREN

## Third Edition

Harry J. Baker, Ph.D.,

Divisional Director, Psychological Clinic
Detroit Public Schools

The Macmillan Company   New York

# *Foreword*

"My child is different!" This statement is heard frequently by teachers and administrators as they talk with parents. It is true, and one of the things which makes teaching a never ending challenge. In what way is the child different from everyone else? Are the differences ones which will aid or handicap his ability to learn and to become a competent and wholesome adult? What can or *should* the teacher and the school do to enhance or to minimize the effect of the exceptional abilities or deficiencies? These questions have puzzled educators for a long time. Research, experimentation, and experience have revealed much that can and should make it possible for the informed teacher and the school administrator today to be more understanding and more skilled in dealing with the problems of the child commonly termed "exceptional."

It is increasingly important that education for all pupils be more efficient than it has been. The demands on each individual are greater than ever and it appears these demands will increase rather than diminish. Job opportunities for the unskilled are declining. The need for more, better prepared, able persons increases faster and faster. Failure to refine more efficiently through education the talent of all individuals is to lower the potential of the nation. This we can ill afford.

The teacher or school administrator is increasingly aware that if he would be competent he needs to know more about the causes of special ability or disability of pupils, and to know what to expect from such pupils.

What has research and experience revealed that will help school
personnel to understand better the nature and causes of conditions
which handicap or facilitate learning of children who are commonly
classified as "exceptional"? How can the school provide the best conditions for these pupils? Dr. Harry Baker has the advantage of a lifetime of study and experience in relating research on problems of the
exceptional child to school practice. With this background he has
been able to make available in this book a wealth of information
which practicing and prospective teachers and administrators will
find useful. As this knowledge is applied wisely it is reasonable to
expect that more and more parents will thank the schools for recognizing how and why their child is different and for seeing that
schooling best adapted to his individual needs is provided.

S. M. Brownell

Superintendent of Public Schools
Detroit, Michigan

# Preface to the Third Edition

THE FIRST EDITION of this book was published in the War Year of 1944. It was a time when education was being reviewed with the stern eye of a nation in desperate need of a citizenry highly trained and resourcefully efficient. This scrutiny sought out not only the most highly trained segments of the population but demanded the full utilization of all citizens including the handicapped. It was a natural time to survey and to review the characteristics and the needs of all handicapped adults and children.

The demand for interpretation of exceptional children was so great that a Spanish edition of the first edition was published in Argentina. The second edition was published in 1953 and by that time the personnel trained in many areas of adjustment had returned to civilian duties, bringing with them a wealth of information with a new orientation on the education of exceptional children. Education now realized that the handicapped and the exceptional had potentialities which made them assets rather than liabilities. New interest was focused on the current generation of handicapped and exceptional children which included more extensive facilities for identification, diagnosis, education, vocational training, and placement.

The third edition is scheduled at an opportune time in the affairs of exceptional children. There has been a most encouraging development of "the team" approach to problems of exceptional children. The medical specialist, the psychologist, the social worker, the nurse, the teacher, the parent, and others often meet together and plan for the many phases of problems in this important area. This plan changes the orientation from isolated segments to the coordination of all factors which affect the entire child. All of these team members have brought in new discoveries and interpretations from their respective fields. The various specialists are sharing these findings liberally through their published accounts, and by personal appearance and their scientific papers given on convention programs such as at the International Council for Exceptional Children.

In preparation for the White House Conference on Child Health and Protection in 1930, it was the author's privilege to be chairman of one of eleven subcommittees on Special Education under the general chairmanship of Dr. Charles S. Berry. This assignment by President Hoover was the first serious and official attempt to coordinate a comprehensive plan for the educational needs of all exceptional children. In a two-day meeting of all subcommittee chairmen and in later meetings of all committees, most encouraging progress was made in cooperative planning. Possible differences in philosophies, in administrative policies, and in overlapping interests were handled judiciously and it was realized that through united effort much more could be accomplished. Present at these meetings were such individuals as Jane Neil of Chicago; Mrs. Winifred Hathaway from the National Society for the Prevention of Blindness; Dr. Wendell Phillips, founder of the American Federation of Organizations for the Hard of Hearing; Dr. Lee Travis from the University of Iowa Speech Clinic; Dr. Adele Smith in charge of education for the physically handicapped in New York City; Dr. Henry H. Goddard, with interest in the gifted, and other well-known leaders in the various fields.

In the preparation of this edition the author is greatly indebted to many individuals and organizations for pictures and illustrations which add immeasureably to the verbal descriptions. Thanks are also extended to many authors and publishers for short but important quotations, in which a sincere attempt has always been made to keep them within the meaning of their own contexts. Special appreciation is extended to Dr. Samuel M. Brownell, Superintendent of the Detroit Public Schools, for preparation of the Foreword in which his comprehensive philosophy of education for the exceptional has been ably stated.

Of greatest assistance has been the help and encouragement of my wife, Mrs. Hazel Joy Baker, for preparation of source materials and for many tasks necessary in the preparation and editing of this revised edition.

Harry J. Baker

# Contents

xi

# List of Tables

# List of Diagrams

# PART 1

*Introduction to the Field*

# CHAPTER 1

## General Education and Special Education

ONE OF THE principal goals of education is to insure that handicapped and exceptional children shall have equivalent, although not necessarily identical, education to that of nonhandicapped children. The exceptional differ from the nonhandicapped mainly in degree, rather than in kind. Because of the impairments and handicaps of the exceptional, some methods and procedures must be varied, but the general aims and purposes must be the same. Unless such aims and purposes are always kept in mind, the education of exceptional children becomes a thing apart, foreign and unrelated to the education of all children.

### Trends in American Educational Philosophy

As summarized by Taylor[1] there are three trends in American educational philosophy which furnish the background for education. The first of these is naturalism and instrumentalism, based on science. Its central emphasis is empirical, and reflects the thinking of William James and John Dewey. The second trend is rationalism which seeks to apprehend universal truths from the Greek philosophy of Aristotle and the medieval period of St. Thomas. The third trend is to analytical philosophy, which embodies the theory of knowledge,

[1] H. Taylor, "General Education," *Fifty-first Yearbook, Part I*, National Society for the Study of Education, The University of Chicago Press, Chicago, 1952, pp. 20-45.

3

the analysis of propositions, and the reduction of meaning to symbols and logical forms. Since these schools of philosophical thought represent quite widely differing ideas, and since each of them seeks to control education trends, there is some confusion in the basic foundations of education. The problem of a sound philosophy becomes more complex when dealing with the education of exceptional children.

### Education and Democracy

The colonization of America by the oppressed people of Europe, which eventually developed into the present democracy, was motivated by a need of and impulse for freedom. The democratic way of life was paralleled by the concept that only through universal education could such a democracy be developed and preserved. In it all the people must be intelligently informed and able to participate. Although education was left primarily to the states, the national government has from the start encouraged universal education. In Article III of the Ordinance of 1787 it was declared that: "Religion, morality, and knowledge being necessary to good government and the happiness of mankind, schools and the means of education shall forever be encouraged."

Education has always been related to the ways of life so that changes in the latter bring changes in the former. The early American needs for education were confined mainly to the three R's as a means for carrying on the simple transactions of rural life. With the development of a complex urban life, with modern inventions, and with the shift from individual ownership of farms and small businesses to employment in large industries, education has taken on much more important, complicated, and far-reaching aims, methods, techniques, and procedures.

In this complexity of modern life there is always the challenge that education shall not lag behind society and merely propagate what society has already experienced. It must not only interpret the past and relate it to the present, but set goals and ideals for the future as well. Just how effectively education has been able to perform this important function is still subject to differences of opinion. How well it is adjusted to the needs of exceptional children in this modern setting is as yet a greater problem.

In many countries education has been used as a dangerous but effective tool to foster philosophies of government and ways of life quite different from those in America and other democratic countries. In an article, "Education under the Nazis," Beard[1] states:

> Decree after decree shows that it is . . . openly hostile to every manifestation of free inquiry and discussion in the schools from the bottom to the top. The subjects taught, the books admitted to schoolrooms, the papers and magazines bought for libraries, and the very spirit of instruction are prescribed in minute detail. No room is left for private opinion.

Although that particular system of education fell to the superior military achievement of democracies, somewhat similar forms continue to rise elsewhere and challenge educational freedom. Very insidious forms, known as "brain-washing," attempt to change the beliefs and attitudes of adults without waiting for longer change in maturing children.

### Education of American Adults

Since education of all the people is an important goal in free democracy, it is timely to consider the educational status of American adults. Although the picture is far from ideal, it is still ahead of most other countries. The United States Census of 1950 showed that the average grade reached by adults over twenty-five years of age was 9.3. Table I shows the details.

In the decennial period from 1940 the average grade had moved up one full grade; the per cent with no school had been reduced from 3.8 to 2.5; and the per cent finishing college had increased from 4.6 to 6.0. Particular attention should be directed to the more than two million who had no schooling and to those who reached grades 1 to 4. Undoubtedly many of them were handicapped by some physical, sensory, mental, or emotional disability, and for whom some special

[1] C. A. Beard, "Education under the Nazis," *Foreign Affairs*, 1936, 14, pp. 437-452.

TABLE I

Grades Reached by American Adults over Twenty-Five
Years of Age, 1950 Census

| Grade Reached | Number | Per cent |
|---|---|---|
| None | 2,184,355 | 2.5 |
| 1-4 | 7,270,465 | 8.3 |
| 5-6 | 7,975,945 | 9.1 |
| 7 | 5,985,955 | 6.8 |
| 8 | 17,741,510 | 20.2 |
| Hi. 1-3 | 14,857,660 | 17.1 |
| 4 | 17,678,930 | 20.2 |
| Col. 1-3 | 6,261,635 | 7.2 |
| 4 | 5,284,445 | 6.0 |
| Not reported | 2,329,675 | 2.6 |
| Total | 87,570,575 | 100.0 |

educational provision should have been made. At the other extreme, only one out of every sixteen adults had completed a four-year college course at a time when leadership was most urgently needed. A comprehensive and realistic view of education becomes the order of the day.

## Educational Objectives

Excellent attempts have been made in statements of educational objectives. Many authors were puzzled and confused about how to isolate specific issues independently of each other since life itself is complex. Education and life should be so synonymous that the objectives of one are the objectives of the other. In the search for specific educational objectives, areas of human activity have been minutely subdivided. Frederick and Farquear[1] made a survey of educational objectives and tabulated forty-four classifications with a total of 349 areas listed. Any list which attempts to divide objectives into too many areas becomes cumbersome, whereas one that is too simple and brief may be so general that it lacks useful, specific force. A middle ground

[1] O.I. Frederick and L.J. Farquear, "Problems of Life," I and II. *School Review*, 1938, 46, pp. 337-345 and 415-422.

is more desirable. In 1861 Herbert Spencer[1] offered a practical five-fold classification of human activities as a basis for educational objectives:

(1) self-preservation
(2) securing the necessities of life
(3) the rearing and discipline of offspring
(4) the maintenance of proper social and political relations, and
(5) the activities which make up the leisure part of life, devoted to the gratification of the tastes and feelings.

A widely quoted list of aims was contained in the 1918 Report of the Commission of Reorganization of Secondary Education of the National Education Association.[2] These aims were known as the seven cardinal principles of education and are as follows: (1) health, (2) command of the fundamental processes, (3) worthy home-membership, (4) vocation, (5) citizenship, (6) worthy use of leisure, and (7) ethical character.

The Department of Superintendence of the National Education Association[3] in 1928 listed four areas of the curriculum related to the individual as: (1) to his own growth and development, (2) to the world of nature, (3) to the systems of organized society, and (4) to the Power which in some ways orders the development of man and his universe.

### The Purposes of Education in American Democracy

The Educational Policies Commission of the National Education Association and the American Association of School Administrators[4] prepared a comprehensive statement of purposes of education in American democracy. They are: (1) self-realization, (2) human rela-

---

[1] H. Spencer, *Education*, D. Appleton-Century Company, Inc., New York, 1861, p. 32.

[2] U.S. Department of the Interior, Bureau of Education, *Cardinal Principles of Secondary Education*, Government Printing Office, Washington, D.C., 1918, p. 32.

[3] National Education Association, Department of Superintendence, *The Development of the High School Curriculum*, Sixth yearbook, Department of Superintendence, Washington, D.C., 1928, pp. 51-56.

[4] Educational Policies Commission, *The Purposes of Education in American Democracy*, National Education Association, Washington, D.C., 1938, 157 pp.

tionships, (3) economic efficiency, and (4) civic responsibility. Each of these is related to each of the others in the total life of the individual and in the total educational program. Each of these four is capable of further subdivision; for example, the objectives of self-realization are as follows:

## The Objectives of Self-Realization[1]

*The Inquiring Mind.* The educated person has an appetite for learning.
*Speech.* The educated person can speak the mother tongue clearly.
*Reading.* The educated person reads the mother tongue effectively.
*Writing.* The educated person writes the mother tongue effectively.
*Number.* The educated person solves his problem of counting and calculating.
*Sight and Hearing.* The educated person is skilled in listening and observing.
*Health Knowledge.* The educated person understands the basic facts concerning health and disease.
*Health Habits.* The educated person protects his own health and that of his dependents.
*Public Health.* The educated person works to improve the health of the community.
*Recreation.* The educated person is participant and spectator in many sports and other pastimes.
*Intellectual Interest.* The educated person has mental resources for the use of leisure.
*Esthetic Interests.* The educated person appreciates beauty.
*Character.* The educated person gives responsible direction to his own life.

These worthy objectives are a challenge in the education of the non-handicapped child, but are doubly so for the exceptional child. At once it is realized that exceptional children are deficient in some of the very tools with which to attain self-realization. Many are defective in sight or are totally blind. Others are hard-of-hearing or totally deaf; some have speech defects, lowered vitality, limited mental processes, defects of character, and other handicaps. The challenge readily becomes clear that all remediable defects must be corrected, that the uncorrectable one be utilized intelligently and effectively, and that, so far as possible, others be substituted and utilized in maximum ways.

[1] Education Policies Commission, *ibid.*, p. 50. Quoted by permission.

This first objective of self-realization implies the optimum utilization of normal physical and mental faculties, yet the very tools of self-realization themselves are faulty and inadequate. The real significance of an education suited to the needs and the abilities of exceptional children becomes apparent in a very striking way.

*Human relationships.* This second objective faces problems in various kinds of exceptional children. Friendship and cooperation are basic factors, but they are difficult to achieve if the individual cannot meet his associates on an equal basis. He may be accepted in an apologetic way, out of sympathy, which he rejects as distasteful; or he may be rejected outright by an uncharitable and selfish world. The mentally retarded child cannot match wits against more favored associates, the crippled child cannot take his place in the football game, and the poor reader is not accepted by his classmates. Many of the exceptional set up barriers of aloofness, of unsocial behavior, or of inferiority feelings to offset their inadequate and unsatisfactory human relationships. Many of the things which are taken for granted in the nonhandicapped child for the establishment of good human relationships must be nurtured and developed in exceptional children before they can be put to effective use. Yet the goal of good human relationships is possibly of greater importance in the case of the exceptional so that they may achieve the other objectives as well.

*Economic efficiency.* This objective includes satisfaction of good workmanship, wise occupational choice, good judgment in buying, and in personal economics. Since it is difficult for the nonhandicapped to achieve these objectives it may be doubly hard for the exceptional. The difficulties of wise occupational choice and adequate workmanship are well known in the fields of the handicapped, yet they are very necessary if life is to be maintained on a level above charity. With limited incomes and with unusual expenses for health protection, wise personal economics far beyond those of the nonhandicapped are necessary and must be realized. These problems will be discussed to some extent in the sections about various types of the handicapped.

*Civic responsibility.* Civic responsibility includes social activity, social understanding, tolerance, political citizenship, and devotion to democracy. Unless the first three objects are realized without undue strain, it is a very trying problem to accept one's civic responsibility with zeal, with enthusiasm, and with pleasure. It is only by wide understanding and by judicious training that the exceptional are able to face life's problems from this point of view. A small but increasing percentage of the exceptional have any recognition or special education and those who do not are obviously faced with discouragement in regard to their civic responsibility. Some of them resign themselves to inevitable pessimism and discouragement, others actively rebel against society with deviant behavior and personality maladjustments even at an early age.

While these four objectives are worthy and highly desirable for the exceptional, as well as for the nonhandicapped, it must be realized that they are inherently more difficult for the handicapped. The greater the task, the greater is the challenge. The examples of many famous individuals with such extreme handicaps as complete deafness, blindness, and other disabilities furnish proof that worthy objectives may be attained.

### Definitions of the Exceptional

There is no single term which appropriately describes all types of exceptional children. The term "exceptional" is probably the most suitable of several, although in the popular mind it means only the mentally gifted. According to dictionary definitions, the term gives the impression of something very unusual, outstanding, extraordinary, or rare. One of the greatest obstacles to a better and more complete program of special education for exceptional children arises from the widespread misconception that they represent a class, separate and distinct from normal children. An important objective is to relate the education of the exceptional to that of normal, average children in logical and meaningful ways. Many exceptional children with lesser handicaps continue to be taught in regular grades and the present philosophy stresses intermingling with the nonhandicapped as far as possible.

The types of exceptional children discussed in this book cover a wide range for two reasons: (1) to bridge a gap between the normal or average child and the extremely handicapped or exceptional, and (2) to interpret the needs of the mildly handicapped who are often more neglected and misunderstood than are those with extreme deviations. "Exceptional" is a more inclusive term than "handicapped," since it includes children at both extremes of several different factors. The committee of the National Society for the Study of Education dealing with the education of exceptional children proposed the following definition: "those who deviate from what is supposed to be average in physical, mental, emotional, or social characteristics to such an extent that they require special educational services in order to develop to their maximum capacity."[1]

In this definition emphasis is upon "services" which is an all-inclusive term. It may mean a teacher assigned to teach children confined to bed in hospitals or at home; it may mean an itinerant teacher who helps the regular teacher at stated times; it may mean a special class in which exceptional pupils learn the professional phases of their schooling, but join regular pupils in class discussion; or, it may mean a completely segregated class or special school.

### Types of the Exceptional

There are many types of exceptional children. There is no completely satisfactory order in which they should be discussed. One of the major obstacles to a satisfactory sequence is the fact that many exceptional children represent combinations of emotional, physical, social, and mental characteristics. It is necessary from time to time, at the risk of being repetitious, to call attention to discussions of related handicaps appearing in earlier or in later chapters. The order of chapters has been changed from the two earlier editions of this book in which the sensory disorders and defects were introduced first. They have been replaced by the four chapters of Part 2 which deal with disorders of mental health and deviant behavior which presently seem to be the topics of most concern to teachers, school administrators, and parents.

[1] National Society for the Study of Education, *Forty-ninth Yearbook, Part II,* University of Chicago Press, Chicago, 1950, p. 3.

Part 3 consists of five chapters on the general topics of neurological disorders and diseases. After a description of the nervous system, other problems discussed will include convulsive disorders, cerebral palsy, brain injuries, and mental disorders and diseases. Children with some of these impairments are sometimes incorrectly considered as showing deviant behavior from causes other than those of neurological origin.

Part 4 has four chapters which discuss intellectual abilities and aptitudes. After a general description, chapters follow on the mentally retarded and the mentally accelerated. A fourth chapter touches upon the slow-learning and the rapid-learning who are usually enrolled in regular classes, but whose problems are different enough from those of average children to warrant some interpretation.

Part 5 has two chapters on deviations in educational achievement. Pupils in this category appear to have no obvious physical, mental, or other defect and yet do not progress satisfactorily in school. They often have particular difficulties in reading. Descriptions of some programs are offered and suggestions are made about what the schools should do for these students.

Part 6 contains six chapters. The first three are concerned with visual defects and disorders and the second three are about impairments of hearing. In each set of chapters a general description of the anatomy and physiology of the eye or ear is presented. There is a second chapter about partial handicaps requiring special educational services, and a third chapter on the totally impaired.

Part 7 contains six chapters on various physical disorders and defects. The two chapters on speech and its disorders might well be included in Part 2, since they involve many problems of mental health in addition to the physical basis of some speech disorders. Speech disorders point up the need for a very comprehensive approach to the entire child. There is a chapter on orthopedic defects, another on defects and disorders in vitality, another on growth, and a chapter on a miscellaneous group of physical defects.

Part 8 closes with three chapters on sociological and community responsibility for exceptional children. In this part an attempt has been made to show that the schools alone cannot or should not be expected to carry the complete responsibility for exceptional children.

## The Curriculum

Within general limits there are certain basic portions of the school curriculum which should be provided for all children. In many kinds of exceptional children the modern philosophy requires that they shall participate as far as possible with pupils in regular classes to gain the benefits of a normal situation. Preparation may have to be made under the direction of a teacher especially trained in their particular types of handicaps. In such cases the special teacher must keep abreast of curriculum materials and must have constant conferences with teachers of regular classes. In instances where it is not possible to have participation with regular classes, the special teacher must keep herself informed of and be familiar with the curriculum suitable to the grades and ages of her pupils.

For many types of exceptional children, the teacher has a second important problem of opening up the avenues of communication so that the curriculum may function. For example, the development of speech and understanding in the totally deaf child must proceed in its early stages before learning of fundamental subjects may be undertaken, and, hence, should begin earlier than the usual age of school entrance. The mentally retarded child must have a minimum curriculum, while the mentally gifted individual deserves enrichment with a possibility of acceleration. Many hospitalized and home-bound children are receiving the benefit of special teachers who must not only instruct but also attempt to preserve the spirit and atmosphere of study and class participation as best they can. Particularly difficult are cases in which no physical activity is possible so that even handwriting or other handwork cannot be undertaken.

While a great amount of curriculum materials has been adapted, any changes in the regular curriculum sometimes work hardships and add additional expenses; for instance, transforming it into Braille for the blind or printing it in the large, Clear Type for the partially-seeing. In any event, problems of curriculum for exceptional children are a constant challenge which must be shared by the special teacher and the regular teacher. There are probably many ways of learning used by the special teacher which might be beneficial to the regular classes in modified form. The field of exceptional children is necessarily an experimental laboratory of education which has uses beyond those of its own groups.

### Teachers and Teacher Training

Enough has just been said about the curriculum to show that the characteristics and training of special teachers for exceptional children is not a simple and minimum requirement. The special teacher must take required courses leading to knowledge and mastery of subject matter and its adaptation to exceptional children. In addition she must take broad training in the psychology of exceptional children, in the anatomy and physiology of handicaps and in how to develop the capabilities of such children. The special teacher must be versatile in dealing with children who are basically frustrated or confused. She must cooperate with their parents, with the medical profession, and with the regular teachers so that her special class or group is an integral part of the school. Because of these many requirements, there is always a shortage of teachers for exceptional children. This shortage exists although classes are usually smaller and some school systems provide an additional salary increment. This shortage existed in the depression days when there was an oversupply of regular teachers.

### Organization and Administration

The organization and administration of a department of special education is a principal responsibility of the school administrative staff. Since this area is highly specialized, a few teachers who have had some training could be organized into a team to work with the administration in setting up the program. Many State Departments of Public Instruction are now employing specialists to assist local systems with such problems, and in some states, such service is provided by counties.

A first step is the survey of needs to determine what areas should be covered. In some states it is possible to plan on a whole area of school districts as a unit, although this requires cooperative action. Special units of regular buildings, or, in large communities, entire buildings may be planned for several groups of exceptional children. A good example is the Jane Neil School for the Physically Handicapped in the Chicago public schools. Since many types of exceptional children require special equipment, rooms should be selected which are relatively permanent. In general, rooms should be cheerful and well lighted since many exceptional children have been discouraged and frustrated by their handicaps. Giving them the least attractive and basement rooms or the oldest buildings does them a great disservice.

Administration has many other problems in the education of handicapped and exceptional children. Special transportation, lunch room service, selling the program to parents and the public, and continually giving the attention which it merits are only a few of them. Above all, it must be remembered that the exceptional children are *children* and should be made to feel welcome, comfortable, and a real part of the school or school system.

## General Plan of Presentation

In a preceding section exceptional children were classified into several principal groups with many subdivisions under each. The total field is large and its coverage needs to be comprehensive since each subtype is worthy of very extensive discussion. In this presentation there is no set or uniform pattern of subtopic presentation since each type of the exceptional has unique problems and characteristics. Attempts will be made to give satisfactory definitions. In the field of diagnosis some general clues are offered which teachers may observe; the more detailed diagnostic procedures by specialists are outlined if they also give further insight into unique characteristics. The assistance of medical specialists who are becoming more available is a very hopeful assist in interpreting the assets and the limitations of the handicapped. The number of cases gives useful information about the extent of the problem. Some attempt is also made to distinguish between types of pupils who may remain in regular classes, those who may succeed in special classes, and those whose handicaps are so severe that hospitalization or permanent care is necessary. The history of what has been known about the handicap and what has been done about it over the years adds perspective to the present problem. The causes, remedies, and preventive measures often go hand in hand and are sometimes presented as a unit.

At the ends of the chapters there are questions and topics for further discussions which could easily carry the interested student much beyond the minimum outline of the chapter itself. The bibliographies list many entire books devoted to a single type of handicap and the references to periodical literature report many current studies and investigations. There has been a great and encouraging increase in the number of local, state, national, and international organizations of parents, or professional workers in many specialized fields of the handicapped. They publish periodicals and do much to promote interest in and provision for the particular handicap. Many of them have reprints of articles or other interpretations which are distributed free or for a nominal price. Some listing of films has also been attempted, since a visual presentation often tells much more than the printed word. By the effective use of these outlines and references, it is possible for students and for teachers individually, in groups, or by workshop methods to expand their interests in any field of the exceptional.

Finally it should be emphasized that all discussions of the handicapped and the exceptional imply a warm and intimate understanding of children. Although diagnostic devices seem somewhat impersonal, it is never to be implied that they are administered or interpreted in a cold, matter-of-fact manner. It is the purpose of all treatment that the best shall be developed in each exceptional child.

## Questions and Topics for Discussion

1. Make a more detailed report on the types of objectives cited by Frederick and Farquear (see footnote reference).
2. Make a further report on the objectives as outlined by the Educational Policies Commission.
3. Discuss any special aims and objectives which you believe should be developed to apply especially to exceptional children.
4. Give your own first impression of any exceptional children whom you have known earlier as classmates.

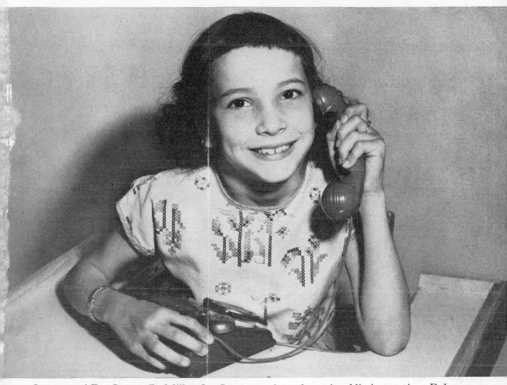

The exceptional child is first of all a child.

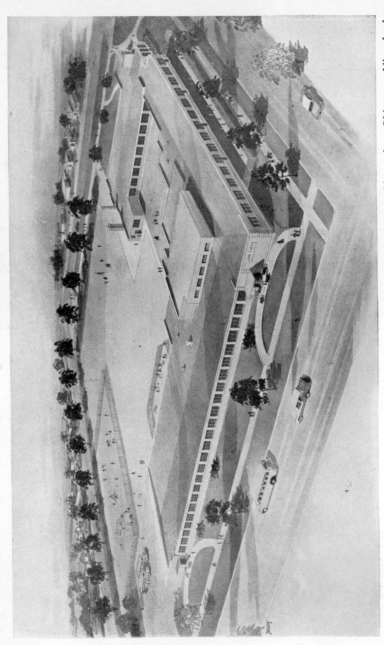

*Courtesy of photographic services, Chicago public schools.*

Jane A. Neil School for physically handicapped children, Chicago.

5. Report on any type of special class which you have visited.
6. List some ways in which special education can be made similar to that of regular classes.

## A. *Organizations*

1. American Association of School Administrators, Washington, D.C.
2. American Council on Education, Washington, D.C.
3. American Educational Research Association, Washington, D.C.
4. Association of Supervision and Curriculum Development, Washington, D.C.
5. Council for Exceptional Children, Washington, D.C.
6. National Education Association, Washington, D.C.
7. Society for the Advancement of Education, 1834 Broadway, New York 23.

Note: For national organizations in specific fields of exceptional children see organizations at end of various chapters.

## B. *Periodicals*

1. *American School Board Journal* (monthly), Bruce Publishing Company, Milwaukee, Wis.
2. *Educational Administration and Supervision* (monthly except June and September), Warwick and York, Baltimore, Md.
3. *Elementary School Journal* (monthly October to May), University of Chicago Press, Chicago.
4. *Educational Leadership* (monthly October to May), Association of Supervision and Curriculum Development of the National Education Association.
5. *Exceptional Children* (monthly October to May), Council for Exceptional Children, Washington, D.C.
6. *Journal of Teacher Education* (quarterly), National Committee on Teacher Education and Professional Standards, National Education Association.
7. *Nation's Schools* (monthly), 919 N. Michigan Ave., Chicago 11.
8. *N. E. A. Journal* (monthly), National Education Association, Washington, D.C.
9. *Review of Educational Research* (five numbers annually), American Educational Research Association, Washington, D.C.
10. *School and Society* (biweekly except July and August), Society for the Advancement of Education, 1834 Broadway, New York 23.

## C. Books

### Section I. General Education

1. American Educational Research Association, "Educational Organization, Administration, and Finance," *Review of Educational Research*, Vol. XXV, No. 4, October, 1955, pp. 277-364.
2. Bode, B.H., *Fundamentals of Education*, The Macmillan Co., New York, 1921, 245 pp.
3. Breed, F.S., *Education and the New Realism*, The Macmillan Co., New York, 1939, 237 pp.
4. Broudy, H.S., *Building a Philosophy of Education*, Prentice-Hall, Inc., Englewood Cliffs, N.J., 1954, 214 pp.
5. Cole, L.W., *A History of Education*, Rinehart and Co., Inc., New York, 1950, 700 pp.
6. Dewey, J., *Democracy and Education*, The Macmillan Co., New York, 1916, 434 pp.
7. ———, *Experience and Education*, The Macmillan Co., New York, 1938, 116 pp.
8. Educational Policies Commission, *Education for All American Children*, National Education Association, Washington, D.C., 1948, 292 pp.
9. ———, *The Education of Free Men in American Democracy*, National Education Association, Washington, D.C., 1941, 115 pp.
10. ———, *The Purposes of Education in American Democracy*, National Education Association, Washington, D.C., 1938, 157 pp.
11. ———, *The Structure and Administration of Education in American Democracy*, National Education Association, Washington, D.C., 1938, 128 pp.
12. Fitzpatrick, E.A., *Philosophy of Education*, Bruce Publishing Co., Milwaukee, Wis., 1953, 477 pp.
13. Kilpatrick, W.H., *Education for a Changing Civilization*, The Macmillan Co., New York, 1926, 143 pp.
14. Lawson, D.E., *School Administration*, The Odyssey Press, Inc., New York, 1953, 405 pp.
15. Mickelson, P.P., and K.H. Hansen, *Elementary School Administration*, McGraw-Hill Book Co., Inc., New York, 1957, 335 pp.
16. Mort, P.R., and D.H. Ross, *Principles of School Administration* (rev. ed.), McGraw-Hill Book Co., Inc., New York, 1957, 451 pp.
17. National Education Association, Department of Elementary School Principals, *The Elementary-School Principalship—Today and To-*

morrow, Twenty-seventh Yearbook, Washington, D.C., 1948, 412 pp.

18. National Society for the Study of Education, *General Education*, Fifty-first Yearbook, Part I, University of Chicago Press, Chicago, 1952, 377 pp.
19. Sayers, E.V., *A First Course in Philosophy of Education*, Henry Holt and Co., Inc., New York, 1950, 399 pp.
20. Wahlquist, J.T. et al., *The Administration of Public Education*, Ronald Press Co., New York, 1920, 611 pp.

## Section II. Special Education

1. American Educational Research Association, "The Education of Exceptional Children," *Review of Educational Research*, Vol. XXIII, No. 5, December, 1953, pp. 387-554.
2. Cruickshank, W.M. (ed.), *Psychology of Exceptional Children and Youth*, Prentice-Hall, Inc., Englewood Cliffs, N.J., 1955, 594 pp.
3. Cruickshank, W.M., and G.O. Johnson, (eds.), *Education of Exceptional Children and Youth*, Prentice-Hall, Inc., Englewood Cliffs, N.J., 1958, 723 pp.
4. Frampton, M.E., and E.D. Gall (eds.), *Special Education for the Exceptional*, Vol. I, 453 pp.; Vol. II, 677 pp.; Vol. III, 699 pp. Porter Sargent Publisher, Boston, 1955 and 1956.
5. Frampton, M.E., and H.G. Rowell, *Education of the Handicapped*, Vol. I, *History*, World Book Co., Yonkers, N.Y., 1938, 260 pp.
6. ———, and ———, *Education of the Handicapped*, Vol II, *Problems*, World Book Co., Yonkers, N.Y., 1940, 440 pp.
7. Garrison, K.C., *The Psychology of Exceptional Children* (rev. ed.), Ronald Press Co., New York, 1950, 517 pp.
8. Goodenough, F.L., *Exceptional Children*, Appleton-Century-Crofts, Inc., New York, 1956, 428 pp.
9. Hayes, E.N. (ed.), *Directory for Exceptional Children* (2nd ed.), Porter Sargent Publisher, Boston, 1956, 247 pp.
10. Heck, A.O., *The Education of Exceptional Children* (2nd. ed.), McGraw-Hill Book Co., Inc., New York, 1953, 513 pp.
11. Louttit, C.M., *Clinical Psychology of Exceptional Children* (3rd ed.), Harper & Brothers, New York, 1957, 573 pp.
12. Michal-Smith, H. (ed.), *Management of the Handicapped Child*, Grune and Stratton, Inc., New York, 1957, 276 pp.
13. National Society for the Study of Education, *The Education of Exceptional Children*, Forty-ninth Yearbook, Part II, University of Chicago Press, Chicago, 1950, 350 pp.
14. Pintner, R., J. Eisenson, and M. Stanton, *The Psychology of the Physically Handicapped*, F.S. Crofts Co., New York, 1940, 391 pp.

15. Scheidemann, N.V., *The Psychology of Exceptional Children*, Houghton Mifflin Co., Boston, 1931, 520 pp.
16. ———, *The Psychology of Exceptional Children*, Vol. II, Houghton Mifflin Company, Boston, 1937, 460 pp.
17. Wallin, J.E.W., *The Education of Handicapped Children*, Houghton Mifflin Co., Boston, 1924, 394 pp.
18. White House Conference, *Special Education: The Handicapped and the Gifted*, D. Appleton-Century Co., New York, 1931, 604 pp.
19. ———, *The Handicapped Child*, D. Appleton-Century Co., New York, 1933, 452 pp.

### D. Films and Filmstrips

1. *Defining Democracy*, 18 minutes, sound. An excellent short definition of democracy for teachers. Encyclopaedia Britannica Films, 1150 Wilmette Ave., Wilmette, Ill.
2. *Design of American Public Education*, 16 minutes, sound. Aims and organization of our democratic school system. McGraw-Hill Text-Film Department, New York.
3. *The American Teacher*, 20 minutes, sound. Increased responsibility of citizens in a modern democracy for the education of youth. March of Time.

At the national level the Federal Security Agency, Office of Education, publishes a series of bulletins and pamphlets under the editorship of Dr. Romaine Mackie and others on many types of exceptional children and encourages research and promotion of their education. The United States Government Printing Office, Washington, D.C., lists the costs of these reports and publications in its current catalogue.

# CHAPTER 2

## Inventories of
## Pupil Populations

It has just been noted that in the problems of general education and in the organization and administration of special education for exceptional children major attention is necessarily directed to entire classes, schools, and entire school systems. Behind this general background attention must necessarily be given to the individual characteristics and needs of each child. The major emphasis in this book is upon the individual child who is afflicted with some type of handicap or who possesses abilities different from those of the average child. Parents are interested in a general way in the excellence of education for all children, but they are more specifically interested in what the school is able to do for their own children. Any exceptional child commands unusually high parental interest, since he must succeed regardless of handicap. Ideally, extra care should be given to the education of the exceptional child so that it may compensate for his handicap.

If there is to be individual attention to all handicapped and nonhandicapped children, inventories of their many qualities and their characteristics must be available. Some of the more important types of inventories and basic information will be discussed. It is assumed that appropriate recording forms should be available.

*Identifying data.* The full name, with correct spelling is first in order. If there are broken families and if two different names are used, or names have been changed by adoption, both should appear

21

on records and a cross reference will permit them to be located under alphabetical filing according to surnames. In a similar manner names of parents or legal guardians should be entered. The residence address with telephone number should be recorded and additional spaces provided since many parents occasionally move. If there is a family physician his name and telephone number should be available in case of emergency. The birthdate of the child should be correctly verified by medical registration, baptismal certificate, or other official papers. In many states no identification by race or color is permitted. The sex record should be entered since names are often confusing.

*Health record.* Because there is a large concentration of children in school buildings, there are dangers of epidemics from contagious diseases. For this reason, as well as for the health and safety of all individual pupils, a comprehensive examination and record of results should be available. Before school entrance, and preferably in the early years of childhood, various inoculations and vaccinations should be made as a major responsibility of parents. Reports should be furnished to schools; this is more commonly done by parents in advance of first school registration. Whenever such precautions have not been taken, they should be required, unless there is religious objection by parents.

It is particularly important that reports of general physical examinations should also be available. The conditions of vision and hearing are among the most vital factors. If they are greatly impaired, communication is impossible and regular schooling is obviously ineffective. The general state of nutrition and the condition of the heart and other vital organs should be known. There is a general trend to enter on health records only conditions which are known to be in need of correction. The teacher is usually required to make a quick inspection each morning to note signs of high temperature or other symptoms that suggest a sick child. Although there is less significance attached to height and to weight than before, some authorities have found relationships between fluctuations in growth and variations in personality attributes. For a few individuals who vary quite markedly from the usual norms, measurements of height and weight are of considerable importance.

*Scholastic records.* Various school systems have many types of scholastic records. Some are on a letter basis, usually at least four or five letters; others mark "satisfactory" or "unsatisfactory"; a few use the one hundred per cent basis; and some have no formal marks but substitute explanatory letters to each parent. Secondary schools keep a cumulative scholastic record. The usual practice in elementary schools is to keep such records either annually or by semesters, with little continuity from year to year. Parents may use them effectively to prove some particular point in their favor.

Achievement test records are valuable and are quite universally used. In their simpler forms they may be used as early as in the first grade. In the intermediate or upper elementary grades achievement tests are given in almost all subjects while in high schools they are also available in the regular and special subjects. Several publishing companies have catalogues with complete lines of achievement tests for commercial use. Many of them also provide for machine scoring and mechanical reporting of results.

*Tests of aptitudes.* A great variety of group tests of mental ability are in very common use. There are also tests of mechanical and clerical aptitude, musical and artistic aptitude, and of various aptitudes in other fields. Many of these tests are repeated with alternate forms as often as every two or three years. The achievement tests may be given as often as once a year and some short forms may be used throughout the school year.

Personality inventories are coming into more common use. In the early primary grades the ratings may have to be made by the teachers, or if the tests are in pictorial form, the pupil may choose an appropriate answer to a question about the story which is orally presented or printed in simple language. In higher grades pupils read and check from five-choice answers or from "yes," "no," or "neutral" opinions. Some of these inventories will be discussed in Chapter 6.

*Other records.* Schools may have a somewhat confidential file of facts about family history, such as records of adopted children or guardianships of unusual character, which may be pertinent to the welfare of the child. A small percentage of emotionally disturbed parents are constantly visiting the schools and filing complaints based on children's interpretations which are often far from the actual facts. School administrators must use unusually good judgment in the selection and filing of such materials.

## Record Systems

Many kinds of information have been suggested. In most instances, perhaps as a result of formal tests, record forms are provided by the authors and publishers. Health and attendance forms are published by large systems; in some states there are state-wide forms for some items. The total result may be a large number of separate forms of varying sizes. It is possible to insert all of them in a large envelope for each pupil and alphabetize them in a central file in the principal's office. For the more specific and frequent use of the classroom teacher some records should also be available in her room, but provision for secrecy from pupil scrutiny is necessary. Within the envelope for each pupil there should be an orderly and uniform arrangement of these various records if they are to be of any practical use. This list of materials should either be printed on the outside of the master envelope or be the first item for easy reference.

From time to time school systems make surveys of certain facts about a large number of pupils from all schools of the district. Results of achievement or aptitude tests, age-grade reports, or age-grade-progress are some examples. In such projects it is possible to code the data for mechanical tabulation since tabulations by hand would be very slow and laborious and would permit a greater percentage of error. Such methods are not useful within a single school building, but they would be possible if sufficient clerical help were available. The principal of a building or individual teachers should keep special lists of such information as children with chronic illness, those with poor attendance, those in need of mental hygiene services, and potential candidates for various types of special classes for exceptional children.

In addition to the records kept within each school there are central bureaus which must keep records according to state laws in connection with state aid for local systems. Such records are usually kept according to families and addresses which are obtained from an annual compulsory house-to-house canvas in some states. Records are kept of transfers to and from other school districts and also enumerate enrollments in private and in parochial schools as well as in public schools. Since questions of importance with possible legal implications may occur at any time in the individual's life, the pupils' records are usually kept in the regular buildings for many years.

Clinics and bureaus of child study, child guidance, and psychological testing usually keep a set of special records in a central location. These records are mainly limited to a comparatively small but important segment of the school population. Requests by schools for such service, results of tests and interviews, and reports to schools or to interested community agencies are on file. A more detailed family and case history is part of the record. If a child has been serviced several times during his school life, a file record of considerable proportions has developed. It is becoming more and more important that these special records be kept during the lifetime of the individual. As time progresses records of families for several generations may be assembled which offer practical, rather than merely theoretical, information in sociological areas. Information from such records has been extremely useful in the selection and evaluation of draftees for military duty whenever a minimum of time and facilities are available for thorough investigations. Similarly, organizations such as the Veterans Administration are able to get a more accurate longitudinal description of individuals who are currently in disturbed emotional states and whose pre-service status or condition should also be known. Many other governmental and community agencies find these records, as well as those kept in school buildings, to be of great value. Because of the volume of such records in various communities, microfilming them for economy in filing space is coming into more common use. In the Psychological Clinic of the Detroit Public Schools, one and one-half million such records dating back to the year 1910, when the Clinic was organized, are on microfilm.

In addition to these records there are specialized records for children with physical, sensory, emotional, or other handicaps which should be kept in connection with their special class. Such records may include the detailed analysis of hearing loss in either ear, the status of eyes in impaired vision or total blindness, the analysis of specific causes and conditions in impaired speech, orthopedic conditions, and many others. If there are special teachers of such exceptional children, they need to confer and to interpret such records to regular teachers who may be sharing educational programs with them. In the event that there are no special teachers it is important for the regular teacher to understand the principal implication of such records for which she is responsible.

### Records and the Teacher

For the various areas of records which have just been outlined, it is necessary for the school administration and teachers to keep a proper perspective. On the negative side it must be recognized that teachers have other duties in the instruction of children which occupy most of their professional teaching time. If teachers must spend much time in addition to their regular duties in gathering and recording data, the beneficial results may be heavily discounted. In many instances the scoring and the recording of achievement, aptitude, and adjustment inventories add to the clerical work, although it may be somewhat lessened by mechanized scoring techniques. Teachers must recognize specific values in all types of records for their own use and in interpreting the needs of their pupils to offset the detailed work involved in developing and keeping them.

In addition to the general use of records which identifies the over-all pattern of the class, many of the specific records about each individual pupil may not necessarily be reviewed every day since their status has become generally familiar to the teacher. However, when unusual conditions arise, or when conferences are necessary with parents of representatives of community agencies, this reserve of additional information is invaluable. At such times it establishes that, although the schools deal with great numbers of children, they are also, as parents expect, acquainted with the characteristics and needs of each individual child. Some teachers find that extensive anecdotal records are also very helpful.

The specialized teachers of exceptional children must be familiar with a great variety of records beyond those used by regular teachers. They must make greater daily use of them since the pupils' handicaps interject additional problems in teaching. The teaching of exceptional children emphasizes that the child rather than the class is the principal focus and, therefore, detailed records play a very important part.

In the use of all records both by regular and special teachers, professional ethics should guide in proper and wise interpretation. Teachers should regard them with the same care exercised by the family physician, the dentist, the attorney, or the banker. Records may be both beneficial and dangerous; for this reason, proper perspective must always be maintained. Certain records should be so confidential that they are not usually subject to local or state subpoena. Care must be exercised in this important area.

## Questions and Topics for Discussion

1. Make up a sample record form of identifying data.
2. Discuss samples of health record forms from your local school system.
3. Describe and discuss the various systems of scholastic marks or grades.
4. Have a qualified psychologist discuss and explain tests of achievement, intelligence, and personality.
5. Discuss systems of permanent records.

## A. Organizations

1. American Educational Research Association, 1201 16th St., N. W., Washington 6, D.C.
2. National Conference for Measurements Used in Education, R.D. North, Secretary-Treasurer, 21 Audubon Ave., New York 32.

## B. Periodicals

1. *Education* (monthly September to May), The Palmer Co., Hingham, Mass.
2. *Educational and Psychological Measurement* (quarterly), G.F. Kuder (ed.), College Station, Durham, N.C.

3. *Journal of Applied Psychology* (bimonthly), American Psychological Association, Washington 6, D.C.
4. *Journal of Educational Research* (monthly), Dembar Publications, Madison, Wis.
5. *Review of Educational Research* (five numbers annually), American Educational Research Association, Washington, D.C.

## C. Books

1. Buros, O. (ed.), *The Fourth Mental Measurements Yearbook*, The Gryphon Press, Highland Park, N.J., 1953, 1163 pp.
2. Greene, H.A., A.N. Jorgensen, and J.R. Gerberich, *Measurement and Evaluation in the Elementary School*, Longmans Green and Co., New York, 1953, 617 pp.
3. Lindquist, E.F. (ed.), *Educational Measurement*, American Council on Education, Washington, D.C., 1955, 819 pp.
4. Thorndike, R.L., and E. Hagen, *Measurement and Evaluation in Psychology and Education*, John Wiley and Sons, Inc., New York, 1955, 575 pp.
5. Torgerson, T.L., and G.S. Adams, *Measurement and Evaluation*, Dryden Press, New York, 1954, 489 pp.
6. Wheatley, G.M., and G.T. Hallock, *Health Observation of School Children* (2nd ed.), McGraw-Hill Book Co., Inc., New York, 1956, 488 pp.

## D. Test Publishers

1. C.A. Gregory Co. (and Public School Publishing Company), 345 Calhoun St., Cincinnati 19, Ohio.
2. The California Test Bureau, 5916 Hollywood Blvd., Los Angeles 28.
3. Committee on Diagnostic Reading Tests, Inc., 415 W. 119th St., New York 27.
4. The Educational Test Bureau, 720 Washington Ave., S. E., Minneapolis, Minn.
5. Educational Testing Service, 20 Nassau St., Princeton, N.J.
6. Houghton Mifflin Co., Boston.
7. The Psychological Corp., 522 5th Ave., New York 36.
8. Personnel Press, Inc., 188 Nassau St., Princeton, N.J.
9. Science Research Associates, 57 W. Grand Ave., Chicago 10.
10. Stanford University Press, Stanford University, Calif.
11. Western Psychological Services, 10655 Santa Monica Blvd., West Los Angeles 25, Calif.
12. World Book Company, Yonkers, N.Y.

# PART 2

Disorders of Mental Health
and Deviant Behavior

# CHAPTER 3

## Mental and Physical
## Hygiene and Health

THE PRINCIPAL THEME of this book is the understanding and interpretation of exceptional children. It is concerned with their health, both mental and physical, since impaired health and physical disabilities are common denominators of the exceptional. Hygiene is the science by which health is restored and maintained. Good physical health implies freedom from physical illness, suitable stamina and strength, and absence of or correction of physical and sensory handicaps. Good mental health implies freedom from mental illness, happiness, and a wholesome development of character and personality. In both the physical and the mental realms, health and hygiene are not synonymous terms, although they are commonly confused in popular usage. Health is a *condition* which may be good, average, or poor and is subject to change. Hygiene is the *science* or process by which health is modified, if necessary, or maintained at a satisfactory level. These terms apply equally to physical and mental hygiene and health.

### Interrelationships

Thus far, the statements above may have given the impression that the physical and the mental are separate and mutually exclusive entities. Actually, nothing could be further from the truth, for they are closely interrelated. Historically, they were too often considered to be separate and unrelated. Physical illnesses and defects were treated

31

without regard to feelings, attitudes, or other psychological complications. A broken back was a broken back and nothing else. Likewise, it was often believed that mental illness was purely in the mind and had no relation to the body. In theory there are undoubtedly a few examples in both the physical and mental fields in which this separation is relatively complete, but they are more likely to be the exceptions rather than the rule. The mental interests and outlook of an individual who has spent a few weeks in bed from an accident or from a long-time illness are soon noticeably different from his usual attitudes toward life. Throughout these chapters that discuss many types of exceptional children there is general evidence of the interrelationship of the physical and mental phases of their impairments.

## The Evaluation of Health

If there is to be satisfactory physical or mental health, or both, an evaluation is necessary; this is particularly true of impaired conditions. In the various fields concerned with exceptional children this phase has not been neglected. Complete systems of examination will not be outlined but enough of the external symptoms will be mentioned to alert teachers and parents to possible impairments. In many fields, diagnosis by highly skilled specialists, together with their recommendations for, and services in remedial treatment, is desirable and necessary. If there are weaknesses in the total health picture they are more likely to be in how to maintain good physical and mental health after it has been attained, rather than in the process of gaining it. The major emphasis in this chapter will be directed to the hygiene phases, rather than to the health phases, of exceptional children.

## Physical Hygiene

As will be the case in mental hygiene, physical hygiene has two phases, both equally important. The first phase is restorative or preventive. Klein[1] defines it as *prophylactic* hygiene.

Bacteriologists have furnished a number of such prophylactic techniques which the physician employs whenever he endeavors to *prevent* diphtheria,

[1] D.B. Klein, *Mental Hygiene*, Henry Holt and Co., Inc., New York, 1944, p. 15.

typhoid fever, or lockjaw from developing. To the extent that he urges his patients to include particular vitamin-containing foods in their diets in order to prevent such diseases as pellagra, or scurvy or rickets, he may be said to be practicing prophylactic or preventive medicine.

In a broad sense, the preventive and restorative measures outlined in the twelve chapters of Parts 6 and 7 on physical and sensory defects, are prophylactic measures. The correction of visual defects with glasses or auditory defects with the hearing aid are examples of restorative medicine. One of the major goals throughout this book is to discover and recommend remedial and preventive measures so that normal functioning may either be restored, or approached as closely as possible. Wheatley[1] and Hallock in their *Health Observation of School Children* provide a guide for helping teachers and others to observe and understand the school child both in health and illness. The literature in the field of remedial and preventive medicine is voluminous because of the number of children afflicted in various ways.

The second phase of physical hygiene is oriented toward the preservation of good health once it has been attained. Great amounts of time and money are spent upon the prophylactic measures which should make a lasting impression on the health. Human nature has fortunate or possibly unfortunate ways of easily and quickly forgetting as soon as health is restored. Meliorative measures which could preserve the improved or restored status are no longer remembered. Glasses which were properly fitted and adjusted continue to be worn long after their size and correction have outlived maximum usefulness. Care must be taken to insure that reasonable and balanced diets are regularly followed. Physical exercise suited to the individual may be entirely neglected. Proper amounts of restful sleep are too easily cut short with late television shows. Increasing attention is being paid to meliorative measures in the many commercials on radio and television and in the advertisements in the press and in popular periodicals. Even with all of these reminders a disproportionately large amount of time and effort go into the preservation of a minimum

[1] G. M. Wheatley and G. T. Hallock, *Health Observation of School Children* (2nd ed.), The Blakiston Division, McGraw-Hill Book Co., Inc., New York, 1956, 488 pp.

level of health as compared to the energy spent on the prophylactic and restorative measures. Because of these deficiencies, many children and adults function on a minimum level, just above incapacitating illness, rather than on a level of vigorous physical health in which stamina is more easily fostered and preserved.

## Mental Hygiene

The characteristic patterns of mental hygiene parallel those of physical hygiene. The content of mental hygiene and its operations are somewhat different than those of physical hygiene. Redl[1] and Wattenberg contrast them as follows:

The subject matter of mental hygiene is the entire mind and the entire personality. It deals with such things as emotions, character structure, attachments, and feelings. These are not visible, and most of them are difficult to observe. Moreover, they have no existence independent of human beings. You cannot take a sample of an inferiority complex out of one person and introduce it into someone else. Because the conditions underlying psychological disturbances involve the whole life history of a person, it is much harder to duplicate the situations for experimental purposes.

There are millions of individuals suffering from disturbances in mental health. They range from severe types of the institutionalized mentally ill to mild states of temporary unhappiness which are very common. The field of deviant behavior, described in Chapter 5, includes many varieties of unsatisfactory mental health conditions. The frustrations which accompany all kinds of physical and sensory handicaps have many implications for mental as well as physical health, and re-emphasize the strongly interrelated nature of the mind and body.

The prophylactic phase of mental hygiene is a science of recent origin. Electric shock therapy, insulin, and various tranquilizing drugs are as yet in the stage of experimentation but have demonstrated some hopefully encouraging results for the mentally ill. For the less seriously disturbed, many methods of treatment are currently in use and wide experimentation is in process. Psychotherapy, play therapy, group

[1] F. Redl and W.W. Wattenberg, *Mental Hygiene in Teaching*, Harcourt Brace and Co., Inc., New York, 1951, pp. 27-28.

activities, programs of child guidance clinics, and school social workers, known as visiting teachers, institute a variety of mental hygiene practices to restore mental health. Improved home atmosphere, foster home placement, and many other projects are described more extensively in Chapter 6. Treatments range from kindness and sympathetic understanding to commitment to penal institutions for punishment and reform. Eventually, through one of the many avenues open to doctors and other professional people, some individuals with these problems may reach a satisfactory stage of mental health.

As in the case of physical health, once a recovery or restoration of improved mental health has been made, it is difficult to utilize mental hygiene practices which are meliorative. The unhappy days are easily forgotten, along with the conditions and practices which caused them. Unconsciously, they may recur but so gradually that they are not noticed until overt lapses begin to reappear. In complex modern society there are so many opportunities for the development of tensions and frustrations that deviations from mental health may occur unless the practices of good mental hygiene are observed. Praise and recognition for tasks well done at home and at school, confidence that children will eventually succeed, and that love and security will always be present are among the best meliorative phases of mental hygiene. Many details of this positive approach are presented and discussed in Chapter 6.

### Historical Orientation

Medical treatment for physical illnesses dates back into prehistoric days. The "medicine man" is a legend in the earliest recordings of history and he persistently survives even now in modern garb. The treatment of mental illness has had a much more recent development, although some of its early features antedate the remarkable current discoveries in physical health and hygiene. In the golden era of Ancient Greece, history records that Hippocrates practiced medicine according to scientific principles. His ethical principles and standards were on such a superior plane that even today at commencement exercises medical graduates are charged with the Hippocratic oath.

In the light of what is now known about sanitation, it is a miracle to us that man was able to survive. In fact, at times he was dangerously close to extinction. During the Hundred Years' War, which encompassed all of Europe in the fourteenth century, the bubonic plague swept in from the Orient. It was known as the Black Death and reached its height from 1348-1349 when there were estimates that from one-fourth to more than one-half of the population succumbed. This scourge had such profound effects that mankind began in earnest to seek for a better mode of existence. Writers, scientists, artists such as Leonardo da Vinci, and explorers such as Columbus, devoted their efforts to this end.

Advances in knowledge about physical health have come most rapidly in the past hundred years. Up to that time the cure for many diseases, such as fevers and pneumonia, was the standard procedure of letting blood which was supposed to reduce the body temperature. President George Washington's death was probably hastened, rather than retarded, in this way, when he was in the advanced stages of pneumonia. In 1860 Pasteur discovered that fermentation was caused by the growth of organisms rather than by chemical change. He demonstrated vaccination in 1881 and inoculation against rabies in 1885. Robert Koch discovered the tubercle bacillus in 1881 and the germ of Asiatic cholera in 1883. Joseph Lister discovered the principle of antiseptics in 1866 but it was twenty years later before hospitals made general use of it. Fleming discovered penicillin as recently as 1943 and the Salk vaccine for infantile paralysis was announced in 1955. These years are truly the golden age of discovery in disease and preventive medicine.

Progress in the treatment of mental disease and impaired conditions of mental health have had a less fortunate history. For centuries the mentally ill were treated with the utmost cruelty, persecuted, put to death for inability to subscribe to certain religious beliefs, or were burned at the stake as witches. Although state hospitals were generally established in the nineteenth century, harrowing tales of overcrowded conditions and inadequately trained staffs were reported. Attention was sharply focused on these conditions with the publication of *A Mind That Found Itself*, written in 1908 by Clifford Beers who had recovered from mental illness while in a mental hospital. Some of the recent discoveries in mental hygiene for the mentally ill have already been mentioned and will be discussed further in Chapter 11 on Mental Disorders and Diseases.

Organizations for the interpretation of hygiene procedures for improved mental health have expanded rapidly in recent years. There are several such organizations of various professions in which the personnel join together in attacks on common problems.

Connecticut founded the first state Society for Mental Hygiene in 1908. This was followed the next year by establishment of the National Committee for Mental Hygiene. The First International Congress on Mental Hygiene was held in 1930. All states now have local organizations and it is well represented in Canada and in western European countries. The American Orthopsychiatric Association, whose membership is drawn from many professional fields, was organized in 1923; its quarterly *American Journal of Orthopsychiatry* is subtitled *Journal of Human Behavior.*

The field of social work was beginning to be active soon after the turn of the century. Before that time it was concerned chiefly with relief for the poor. As early as 1906 social agencies and civic groups became interested in social work which would bridge the gap between home and school. After some years of private financial support, Rochester and Mount Vernon, New York, started programs under their boards of education in 1913-1914. The movement spread rapidly and by 1919 the American Association of Visiting Teachers was formed. In 1921 the Commonwealth Fund established thirty centers of visiting teachers in various cities throughout the country. Its programs were so successful that at the end of the demonstration period twenty-one communities took over the financing and management and continued these school social work programs. The visiting teacher movement has continued to spread with subsidies from state legislatures to local school systems. Michigan initiated such an expanded program in 1944-1945 and the Detroit public schools currently have forty visiting teachers. The visiting teachers have joined with all other fields of social work; this combined group is now organized as The National Association of Social Workers. Quarterly numbers of its journal *Social Work* began publication in January, 1956. The term "visiting teacher" is rather commonly used although it is sometimes confused with the program for teaching homebound and bed-ridden children. As a group, these teachers prefer the term "school social workers" since it emphasizes the professional nature of their training and activities.

### Problems of Exceptional Children

In the interest of clarity, these descriptions of physical health and hygiene and mental health and hygiene were presented in a general theoretical manner as if they were applicable only to the normal child. Even when set in this pattern of relative normality, health and hygiene, both physical and mental, are complex in nature and intricate in their interrelationships. The problems in these fields are much more complicated in areas of exceptional children.

In all types of exceptional children it is good practice to start with the state of physical health and an examination of physical and sensory defects. Such physical examinations should be the regular practice even for children in whom the chief problem is deviant behavior, psychological deficit, or educational retardation and disability. A quick survey of the chapter headings discloses the great number and variety of types of exceptional children. The next logical step is the application of physical hygiene which corresponds to the variety of physical and sensory defects and disabilities. This portion of the program is a monumental task.

The mental health of exceptional children is fully as important as their physical health. Mental health problems often occur in individuals whose primary problems are in physical health. Evaluation procedures in mental health are being rapidly developed for all types of exceptional children. In the various chapters on physical and sensory impairments many illustrations of mental health characteristics different from those of the nonhandicapped will be noted. The application of mental hygiene to this field is much more difficult and complex than in the case of normal children. At best these problems are sketched in broad outlines rather than spelled out in detail.

Physical health, physical hygiene, mental health, and mental hygiene are not four simple and distinct entities which can be singled out and treated independently. Physical health and mental health have phases in common which cannot always be clearly differentiated. Individuals with mental health impairments may firmly believe that their physical health is imperfect, or that bodily imperfections exist although detailed physical examinations show no such conditions. In like manner physical hygiene and mental hygiene may have much in common. When one is improved, the other may also respond favorably. The next step is consideration of the personality structure with its complex interrelationships.

## Questions and Topics for Discussion

1. Give further illustrations and definitions of physical health, mental health, physical hygiene, and mental hygiene.
2. Cite examples of relationships between physical and mental health.
3. Report on devastating plagues other than the bubonic with its Black Death.
4. Study and report on the Hippocratic Oath.
5. Discuss the psychology of forgetting such events as operations or critical illnesses.
6. Distinguish between prophylactic and meliorative measures.

## A. Organizations

1. American Medical Association, 535 N. Dearborn St., Chicago 10.
2. American Public Health Association, 1790 Broadway, New York, 19.
3. American Association for Health, Physical Education and Recreation, 1201 16th St., N. W., Washington 6, D.C.
4. National Association for Mental Health, 1790 Broadway, New York 19.
5. National Health Council, 1790 Broadway, New York 19.
6. Society for Research in Child Development, Northwestern University, Evanston, Ill.

## B. Periodicals

1. *American Journal of Orthopsychiatry* (quarterly), American Orthopsychiatric Association, 1790 Broadway, New York 19.

2. A.M.A., *American Journal of Diseases of Children* (monthly), American Medical Association, Chicago.
3. *Journal of the American Association for Health, Physical Education, and Recreation* (monthly), American Association for Health, Physical Education, and Recreation, Washington, D.C.
4. *Mental Hygiene* (quarterly), National Association for Mental Health, New York.
5. *Social Work* (quarterly), National Association of Social Workers, 95 Madison Ave., New York 16.

## C. Books

1. Baker, H.J., *The Art of Understanding*, Christopher Publishing House, Boston, 1940, 400 pp.
2. Carroll, H.A., *Mental Hygiene: The Dynamics of Adjustment* (3rd ed.), Prentice-Hall, Inc., Englewood Cliffs, N. J., 1955, 428 pp.
3. Crow, L.D., and A. Crow, *Mental Hygiene in Home and School Life*, McGraw-Hill Book Co., Inc., New York, 1942, 474 pp.
4. Cutts, N.E., and N. Moseley, *Practical School Discipline and Mental Hygiene*, Houghton Mifflin Company, Boston, 1941, 324 pp.
5. Fenton, N., *Mental Hygiene In School Practice*, Stanford University Press, Stanford University, Calif., 1949, 455 pp.
6. Irwin, L.W., J.H. Humphrey, and W.R. Johnson, *Methods and Materials in School Health Education*, C. V. Mosby Co., St. Louis, Mo., 1956, 367 pp.
7. Kellogg Foundation, *An Experience in Health Education*, Kellogg Foundation, Battle Creek, Mich., 1950, 174 pp.
8. Klein, D.B., *Mental Hygiene* (rev. ed.), Henry Holt and Co., Inc., New York, 1956, 654 pp.
9. Lindgren, H.C., *Mental Health in Education*, Henry Holt and Co., Inc., New York, 1954, 561 pp.
10. Morgan, J.J.B., *How to Keep a Sound Mind*, The Macmillan Co., New York, 1946, 404 pp.
11. Paul, B.D., and W.B. Miller, *Health, Culture, and Community*, Russell Sage Foundation, New York, 1955, 493 pp.
12. Redl, F., and W.W. Wattenberg, *Mental Hygiene in Teaching*, Harcourt Brace and Co., Inc., New York, 1951, 454 pp.
13. Schwebel, M., and E.F. Harris, *Health Counseling*, Chartwell House, Inc., New York, 1951, 238 pp.
14. Sherman, M., *Mental Hygiene and Education*, Longmans Green and Company, New York, 1934, 295 pp.
15. Thorpe, L.P., *The Psychology of Mental Health*, Ronald Press Co., New York, 1950, 747 pp.

16.  Walker, H., *Health in the Elementary School: The Role of the Classroom Teacher*, Ronald Press Co., New York, 1955, 228 pp.
17.  Weiss, E., and O.S. English, *Psychosomatic Medicine*, W.B. Saunders Co., Philadelphia, 1943, 687 pp.
18.  Wheatley, G.M., and G.T. Hallock, *Health Observation of School Children*, McGraw-Hill Book Co., Inc., New York, 1956, 488 pp.

## D. Films and Filmstrips

1.  *As Others See You*, 33-frame filmstrip. How to stand and walk; good grooming habits. McGraw-Hill Text-Film Department.
2.  *Functions of the Body*, 15 minutes. Demonstrates interdependence of all bodily systems. United World Films, New York.
3.  *How the Organs of the Body Function*, 30 minutes. Breathing, digestion, circulation, etc. Bray Studios, New York.
4.  *Teacher Observations of School Children*, 18 minutes, 43-frame filmstrip with 33⅓-r.p.m. disk. Visualizations of signs of good health and certain noticeable deviations from it. Metropolitan Life Insurance Company, New York.
5.  *Mental Health*, 12 minutes, sound. Basic structure of personality and ways in which mental health can be maintained and improved. Encyclopaedia Britannica Films.
6   *Nation's Mental Health*, 18 minutes. Since seven million citizens suffer from mental disorder, the National Mental Health Act was passed in Federal legislation. McGraw-Hill Text-Film Department.

# CHAPTER 4

## Mental Health
## and the Personality Structure

A WELL-BALANCED personality structure is essential for effective mental health. Many separate and disparate elements of life must be harmonized and coordinated within each individual or there would be no intelligent direction of human affairs. Motivations, conflicts, desires, purposes, ideals, influences, perceptions, rationalizations, aches, and pains all enter into this confusing hopper. It is mainly undifferentiated in the earliest years but out of this there must come some order, balance, coordination, and integration. There is little use in trying to conceal the fact that this process is not simple. However, if there is to be understanding, some simplification must be attempted. The process of explaining factors and their interrelationships in the personality structure which lead to mental health is implemented by mental hygiene as noted in the preceding chapter.

### Nature of the Personality Structure

In common with other structures, such as the human body, personality has many parts. They must have some connection, just as, in much the same manner, the muscles function in relationship to the bones in the bodily structure. The personality structure differs from the bodily structure in that many of the elements are intellectual, emotional, or temperamental, or may have ethical or moral implications. The personality has a time sequence which begins with little or practically no characterization in the early months of babyhood

42

but develops into relative completion some time in adulthood. Well-recognized conflicts arise at specified times and are resolved with varying degrees of success in accordance with the circumstances of handling and treatment. Although there is a time sequence and a general progression of cause and effect relationships, the direction of such trends may sometimes be reversed so that regression into infantile or earlier behavior occurs. The personality structure is the interacting product of heredity and environment and neither can be claimed as the sole influence. With these reservations and conditions in mind the principal elements will be discussed.

### Basic Elements of the Personality Structure

The elements of the personality structure have various properties and dimensions. The first three to be discussed exist in some form at birth and many of the others are derived from them.

*The unlearned needs and drives.* There are a few unlearned needs and drives which appear immediately at birth and dominate the behavior. Learning and experience begin to modify the manipulations of these needs within a few hours so that the baby learns that by crying he will be fed. The satisfaction of food does not remove or eliminate the periodic need for food. Responses to cold, warmth and other factors of physical comfort which dominate the infant's demands are paramount in his elementary needs. Self-preservation is his primary goal and it is mainly unconscious. His need for security brings him into social *rapport* with his mother. This is the first step in interpersonal relationships and is generally a pleasurable experience suggesting repetition. While there is progress in the control of these basic drives by the end of the first year, throughout this early period they are the chief ingredients of the personality structure.

Various descriptive terms have been used to define what is meant by these early drives. The term *instinct* has sometimes been used but at some period of psychological history it fell into disrepute. The definition of instinct as a natural or innate quality was challenged many years ago by John Watson who demonstrated that conditioning and learning soon take over. His experiments implied that any natural or unlearned behavior was soon eliminated. *Instinct* had an unsavory implication after animal experimentation disclosed that most animal behavior was instinctive and the comparison was unpleasant. Any references to this area of human nature practically disappeared from the literature of psychology, but the unlearned behaviors tended to persist. Modern warfare with its dangers, fears, and insecurities, starvation and fatherless families, lost hope—all reminded society that unlearned needs and drives had not been completely erased. They continued to function not only in the lives of children, but in adults as well. It had been discovered that the "push-button" conveniences of automatic heating and self-serve, precooked foods were not sufficient to meet all of man's basic needs.

In the meantime, quietly behind the scenes a different type of psychology was being identified in which the unlearned needs and drives were found to play an important role in the motivations of human behavior. The conscious and intellectual phases of human nature which were supposed to explain and govern all actions and all ideas were found to have some hidden or unconscious partners. They take the form of self-preservation, race preservation through strong sexual drives, and the need for pleasurable gratifications. The word *id*, because of its early Latin meaning, was chosen to encompass this mass of life tendencies. *Id is* one of the basic terms in Freudian psychology and it is used to describe that portion of the personality which is concerned with the unlearned needs and drives. Its relationship to other portions of the personality and to other Freudian terms will be discussed after some other basic elements of the personality structure have been presented.

*Bodily attributes.* The human body is a vital and significant portion of the personality structure. This fact is profusely illustrated in many entire chapters of this book. The anatomy and physiology of the eye and ear and their functions in the process of living are described in a series of six chapters in Part 6. Bodily attributes which determine vitality, rates of growth, speech development, and some orthopedic defects project their influences into various portions of the personality structure. Two terms descriptive of these interrelationships are coming into usage: (1) somatopsychology is preferred by psychologists; and (2) psychosomatic medicine by physicians, especially by psychiatrists. Deviations in height and weight and general health and stamina affect the personal and social attitudes as they act and react in the process of social living. Personal appearance, facial blemish, and the status of teeth may be less important but are, nevertheless, effective causative factors. If all the facts could be known there would undoubtedly be many logical explanations of personality and behavior problems in the minor as well as major physical defects.

The nervous system is the most significant of all bodily attributes. There are two principal phases: (1) One aspect includes the injuries which cause convulsive disorders, cerebral palsy, other brain injury, and some mental illnesses outlined in the chapters of Part 3; and (2) the other phase is related to the general level of intellectual ability with its great range of general abilities, and variations in special aptitudes outlined in the chapters of Part 4. Throughout the other portions of the personality the effects of bodily conditions will continue to appear. For example, some interesting relationships have been found between the type of body build and characteristics of temperament. Physical or sensory impairments are known to have marked effects on the self concept of the afflicted individual. This, of course, makes his outlook on life different from that of the nonhandicapped. Despite these hindrances, the accomplishments of the handicapped are a fascinating page of history.

*Abilities and aptitudes.* A series of abilities and aptitudes constitute an entire area of the personality structure. They give insight and direction into the conscious activities and provide the reasoning which produces the talent that has brought about the principal advances in human achievement. Analysis of slow and backward minds has provided helpful new insight for the fields of psychology. Detailed discussion of abilities and aptitudes will be presented in Part 4.

To summarize up to this point, the unlearned needs and drives, the bodily attributes, and the abilities and aptitudes are basic elements or ingredients in the personality. While the unlearned needs and drives are very predominant at birth and in the early childhood years, the development of the full personality structure includes their restraint, training, and constant direction into socially and ethically acceptable codes of behavior. The bodily attributes exist in miniature form but their general status is set within restricted limits. The possibilities of minor improvement are less potent than the many major impairments which may already exist or be acquired. Except for some unusual condition of endocrine imbalance, the ultimate height of any individual has already been approximately determined at or before birth. Negative forces may lessen the potential abilities and aptitudes but little is known of any agents which can markedly increase their status or efficiency.

In evaluating the personality of each individual an inventory should be made in these three areas so that a realistic attitude may be developed. There are congenital factors, determined in large measure by heredity. While some of the derived factors also undoubtedly have congenital and hereditary causes, they are not defined so definitely as the first three which have been presented.

These qualifying remarks intimate that environmental causes and conditions will be presented not as competition or rivalry but as the other important member of a cooperating team. The environment will be found to have effects not only as a result of specific episodes, but also in the form of cumulative influences from the passage of time and experience. Individuals must be born and they must have environmental experiences if they are to develop wholesome and well-integrated personalities. From this point the description of integration will be undertaken.

### Derived Elements of the Personality Structure

In addition to the three basic elements of the personality structure several others are derived from the impact of life and environmental experiences. Some of these effects are characterized as being brief, others as having long duration. While there is progression in one direction there may also be interaction as noted in psychosomatic medicine and in somatopsychology. In order to clarify this presentation, certain elements will be discussed as separate entities but with full realization that each of them has many close interrelationships with all others.

*The feelings.* Among the first impressions in the life of the new-born infant are sensations of cold, warmth, or pain. These impressions are phases of feelings. Sensations arise from the unique sensitivity of the infant's body which reacts with added force if time does not bring relief. This simple episode illustrates the interaction of body and environment plus the time factor. If the sensation becomes extreme the urgency for relief reaches back into the unlearned needs and drives. The aroused nerve impulses become sufficiently strong to arouse conscious attention by the intellectual faculties. Such bodily sensations are likely to be unpleasant, whereas relief and positive attention are pleasant. The sensation itself is physical, but the conscious awareness of it may be expressed as feeling in the psychological meaning.

While the many sensations of the newborn infant are important and seemingly overemphasized, they slowly diminish during early childhood. However, the perceptions of pleasantness and unpleasantness which accompanied them may not subside and may set general feeling tones. These feelings may be based not only on the sensations but are related to relief from unconscious or conscious anxiety about survival in times of danger. Intellectual impressions are pleasant, neutral, or unpleasant and hence are interrelated to the feelings. It is evident that feelings may be based on intellect, on bodily conditions, on the unlearned needs and drives, or on combinations of two or more of them. Time, environment, and experience join with them to produce, affect, and mold the feelings.

Feelings have many dimensions. Feelings may be mild or severe, shallow or deep, of short or long duration, anticipatory or retrospective as well as current in character. Feelings stand at the crossroads of the many forces which affect the unfolding and developing of the personality structure. They are an important link in a series of factors which are coordinated into the complex known as the personality. Within limits, the feelings can be trained into positive channels, or they may be allowed to run rampant so as to disorganize character and personality.

*The emotions.* The next factor in the personality structure is the emotions. Although there are differences between emotions and feelings they have much in common. Emotions may be pleasant or unpleasant, but they also have characteristics which lie deeper. Feelings which become very intense change their character and are more properly considered as emotions. This change adds bodily reactions which makes emotions run deep and potent in human affairs. Emotions increase the rate of heart beat, raise the blood pressure, upset the digestion, cause sleepless nights and create general disturbance of bodily functions. When feelings are prolonged in time and in intensity, emotional episodes logically follow.

A few compensating pairs of emotions are illustrative, such as joy and sorrow, love and hate, and fear and anger. Fear is also paired with courage, although anger is often the compensating reaction after fear; as an example, the reactions to a traffic accident. Many of these paired reactions are puzzling since they temporarily put the individual out of character. For example, there may be expressions of joy when sorrow is in order, or vice versa. Love and hatred add their confusions, existing concurrently and known as ambivalence. A flippant attitude takes over when seriousness is the obvious reaction. Nature has probably provided embarrassing situations as compensation for incidents which might become too overwhelming if unduly prolonged. This restoration to emotional balance is probably parallel to the phenomenon of restoration of bodily condition known as homeostasis.

Time, experience, and environment function in setting emotional tones and in causing them to fluctuate in intensity and direction. In the ordinary affairs of adult life emotions may not be manifesting unusual trends, but children undoubtedly live much more closely to their emotions. Considered as a unit of the personality structure, feelings and emotions are at the focal point in personality development. They have close relationships with the three basic areas of unlearned needs, bodily attributes, and intellectual abilities. If feelings and emotions are greatly disturbed, they are linked closely with the unlearned needs, and emotions are characterized by bodily accompaniments. The interrelationship of intellectual abilities and the emotions is very significant. It is difficult to develop and maintain a balance between them. When emotions run high, reasoning and good judgment may be overshadowed and mob psychology becomes the rule.

Some problems can be resolved through play.

*Courtesy of Dr. George R. Miller, Jr., State superintendent of public instruction, Delaware.*

Little mechanical town made by a class of socially maladjusted younger boys.

It may be equally unfortunate to have intellect control feelings and emotions at all times so that the individual becomes only a strictly logical being with no warmth of personality. In young children feelings and emotions may easily overrule intellect. The mentally retarded of all ages have similar difficulty, whereas the opposite may characterize the intellectually gifted. Insight into feelings and emotions has recently become an important feature of education, home life, and general society. In terms of time sequence, feelings and emotions follow rather than precede the unlearned needs, the bodily attributes, and the intellectual abilities and aptitudes. Obviously the feelings and emotions are factors in the personality structure. They should be susceptible to education and training. Therein lies the hope for improvement in human behavior and human happiness.

*The temperament.* Temperament is a term commonly used to describe an area of the personality structure. It is difficult to place it in a sequence of developing and contributing factors. Temperament falls somewhere between the three basic factors and the final statement of personality. Webster's Unabridged Dictionary defines temperament as "the characteristics of an individual which are revealed in his proneness to certain feelings, moods, and desires, and which may depend upon the glandular and chemical characteristics of his constitution." This well-stated definition identifies temperament as having some dependence upon bodily attributes and hence follows it in time sequence as is true with regard to feelings and emotions. In his presentation, Allport[1] defines temperament as follows:

> Temperament refers to the characteristic phenomena of an individual's emotional nature, including his susceptibility to emotional stimulation, his customary strength and speed of response, the quality of his prevailing mood, and all peculiarities of fluctuation and intensity of mood; these phenomena being regarded as dependent upon constitutional make-up and, therefore, largely hereditary in origin.

There are various influences such as feelings and emotions which affect the temperament. Continued periods of hatred affect the temperament in an adverse manner, but positive emotional tones have beneficial influences upon it. Individuals often make serious attempts

[1] G.W. Allport, *Personality*, Henry Holt and Co., Inc., New York, 1937, p. 54.

to develop favorable temperament as an aid to better interpersonal relationships. Temperamental moods are reflected in the feelings and emotions.

Sheldon[1] has developed a somewhat specific classification of temperament under three principal headings. Each of them is rated or defined on a seven-point scale with "1" being the least amount and "7" the greatest amount or manifestation. The first component is viscerotonia, in which the individual is characterized by love of comfort, by sociability, by affection, with emphasis upon food. "The digestive tract is king, and its welfare appears to define the primary purpose of life." Frequently an individual is observed who seems to relate his life to this component, although the other two components are present in some degree. The second component is somatotonia in which bodily expression and great muscular activity predominate. The principal emphases of life's activities are physical movements, sports, and locomotion. The third component is cerebrotonia or a desire for concealment, avoidance of social contacts, and love of privacy. Rather than acting out their moods and problems or talking them out over the festive table, these individuals prefer to withdraw and rationalize about them. In Sheldon's organization the three components are rated in the order of viscerotonia, somatotonia, and cerebrotonia. A rating of 6-3-1 would describe the temperament as strongly viscerotonic, less than average somatotonic, and very low in cerebrotonic qualities. The majority of individuals are near the average rating of 4 in all three ratings. The minority with extreme ratings are more easily understood and described by this classification method. Sheldon comments that many individuals have a preponderance of two components, with a relative lack of the third.

This system of classification takes on added significance when it is related to Sheldon's[2] investigations into the varieties of human physique in which three components have also been identified. The first component is endomorphy, in which the digestive viscera are massive and highly developed; the second is mesomorphy, in which the muscu-

[1] W.H. Sheldon, *The Varieties of Temperament*, Harper & Brothers, New York, 1944, 520 pp.
[2] W.H. Sheldon, S.S. Stevens, and W.B. Tucker, *The Varieties of Human Physique*, Harper & Brothers, New York, 1940, 347 pp.

lar phases of bodily structure are predominant; and ectomorphy, in which long, slender, and poorly muscled extremities predominate. The seven-point scaling method also applies to this system of classification. There are positive relationships between the relative components of temperament and types, with endomorphy related to viscerotonia, mesomorphy to somatotonia, and ectomorphy to cerebrotonia. Negative relationships exist in all instances when any other pairings are made between bodily type and temperament. Sheldon notes that when the relationship does not run to form the individual lives under great stress trying to harmonize two contradictory trends. These connections between bodily type and temperament illustrate that many factors of the personality structure are interrelated to form a constitutional entity which is unique for each individual.

*The will.* Among the various elements in the personality structure is the will. In popular usage the will is often described as either strong or weak. In a practical sense the will is a dominating factor in character and personality. The will is dependent upon many of the structural factors which have been discussed. It is influenced by environmental forces such as admonitions by parents and associates, but it is also influenced by bodily strength and stamina, by intellectual insight, and by the controlled exercise of unlearned needs and drives. Whenever these interacting forces are in conflict to such an extent that feelings and emotions are unduly disturbed the will becomes distorted. It may regress into a negative phase or develop into an extremely positive state of stubbornness which defeats its own purposes. In general, a reasonably strong will is commendable and gives status to the individual. Abnormal deviations of the will affect the entire personality and throw it out of balance and proportion. Within certain limits the will is capable of being trained and hence is one of the improvable factors in the personality structure.

*Morality.* Morality may be defined as knowledge of moral principles, the quality of that which conforms to constructive or positive ideals or principles of human conduct. Ethics is the science of moral duty; more broadly, the science of the ideal human character and the ideal ends of human action. Morality should not be confused with religion, although religion is an agent in moral training and different religions emphasize different phases of morality. Successful citizenship is also an important ingredient of morality.

The foundations of morality are broad and diverse. For the majority of individuals direct training in home, school, and church is reflected in improved moral behavior, but this is not a universally guaranteed formula. A few individuals do not respond, or may actually revolt; others who have been exposed to negative moral influences may develop very fine moral qualities. The exceptions constitute a challenge in the psychology of behavior. It is somewhat beyond the scope of this chapter to enter into a description of fluctuating trends in morality for entire communities, for nations, or possibly for the world.

At this point it is timely to make further comment on the pattern of Freudian psychology with its id, ego, and superego. In the earlier discussion of unlearned drives and needs, the id, seeking personal satisfactions even at the expense of moral codes, played an important role. The superego with its emphasis upon social good and rules of ethical conduct is directly related to these moral codes. Freudian psychology places great emphasis upon the struggle between the id and the superego, i.e., between the unlearned needs and drives against the morality. The id is buried in the subconscious or in the unconscious where it exercises subtle influences. The superego is generally in the conscious, trying openly to fight an unseen and unrecognized foe. Many struggles take place which involve the feelings and the emotions. The referee or arbitrator is the ego. Thus far the ego has not been introduced as a factor or element in the personality structure. In order to clarify the meaning of the ego the term *homeostasis* should be considered. Whenever the physical systems of the body are thrown out of balance by disease, accident, or other causes there are forces which seek to restore that balance. This principle or process of restoration is known as homeostasis. In like manner, when the factors of the personality structure are thrown out of balance the principle or process of homeostasis goes into action to restore the balance. In the author's opinion, this force or process of homeostasis in the personality structure defines or constitutes the ego. It attempts to dissipate conflicts between the forces of the id and of the superego, or between any other conflicting factors of the personality structure. In psychoanalysis the libido is defined as the sum total of all instinctual forces represented in the unlearned needs and drives. Sometimes the libido is defined more narrowly as the sexual drive. In Freudian psychology emphasis is laid on the influences of the unconscious forces which conflict with acceptable codes of behavior. Bringing these subtle influences into consciousness out of control of the censor, analyzing why they exist, and attempting to discover how to neutralize them are some of the principles of Freudian psychology.

*Character.* Although character and personality have some elements in common, there are differences between them. Character has been defined in many ways and has been a subject of study since man developed into a civilized being. Character is made up of such a complex of factors and forces that any simple definition is practically impossible to formulate. Character is a continuous entity which expresses the uniqueness of each individual. It embraces all of the factors of the personality structure which have just been described. Yet it is something in itself beyond their sum total. Will power is an important ingredient of character. Wholesome feelings and emotions give a healthful tone to character and a well-developed moral sense is a basic requirement. Unless the three basic factors of unlearned drives, bodily attributes, and intellectual capacities are of high quality, the development of satisfactory character is difficult but not impossible. This is attested to by the many individuals with some degree of defect in one or more of the various factors who are able to develop very fine characters.

There are many trait names used to define or to describe character and which throw more light upon its meaning. The most comprehensive compilation of such trait-names was made by Allport and Odbert[1] from the terms in Webster's Unabridged Dictionary which yielded a total of 17,953 terms or 4½ per cent of all dictionary words. They are divided into four groups as follows:

4,504 Neutral terms designating possible personal traits, such as "absent-minded."

[1] G.W. Allport and H.S. Odbert, "Trait-Names, A Psychological Study," *Psychological Monographs*, 1936, 47, 171 pp.

4,451 Terms primarily descriptive of temporary moods activities, such as "abusive."

5,226 Weighted terms conveying social or characterial judgments of personal conduct, or designating influence of others, such as "agreeable."

3,682 Miscellaneous: designations of physique, capacities, and developmental conditions; metaphorical and doubtful terms, such as "adroit."

Since character has many attributes it would seem logical to assay them and add them up on an inventory list to attempt to delineate and differentiate the elements which contribute to character. Within certain limits the lay person tries this method of evaluation; usually, however, it results in elaborating on a few descriptive terms which are either strongly positive or negative. The trained observer is somewhat more cautious, because he realizes that even with long acquaintance, he is not well informed about certain aspects of the individual's character. In order to clarify some considerations about personality the hypothesis of an inventory of character dimensions will be tentatively accepted.

*Personality.* Although the terms "character" and "personality" are often used synonymously, there are certain differences between them. Any individual has as many personalities as people whom he meets. Character plus the social impressions constitute the personality or the personalities. By our attitudes it is possible to bring out the positive or negative traits in others. It is ideal when an individual of wholesome character is able to preserve it under all circumstances and with all kinds of people.

Reciprocally the individual's contacts with a host of his associates have their effects on him. His experiences are similar to the symmetrical or asymmetrical images which he sees of himself when he passes in front of symmetrical or asymmetrical mirrors. He sees himself mirrored in reactions which may be pleasant or unpleasant, charged with anger, or tempered by love and affection. When the general impressions of character and personality are nearly identical and wholesome, the individual is able to live a more stable and satisfying life. If first impressions are favorable, but long acquaintance discloses traits of character and personality which do not measure up to earlier promises, rejection brings disappointment and disillusionment. Initially unfavorable impression of character based upon some deviate physical feature may be discounted later when neutralized by favorable qualities.

Allport[1] offers the following definition of personality:

Personality is the dynamic organization within the individual of those psychophysical systems that determine his unique adjustments to his environment.

All portions of this definition are very pertinent—that personality is a "dynamic organization" which occurs "within the individual" of "those psychophysical systems" which are many and which arise from the physical and psychological factors and form an interacting team. The individual makes "his unique adjustments" to his particular environment.

A summary of the pattern of personality structure is shown in the accompanying diagram. The basic factors, such as the unlearned drives, are affected by the environment as shown at the left. Environment affects all phases of the personality structure. Time and experience continue to move along and add their daily influences from month to month, and year to year. Beginning with feelings and continuing through personality, there is an increasing time element in the various factors. Feelings are relatively brief and transitory, character and personality are relatively long and enduring. As emphasized in earlier paragraphs while there is a progressive trend toward character and personality, various factors may sometimes reverse their trends. A seriously disturbing episode may upset the feelings and emotions so as to set off a chain of unfavorable and violent reactions throughout the entire personality structure.

## The Significance of the Personality Structure

If there is to be some understanding of human nature and human behavior, some framework or structure such as that shown in the ac-

[1] G.W. Allport, *Personality, A Psychological Interpretation*, Henry Holt and Co., Inc., New York, 1937, p. 48.

**Pattern of Personality Integration**

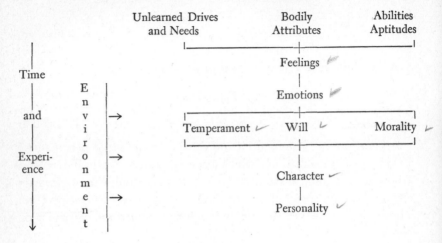

DIAGRAM I

companying diagram is necessary. Each part must fit and coordinate with all other parts if there is to be an effective and workable personality. A distortion or impairment of any part may throw the entire structure out of balance. In handicapped and exceptional children impairments do exist and contribute to such results. In Chapter 3 we showed how physical hygiene contributes to physical health and how mental hygiene contributes to mental health. These operative principles will be discussed in terms of actual practice in the succeeding chapters. Each chapter should be considered in the light of the present chapter and continual reference should be made to it.

### Questions and Topics for Discussion

1. Formulate your own definition of the personality structure.
2. What is the present status of *instinct* in the field of psychology?
3. Make some distinctions between feelings and emotions.
4. Discuss the balance between intellectual controls and the influence of feelings and emotions.
5. Report in more detail on Sheldon's study of the relationship patterns between physique and temperament.

6. Discuss the question of general versus specific moral and ethical principles and practices.
7. Make contrasts between the nature of character and of personality.

## A. *Organizations*

See *Organizations* at end of Chapter 3.

## B. *Periodicals*

1. *American Journal of Psychology* (quarterly), University of Texas, Austin, Tex.
2. *Journal of Abnormal and Social Psychology* (bimonthly), American Psychological Association, Washington, D.C.
3. *Journal of Applied Psychology* (bimonthly), American Psychological Association, Washington, D.C.
4. *Journal of Personality* (quarterly), College Station, Durham, N. C.
5. *Journal of Social Psychology* (quarterly), Provincetown, Mass.

## C. *Books*

1. Allport, G.W., *Personality, A Psychological Interpretation*, Henry Holt and Co., Inc., New York, 1937, 588 pp.
2. Arnold, M.B., and J.A. Gasson, *The Human Person*, Ronald Press Co., New York, 1954, 593 pp.
3. Baker, H.J., *The Art of Understanding*, Christopher Publishing House, Boston, 1940, 400 pp.
4. Blum, G.S., *Psychoanalytic Theories of Personality*, McGraw-Hill Book Co., Inc., New York, 1953, 219 pp.
5. Brand, H., *The Study of Personality*, John Wiley and Sons, Inc., New York, 1954, 581 pp.
6. Cattell, R.B., *Description and Measurement of Personality*, World Book Company, Yonkers, N. Y., 1946, 602 pp.
7. Eysenck, H.J., *Dimensions of Personality*, Routledge and Kegan Paul, London, 1947, 308 pp.
8. ———, *The Scientific Study of Personality*, The Macmillan Co., New York, 1952, 320 pp.
9. ———, *The Structure of Human Personality*, John Wiley and Sons, Inc., New York, 1953, 348 pp.
10. Ferguson, L.W., *Personality Measurement*, McGraw-Hill Book Co., Inc., New York, 1952, 457 pp.
11. Healy, W., *Personality in Formation and Action*, W.W. Norton and Co., New York, 1938, 204 pp.

12. Kluckhohn, C., and H.A. Murray (eds.) *Personality in Nature, Society and Culture*, Alfred A. Knopf, New York, 1949, 561 pp.

13. Lewin, K., *A Dynamic Theory of Personality*, McGraw-Hill Book Co., Inc., New York, 1935, 286 pp.

14. Lotkin, J.S., *Personality Development*, Harper & Brothers, New York, 1952, 504 pp.

15. McCary, J.L., *Psychology of Personality*, Logos Press, New York, 1956, 383 pp.

16. McClelland, D.C., *Personality*, William Sloane, New York, 1951, 654 pp.

17. McKinney, F., *Psychology of Personal Adjustment: Student's Introduction to Mental Hygiene* (2nd ed.), John Wiley and Sons, Inc., New York, 1949, 752 pp.

18. McNemar, Q., and M.A. Merrill (eds.), *Studies in Personality*, McGraw-Hill Book Co., Inc., New York, 1942, 333 pp.

19. Murphy, G., *Personality*, Harper & Brothers, New York, 1947, 999 pp.

20. Patty, W.L., and L.S. Johnson, *Personality and Adjustment*, McGraw-Hill Book Co., Inc., New York, 1953, 403 pp.

21. Notcutt, B., *The Psychology of Personality*, Philosophical Library, New York, 1953, 259 pp.

22. Sappenfield, B.R., *Personality Dynamics*, Alfred A. Knopf, New York, 1954, 412 pp.

23. Stagner, R., *Psychology of Personality* (2nd ed.), McGraw-Hill Book Co., Inc., New York, 1948, 485 pp.

24. Stern, G.G., M.I. Stein, and B.S. Bloom, *Methods in Personality Assessment*, The Free Press, Glencoe, Ill., 1956, 271 pp.

25. Thorpe, L.P., *Personality and Life*, Longmans Green and Co., New York, 1945, 266 pp.

26. Wallin, J.E.W., *Personality Maladjustments and Mental Hygiene* (2nd ed.), McGraw-Hill Book Co., Inc., New York, 1949, 581 pp.

27. Young, K., *Personality and Problems of Adjustment* (2nd ed.), Appleton-Century-Crofts, Inc., New York, 1952, 716 pp.

## D. Films and Filmstrips

1. *Children's Emotions*, 22 minutes, and follow-up filmstrip. Analysis of children's major emotions and guide for parental handling. McGraw-Hill Text-Film Department.

2. *Facing Reality*, 10 minutes, sound. Explanation of common defense and escape mechanisms. McGraw-Hill Text-Film Department.

3. *Genesis of Emotions*, 30 minutes, silent. Shows the wide gamut of

emotions by the end of the first year. New York University Film Library.

4. *Improve Your Personality*, 10 minutes, sound. How personality can be developed and controlled through self-awareness. Coronet Instructional Films.

5. *Individual Differences*, 23 minutes, sound. Case study of a shy boy over-shadowed by a more adept brother. McGraw-Hill Text-Film Department.

6. *Judging Emotional Behavior*, 20 minutes, sound. Observer is given an opportunity to test his own sensitivity to the feelings of others. Churchill-Wexler Productions.

7. *Personality and Emotions*, 16 minutes, sound. Development from infancy and early childhood to maturity. Encyclopaedia Britannica Films.

8. *Shy Guy*, 15 minutes, sound. Lonely high school boy helped through a difficult period. Coronet Instructional Films.

9. *Shyness*, 23 minutes, sound. From the lonely existence of one boy, the film turns to the study of three children. McGraw-Hill Text-Film Department.

10. *Sibling Relations and Personality*, 22 minutes, sound. Sibling relationships in personality shaping. McGraw-Hill Text-Film Department.

11. *Two Children. Contrasting Aspects of Personality Development*, 20 minutes, silent. Contrasts in many areas of development. New York University Film Library.

12. *Unity of Personality*, 18 minutes, silent. Consistency of expressive movements are shown in five different personalities. Psychological Cinema Register, University Park, Pa.

# CHAPTER 5

## *The Characteristics and Causes of Deviant Behavior*

DEVIANT BEHAVIOR in children is a universal problem for teachers, parents, and all agencies concerned with their welfare. It is expressed in many ways and has causes so numerous that remedies and preventions are drawn from many sources and facilities. Pure forms of deviant behavior seldom exist by themselves but usually are found in conjunction with mental, sensory, and physical defects. Later chapters dealing with such defects include descriptions of deviant behavior. After the characteristics of these handicapped and exceptional children have been studied and interpreted, a review of these chapters will show that the number of unexplained characteristics and causes of deviant behavior has been greatly reduced.

There are many unique features of deviant behavior. Aggressive behavior affects not only the individual himself but also those who are associated with him. Their lives and activities are disturbed and affected in countless ways and, as a result, their feelings and emotions are aroused. Aggression tends to be countered with aggression, although deafness is not countered with deafness. Unless personal feelings and emotions can be kept in check, those who must deal with deviant behavior are working under personal handicaps which may neutralize their good intentions. Because of the human element such relationships are much easier to explain in theory than to put into practice. Even though personal reactions of adults may be kept under control, deviant behavior disturbs the routine of classrooms and affects a large group of associates. At home the planned activities and periods of quiet are disturbed for the entire family. Although withdrawing behavior has less disturbing features than aggressive acts, observant teachers and parents are becoming increasingly aware of it and are realizing its true importance.

## Differing Views on Deviant Behavior

Differing views on deviant behavior are barriers to improvement. Teachers and parents who seek immediate relief from disturbances often resort to physical restraint, scolding, denial of privileges, or other forms of punishment. They are facing a very specific and urgent problem. Specialists in diagnosing and prescribing remedies are not so personally concerned with handling current episodes. Since their remedial measures are directed toward changes in basic causes, they expect improvements later. Teachers and parents are often disappointed when specific prescriptions and immediate easement are not provided. At best, they are advised to be very patient, to constrain their own personal feelings, and to trust that improvements will eventually come.

Specialists in the various diagnostic methods include clinical psychologists, psychiatrists, when available, trained social workers attached to school systems or to child guidance clinics. They are dedicated to discovering formulas for the prevention and cure of deviant behavior. They must also be aware of the behavior of children at school, at home, and in the community. Such behavior may be quite different from that which is shown to diagnosticians. This condition is being remedied by observing children in action situations. Often a diagnostician is asked how to prevent a particular child from stealing, from disturbing the classroom, or from performing other overt acts. He feels that he must base his answer upon the nature of the particular individual and his training and treatment throughout childhood. However, since gathering and interpreting such contributory information requires time, he may hesitate to express what he believes may be a snap judgment. In the past few years there has been considerable improvement in teacher-diagnostician relationships. Teachers in training are able to study the psychology of behavior and the principles of mental health and diagnosticians serve internships in action situations as well as in theory. With these differing views and attempts to meet them in mind some specific deviant behavior surveys will be presented.

### Surveys of Deviant Behavior

Deviant behavior is of wide scope. There are at least three environments for which deviant behavior is characteristically different—the school, the home, and the community. A fourth less-recognized environment is the individual himself and his personality structure. The struggle between morality and unlearned drives may rage violently and, although morality may win, the personality may have been affected. Too often it has been mistakenly assumed that the individual is something apart from his external environment when, in actuality, the individual and his environment should be considered as a continuum. The ethics of social behavior not only become integrated within the individual but are also expressed in overt behavior and attitudes toward others.

*School behavior.* One of the early surveys of behavior was made from observations made in a Cleveland school and was reported by E. K. Wickman.[1] The teachers reported the behavior of 874 pupils without the use of a check list. Results are shown in Table II.

Table II is interpreted to read that 74.7 per cent of all pupils whispered and that 41.0 per cent did it habitually. The ratio of total incidence to frequency of habitual incidence shows some interesting contrasts, for example the per cents of the latter are approximately one-half as much as the former. Further, "disorderly in class" had per cents of 38.8 for total incidence but 18.4 for frequency of habitual incidence. 19.6 per cent of all the pupils were characterized as being "lying, untruthful," but only 3.3 per cent were habitually lying or untruthful. "Destroying property" was reported nearly seven times as much as an incident as it was reported as an habitual characteristic. If the frequency of habitual incidence had equalled

---

[1] E.K. Wickman, *Children's Behavior and Teachers' Attitudes,* The Commonwealth Fund, New York, 1928, p. 30.

## TABLE II

### Total Incidence and Frequency of Habitual Incidence in 874 Pupils of a Cleveland School

| Type of Problem | Per cent of Incidence in 874 Pupils | | Type of Problem | Per cent of Incidence in 874 Pupils | |
|---|---|---|---|---|---|
| | Total Incidence | Frequency or Habitual Incidence | | Total Incidence | Frequency or Habitual Incidence |
| Whispering | 74.7 | 41.0 | Fearful | 9.3 | 1.8 |
| Inattentive | 59.0 | 29.1 | Physical coward | 8.8 | 1.2 |
| Careless in work | 44.4 | 23.9 | Nervous | 8.7 | 3.5 |
| Tattling | 42.0 | 11.5 | Willfully | | |
| Disorderly in class | 38.8 | 18.4 | disobedient | 8.2 | 3.7 |
| Interrupting | 38.7 | 18.6 | Destroying | | |
| Failure to study | 36.2 | 17.5 | property | 8.2 | 1.2 |
| Shy, withdrawing | 35.2 | 18.2 | Unhappy, | | |
| Daydreaming | 33.4 | 13.5 | depressed | 8.0 | 1.4 |
| Lack of interest | 31.8 | 10.8 | Quarrelsome | 7.9 | 2.5 |
| Overactive | 30.9 | 16.5 | Stubborn in | | |
| Cheating | 29.5 | 8.7 | group | 7.5 | 1.8 |
| Oversensitive | 25.2 | 8.3 | Rude, impudent | 6.7 | 3.8 |
| Neglectful | 25.4 | 9.9 | Impertinent, | | |
| Physically lazy | 20.8 | 10.7 | defiant | 5.6 | 1.7 |
| Lying, untruthful | 19.6 | 3.3 | Carrying grudges | 4.9 | 0.8 |
| Unnecessary | | | Stealing articles | 4.0 | 0.6 |
| tardiness | 17.6 | 3.5 | Masturbation | 3.9 | 0.9 |
| Acting "smart" | 14.6 | 7.4 | Enuresis | 3.9 | 0.8 |
| Overcritical | 14.2 | 5.3 | Sissy (or tomboy) | 3.6 | 1.2 |
| Imaginative tales | 13.3 | 3.7 | Suspicious | 2.1 | 0.3 |
| Meddlesome | 12.6 | 4.2 | Cruel, bullying | 1.7 | 0.7 |
| Sullen, sulky | 12.5 | 2.5 | Profanity | 1.7 | 0.0 |
| Domineering | 12.1 | 5.9 | Truancy | 1.6 | 0.2 |
| Slovenly | | | Temper outbursts | 1.5 | 0.3 |
| appearance | 11.8 | 4.8 | Stealing money | 0.7 | 0.3 |
| Suggestible | 9.4 | 4.5 | Stealing food, | | |
| | | | sweets | 0.7 | 0.2 |
| | | | Obscene notes, | | |
| | | | talk | 0.3 | 0.0 |
| | | | Smoking | 0.2 | 0.1 |

the total incidence it would not be difficult to imagine how impossible it would have been to maintain reasonable discipline within the school. Fortunately many of the more frequently reported items such as "daydreaming" and "failure to study" did not have as serious consequences to school discipline or possibly to individual pupils as "destroying property" or "stealing money" which were reported less frequently.

Baker and Traphagen[1] summarized an alphabetized check list of twenty-six behavior traits on a survey of elementary school children in the Detroit public schools in 1929. Replies were received on 1,357 pupils—approximately one per cent of the school population. Approximately 85 per cent were boys and 15 per cent were girls. There was an average of 6.8 items listed per pupil, and approximately seven pupils were reported per school. Results are shown in Table III.

There was more aggressively deviant behavior reported in this list than in the Cleveland study in which no check list was given. In the area of withdrawing behavior, ninety-seven pupils were characterized as quiet and seclusive and eighty-four as timid and avoiding others.

In order to approach solutions to problems of deviant behavior lists of items and traits such as shown above need to be summarized and grouped into fewer general classes. Such a classification was made for 279 children by the California Association of School Psychologists and Psychometrists.[2] This study included 207 boys and 72 girls, an approximate ratio of three boys to one girl. Classification is shown in Table IV.

The fact that several items or traits are noted for each boy or girl in these surveys shows the complex nature of deviant behavior, its multiple causes, and the inherent difficulties in improvement.

The Detroit public schools have a staff of thirty-eight visiting teachers, whose titles should more properly be school social workers, to whom 2,799 pupils with problems were referred in the school year

[1] H.J. Baker and V. Traphagen, *The Diagnosis and Treatment of Behavior-Problem Children*, The Macmillan Co., New York, 1935, pp. 370-377 (out of print).
[2] California Association of School Psychologists and Psychometrists, Research Committee, "Emotionally Disturbed Children in California," *California Journal of Educational Research*, 1954, 5, pp. 116-120.

TABLE III

Frequencies of the Behavior Items, 1929 Detroit Behavior Survey

| Items or Traits | Number | Per cent of Maximum Possible Occurrence | Per cent of All Items Occurring |
|---|---|---|---|
| Interferes, disturbs | 871 | 64.2 | 9.4 |
| Argues, talkative | 848 | 62.5 | 9.2 |
| Fights, quarrelsome | 810 | 59.7 | 8.7 |
| Defiant, stubborn | 647 | 47.7 | 7.0 |
| Lies, deceitful | 556 | 41.0 | 6.0 |
| Bullies, boasts | 549 | 40.5 | 5.9 |
| Resents correction | 520 | 38.3 | 5.6 |
| Cruel, teases | 473 | 34.9 | 5.1 |
| Cheats in school or at play | 469 | 34.6 | 5.1 |
| Obstinate, sullen | 465 | 34.3 | 5.0 |
| Smart aleck | 333 | 24.5 | 3.6 |
| Impulsive, erratic | 324 | 23.9 | 3.5 |
| Daydreams, absent-minded | 305 | 22.5 | 3.3 |
| Overactive, nervous | 295 | 21.7 | 3.2 |
| Steals | 292 | 21.5 | 3.2 |
| Disliked, repulsive | 252 | 18.6 | 2.7 |
| Truant (school) | 231 | 17.0 | 2.5 |
| Temper tantrums, rage | 204 | 15.0 | 2.2 |
| Profane, vulgar, obscene | 182 | 13.4 | 2.0 |
| Selfish | 135 | 9.9 | 1.5 |
| Hysterical, cries | 124 | 9.1 | 1.3 |
| Quiet, seclusive | 97 | 7.1 | 1.0 |
| Truant (home) | 97 | 7.1 | 1.0 |
| Sex abuse | 87 | 6.4 | 0.9 |
| Avoids others, timid | 84 | 6.2 | 0.9 |
| Sets fires | 14 | 1.0 | 0.2 |
| Totals | 9264 | —— | 100.0 |

## TABLE IV

### Type and Number of Socially and Emotionally
### Disturbed Children (California)

| Type | Per cent |
| --- | --- |
| Personality Problems, such as withdrawal | 17 |
| Learning and academic problems | 16 |
| Emotional problems, temper outbursts | 13 |
| Social relationships, dangerous | 14 |
| Behavior problems, stealing, lying | 14 |
| Nervous habits, enuresis, thumb-sucking | 11 |
| Discipline and authority, defiance | 10 |
| Somatic symptoms, fatigue | 5 |
| Total | 100 |

## TABLE V

### Reasons for Referral for Visiting Teacher Service

| | Boys No. Per cent | | Girls No. Per cent | | Total No. Per cent | |
| --- | --- | --- | --- | --- | --- | --- |
| Aggressive behavior | 308 | 16.0 | 113 | 12.3 | 421 | 14.8 |
| Personality disturbance | 256 | 13.2 | 147 | 15.9 | 403 | 14.2 |
| School citizenship | 292 | 15.1 | 110 | 12.0 | 402 | 14.1 |
| Scholastic difficulty | 285 | 14.7 | 76 | 8.3 | 361 | 12.7 |
| Home status | 191 | 9.8 | 138 | 15.0 | 329 | 11.5 |
| Generally antisocial | 223 | 11.5 | 73 | 8.0 | 296 | 10.3 |
| Home citizenship | 87 | 4.5 | 73 | 8.0 | 160 | 5.6 |
| Mental status—health | 85 | 4.4 | 68 | 7.4 | 153 | 5.3 |
| Physical status—health | 80 | 4.1 | 38 | 4.1 | 118 | 4.1 |
| Regressive behavior | 63 | 3.2 | 30 | 3.3 | 93 | 3.2 |
| School-home relationships | 51 | 2.6 | 32 | 3.5 | 83 | 2.9 |
| Miscellaneous | 17 | 0.9 | 20 | 2.2 | 37 | 1.3 |
| Total | 1938 | 100.0 | 918 | 100.0 | 2856 | 100.0 |

1955-1956. The reasons for referrals by school principals, counselors, and other personnel are shown in Table V.

In Table V, aggressive behavior leads the list for boys but ranks third in frequency for girls whose primary reason for referral was personality disturbance. Girls had less scholastic difficulty than boys but more difficulty with the social climate of their homes. A few pupils had more than one referral.

*Annoyances observed by parents.* A somewhat different type of list was compiled by Sherman[1] in an investigation conducted by parents of good intelligence who carried notebooks for one week in which they recorded acts of their children which annoyed them. They listed fifty-one separate items which recurred a total of 2,214 times. The main results are shown in Table VI.

### TABLE VI

Annoyances Observed by Parents (Sherman)

| Description | Number of Times Recurring | Per cent |
| --- | --- | --- |
| Noises and interruptions | 380 | 17.9 |
| Disobedience | 304 | 14.3 |
| Bad manners | 154 | 6.6 |
| Slowness, laziness, tardiness | 137 | 6.4 |
| Untidiness | 126 | 5.9 |
| Restlessness | 112 | 5.2 |
| Physical annoyance to others | 98 | 4.6 |
| Dirty habits | 89 | 4.1 |
| Bad humor, crying, temper | 70 | 3.2 |
| Teasing | 69 | 3.2 |

There are some similar observations noted for school behavior but there is more emphasis upon untidiness. Dirty habits are usually remedied before the child leaves for school. In the main, parental observations do not include many problems which seem as serious as those reported in school, but the general culture of these homes was probably somewhat above average. Since children's behavior is based on causes from all their environments, it follows that remedial programs should include parents as well as teachers.

*Delinquency.* In addition to conditions of deviant behavior reported

[1] M. Sherman, *Basic Problems of Behavior*, Longmans Green and Co., New York, 1941, p. 334.

in the several tables above there are more serious types of problems which bring individuals to the attention of the police and courts where they may also be studied by clinical, sociological, and penal agencies. In a study of one thousand juvenile delinquents the Gluecks[1] compiled the list of offenses shown in Table VII.

### TABLE VII

Offenses Committed by 1,000 Juvenile Delinquents (Glueck)

| Offenses | Number |
| --- | --- |
| Larceny and similar offenses | 505 |
| Burglary and similar offenses | 231 |
| Stubbornness (including waywardness, disobedience) | 107 |
| Running away from home | 46 |
| Truancy | 30 |
| Assault and battery; disturbing the peace | 24 |
| Trespassing and similar offenses | 10 |
| Sex offenses | 9 |
| Gaming, or being present at gaming | 7 |
| Various other offenses | 31 |
| Total | 1,000 |

Various forms of theft accounted for slightly more than one-half of all offenses, with burglary including approximately one-fourth of the total. Various forms of stubbornness, which comes principally under the area of *will* in the personality structure, accounts for one of every ten offenses.

*Police investigations.* A sample survey of all offenses which come to police departments of large cities is shown in Table VIII. These offenses occurred in the month of July, 1957, and the statistics were compiled by the Youth Bureau of the Detroit police department.

This list includes only boys above ten years of age. Younger boys are serviced by the Women's division of the police department. This list, compiled about two decades later than that of the Gluecks, is quite similar in rank order but shows less larceny and more offenses

[1] S. Glueck and E.T. Glueck, *One Thousand Juvenile Delinquents*, Harvard University Press, Cambridge, Mass., 1939, p. 100.

of immoral nature against persons. Of the total of 711 boys, 329, or 47.2 per cent, were not detained. Complaints on three hundred ten cases were filed with the juvenile court. Approximately three-fourths of the boys were fourteen, fifteen, or sixteen years old.

### TABLE VIII

Juvenile Offenses Reported by the Youth Bureau of the Detroit Police Department for July, 1957

| Offenses | Number | Per cent |
|---|---|---|
| Larceny-theft, except auto theft | 162 | 22.8 |
| Burglary, breaking or entering | 143 | 20.1 |
| Miscellaneous, truancy from home, etc. | 96 | 13.4 |
| Auto theft | 94 | 13.2 |
| Robbery | 41 | 5.7 |
| Assault and battery | 41 | 5.7 |
| Disorderly conduct | 36 | 5.1 |
| Felonious assault | 27 | 3.9 |
| Investigated on suspicion | 21 | 3.0 |
| Sex offenses, immoral | 17 | 2.4 |
| Rape | 10 | 1.4 |
| Carrying concealed weapons | 9 | 1.3 |
| Others, including murder | 14 | 2.0 |
| Total | 711 | 100.0 |

On a city-wide basis for Detroit from 1952 to 1956 for boys ten to sixteen years of age there had been an increase from 6.0 to 8.1 per 100 boys with the total offenses increasing from 5,052 to 7,295. For the first nine months of 1957 this rate had declined to 6.7 per 100. Because of repeaters the number of offenses was greater than the number of offenders, rising from 3,542 in 1952 to 5,056 in 1956. The Federal Bureau of Investigation reported that, on a nation-wide basis, arrests of young people under 18 years increased 17.3 per cent in 1956. It is evident that the problems of juvenile delinquency are very grave.

*Other forms of deviant behavior.* There are other forms of deviant behavior which are broadly classified as abnormal, but which may be included in some of the items shown in the various tables above. These types of problems will be discussed in Chapter 11 on Mental Disorders and Diseases.

Enough data have been reported about the many forms of deviant behavior to show that there are no simple solutions, no quick remedies, or no possibilities that it will suddenly subside. It is necessary to take an extended look into causes if some improvements are to be made.

## Classification of Causes

There are three main types of causes, similar in some respects, but differing in points of origin or in areas of effect: (1) sensory or physical impairments or deviations within the individual; (2) developmental conflicts characteristic of specific ages or levels; and (3) environmental causes reacting on the individual. While there is considerable overlapping in these areas, they will be considered separately in the interests of clarity.

1. *Conditions within the individual.* In the various chapters of Part 3 there are many illustrations of deviant behavior inherent in the personality structure. The perseveration activities of the cerebral palsied have no implications of moral misbehavior but nevertheless they may be distracting to associates. The brain-injured child cannot structure his mental impressions in the usual ways and hence his outlook deviates from the normal. In rather severe cases of brain injury the behavior is very erratic, relatively uncontrollable and the individual shifts attention very quickly. The very extreme types are so deviant in behavior that many of them must be hospitalized as mentally ill or psychotic patients. The chapters in Parts 6 and 7 present some phases of the characteristic behavior of sensory and physical impairments and diseases. Whenever these conditions are recognized as such they are usually taken into account in evaluating deviant behavior.

2. *Developmental conflicts.* There are some conflicts through which all individuals must pass and most of us are able to resolve them quite successfully. However, a few people block and are never able to reach satisfactory solutions. The structure of a conflict offers two alternate avenues of action or choice which seem diametrically opposed. In attempting to arrive at solutions, the individual's personal choice is

often denied him by adults or by his associates who offer choices which seem unreasonable if not impossible. In extreme cases there may be complete withdrawal into flights of fantasy where solutions seem easy. If the solutions are actually made, they are often accompanied by gross disturbances of the feelings and emotions so that distortions may throw the personality structure out of balance. Eventually the ideal solution results when the two horns of the dilemma seem to have some elements in common and a practical and workable compromise is reached.

In infancy and in the earliest years of childhood, the conflict lies between the unlearned drives on the one hand, and the necessity of learning to accept some delay and training to meet these needs on the other. Successful toilet training is a practical illustration. Another crisis occurs when delays caused by the better preparation of food must be balanced against the immediate satisfaction of hunger pangs. Scenes of loud crying are gradually balanced against social approval when acceptable behavior is found to be more satisfactory. These important decisions are actually much more critical than some parents who think that the only issue is simple, direct training may believe. In these early years the child has learned to accept some compromise.

In the principal years of childhood from preschool days to adolescence a second conflict arises. Actions which satisfy selfish ends conflict with actions that take into account the welfare of others. The desire to eat two pieces of candy instead of sharing them with someone else is a simple illustration. What the individual actually does is not acceptable to others; what they expect him to do is not acceptable to him. The principle of personal sacrifice for the happiness of others is not easily understood. In theory, there are supposed to be some personal satisfactions in the form of thanks from the one who receives. If the earliest experiences in giving and in serving others are not successful, important ground is lost. As early as preschool days a few children have already decided that there is only loss and no gain in sharing. If the frustrations are particularly severe the individual may lapse into fantasy in which he believes that he has achieved social acceptance. However, if the lessons are not too severe or too unsuccessful there comes a recognition that in serving and sharing with others there is also satisfaction for self. Childhood is filled with a steady flow of this basic conflict which requires that the individual make compromises. Whenever the emotions are violently aroused they overpower reason so that quiet concentration at school becomes difficult. Teachers and parents should remind themselves that children have not solved this important conflict which they themselves have already experienced.

The third conflict comes at adolescence. While much has been written and said about the physical changes at adolescence, the psychological change and the conflicts accompaning that change are equally, if not more, important. There are two drives which seem contradictory in nature. One side was and is childhood which was characterized in the main by the fact that decisions were made by adults. In looking toward his own adulthood the evolving adolescent strives to make decisions for himself. Society does not release him into this new realm of self-sufficiency as suddenly as he wishes. When he goes a little too far off limits he is reminded that to have asked would have been better. This, of course, places him back into childhood. With some caution he may try again, with or without success. The mechanics of this conflict operate in the same general way as did the self-versus-social satisfactions in childhood. Emotional disturbances, failure in school, and flight to fantasy are resulting by-products. The individual may resign himself to remain in the childhood role or he may violently erupt by running away from home. After a few stormy years he is fortunate if he has learned the importance of compromise. At twenty-five years of age he is more likely to seek advice from parents or others than he was at fifteen years.

Parents and other adults dealing with adolescents who are in the beginning stages of this conflict can either help or hinder them in resolving these problems. The adolescent goes through a stage of embarrassment when he realizes that as a novice adult he may be making errors that disclose his amateur status. If he is not treated wisely, permanent feelings of inferiority may develop. Since the ability to make wise decisions is one of the prerequisites of successful adulthood, opportunities for making decisions should not be delayed until the late date of adolescence. In its simpler forms it should be cultivated in matters of comparatively small importance throughout childhood, so that there will be no sudden and violent change necessary. Undoubtedly many of the citations of deviant behavior listed in the tables earlier in this chapter are results of unsolved conflicts arising from unwise treatment in infancy, in childhood, and in adolescence. License to drive a car is becoming a specific symbol that adulthood has been reached. Less fortunate identifications are excessive smoking, drinking, and sexual promiscuity which may be only violent escapes from childhood.

The fourth conflict or series of conflicts arise in adulthood. Many complex decisions must be made and choice is not easy. If the decision seems too difficult, the basis for decision fluctuates between the hard facts of reality and the fantasy of highly successful accomplishment. While a little fantasy and imagination are desirable elements in human affairs, if they become so extreme that they dominate, the individual may have reached a dangerous state of mental illness. Mental illness has some foundations in this area as well as in impairment of the nervous system.

These four conflicts are actually much more complex than the basic descriptions imply. Conflicts between the id phases of the unlearned needs and drives and the standards of ethical and moral behavior of the superego shake the very foundations of the personality structure. The principle of homeostasis or restoration of personality balance emerges as the ego which is the arbitrator between conflicting forces.

3. *Causes primarily environmental in nature.* In the third general classification of behavior deviations there are some environmental ingredients. Such a statement must be accepted with caution, since there are many exceptions. Reference should be made to Allport's definition of personality in the preceding chapter, i.e., the "unique combination of factors, etc." There has been a great amount of this kind of fallacious reasoning: when an unwholesome home environment leads to delinquency in an individual, it is concluded that this is a universal relationship. Caution must be observed in such a generalization since other children from the same home may not be delinquent. These differences occur in fraternal twins, and even in identical twins. It is becoming apparent that several identical factors must operate to produce approximately identical normal or deviant behavior. Un-

limited research needs to be done before very many generalizations can be safely made. With these limitations in mind, some illustrations will be given of possible social conditions plus personal elements which result in deviant behavior.

(1)    The first is the harmless although irritating fun which a highly intellectual child may interject into classroom episodes. He sees the comical side, he senses some incongruity and he delights in matching wits against the teacher. Unless such episodes can be taken in stride, poor interpersonal relationships arise which may develop into sullenness and bona fide antisocial behavior. Guidance workers occasionally find bright children with no malice in heart, who have so harassed their teachers that they are considered to be confirmed delinquents. Other characteristics of the mentally gifted will be discussed in Chapter 14.

(2)    Attention-getting is a second type of deviant behavior. The need for attention and approval is practically universal. It becomes a major factor in human affairs as social developments assume greater importance. In ordinary affairs of school, home, and community, there are many opportunities for recognition which satisfy social needs. However, there are many ways in which these needs are blocked—the sensory handicap of blindness or the inability to read as well as classmates. Because of such limitations the individual child may be overlooked in contrast to his more adept and able associates. He feels neglected and hence makes a bid for attention. If acceptable accomplishments are not possible, he is tempted to commit some overt act of deviant behavior which attracts the attention of teacher and class. It may happen at home. Such a child is willing to run the risk of some form of punishment for the satisfaction of being in the spotlight. Finding and developing desirable and acceptable activities is an obvious need but is not easily done. If opportunity were to be given, the greatest majority of such children would be very willing to trade deviant for acceptable behavior.

Some of the more delinquent forms of deviant behavior are less easily diagnosed. They may be similar in form but differing in intensity from some of the patterns already discussed. Violent reactions to the conflicts of adolescence may furnish an indirect desire to disgrace parents by causing them to appear in court or to make restitution for damage at school or in the community. Stealing and burglary which lead the list of delinquency offenses seem to be motivated by a practical need for spending money in view of the high cost of everything. Stealing cars is largely a matter of adventure since they are generally driven on short trips and abandoned when out of gasoline. Immoral sex offenses may have more deeply seated causes. A common denominator of some types of delinquency is the influence of the gang. Airing of similar grievances arising from the home, the school, and the community often add reinforcement to bravado. These suggestions represent only a few of the many motivations which lead youth into deviant behavior.

### The Number of Cases

It is evident from the various tables and discussions that the many forms of deviant behavior represent a large number of children and youth. Comparatively few individuals resort to such extreme acts as murder. When the list is extended to include many minor classroom interruptions, the number mounts rapidly. Some practical middle ground should be agreed upon as the upper limit for those who require considerable time of teachers and parents, as well as the services of diagnostic and remedial agencies. If a limit as low as one per cent of deviant behavior is set, the cases are quite extreme. If 5 per cent is the standard, many lesser types are included; 2 per cent seems to be the generally accepted standard. One professional worker for every 2,500 of the pupil population provides for service for a maximum case load of fifty individuals. Communities vary in number of individuals requiring such attention according to cultural and economic conditions. However, more favorable physical conditions do not guarantee complete happiness or perfect personality adjustment.

The present chapter has outlined some of the major areas of deviant behavior and many of its causes. The following chapter will outline methods of diagnosis and treatment, and describe agencies providing such services.

## Questions and Topics for Discussion

1. Discuss some inclusive definitions of deviant behavior.
2. Describe one or more cases of deviant behavior with whom you have had to deal in school or elsewhere.
3. What help or assistance was available in such a situation?
4. Point out some relationships which you believe exist between the deviant behavior and the underlying causes.
5. List more actions than given in this chapter which you consider to be deviant behavior.
6. Report on additional surveys of deviant behavior.

Note: Consult reference material at the end of Chapter 6.

# CHAPTER 6

## Remedial Programs
## for Deviant Behavior

THE PAST THREE or four decades have witnessed a remarkable growth of interest in deviant behavior. This interest has gradually proceeded from the listing of the behavior itself to diagnoses, remedies, and preventions. At present there are several professions attacking the problem and many agencies providing various types of service. None of these facilities, singly or in combination are at present able to fill the demands for service. A few of the principal features of these programs will be presented.

### The Role of Teacher or Parent

Since the teacher has full-time responsibilities for instruction, it is beyond her field of training to give treatment to the individual deviant. However, her general philosophy, patience, and methods of group control may have a salutary effect upon the individual deviant. She should be advised of practical remedies which are easy to administer in a minimum of her time. Otherwise she must depend upon the services of personnel trained in mental hygiene to carry that program. She should be an active member of a team dealing with any of her pupils. The burden of carrying on with deviant cases in daily schedules is always her responsibility whereas the nonteaching agencies and services are free from this major responsibility.

Parents and the home are the most important influences in determining standards of behavior. The author remembers vividly the

77

admonitions of President Hoover at the White House Conference on Child Health and Protection in 1930 that no matter how many agencies were working in this field the prime responsibility continued to rest in the home. The early years of family life before school entrance and before most diagnostic services are available set the general tone of the child's life. That parents are seeking help is attested to by the great expansion of the parent-teacher movement, of child-study clubs, and of allied organizations.

In ordinary affairs resourceful parents are able to handle most situations. When deviations become quite marked, parents should seek help and professional advice. It may help to explain to them that the physician and the dentist usually feel that they are too close to problems in their own families to trust their own treatments. They, too, seek outside help.

Since there are many causes of deviant behavior there are also many types of service, methods of diagnosis, and treatment. This multiplicity of approaches has advantages and disadvantages, although the advantages probably outweigh the disadvantages since there is likely to emerge one or more systems which incorporate the best features of several methods. Other fields of human endeavor have had similar experiences and have eventually gained from them. Some of the principal approaches in the study of deviant behavior and some common benefits resulting from them will be described.

### Group and Individual Approaches

In every large community there are group recreational and character-building activities. Some of these are financed by public funds and are known as departments of recreation. Trained personnel are employed to supervise playground activities and to arrange amateur games and sports which are modified in indoor facilities in winter months. Privately financed activities such as scouting provide character-building programs for large numbers of children and youth. The benefits of such programs cannot be measured by numbers served since they provide experiences in social living as well as filling otherwise unused hours of idle time. The land space and properties reserved for such activities in the midst of large urban areas testify to their importance. The principal purpose is to provide opportunities for the rank and file of children and youth. Treatment and cure for deviant behavior are indirectly implied. There has been ample evidence that the use of such recreational facilities has succeeded in attaining its principal goals. However, success has not been complete in some types of deviant behavior.

The study of deviant behavior is also approached through the study of the individual and his unique problems. Diagnosis and treatment are provided for his specific difficulties. This process is termed the *individual method* in contrast to the group method of approach noted above. From time to time conflicting claims have been made about the effectiveness of the group versus the individual method in treating deviant behavior. Greater amounts of money have often been expended upon group recreational programs and there has been more favorable publicity for it because of the large numbers of individuals who participate. The individual deviant in the quiet and somewhat secluded quarters of a child guidance clinic does not make such a spectacular impression on the press or the public. Society naturally puts less emphasis upon individual study than upon the group projects. As a result there has been less expansion of financial support for individual diagnostic and remedial facilities than for group recreational programs.

The real issues are slowly coming to light. The more extreme behavior deviant usually does not patronize the group facilities. If he does attend, the recreational leader is in much the same position as the teacher. There is no time to deal with him so that this leader also feels the need for and recognizes the value of the specific diagnostic services. The individual diagnostic service has as one of its important goals successful adjustment of the individual deviant so that he may join with and be accepted in group activities. Rather than competition of services they are found to be complementary with each supplementing the other. In the modern "team" approach, both services are represented.

Some promising programs have been initiated in recent years in which small groups of deviants are brought together for group activities under leaders trained in casework and in group techniques. They are able to apply both the individual and the group approach in very effective ways. This economy of effort should be greatly expanded.

### Procedures in Individual Diagnostic Programs

Within the individual diagnostic and remedial fields there are a few principles and conditions of procedure which need to be taken into account. Such service is necessarily expensive and time-consuming to the trained staff personnel. Whenever possible, the deviant should take self-administering adjustment inventories upon which he can check and evaluate himself. These inventories may be administered to a small group of deviants under the direction of a trained diagnostician. He may also administer one or more group intelligence examinations and other aptitude tests to a small group. The diagnostician may use them as the basis for further exploration in individual conference. Many such inventories give not only a general evaluation of status or problems, but specific areas of strength and weakness. The time which has been saved may then be used to better advantage in more intensive and extensive individual examinations of especially affected areas. Such programs of action are particularly feasible when diagnostic facilities are attached to school systems. Several pupils of approximately the same age may be examined as a group. Certain group tests of intellectual aptitude in pictorial form may be given as early as kindergarten or first grade and tests involving simple reading materials may be used as early as the third or fourth grades.

In addition to the time-economy factor many deviants will respond more naturally and without emotion to examinations in the group setting to which they have become accustomed in school. In the face-to-face interview technique with an adult, the trained worker must very carefully establish a free and satisfactory *rapport* with the deviant in order that emotional tones from such a contact may be reduced. Similarly some of the therapeutic and remedial suggestions may be given in printed form rather than by word of mouth to avoid the implication that adults are lecturing. Although the deviant may smile in apparent acceptance his basic hidden attitudes toward such guid-

Courtesy of Ralph D. Rabinovitch, M.D., director.

Hawthorn Center for emotionally disturbed children, Northville, Michigan.

Courtesy of Ralph D. Rabinovitch, M.D., director.

Activity projects Hawthorn Center for emotionally disturbed children, Northville, Michigan.

ance are not always as evident as the surface symptoms may indicate. Hamilton[1] devotes one chapter to the importance of such face-to-face relationships.

Which techniques and methods of diagnosis are used, and which methods of therapeutic counseling and guidance are employed are somewhat incidental to achieving the final goal. This goal is insight by the deviant himself and his determination to reach the desired end. Unless the techniques have been understandable and he has accepted them as his own, results will be unsuccessful. This state of affairs is similar to classroom situations in which some particular method of teaching may or may not be effective but its use is nevertheless continued. These same principles must also apply to the attitudes of parents whose guidance of the deviant is also involved.

## The Physiological Examination

Deviant behavior does not exist without cause. There are many possible causes some of which may be bodily disorder, defect, or disease. A complete physical examination should either account for or rule out such factors. In more cases than is generally believed true bodily defects or impaired conditions are present. This will be further illustrated in the twelve chapters of Parts 6 and 7. Any type of disabling physical handicap may disrupt normal activities, lead to frustrations, emotional blockings, and distortions of the personality structure, as we have noted in Chapter 4. Examinations should extend much beyond simple tests of vision and hearing to include the circulatory, respiratory, digestive, endocrine and nervous systems. If all correctable physiological defects could be remedied and suitable educational provisions for all uncorrectable defects be provided, there would undoubtedly be fewer cases of deviant behavior.

The relationships between bodily impairments and emotional disturbances seldom yield to distinct and easy clarification. Whenever a deviant has some emotional disturbance it may seem easier to seek social or psychological causes than to undergo a complete physical examination. There is a further temptation to hope that reduction of

[1] G. Hamilton, *Theory and Practice of Social Case Work*, Columbia University Press, New York, 1956, 328 pp.

the psychological components will relieve the physiological impairment, since this is true in some instances. The author believes that many emotional disturbances are successfully weathered if there is no bodily ailment, but, if such ailment exists, the chances of success are considerably reduced.

## The Aptitudes Examinations

There is no purely mechanical sequence of examinations which should be automatically followed in all cases of deviant behavior. Often the deviant is in a highly disturbed emotional state upon the first interview. He would benefit by some assurance of what examinations are likely to be given and for what purpose. The psychologist is aware of the deviant's mental and emotional state and governs his procedure and time of examination accordingly.

Each individual has not only a general level or degree of ability, but variations from this level in many simpler aptitudes. Some of the current intelligence tests yield not only a general result but, as in the Wechsler examination, separate verbal and nonverbal scores. The Detroit Tests of Learning Aptitude portray test results in a profile of several subparts, as will be described in Chapter 12. Further light will be thrown upon the functioning or malfunctioning of psychological processes in the five chapters of Part 3. Reference should also be made to the important function and position of abilities and aptitudes in the personality structure cited in Chapter 4.

Cases of deviant behavior usually "scatter" over a wide range of abilities on aptitude examinations. Impairment of various portions of the central nervous system are reflected and paralleled by such ranges. The deviant finds that his aptitude for learning has sharp deviations above and below his general intellectual level. When any particular learning process utilizes his higher abilities he feels exhilarated but when the opposite occurs he becomes frustrated and emotionally disturbed. Some causes of deviant behavior lie here rather than in any social or environmental causes. In any case, a complete series of aptitudes examinations is a very significant part of the thorough examination program.

The aptitudes examination should not be limited to intellectual capacities only but should extend to artistic, literary, musical, mechanical, and other abilities. The deviant behavior pupil may well have some surprisingly high abilities in some of these fields about which neither he, his family, nor his teachers are aware. Utilizing these special abilities for constructive goals is one of the best means of gaining recognition for worthwhile accomplishments and substituting them for undesirable forms of behavior.

### Projective Techniques

Another type of examination has been devised to seek out clues to hidden feelings and emotions. A commonly used device is the Rorschach test which consists of a standardized set of ink blots of irregular shapes, colors, and forms which the pupil is encouraged to interpret as they impress him. The examiner studies these clues and by skillful questioning and indirect suggestion leads him into further disclosures about these impressions. Various types of personalities are brought to light. In recent years a school of psychologists have made intensive studies of the Rorschach method and have attempted to standardize the techniques of examination, scoring, and interpretation. The Rorschach test has proved to be a very useful technique in analyzing many forms of deviant behavior. Extensive research is continuing and is summarized in the Fourth Mental Measurements Yearbook.[1]

There are other incidental projective techniques which have as their common purpose the release of hidden attitudes, feelings, and emotions. In simple forms they may occur in the presence of the teacher when a pupil becomes very enthusiastic about some successful or interesting activity. He suddenly bursts out with a statement about his home or parents which is entirely unrelated to the task at hand. Although the alert teacher may recognize the significance of such unrelated behavior, she must proceed as if it had not occurred. She may wisely recognize the basic significance of such incidents. A similar

---

[1] O.K. Buros, ed., *The Fourth Mental Measurements Yearbook*, The Gryphon Press, Highland Park, N.J., 1953, pp. 117-128.

situation may develop at home or in some happy period when parent and child are enjoying a mutual task.

Informal activities with young children such as playing house yield unsolicited information about jealousy of a younger sibling. Punishment given to the doll typifies an attitude toward the newborn baby. These types of play therapy give not only an opportunity for projecting the feelings but also for acting them out since children of this age are too young to formulate them into words.

Cruickshank[1] has devised a projection technique of open-end sentences to be completed by the pupils in whatever way seems most meaningful to them. The responses which he received from pupils with orthopedic handicaps differed from the nonhandicapped in that they showed more concern and anxiety about self and relationships with the nonhandicapped. Further discussion is in Chapter 26.

### Personality Adjustment Inventories

After successful use of group paper-and-pencil tests of intelligence, other aptitudes, and educational achievement were used, attention was turned to similar procedures for character and personality. As early as 1927 the author was requested to make such an inventory to measure the effectiveness of formal instruction in character training for a committee in the Detroit Public Schools. Classes of pupils in grades four to six were divided into experimental and control groups and an eighty-item inventory was prepared and administered with three-choice responses. It included practices and attitudes toward school, home, play, social, and ethical-moral areas. In test construction a principle similar to that used in intelligence tests was employed by sampling judgments about items drawn from environmental experiences. This test was given both as the initial and final survey of one semester, and was known as The Things I Do test.[2]

The interpretation of results did not follow the traditional pattern of improvement in total scores between initial and final testing as is

[1] W. M. Cruickshank, Psychology of Exceptional Children and Youth, Prentice-Hall, Inc., Englewood Cliffs, N.J., 1955, pp. 285-344.

[2] H.J. Baker, The Things I Do, Public School Publishing Company, Cincinnati, Ohio, 8 pp. (out of print).

true in a test of educational achievement. The effectiveness of character training was measured by the changes which occurred in pupils' attitudes and ideas as a result of the classroom training. In control classes where there was only incidental instruction in character, the pupils rated themselves similarly on initial and final tests, whereas in the experimental group there were changes in scores, with some rating themselves higher, others lower, so that the correlation between initial and final testing was less for the experimental than for the control classes. The shifts in ratings were generally considered to reflect desirable changes in attitudes. Those who rated themselves too low on the initial tests had a higher opinion of themselves as a result of the character training, and the opposite was also true.

A revised Gamma form of this inventory for grades three to six, carrying the principal caption *Telling What I Do* is published by the C.A. Gregory Company. The number of items is increased to 128 with three-choice responses. Each item is scored on a two-dimensional rather than on a one-dimensional basis and yields more meaningful results. The first dimension describes certain attitudes toward the environments in which an individual lives. This dimension also includes certain attributes which the environments stimulate in the individual. These attitudes and attributes include such items as the general physical status of the environments; the social reactions toward them; the feeling and emotional tones; and the ethical and moral attitudes and practices in these areas. For example, a child may express a fear about punishment at home. This fear may be stimulated by actual experience, or it may be caused by predispositions or attributes within the child himself. For the moment the chief interest is not in the actual status of punishment or in the child's predispositions towards it, but rather on the fact that he expresses an attitude about it. These matters are considered in the diagnostic process which follows later.

The second dimension of each item is the environment, or rather, the environments. While the term "environment" describes the general surroundings, in practical usage environment is subdivided into specific areas, such as school, home, and neighborhood. In this Gamma form of Adjustment Inventory four subdivisions of environments are delineated. These environments are ranked in a line of distances whose principal element is not necessarily physical distance but the distances of social and emotional control and intimacy. The neighborhood or community is the most distant environment in terms of the individual's control by parents or by other authorized adults. The next in order is the school with control by the teacher but still away from home and parental control. The next environment is the home with parental control and with more emotional and personal elements which characterize it. The last and most immediate environment consists of qualities and factors interwoven into the individual himself or very close to him. These include the clothes he wears, his personal hygiene, and similar characteristics by which he is identified. Items more intimately associated may be a scarred face, a body that is thin or fat, eyes that see clearly or dimly, and hearts that are weak or strong. It is difficult to determine where environment ends and the self begins. Possibly such a limit is beside the point. The individual establishes ethical attitudes and reactions in relation to his neighborhood, his school, his home, and himself. Likewise he has a series of emotional and feeling tones toward each of these four environmental areas, a series of attitudes in which he plays a social role; finally he develops characteristic habits, or evaluation of status in each of them including himself.

The general plan of this two-dimensional pattern is shown in Diagram II. The evaluation of status and habits are first in order since they give practice in judging elements which are relatively more factual than social or ethical judgments. These first series of evaluations are taken in the order of: (1) the individual; (2) the home; (3) the school; and (4) the community or neighborhood. Then environments proceed from the immediate to the more distant, starting with the individual and ending with the community. The social attitudes and attributes constitute the second reaction series and extend through the four environments. The emotional reactions and, finally, the ethical reactions complete the pattern.

The body of Diagram II contains sixteen cells with two-dimensional qualities in each. Totals by reactions appear on the horizontal lines at the right, the environmental totals at the bottom. At the lower right a grand total score may be entered. Each of the sixteen cell scores reveals strengths or weaknesses and discloses some interesting variations from environment to environment and from reaction to reaction. In each cell there are eight items, each with a three-choice response. The score values range from one for the least desirable responses to three for the most desirable. The total score for each cell has a minimum of eight points and a maximum of twenty-four points. A tentative or informal standard of less than seventeen points was determined as the "cutoff" point below which individuals would profit by some interpretation and suggestions for improvement. A series of sixteen remedial leaflets, corresponding to the sixteen cells of Diagram II was prepared for the guidance of parents and designed to be of assistance to teachers as well.

**Individual Pattern of Reactions to Environments**

Environment

| Reaction | Individual | Home | School | Community | Total |
|---|---|---|---|---|---|
| Habits or status | | | | | |
| Social | | | | | |
| Emotional | | | | | |
| Ethical | | | | | |
| Total | | | | | |

**DIAGRAM II**

*Basis of treatment.* Upon the basis of practical case study methods by visiting teachers, serving as school social workers, some general standards of pupils' needs were determined according to the number of cells with scores of less than seventeen points. If none or only one leaflet was indicated, the pupil's problem was generally slight and required only one incidental discussion between teacher and parents; if two or three leaflets were needed there should have been several conferences between teachers and parents using the leaflets as the basis of discussion; if four or five leaflets were indicated the visiting teacher should have been added to the conference team in a consultive capacity; and, if six or more leaflets were indicated, the case needed intensive study by the trained social worker or visiting teacher working with the pupil, the teacher, the parents, and all other parties having some contributions to make.

A *Detroit survey.* Four Detroit elementary public schools were surveyed in grades four through six using this Inventory. Schools A and B served low economic and social areas of crowded rooming houses and old apartment buildings whereas schools C and D were located in single-home-owned neighborhoods of a little above average economic status. In schools A and B sixty-seven out of 585 pupils or 11.5 per cent showed the need for intensive case treatment, and in schools C and D twenty-eight out of 718 pupils or 4.2 per cent needed such treatment. In addition to the specific cases needing individual treatment certain sociological problems were disclosed. In the less favored areas the girls showed many emotional disturbances from discord in the home, lack of privacy, and crowded confusion whereas the boys in these areas were less aware of these problems but protested about lack of playground space and the attendant hours of enforced idleness.

Other forms in this Detroit Adjustment Inventory Series include the Delta Form for children five to eight years of age in which the teacher in cooperation with the parents does the rating. The same general plan of reactions to environments is followed and there are sixteen remedial leaflets for the guidance of teachers and parents. The Alpha Form is available for pupils in junior and senior high school and covers in one dimension, twenty-four areas, such as health, habits, home, personality traits, and ethical standards. The remedial leaflets are designed for use by the pupils themselves. A form for adults with remedial leaflets is available but designed for interpretation by a trained counselor. All forms in this series are available through the C.A. Gregory Company, Cincinnati, Ohio.

The California Test of Personality has a series of five forms ranging from kindergarten through to the adult level and is available through the California Test Bureau, Los Angeles. Science Research Associates of Chicago publishes a Junior Inventory for grades four to eight. The Mooney Problem Check Lists, published by the Psychological Corporation, New York, has forms for junior and senior high school and college. The Bernreuter Adjustment Inventory for college students and adults is available through the C.A. Gregory Company.

All of these inventories are valuable for survey purposes and for locating pupils who appear to have the greater number of problems. The specific areas in which problems are found furnish the school social worker or the psychologist with clues for professional interpretation in their diagnostic programs. The remedial leaflets supplement their interpretations with opportunity to read and study in privacy suggestions for improvements. None of the authors of such inventories claim they are complete diagnostic and remedial instruments without professional interpretation, but within these limits they are useful and economical of professional time.

## The Case-Study Method

At some point in the study of the deviant in behavior a thorough and comprehensive case study is prepared by a trained social worker. It may precede or follow the aptitudes and the physiological examinations or the various personality inventories. The case history gives insight into the general background of family. The ages of parents, their health, education, occupation, economic status, and attitudes toward the deviant are evaluated in regard to effects upon the deviant himself. The list of siblings is also covered in the same manner and for the same reasons. Descriptions of grandparents frequently provide clues as to hereditary diseases and influences upon the deviant's parents.

The health and developmental history of the deviant are surveyed in detail, i.e., prenatal conditions, birth conditions, age of walking and talking, childhood diseases. Interpretations are sought for conditions which have resulted in personality distortions and causes of deviant behavior. The personal description of the deviant often yields clues about such causes as unfavorable facial features resulting in social rejection. Community agencies in addition to schools which should provide auxiliary service to the deviant or to his family are taken into account. The registration bureau services in larger cities furnish important information about what agencies have been active in behalf of the deviant or his family. The deviant's associates and their activities furnish important clues about his interests, his hobbies, and use of his spare time. His progress in school and his behavior furnish a picture of his attitude toward school.

The case history is by no means a mechanical process of questions and answers, but is designed to be a practical means for becoming acquainted with the many phases of the deviant's problems. Parents participate and receive some interpretations which reveal how their attitudes and their general disciplinary policies have affected the deviant. Information, interpretation, and therapy proceed hand in hand. There are two variations of the therapeutic process which should be mentioned. In the nondirective therapy the counselor, psychologist, or school social worker refrains from offering direct advice, but believes that with liberal explanation and understanding of the problems the deviant himself or his parents will see and carry out what should be done. Rogers[1] describes this nondirective therapy in his *Counseling and Psychotherapy*. A somewhat different approach is to give some direct therapeutic advice and suggestions in the belief that, although problems have been discussed, their solutions may not be so obvious to parent and deviant who are too close to the problem to see it clearly. In an ideal situation the nondirective process is relatively more desirable because it has been originated and understood by the individual himself, and hence he has his own motivation for improvement. To the extent that he or his parents prefer to rely upon what they consider to be more professional advice by the trained worker than their own judgment some directive counseling is welcomed. It is probably true that much of the case technique is a combination of the two methods. In the final analysis the individual must understand and accept the conditions of treatment himself, otherwise it is likely to fail.

[1] C.R. Rogers, *Counseling and Psychotherapy*, Houghton Mifflin Co., Boston, 1942, 450 pp.

enrolled there or with schools where such pupils were soon to be enrolled.

*Distribution of visiting teacher time.* The distribution of visiting teacher time is shown in Table X. One-third of their time is spent with the pupils themselves, 15 per cent with teachers and other staff members, and approximately 8 per cent is devoted to conferences with other organizations interested in the welfare and progress of children.

TABLE IX

Agencies and Organizations Consulted

| Type | Individual Pupils | | Times Consulted | |
|---|---|---|---|---|
| | No. | Per cent | No. | Per cent |
| Clinics, psychological-guidance | 717 | 22.8 | 2984 | 28.8 |
| Schools | 466 | 14.9 | 1436 | 14.0 |
| Family agencies | 363 | 11.5 | 1106 | 10.8 |
| Clinics, health | 379 | 12.1 | 1065 | 10.4 |
| Child care | 309 | 9.8 | 1015 | 9.9 |
| Courts | 326 | 10.3 | 971 | 9.4 |
| Miscellaneous | 157 | 5.0 | 504 | 4.9 |
| Recreation | 140 | 4.4 | 399 | 3.9 |
| Camps | 130 | 4.1 | 331 | 3.2 |
| Institutions | 84 | 2.7 | 256 | 2.5 |
| Churches | 76 | 2.4 | 226 | 2.2 |
| Total | 3,147 | 100.0 | 10,293 | 100.0 |

*Types of adjustment of closed cases.* Approximately two-thirds of all the cases had made a satisfactory or fair adjustment upon closing. There were various reasons to explain the 10 per cent who remained unsatisfactorily adjusted; for instance, refusal of the family to cooperate or children suspended for some sudden overt action.

Similar programs are being instituted in many other Michigan cities and programs have also been started in many other states. The visiting teachers are also known as school social workers and affiliate as a division of the National Association of Social Workers. In the Detroit programs they are required to have preparation as teachers

TABLE X

Distribution of Visiting Teachers' Time

| Activity | Per cent of Time |
|----------|------------------|
| Pupils | 32.3 |
| Teachers and staff | 15.5 |
| Parents | 12.2 |
| Organizations | 7.9 |
| | |
| Speeches | 0.5 |
| Travel | 9.8 |
| Reports, meetings | 20.0 |
| Miscellaneous | 1.8 |
| Total | 100.0 |

with regular permanent teaching certificates, and, in addition, must have professional training in schools of social work in recognized universities. Many of them have the two-year master's of social work degree or two regular master's degrees, one of which fulfills the requirements for full qualification as a visiting teacher. Child Guidance Clinics are being established under the auspices of such agencies of state governments as mental health commissions. These clinics provide the various services of psychiatrist, psychologist, social worker, nurse, and educational diagnostician. They are successful to the extent that there is full cooperation with school systems in the services to pupils with behavior and personality problems.

### Educational Provisions

In addition to the various diagnostic and remedial services, schools must provide for continued enrollment in regular or special schools or classes. Many school systems have found it necessary to establish special facilities because it becomes impractical and impossible to conduct regular classes with one or more of these deviant cases in attendance. Detroit public schools have three schools for older boys with a diversified program of academic, shop, and vocational courses. There are also fifteen classes for boys eight to twelve years of age that have not more than fifteen pupils enrolled in each and are under the direction of a well-trained and understanding teacher. The Chicago public schools have centers for older boys and a similar school for older girls. In both cities diagnostic facilities and visiting teacher programs are provided.

There is a small number of extremely disturbed children who cannot fit into such special facilities and need periods of hospitalization with a minimum school program provided in the hospital. The Hawthorn Center, the Lafayette Clinic and Hospital, as well as children's wards of State Mental Hospitals in or near Detroit are providing facilities for a limited number of such cases. The research activities of these hospitals and clinics are throwing new light upon the nature of extreme disturbances.

## Research Findings in Deviant Behavior

From the information provided in earlier sections of this chapter it is evident that the causes of deviant behavior are multiple in character, although, of course, some cases may have only a few causes. Others have many causes whose interrelationships are extremely puzzling. By contrast most of the sensory and physical handicaps such as impaired vision have their origin in a specific imperfection in the crystalline lens, in muscle imbalance, or as a result of an accident or injury.

A few investigations have disclosed evidences of principal factors in juvenile delinquency. Sheldon and Eleanor Glueck[1] made an extensive study of one thousand such cases and out of some sixty factors which existed in predelinquency days the following six were considered to be the most significant: (1) unsound discipline by father; (2) by mother; (3) school retardation of three years or more; (4) school failure or other misconduct; (5) early age of first-known behavior disorder; and (6) length of time between onset of delinquency and the child's examination by the Judge Baker Foundation.

Within these factors there is a variety of modifying conditions. Unsound discipline may be extreme either in too great leniency or in

[1] S. Glueck and E. Glueck, *One Thousand Juvenile Delinquents*, Harvard University Press, Cambridge, Mass., 1939, 341 pp.

excessive severity or in unpredictable fluctuations between them. Standards of discipline by parents reflect their own childhood disciplinary experiences and are combined with the current social family atmosphere. School retardation of three years or more usually has as one of its principal causes some degree of mental retardation, which may be the primary factor rather than the school retardation itself. However, some cases of school retardation are not mentally retarded as will be noted in the chapters of Part 5. The frustration resulting from the school retardation is known to be painfully evident. School failure has obviously been a prelude to school retardation and with much the same consequences. Unsound discipline by parents started at the child's early age sets his pattern of deviant behavior in his highly formative years. The sixth and final item is self-evident that the longer the unwholesome conditions remained untreated, the more ominous were their effects. This discussion of what appeared to be six relatively simple factors discloses that all of them in turn were based on multiple causes or had multiple effects themselves.

Sheldon[1] and his associates related the varieties of delinquent youth to their system of somatotyping outlined briefly in the discussion of temperament in Chapter 4. Delinquent youth was found to be strongly muscular or mesomorphic and had a below-average score on endomorphy and a definite lacking in ectomorphy or linearity of body. Mothers of delinquent youths were somewhat obese, yet muscular, and powerful, and had an apparent tendency to reject their errant offspring. Sheldon indicated a belief that causes of maladjustment were affiliated with body type and its somatic factors rather than with Freudian psychoanalytic processes.

*Cause-and-effect relationships.* One of the baffling problems in the study of deviant behavior is proof of cause-and-effect relationship between seemingly unrelated causes and effects. When two elements exist side by side with equal degrees of intensity it is usually concluded, erroneously or otherwise, that one causes the other. However, concurrent variations may be accidental and may be caused by one or more conditions which are not a common factor in them.

---

[1] W.H. Sheldon, E.M. Hartl, and E. McDermott, *Varieties of Delinquent Youth*, Harper & Brothers, New York, 1949, 899 pp.

Common sense should determine whether the relationships are merely concurrent or if they are indeed valid relationships. With such limitations in mind, the author will propose some relationships and will try to discover if there are any possible cause-and-effect connections.

In some earlier investigations by Baker and Traphagen,[1] sixty-six factors of case backgrounds were rated on a five-point scale for 189 cases of deviant behavior. Each factor was corrrelated with all of the other factors, for a total of 2,145 correlations. In deviants twelve years of age or older there was evidence of some relationship of truancy from school to lack of playthings and recreational facilities in the early childhood home. Lack of play and recreation may have weakened the holding power of the home, led to unrest and feelings of insecurity. Pleasures outside of the home had to be sought in homes of neighbors where there were toys and where playmates seemed happier. Gradually a basic pattern of unrest developed, which became identified with the unlearned needs and drives within the personality structure. This pattern of unrest and of seeking satisfactions elsewhere was transferred from the home to the school as a place of belonging. The obvious results take place. The school is unable to do much more than the home and adventures outside are much more attractive. These same individuals drift from job to job and are transient patrons of skid row. A professional worker versed in populations of skid row verified that the population was transient and constantly drifted from city to city and from flophouse to flophouse. This type of cause-and-effect relationship seems to have a logical and bona fide connection. It may also illustrate a type of Freudian pattern. In the area of prevention it suggests that the present generation of young children should be blessed with happy homes having holding power and a few toys, so that a later generation of truants shall not be developed. Incidentally, this type of relationship might not have been discovered by a study of a single case, but the trends in a large number of such cases cannot be ignored as accidental. The lack of playthings and general recreational facilities are not simple single-

---

[1] H.J. Baker and V. Traphagen, *The Diagnosis and Treatment of Behavior-Problem Children*, The Macmillan Co., New York, 1935, 393 pp. (out of print).

unit factors but are composed of such auxiliary factors as parental love and affection for children and other social ingredients.

Another cause-and-effect relationship was found between a lack of initiative and ambition and physical size. Abnormally large size caused by endocrine disturbances might easily affect the outlook on health and vitality, while below average sizes might be due to illnesses and malnourishment and could lessen initiative and ambition. Another relationship was found between chronic dream disturbances and mothers' ages at birth of such children. If the mothers were much beyond the age of usual child bearing they often had more than usual anxiety and fear of the ordeal and possibly did not want or expect a child at this late period. Similarly some very young mothers were illegitimately pregnant with the attendant feelings of insecurity, guilt, and emotional upset. Whether there is any direct connection between these emotional states during pregnancy and the disturbed mental conditions of the expected babies may still be a matter of speculation, but, in any event, if such conditions exist after the birth takes place they might easily be reflected in the early years of babyhood and infancy.

*Possibilities of improvement.* One of the most important phases of remedial work is to discover what improvements can be brought about in behavior. In many investigations behavior causes have apparently been assumed to be in a state of immobility, whereas it is more meaningful to consider them in a state of flux. Such an approach has been made under the author's direction and reported in a master's thesis.[1] Mobility introduces useful aids to mental hygiene. The problem of improvability was motivated by the knowledge that some causes of maladjustment seemed to be more susceptible to improvement than others. Little was known about what items offered such possibilities. As far as specific items are concerned, two types of changes are possible. One type occurs when the problem itself is capable of improvement; for example, the use of glasses to correct an eye condition. A second type does not involve change in the problem itself but results from an altered and more favorable attitude

[1] A.W. Rodeheffer, "A Study of the Relationships in Behavior Factors," unpublished master's thesis, Wayne State University, Detroit, 1940, 100 pp.

such as a more satisfactory adjustment to an incurable type of blindness.

It seems unnecessary to go into the details of how a formula of pliability or change was developed. One approach was by studying the contrast of item relationships to each other between a delinquent group and a nondelinquent group of approximately two hundred pupils each. The results are shown in Table XI.

The six principal columns of Table XI include the six areas of a case history. Eight items are included in home atmosphere; eleven items in personality and social favors, etc. A score on a five-point scale had been computed for each item within each of the two groups of pupils. The differences between these scores of the items do not appear in the table, but were used to determine the group order of absolute differentiation between the six groupings or columns of the table. The items in the column of *Personality and Social Factors* were found to have the greatest relative differences between the delinquent and the nondelinquent groups in favor of the latter; the school factors were second in order; home atmosphere, third; habits and recreational factors, fourth; physical factors of the home, fifth; and health and physical factors, sixth. In other words the health and physical factors differentiated in favor of the nondelinquent group but not as markedly as did the personality and social factors.

The order of pliability by groups of factors in the various columns is different from the order of absolute differentiation. All of the items were ranked in the order appearing in the table according to a rank order coefficient of correlation which contrasted the delinquent and the nondelinquent groups. Taken together the eight items of home atmosphere ranked first above all the other groups in pliability or susceptibility to change. This trend is a very hopeful sign since it has often been assumed that home atmosphere was very difficult to improve. Actually the improvement is only a return to or restoration of the ideals and high hopes which reigned when the husband carried his bride over the threshold. It is significant that there is a slightly greater possibility of changing the adult attitude than changing that of children. The full significance of this difference has not been fully realized nor appreciated. It is contrary to preconceived ideas

## TABLE XI

### Pliability of the Sixty-Six Items or Causes

Main Classifications of Causes

| Order of Greatest Pliability | Home Atmosphere | Personality and Social Factors | Physical Home Factors | Habits and Recreational Factors | School Factors | Health and Physical Factors |
|---|---|---|---|---|---|---|
| 1 | | | | conditions of eating | | |
| 2 | | | occupation; father's education | | | |
| 3 | | | | | | |
| 4 | | interests or hobbies | | | | |
| 5 | ideals of home | | | | | |
| 6 | | | economic status; mother's education | | | |
| 7 | | | | | | |
| 8 | | | | early recreation; hygiene clothing | | |
| 9 | | | | | | |
| 10 | family recreation | | | | | |

**TABLE XI** (*Continued*)

Main Classifications of Causes

| Order of Greatest Pliability | Home Atmosphere | Personality and Social Factors | Physical Home Factors | Habits and Recreational Factors | School Factors | Health and Physical Factors |
|---|---|---|---|---|---|---|
| 11 | | | | sleeping conditions | | |
| 12 | | personality type | | | | |
| 13 | | | | | | |
| 14 | | | mother's intelligence | home duties | | |
| 15 | parents' social adjustment | | | | | |
| 16 | | | father's personality | | | |
| 17 | attitude toward child | | | | | |
| 18 | initiative and ambition | | | | | |
| 19 | | | home language | | | |
| 20 | discipline | | | | | |

# TABLE XI (Continued)

Main Classifications of Causes

| Order of Greatest Pliability | Home Atmosphere | Personality and Social Factors | Physical Home Factors | Habits and Recreational Factors | School Factors | Health and Physical Factors |
|---|---|---|---|---|---|---|
| 21 | | | | later recreation | | convulsions, seizures; |
| 22 | | | | | | visual defect |
| 23 | | excitement, shock; | | | | |
| 24 | | vocational interests | | | | |
| 25 | | | | | | |
| 26 | child's attitude | social type | | | | |
| 27 | | | | | | |
| 28 | | anger, rage | | | | orthopedic defect |
| 29 | | | father's intelligence | | | |
| 30 | | | | | | |
| 31 | | general behavior | | | | accidents |
| 32 | religion; | | | | | |
| 33 | general home atmosphere | | | | | |
| 34 | | | | | | |
| 35 | | | | | attendance | |

**TABLE XI** (*Continued*)

Main Classifications of Causes

| Order of Greatest Pliability | Home Atmosphere | Personality and Social Factors | Physical Home Factors | Habits and Recreational Factors | School Factors | Health and Physical Factors |
|---|---|---|---|---|---|---|
| 36 | | fear, anxiety | | | | |
| 37 | | | | | | |
| 38 | | | mother's personality; mother's health | | | present health |
| 39 | | | | present self-care | | |
| 40 | | | | | | |
| 41 | | pity, sympathy | | | scholarship | |
| 42 | | | | | | |
| 43 | | | | playmates | | speech defect; |
| 44 | | | | | | early health |
| 45 | | | | | | |
| 46 | | | | time of sleeping | | infectious diseases |
| 47 | | | father's health; | | attitude | |
| 48 | | | broken home | | | |
| 49 | | | | | | |
| 50 | | | | | | |
| 51 | | | | looks or appearance; eating habits | | |
| 52 | | | legal status; father's age | | | |
| 53 | | | | | | |
| 54 | | | | | | |
| 55 | | | | dreams | | |

**TABLE XI** (*Continued*)

| Order of Greatest Pliability | Home Atmosphere | Personality and Social Factors | Physical Home Factors | Habits and Recreational Factors | School Factors | Health and Physical Factors |
|---|---|---|---|---|---|---|
| 56 | | | | early self-care | | |
| 57 | | | other adults | | | nervousness; |
| 58 | | | | | | hearing defect |
| 59 | | | mother's age | | | |
| 60 | | | | | | |
| 61 | | intelligence | | | | motor co-ordination |
| 62 | | | sibling number and position; sibling adjustment | | | |
| 63 | | | | | | |
| 64 | | | | | | size; children's diseases |
| 65 | | | | | | |
| 66 | | | | | | |
| Group order of pliability | 1 | 2 | 3 | 4 | 5 | 6 |
| Group order of absolute differentiation | 3 | 1 | 5 | 4 | 2 | 6 |

Main Classifications of Causes

that change is easier for children than for adults. A forced lip service by children only disguises secret and hidden attitudes which children have continued to retain. Since children's attitudes are difficult to change it is highly important that correct and wholesome attitudes be established at the very outset. Radical changes in child training and educational procedures are indicated from these findings.

In the group of personality and social factors it is much easier to change children's interests and hobbies than to change their basic intellectual outlook. This outlook is the least pliable of all sixty-six factors and should not be confused with minor changes in intelligence quotients. Among the other factors in this area it is more difficult to alter attitudes of pity and sympathy than to control anger or rage.

The items in the physical factors of the home extend over a wide range of pliability. Occupations of fathers were highly susceptible to change in days of depression and unemployment. Along with such conditions the ability to capitalize on the father's education was also a highly fluctuating factor. From a theoretical "Gallup" poll or sampling of these two items in modern life some index of civic and home stability could probably be computed. The comparative diffi culty of improving sibling adjustments and their relationships within families of different sizes are verified by their standings near the bottom of the pliability scale.

Among the habits and recreational factors related to the home the conditions during mealtime are the most susceptible to improvement or change. If the home life has deteriorated it is not too late to make changes for the better. If a family firmly resolves to declare a truce and have at least one daily meal in a pleasant atmosphere, success is so satisfying that the pattern is easily extended to other mealtimes and to an entire program of better living. Unfortunate looks or appearance is obviously difficult to change. Cultivation of social graces is needed to counteract them. The three items of school factors illustrate the old adage that "you can lead a horse to water but you can't make him drink." Attendance at school may be forced by law; scholarship is more difficult to improve after the pupil is forced into school. Attitudes toward school are the most difficult to improve.

Although the actual differences in health and physical factors between the delinquent and the nondelinquent groups are not extreme, improvement or pliability are the least promising of all areas. If a child has been unduly discouraged by chronic illness he may develop a pattern of discouragement toward school and life which is very difficult to change. The obvious corollary is to develop and maintain a high level of health. In the years of rapid physical growth deviations from the norm or standard for the same age group may have unfortunate results. This problem is discussed in more detail in Chapter 28 on Disorders and Defects in Growth. All of these sixty-six factors and many more which may contribute to deviant behavior are deserving of detailed study and treatment.

The implications of factor or item pliability for the individual deviant are grave. If the unfavorable factors are near the pliable end of the scale the chances of marked improvement are good, but if the unfavorable factors or conditions lie mainly at the less pliable end of the scale a very realistic attitude needs to be taken.

### Suggestions for Teachers and Parents

Many sections of this chapter have outlined and described various services which may be provided by the family physician, the medical specialist, the psychologist, and the school social worker. These services are not provided in sufficient numbers, therefore, no more than a small percentage of all deviant cases can be studied and treated. A large majority of cases must continue to be serviced by teachers and parents without such help.

The author has prepared a four-page bulletin of brief paragraphs on thirty topics, entitled *Suggestions for Training Children*[1] and, with the cooperation of Marygrove Faculty, a special edition with Catholic interpretation is also available from the same publisher. Remedial leaflets for the various Detroit Adjustment Inventories mentioned in earlier sections are helpful with or without the use of the inventories themselves. At the secondary level they furnish content materials for

[1] H.J. Baker, *Suggestions for Training Children*, C.A. Gregory Co., Cincinnati, Ohio, 1940, 4 pp.

courses in home and family living and have been found useful for motivating conversation of speech-handicapped high school students. As a practical guide, the author offers the following suggestions:

1. Aim sincerely to understand the deviant and his problems. Understanding removes the mystery of his behavior and helps you to believe in him. He will probably become aware of this attitude after a short time.

2. Arrange a sponsor for him—principal, assistant principal, counselor, or some teacher. Let him choose this person, preferably not his own teacher. Have him report informally about once a week with comments that others may care to send. This plan should not be called probation and no particular pattern is recommended for it; leave it to the ingenuity of pupil and sponsor.

3. Find out his chief grievance and gradually substitute other activities for it without necessarily leading him to believe you are catering to him. An imagined grievance does about as much harm as an actual one.

4. Find some thing or things that he can do well and for which he will get favorable recognition from his classmates. He probably has some interests, either within or out of school which may be capitalized. At first this recognition will tend to "go to his head" since he is not used to it, but he should gradually become accustomed to it and accept it in the same way as other pupils ordinarily do.

5. Gradually enlist the cooperation of a small group of classmates in his progress, by tactfully pointing out how well he is doing and how hard he is trying. A little praise from classmates is sometimes more effective than that from any adult because it comes at his own level.

6. Enlist the parents to believe in him, have them find ways in which he may be praised at home for effort and good behavior. Suggest activities to them for out-of-school projects: scouts, hobbies, music, etc. A busy, interesting program is one of the best antidotes for idleness and mischief.

7. Have his physical defects corrected, including minor ones which

may be affecting his progress. Extend this plan to traits of character and personality as far as possible.

8. Arrange a flexible program in school. Let him realize this is a sympathetic attempt to get him up to a better level. Eventually he should strive to restore the usual program. Frequently a brief rest period is a good antidote for uneasiness and disturbing behavior.

9. Do not become too discouraged and do not let him become disheartened by some lapses. Keep up his confidence and share yours with him. The lapses will become less frequent and severe. Help him to realize that these concessions are not coddling, but are opportunities for him to make good and that this is his responsibility.

10. If this program does not bring some helpful changes after a fair and thorough trial, you may be dealing with a serious case which should be referred to professional, trained personnel for assistance that you are unable to give.

### Other Forms of Deviant Behavior

The chapters of Part 3 give further interpretation of deviant behavior including convulsive disorders and diseases, cerebral palsy, and encephalitis. Although these kinds of disorders sometimes cause disturbances and interruptions of school and family life, their effects are more likely to be discounted because of specific nervous and physical causes than is true of the kinds of deviant behavior discussed in this chapter.

Special reference should be made to Chapter 11 on mental disorders and diseases as causes of deviant behavior. These extreme types of cases are comparatively rare yet very difficult to control and train in regular classes. Many of them find their way into wards of mental hospitals. The four chapters of Part 4 throw additional light on certain forms of deviant behavior which are based on characteristics resulting from intellectual differences. Deviant behavior is a universal denominator of most kinds of exceptional children. If full allowance can be made for the physical, neurological, and intellectual characteristics of children, the entire field of deviant behavior would be greatly reduced with optimum correction, and with suitable educational provision.

## Questions and Topics for Discussion

1. Describe the relationship of group and individual programs in your community.
2. Analyze the time and cost for professional services on typical deviant cases.
3. List the various examinations and treatment which you would recommend for a case of deviant behavior.
4. Report on the principal features of the Rorschach test.
5. Report on Cruickshank's projection technique of open-end sentences.
6. Prepare a discussion of the Detroit Adjustment Inventory Series.
7. Consider further advantages and disadvantages of the directive versus nondirective therapy.
8. Report on the activities of the visiting teacher program in your community.
9. Discuss further implications of pliability as described in this chapter.

## A. Organizations

1. American Orthopsychiatric Association, 1790 Broadway, New York 19.
2. American Psychological Association, Washington, D.C.
3. National Association for Mental Health, 1790 Broadway, New York 19.
4. National Association of Social Workers, 95 Madison Ave., New York 16.
5. National Probation and Parole Association, 1790 Broadway, New York 19.
6. Society for the Prevention of Crime, 114 E. 30th St., New York 16.

## B. Periodicals

1. *American Journal of Orthopsychiatry* (quarterly), American Orthopsychiatric Association, 1790 Broadway, New York 19.
2. *Federal Probation* (quarterly), Supreme Court Building, Washington 25, D.C.
3. *Journal of Abnormal and Social Psychology*, (bimonthly), American Psychological Association, Washington, D.C.

4. *Mental Hygiene* (quarterly), National Association for Mental Health, 1790 Broadway, New York 19.
5. *Quarterly Journal of Child Behavior,* 70 Pine St., New York 5.

## C. Books

1. American Council on Education, *Helping Teachers Understand Children,* American Council on Education, Washington, D.C.
2. Baker, H.J., *The Art of Understanding,* Christopher Publishing House, Boston, 1940, 400 pp.
3. ———, and V. Traphagen, *The Diagnosis and Treatment of Behavior-Problem Children,* The Macmillan Co., New York, 1935, 393 pp. (out of print).
4. Barron, M.L., *The Juvenile in Delinquent Society,* Alfred A. Knopf, New York, 1954, 349 pp.
5. Bloch, H.A., and F.T. Flynn, *Delinquency,* Random House, New York, 1956, 612 pp.
6. Edelston, H., *The Earliest Stages of Delinquency,* Williams and Wilkins, Baltimore, Md., 1952, 200 pp.
7. Gavian, R.W., *Understanding Juvenile Delinquency,* Oxford Book Co., New York, 1954, 74 pp.
8. Glueck, S., and E. Glueck, *Delinquents in the Making; Paths to Prevention,* Harper & Brothers, New York, 1952, 214 pp.
9. ———, and ———, *Juvenile Delinquents Grown Up,* The Commonwealth Fund, New York, 1940, 330 pp.
10. ———, and ———, *One Thousand Juvenile Delinquents,* Harvard University Press, Cambridge, Mass., 1939, 341 pp.
11. ———, and ———, *Preventing Crime,* A Symposium, McGraw-Hill Book Co., Inc., New York, 1936, 509 pp.
12. ———, and ———, *Unraveling Juvenile Delinquency,* The Commonwealth Fund, New York, 1950, 399 pp.
13. Gordon, H.L., *Casework Services for Children,* Houghton Mifflin Co., Boston, 1956, 493 pp.
14. Grinker, R.R., *Psychosomatic Research,* W.W. Norton Co., New York, 1954, 208 pp.
15. Hamilton, G., *Theory and Practice of Social Case Work* (2nd ed. rev.), Columbia University Press, 1956, 328 pp.
16. Hendrickson, R.C., and F.J. Cook, *Youth in Danger,* Harcourt Brace and Co., Inc., New York, 1956, 300 pp.
17. Hoyles, J.A., *The Treatment of the Young Delinquent,* Philosophical Library, New York, 1952, 274 pp.

18. Kahn, R.L., and C.F. Cannell, *The Dynamics of Interviewing*, John Wiley and Sons, Inc., New York, 1957, 368 pp.
19. Kvaraceus, W.C., *Juvenile Delinquency and the School*, World Book Co., Yonkers, N. Y., 1945, 337 pp.
20. Levy, H.P., *Public Relations for Social Agencies*, Harper & Brothers, New York, 1956, 208 pp.
21. Lippman, H.S., *Treatment of the Child in Emotional Conflict*, McGraw-Hill Book Co., Inc., New York, 1956, 298 pp.
22. McClellan, G.S. (ed.), *Juvenile Delinquency*, The H.W. Wilson Co., New York, 1956, 183 pp.
23. National Society for the Study of Education, *Juvenile Delinquency and the Schools*, Forty-seventh Yearbook, Part I, University of Chicago Press, Chicago, 1948, 280 pp.
24. Pearman, J.R., and A.H. Burrows, *Social Services in the School*, Public Affairs Press, Washington, D.C., 1955, 208 pp.
25. Perlman, H.H., *Social Casework, A Problem-Solving Process*, University of Chicago Press, Chicago, 1957, 292 pp.
26. Rogers, C.R., *The Clinical Treatment of the Problem Child*, Houghton Mifflin Co., Boston, 1939, 393 pp.
27. Sheldon, W.H., *Varieties of Delinquent Youth*, Harper & Brothers, New York, 1949, 899 pp.
28. Sherman, M., *Basic Problems of Behavior*, Longmans Green and Company, New York, 1941, 440 pp.
29. Stevenson, G.S., *Mental Health Planning for Social Action*, McGraw-Hill Book Co., Inc., New York, 1956, 358 pp.
30. Stott, D.H., *Saving Children from Delinquency*, Philosophical Library, New York, 1953, 266 pp.
31. Vedder, C.B., *The Juvenile Offender*, Doubleday Doran Company, Garden City, N. Y., 1954, 510 pp.

## D. Films and Filmstrips

1. *Angry Boy*, 33 minutes, sound. Hidden hostility traced to overprotective attitude of well-intentioned mother. Mental Health Film Board.
2. *Feelings of Depression*, 30 minutes, sound. Lifetime tracing of emotional significance of experiences. McGraw-Hill Text-Film Department.
3. *Feeling of Hostility*, 27 minutes, sound. A girl's hostility from early childhood to adulthood. McGraw-Hill Text-Film Department.
4. *Feeling of Rejection*, 23 minutes, sound. Patient has physical disorders without physical cause, understanding results in healthier habits. McGraw-Hill Text-Film Department.

5. *Maintaining Classroom Discipline,* 14 minutes, sound, follow-up filmstrip. Contrasts wholesome and unwholesome handling of classroom discipline. McGraw-Hill Text-Film Department.

6. *Overdependency,* 32 minutes, sound. The effects of an overprotected childhood counterbalanced through self-insight. National Film Board of Canada.

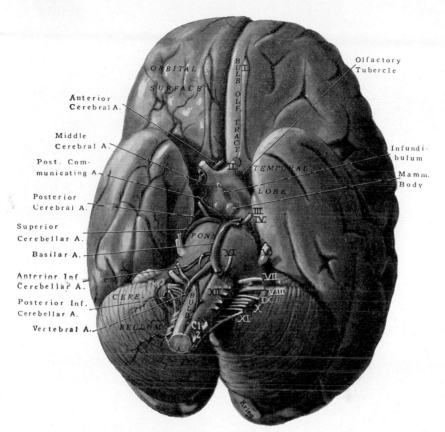

Anterior
Cerebral A.

Middle
Cerebral A.

Post. Com-
municating A

Posterior
Cerebral A.

Superior
Cerebellar A.

Basilar A.

Anterior Inf
Cerebellar A.

Posterior Inf.
Cerebellar A.

Vertebral A.

ORBITAL
SURFACE

BULB OLF.
TRACT

TEMPORAL

LOBE

PONS

CERE-
BELLUM

BULB

Olfactory
Tubercle

Infundi-
bulum

Mamm.
Body

*Courtesy and permission of Wendell J.S. Krieg, Ph.D., author and proprietor of Brain Books. Reproduction from Brain Mechanisms in Diachrome.*

**Basal aspects of the human brain.**

*Courtesy and permission of the owner and manufacturer,*
*Grass Instrument Company, Quincy, Massachusetts.*

The Electroencephalograph.

# PART 3

## Neurological and Mental Disorders and Diseases

# CHAPTER 7

## The Anatomy and Physiology

## of the Nervous System

THE NERVOUS SYSTEM is a focal point in the framework of human action. As an anatomical system of the body, it is director and coordinator of all other bodily systems. It was previously mentioned as a basic factor in the discussion of mental hygiene and mental health. In the next few chapters neurological disorders and diseases are the key to unusual behavior reactions whose indirect causes are easily misunderstood. Deviations in amount and quality of nerve output produce deviations in abilities and aptitudes as will be noted in Part 4. In later chapters which deal with sensory and physical disorders, the nervous system causes or reflects normal and abnormal reactions. A discussion of the nervous system should be an introductory prelude to all succeeding chapters. It has been located strategically to serve as a key to certain disorders and diseases, but it could well be reviewed at all points throughout the text.

The human body is a truly wonderful mechanism in which the nervous system plays a most significant role. There are at least four principal systems of the body which provide some process or media to the other systems. The respiratory system uses air with its vital oxygen content as its principal medium. The digestive system uses the solids and liquids of foods as its medium of communication. The circulatory system uses the blood as its medium to the body. The nervous system also has its medium of communication which is unique. Nothing physical moves along its pathways as in the case of

115

air, food, or blood. The nervous system uses chemical reaction or some electro-chemical medium of communication. Its reaction time is practically instantaneous, whereas digestion of food takes hours and under ordinary circumstances up to three days to complete the expulsion of waste products by defecation. This high priority in speed of communication signifies the paramount importance of the nervous system in protection from dangers, and in intelligent response to a constantly changing array of environmental situations. With these conditions in mind, attention will now be turned to the nature of the nervous system.

### Structure

Complete knowledge is not yet available about all details of nerve action or processes such as is true in an inventory of the bones in the skeletal system. In order to gain a better understanding of the nervous system, it is more practical to start with the simpler types of nerves and continue through the various reception centers such as the medulla to the complexities of the cerebral processes.

*Nerves.* Nerves reach all portions of the body. Some nerves start with tiny receptors integrated closely with muscles and with other bodily organs from which they receive nerve impressions. These dendrite receptors lead into the nerve cell. The axon leads out of the nerve cell and the entire unit is known as the neurone. The cell of the neurone shares with all other bodily cells the characteristic of electric excitation when living and its loss in death. The nerve cells pass nerve excitation through their endings in the axons to other parts of the nervous system or to other body organs. Some neurones are *afferent* or receptors of impressions, others are *efferent* or function in sending back to affected areas orders for movement or other necessary reaction. Another subclassification of nerves is: (1) peripheral, arising from all portions of the body except the head; and (2) cranial or passing directly from the eyes, ears, and other portions of the head directly into the brain. The neurone varies as to length or other dimensions, but its basic pattern remains the same.

*The spinal cord.* The peripheral nerves enter the spinal cord, well encased in the spine, and lead to the brain. There are thirty-one pairs of nerves in the cord, arranged symmetrically, with two roots. The anterior or ventral root is efferent or motor in function, the posterior or dorsal root is afferent or sensory in function. There are also mixed nerves which have both afferent and efferent fibres.

These neurones in the spinal cord are equipped with reflex arcs so that the majority of afferent impressions extend only that far, and are referred over to the efferent nerves for appropriate action. Without such an arrangement human minds would be cluttered by millions of minor bodily adjustments and movements. It is only when some impressions become very extreme that they reach the level of consciousness. Some nerve fibres also extend to the sympathetic ganglia which are adjacent to the vertebral column.

*The sympathetic nervous system.* The sympathetic nervous system has a series of bundles of nerve fibres adjacent to the spinal column and connected with it at key points. Whenever there is any deviation from normal bodily conditions, the sympathetic system is stimulated. The eyes may be affected and tears may begin to flow, the lips and mouth go dry. Constriction of the throat occurs and breathing becomes labored. Marked palpitations of the heart join with these other symptoms. All digestive organs are affected when worries, tensions, or frustrations are experienced. Affected by a double sympathetic system are the kidneys, bladder, colon and rectum, gonads, and external genitalia. The sympathetic nervous system operates through its regular ganglia and in addition, there is also a parasympathetic nervous system. It extends down through the spinal cord and is know as the craniosacral division or outflow. The parasympathetic system also has a bulbar outflow through the VIIth, IXth, and Xth cranial nerves and affecting the lachrymal glands, the heart, and the secretory functions of the digestive organs. The third parasympathetic branch is the midbrain outflow in the IIIrd cranial nerve which causes constriction of the pupil of the eye and contraction of the ciliary muscle. It is generally true that feelings and attitudes are reflected in the visual expressions. Regularly we talk with our eyes. The intimate relationship between mind and body is more easily understood as the functioning of these interconnecting nerve systems become known. In modern language, they represent somopsychologic psychology or psychomatic somotology depending upon the particular school of thought.

Ganglia. The keys to interconnections within the nervous systems are the ganglia. A ganglion is a point in which the nerve terminals from different nerves join closely together for association of impulses. This actual joining or mutual closeness is known as the synapse. Nerve impulses pass through the synapse from one nerve to the next. There is believed to be some relationships between brightness or dullness and the facility with which nerve impulses are transmitted through synaptic connections. Whenever the reflex arcs in the spinal cord fails, some communication may eventually be established through these ganglia. Sherrington made interesting discoveries in this area in 1906 and later experience from injuries has extended knowledge in this significant area.

## The Brain

The brain is the general area of the nervous system which lies within the skull. Although a great majority of afferent impressions are absorbed by the autonomic processes of the spinal cord, the more important and meaningful ones reach various areas of the brain. The brain has four major and several minor divisions with highly specialized functions. The following discussion of the brain will be much more meaningful if constant reference is made to the excellent accompanying diagram of the brain kindly furnished by courtesy of Dr. Wendell J.S. Krieg of Northwestern University Medical School.[1]

The medulla. The medulla oblongata is at the base of the brain and connects from below immediately with the spinal cord and above with the pons. There are many ganglia in the medulla which return more afferent sensations to efferent directions without reaching the major areas of mental awareness. This sorting out or selecting process which began in peripheral areas continues to become more and more discriminating as the higher mental processes are being approached. The principal function of the medulla is the integration of autonomic functions.

[1] W.J.S. Krieg, Brain Mechanism in Diachrome, Brain Books, Evanston, Ill., 1955, 188 pp.

*The pons.* Joined immediately to the medulla is the pons. The term "pons" means bridge, and the pons is indeed a bridge. In it the nerve tracts cross over from one side of the body to the other. This process of crossing over has also begun in the medulla. The real purpose of crossing the nerve tracts is not clear. There is a possibility that in case of incapacity of one hemisphere of the brain, activity would not entirely cease for that entire half of the body.

*The cerebellum.* The cerebellum is a small portion of the brain located in the back and lower part of the skull. It seems to have as one of its principal functions giving smoothness, precision, and force to voluntary muscular action. As such, it acts in a supporting role to voluntary actions initiated in the thought processes of the cerebrum. The cerebellum appears to have no connections with the sensations, but is related in some way to postural tonus. Much of the information about its functions have been derived from diseased conditions and from animal experimentation.

*Intermediary processes.* Between the pons and the cerebrum there are several intermediary processes. There are two areas or cavities known as the IIIrd and IVth ventricles or cavities whose walls operate certain neural functions and mechanisms. The thalamus is a mass of gray matter developed from the wall of the IIIrd ventricle and forms part of the wall itself. It sends projection fibres to the primary sensory areas of the cerebrum and receives fibres from all areas, including the optic tract. The thalamus is an important relay center between vital portions of the nervous system. The hypothalamus lies below the thalamus. It has connections with the auditory nerve and with the entire sympathetic and parasympathetic systems. It is closely related to the endocrine functions of the pituitary gland which is located adjacently in a special bony case known as the sulla tursica. Control of body temperature and general control of sleep or drowsiness are affected by injuries to the hypothalamus. Psychic disturbances may also be related to impaired conditions in this area. The corpus callosum is a broad band of white substance extending under the longitudinal fissure between the cerebral hemispheres. The functions of all these intermediary processes are more extensive than have been sketched, and not all of them are definitely known or understood.

*The cerebrum.* The cerebrum is the principal mass of nerve matter extending over other portions of the brain. Its outer surface is known as the cortex. There is a deep fissure between the hemispheres, and on the surface of each hemisphere are many fissures which furnish greater surface areas. Certain areas of the cortex are localized with respect to specific nervous functions. The occipital area receives the optic sensations, analyzes them, and directs corresponding eye movements. The auditory area is farther forward in the temporal lobe with other sensory areas above it. In front of the sensory areas are the motor areas controlling movements of many bodily parts. The frontal area is the focus of the higher mental processes. While there is considerable localization of various processes, there is also evidence of diverse functioning. It is nature's provision in case of disease, accident, or destruction of specific areas. The cerebral processes guide and direct the voluntary behavior of man, give him the power to think, to reason, to remember, and to project himself into future plans of action.

*Summary of nerve systems.* The various nerve systems are: (1) the central nervous system which includes the brain, the spinal cord, and its afferent and efferent nerves; (2) the autonomic system, which includes the main involuntary functions such as the beating of the heart; (3) the sympathetic system with its ganglia outside of the spinal cord which reflects directly or indirectly unusual sensations or conditions in the various bodily organs; and (4) the parasympathetic system, which affects these same organs but without passing through the sympathetic system. Some authorities use a general term of vegetative system to include the autonomic, sympathetic, and parasympathetic systems.

### Characteristics

The nature of nerve energy continues to be a controversial matter. If it is principally a chemical reaction its rate of reaction is much beyond the usual rate of such reactions. The electrical conduction theory seems to fit more nearly into the rate of response. Although this rate is slightly less than for direct electricity, the many resistance centers of synapses may retard this rate to parallel the nerve energy rate. In the early 1920's the author witnessed such a demonstration in an electrical circuit constructed by Sir Rodney Whitney, who made no other claim except that of rate of response. Nerve conduction may be some unique combination of electro-chemical process not as yet fully discovered and recognized, such as is true of many bodily processes.

On the surface, or cortex, there is an alternating static type of electricity with positive and negative phases at the normal adult rate of approximately ten per second. The fluctuations and deviations of this phenomenon will be presented in the following chapter on convulsive disorders.

The nervous system is relatively well protected from external damage with location of principal parts in the skull and in the spinal cord. Its peripheral branches lie in exposed portions of the body, where it may communicate instantly when it suffers damage along with the skin, muscle, or other tissues. The brain and the spinal cord are encased in bony structures within which they are further cushioned by the cerebrospinal fluid. Along with other tissues of the body, there is a certain chemical composition of the nervous system. Whenever it fluctuates beyond usual limits, various types of convulsive disorders occur.

The nervous system is unique among the bodily systems. In general it does not mend or repair in expected ways as is true of bones or muscles. If a nerve is severed, restoration of nerve function is very slow or in many instances does not take place. When it does mend, it takes a period of months. Some recent research by Sperry[1] provides conclusive evidence that under certain circumstances, regeneration can occur in the central nervous system of animals. There is some evidence that when a nerve is destroyed, the adjacent nerves through their connecting synapses are sometimes activated so that communication is reestablished in this indirect manner. In certain cases of paralysis when the principal nerves cannot be restored, the reflex arcs gradually begin to function so that the various vegetative functions are reactivated. Destruction of a nerve affects the life and condition of members which it formerly served. A hand, an arm, a leg, a portion of the face wither and lose their buoyancy and vitality.

[1] R.W. Sperry. "The Eye and the Brain." *Scientific American*, 1956, 194, p. 48.

## Methods of Diagnosis

From the many complexities of anatomy which have been cited it is evident that methods of diagnosis of impaired function are difficult. Certain portions of the body may become paralyzed when there is nerve failure. Chemical excitation can be traced in some of the peripheral tracts and there has been some similar success in limited cortical areas. When such tracing has been done in connection with electroencephalographic readings, some of the more complicated tracts of the cortex have been identified in animal experimentation. Pneumograms or X-ray pictures of the brain are means for detecting specific areas of impairment. Neurology is a specialized branch of the medical profession which is rapidly advancing more complete knowledge of the entire nervous system.

There are marked individual differences in the nervous stamina of individuals. At one extreme, there are a few persons who remain calm and composed in tense situations, while at the other extreme are those who lack in such stamina. This characteristic is not to be confused with high or low intellectual ability. A bright individual may not have the stamina to continue long at arduous tasks although he has the intellectual ability; in converse manner, a person with limited intellectual ability may be able to endure concentrated mental effort. Parents and teachers should be briefed on how much tolerance children have for prolonged mental tasks. It is much easier to observe evidences of good physical stamina, yet the nervous stamina is equally, if not more, important.

## Brain Injury

The brain-injured child is often a misunderstood child. He does not have the usual tolerance for the average school day, he cannot give undivided attention to his school studies for the usual periods of time. His general behavior does not conform to the rest of his class, and unless his condition is understood he receives reprimands for misbehavior not motivated by malice. His problem is one of health and not of potential delinquency. Punishment which he does not understand aggravates his condition and further disturbs his state of mind. Many of the more severe types of brain injury are obvious to teachers and to parents so that some special type of class, home teaching, or hospitalization are indicated. Individuals with less severe injuries have to be continued in regular classes where the teacher must exercise unusual restraint and proceed with great understanding.

In the next few chapters a few of the more severe types of brain injuries such as convulsive disorders, cerebral palsy, encephalitis and allied conditions arising from fevers, and certain mental disorders and diseases will be discussed. Through an understanding of mild and severe brain injuries there will be a better appreciation of many kinds of socially unacceptable behavior in children. These discussions should lay a better foundation for the understanding of other chapters which follow.

## Questions and Topics for Discussion

1. Report in more detail about some special portion of the nervous system.
2. Report on research on the nervous system in the field of animal experimentation.
3. Report on the latest theories about the nature of nerve conduction.
4. Describe some person whose nervous system has been impaired in some manner.
5. List some of the informal tests which may be used to examine for nerve condition.

Note: Consult reference material at end of Chapter 11.

# CHAPTER 8

## *The Convulsive Disorders*

THE NORMAL CONDITION of the nervous system has been discussed in the preceding chapter. Unfortunately there are some individuals in which this ideal condition is not to be found. When disorders and diseases affect the nervous system many types of unusual, disturbing, and distressing behavior occur. Convulsive disorders constitute one area of such impairments. Convulsive disorders range from a minor tic affecting one particular muscle to extreme attacks of *grand mal* epilepsy in which consciousness is lost and violent physical reactions take place. Whenever there is failure of control by the nervous system it may affect one or more portions of the body.

### I. Grand Mal Epilepsy

A convulsion is an involuntary general paroxysm of muscular contraction. Whenever *grand mal* epilepsy occurs it is liable to bring danger of injury. When its occurrence is sudden and unexpected it becomes a chronic mental hazard to self as well as to associates. The confusion in a schoolroom when a first seizure occurs in the presence of children is a most trying ordeal. Properly caring for and protecting the epileptic from injury and at the same time keeping others calm calls for unusual resourcefulness. The author once observed that when a new draftee had a severe epileptic seizure in a crowded reception center, several hundred others got off to a bad start with additional anxiety about themselves. The afflicted one may have known of his condition but was trying to be accepted for military duty because of his patriotism, or his unknown and latent condition came to light for

124

the first time in the excitement of induction, which was automatically nullified.

## Causes

Convulsive disorders do not always have a single cause, but various causative factors operating in combination. The five major headings of causes listed by Bridge[1] are heredity, brain injury, physiological disturbances, personality maladjustments, and environmental strains. Evidence by Bridge showed that a large majority of epileptics had no family history of epilepsy but there was considerable positive evidence in about fifteen per cent of more than 700 cases. The heredity itself, in a strict sense, is topographical rather than an etiological cause. Brain injuries were found in approximately one-half of the epileptic children; one-half of these injuries occurred during the birth process and the remainder resulted from various accidents and diseases in childhood.

Physiological disturbances which affect the brain are direct causes. Variation in the chemical balance is believed to be a predisposing factor. Epileptics are more susceptible to variations than non-epileptics whose endocrine systems maintain a more uniform control of bodily chemistry. The balance of oxygen and carbon dioxide which fluctuates in the blood stream to the brain alters the physiological condition of that body. Personality maladjustments and emotional strain go hand in hand in causing epileptic episodes. The emotional strain of keeping composed causes fluctuations in adjustment which are reflected in treatment at home. During a trial period of twenty-four-hour programming within the school building from Monday to Friday at the White Epileptic School in Detroit certain epileptic children with tense home relationships returned to school Monday mornings with much greater emotional tension and irritability than when they left on the previous Friday.

## Remedies and Preventions

The several causes of epilepsy suggest some remedies and preventions. Bridge observes that if an epileptic marries, his mate should be

[1] E.M. Bridge, *Epilepsy and Convulsive Disorders in Children,* McGraw-Hill Book Co., Inc., New York, 1949, p. 519.

non-epileptic if the condition is recessive rather than dominant. If both are epileptic, refraining from having children is a highly social motive. Accidental injuries in the process of child birth can be greatly reduced by modern medical precautions. General reductions in accidents involving children in an ever-present need but with more complex living conditions the unfavorable causes grow steadily greater. In the actual physiological conditions themselves the use of dilantin (phenytoin) was introduced by Merritt and Putnam in 1939. Some success had been achieved by the introduction of phenobarbital in 1912 and as early as 1853 Locock first advocated bromides. Some of these latter medications continue to be useful in some types of cases. While dilantin showed considerable promise it produced some unfavorable physical reactions in certain cases. Experimentation has continued with other drug derivatives which reduce the unfavorable reactions. The modern drugs tend to stabilize the chemical balance of the brain cells so that the fluctuations with their attendant seizures may be reduced. Better practices of mental health in the home as described in the chapters of Part 2 should reduce personality disturbances and allied conditions.

### Methods of Diagnosis

Grand mal epilepsy is easily diagnosed when there are frequent visible seizures. The epileptic needs assistance in the form of a cloth or other suitable object placed between the teeth to prevent biting the tongue and general damage to the mouth. Tight clothing, particularly around the neck, should be loosened and provision made against cold air or drafts. In nocturnal epilepsy the condition is not so obvious unless observed by other members of the family who, unless previously informed, may believe that it is only a disturbance from nightmares.

Electroencephalography. Evidence of electrical energy in the cells of the body and particularly in the nervous system was reported in the preceding chapter. In 1929, Hans Berger, a German psychiatrist, reported that electrical activity of the human brain was measurable and from this beginning electroencephalography was born. As electroencephalographs[1] have become perfected, the uses of this measurement technique have rapidly increased. The number of small electrodes which are attached to various positions on the scalp has been greatly increased to give more accurate information about localized disturbances. The variations in brain waves are recorded on a kymograph. Different regions of the brain give distinctive recordings

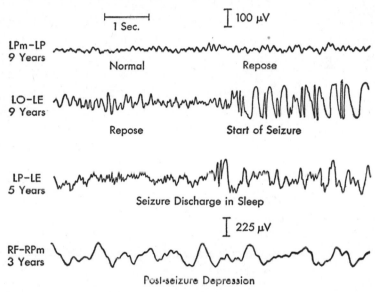

Electroencephalograph tracings.
*Courtesy of A. J. Derbyshire, Ph.D. Detroit*

with alternating plus and minus phases of the alternating current. In infants and young children the baseline sway is at the rate of one or two per second; this gradually increases to about ten per second in later adolescence and adulthood. Normal or non-epileptic readings are fairly regular although certain other neural disorders produce some unique and characteristic readings. In the case of *grand mal* the rate

---

[1] See accompanying illustration of the electroencephalograph, furnished by special permission and courtesy of the Grass Instrument Co., Quincy, Mass., owner and manufacturer.

may increase to as much as fifty or sixty alternations per second and may show an amplitude or spread many times greater than normal. There may be a tremendous chemical reaction at this time which subsides but gradually builds up in a time cycle of varying lengths characteristic of each particular individual. If medication is able to control this imbalance of chemical agents the seizures are less likely to occur in some individuals. The evidence of electrical energy from the electroencephalogram supports the theory that electricity is a possible conductor of nerve impressions although it is static rather than current electricity which shows on the kymograph recordings.

On the illustrations the normal fluctuations are approximately ten per second at the adult level. The epileptic seizure is shown in the second line. Various other disturbances are indicated including neurological deterioration. In view of these conditions it is little wonder that conscious mental activity is disturbed.

*Artificial induction of seizures.* The medical specialist in epilepsy also uses other devices such as artificial induction of seizures. They include overventilation or breathing rapidly 100 times in connection with the electroencephalograph, metrazol injection, and overhydration which affects the chemical balance of the body including the brain.

*Pneumo-encephalogram.* In this procedure some of the cerebrospinal fluid is drained off by spinal puncture or other processes so that air fills in the vacated portions and permits the taking of roentgenogram pictures to show any unusual condition within the brain. This process requires a short period of hospitalization and leaves a peculiar type of headache which slowly disappears as the cerebrospinal fluid is restored to its normal balance and distribution.

*Subdural puncture.* In case of head and brain injury in birth some babies develop blood clots in affected portions of the brain which do not dissolve but which become infected and destroy brain tissue. When such conditions are found an operative process known as a subdural puncture is necessary to drain off the infection. These highly technical medical skills have been responsible for preserving the lives of many babies and restoring them to normal conditions.

## Characteristics of Grand Mal Cases

The lot of the *grand mal* epileptic is an unhappy one. There is no specific condition of the brain which is certain to produce the same characteristics of behavior and personality in all cases. The attempt to isolate and to define a pure type of "epileptic" personality has never been successful and probably should be abandoned. Many of the emotional disturbances noted in epileptic children also occur as a result of other types of illness. Epileptic children may feel that their illness is punishment for being bad and they may sense rejection by parents or the opposite condition of oversolicitude. Some of these conditions in other short-term diseases and illnesses tend to disappear and are soon forgotten, but with the epileptic they continue month after month so that feelings and attitudes become more and more aggravated.

Bridge[1] observes:

Epilepsy even more than other chronic ailments of childhood encourages the continuation or extension of these psychological reactions. The recurrence of seizures at unexpected and embarrassing times destroys confidence and inhibits freedom of action. Fear of physical injury or death becomes increasingly powerful with each relapse. Yet the well-intentioned restrictions imposed by physician and family to minimize these risks give rise to feelings of resentment, discrimination, and even rejection. Finally the epileptic child soon senses that his difficulties are not quickly remedied and that he is faced with an undeserved and discouraging prospect. The result is that the child with epilepsy lives a disheartening life in which both physical and emotional insecurity are ever present.

Such observations point to the need for a whole school of psychological principles and practices which should be an integral part of the home life of all epileptic children.

The general intelligence of epileptics covers a wide range with the median intelligence quotient in the middle nineties. When the structure of the brain is injured or impaired it is remarkable that the intelligence of many cases is so nearly normal rather than extremely limited. Lennox and Collins[2] administered a series of intelligence tests to

[1] E.M. Bridge, *Epilepsy and Convulsive Disorders in Children*, McGraw-Hill Book Co., Inc., New York, 1949, p. 419.

[2] W.G. Lennox and A.L. Collins, "Intelligence of Normal and Epileptic Twins," *American Journal of Psychiatry*, 1945, 101, pp. 764-769.

ninety-three sets of twins and of this number thirty sets had had a history of seizures. The average intelligence quotient for the non-epileptic twins was 108 and for the epileptic twins it was 96. A sampling of twenty-three cases in the White School for Epileptics in Detroit in 1955-1956 showed two with intelligence quotients under 70 and seven with 100 or higher, and a median in the low nineties. A summary of various studies by Pintner, Eisenson, and Stanton,[1] indicates that only a small minority of epileptics show marked deterioration. Further, greater tendencies for deterioration appear among the more severe cases of long duration.

## Number of Cases

There are many factors which enter into the inventory of cases. There are cases of nocturnal seizures whose diagnosis has not been definitely established; others who have only an occasional seizure as compared to some who have chronically frequent occurrences; and pseudo cases such as hysteria which have been incorrectly diagnosed as epilepsy. In addition, fainting spells and trauma from attacks of acute indigestion are not easily distinguishable except by trained specialists who are not always at hand when such episodes occur. There were from three to five times as many children having convulsions that were not diagnosed as epilepsy as those having true epilepsy at the Outpatient Department of the Johns Hopkins Hospital. Surveys from records in World Wars I and II showed that there were about four epileptics in every 1,000 of the population who were subject to seizures at some time in their lives. While this number is relatively small when compared to such conditions as defective vision, nevertheless, the nature of this illness and condition is very grave and affects the total adjustment of the individual, his family, and his associates.

Although this relatively small number of *grand mal* epileptics does not seem to pose much of a problem with respect to the total population, the entire area of convulsive disorders presents a much different story. In later sections of this chapter the many other types of convulsive disorders will be discussed.

[1] R. Pintner, J. Eisenson, and M. Stanton, *The Psychology of the Physically Handicapped*, F.S. Crofts Co., New York, pp. 299-303.

## History of Epilepsy

In such a spectacular disease as epilepsy it may reasonably be expected that it has been mentioned frequently in legend and in historical fact. About 400 B.C. the Greek physician, Hippocrates, described the symptoms of epilepsy in detail: insensibility, contraction of the hands, fixed teeth, and sometimes evacuation of the bowels. In the New Testament it is related that Jesus took a boy who had been convulsing so that he was like a corpse by the hand and lifted him up, and he arose. In a more secular area epilepsy was attributed to the moon goddess, known as Mene, and other equivalent names. The term *lunatic* was applied to both the insane and the epileptic. Courville[1] reports that Hercules was supposed to have been epileptic and for many centuries epilepsy was known as the "disease of Hercules." Epilepsy has been ascribed to divine and demonic origin. Myths have originated in every country and race, including the Japanese, the Mohammedans, and the Indian tribes of North America. As in other fields of the exceptional there have been famous individuals who were epileptic. Alexander the Great, Caesar, and Napoleon were three world conquerors reputed to have been subject to epileptic seizures. It was known that Napoleon had some type of seizure in which he was carefully guarded by a small staff of trusty aides. They unfailingly reported that he was resting and could not be disturbed. It is interesting to relate the cycle of the epileptic to the military psychology of these conquerors. It has been noted that in the period immediately preceding the seizure there is an upsurge of well-being and a feeling and ideas of grandeur. These may have been the periods in which the overly ambitious plans of these war lords were laid. Since the history of the world has been greatly affected by these three military figures, it is evident that epilepsy may have played an important role in the affairs of mankind. Charles Lamb was an epileptic, but it did not interfere with his career as a famous writer. The present and future

[1] C.B. Courville, "Epilepsy in Mythology, Legend, Folk Tale," in Frampton and Gall, *Special Education for the Exceptional*, Vol. III, Porter Sargent, Boston, 1956, pp. 215-226.

may have fewer notables with epilepsy if the modern medical miracles continue to improve.

## Educational Provisions

Educational provision for *grand mal* epileptics has always been a difficult problem. The nature of their condition is such that uninstructed regular-class pupils and teachers are so often taken off guard that they would rather not have an epileptic pupil in the class. Too often epileptic children have been excused from attending school and no provision such as home teaching was made for them. In some cities up to a few years ago it was a common practice to accept them in regular classes or classes for the mentally retarded if they had been given liberal quantities of various bromides so that the seizures did not occur. As a result they were in such a toxic condition that their mental faculties operated only at a very low level.

A survey study of fifty epileptic children was conducted in Ohio through the cooperation of the Ohio State Medical Society and the Ohio Society for Crippled Children with the assistance of various health and social agencies. Dr. J.C. Price[1] reports that twenty-eight of forty in school attended regular classes and eight were enrolled in ungraded classes for the mentally retarded. Two were on home teaching programs and eight were out of school. Through some medication, cooperation of parents and social agencies, and through good understanding upon the part of pupils and teachers quite satisfactory progress was made.

Since the Detroit School for Epileptics, known as the White Special School, was the first and chief educational attempt directed toward epileptics, some mention will be made of its history and program. The Detroit Board of Education in 1933-1934 asked for a survey of epileptic children in order to discover the extent of the problem. The city Department of Health through its nurses and physicians was asked to prepare a list of known cases; these were supplemented by a list prepared by the author in his capacity as Director of the Psychological

[1] J.C. Price, "Epileptic Child in School," Frampton and Gall, *Special Education for the Exceptional*, Vol. III, Porter Sargent Publisher, Boston, 1956, pp. 239-260.

Clinic. His list included many who had been excluded from school. The Board of Education was not satisfied with a mere statement of numbers but requested the name and address of each pupil. From the various sources a list of approximately four hundred names was prepared. It was evident that there was a big problem of epilepsy.

A school was opened in January, 1935, with thirty-five boys as members, in the Schulze School. It was conducted as both a hospital and a school with the children remaining at the building from Monday morning through Friday afternoon. At first it was feared that placing many epileptics together would increase their seizures through suggestion, but it was soon found that these cases had about one-half as many seizures at school as they formerly had had at home. In the following year girls were admitted and used the hospital plan for the first semester while the boys were transported to and from the school daily by bus. At the end of the school year in June, 1939, the hospital plan was abandoned and all children were transported daily. At first there were quite a few seizures on the buses, but these have gradually reduced in number. The period of hospitalization was very valuable because it was possible to give careful study and have full control of diet for the twenty-four-hour periods.

After the epileptic unit was moved to the White elementary school the enrollment reached a peak of 200 pupils, although this number has been gradually reduced since that time. The reduction has been due to better medication, to the more careful screening of pupils with pseudo-epileptic conditions, to cases with nocturnal seizures, and by better understanding of marginal cases whose conditions are interpreted to require regular schools. The White Special School grades ranged from kindergarten to high school and, through an arrangement with a nearby high school, diplomas were granted in its name. In the fall semester of 1957-1958 the pupils were housed in three orthopedic schools of which the White School has become one unit. By this arrangement the distance and time of bus transportation have been greatly reduced. All entrance examinations and medical arrangements continue to be initially cleared at the White School. The total enrollment has been reduced to less than fifty pupils.

## II. Major Focal Seizures

As the term indicates, in focal seizures some specific portion of the brain is affected. Since these impairments are localized, it is possible, in some instances, to treat or to remove them surgically. Penfield and Erickson[1] divide them into four main categories: Jacksonian, masticatory, simple adversive, and tonic-postural seizures. The Jacksonian type may result from some kind of head and brain injury severe enough to affect the brain in the vicinity of the motor area. This condition spreads slowly enough to adjacent areas to be recognized through visible motor movements. In the masticatory seizures there are disturbances of chewing and swallowing; in the adverse seizures, the patient feels his eyes and head turning away from the side in which the lesion is located. Tonic-postural seizures involve the brain stem with subcortical attacks and decerebrate states.

The number of individuals afflicted is large and is particularly frequent in such athletes as boxers, wrestlers, and football players, to whom head injuries are more likely to occur. Reliable data are not available since the final effects may occur years afterward and by then they are ascribed to other causes. High school teaching staffs learn of these later conditions. The author's cousin, who was a noted college football player, succumbed some twenty years later. Injuries from industrial accidents are also highly contributory factors.

## III. Minor Seizures

1. *Simple* petit mal *seizures*. The *grand mal* type of seizure is only one kind of epilepsy. Among others are *petit mal* types with or without convulsions. In its simplest form the *petit mal* attack may go unnoticed except by the trained observer. There are brief lapses of consciousness in which the patient ceases doing whatever is at hand— reading, eating, or walking. Some activities may continue automatically. The lapses probably merge almost imperceptibly into the minor lapses and shifts of attention when any individual, busied with a

[1] W. Penfield and T.C. Erickson, *Epilepsy and Cerebral Localization*, Charles C Thomas Publisher, Springfield, Ill., 1941, pp. 15-17.

large number of different tasks simultaneously, pauses in one to give attention to another.

Cases of *petit mal* may pass as normal, nonhandicapped children but closer observation shows that they are likely to be frail, quiet, inactive, and have low muscular tone. They are characterized as having "sweet" dispositions and are termed "model" children. Some of the same methods of examinations applicable for *grand mal* cases work well for *petit mal*. The electroencephalograph shows a characteristic reading of two or three very slow waves per second alternating with a short and almost instantaneous change having a very wide amplitude known as a spike formation.

Many of the medications used for *grand mal* cases are of no value in the *petit mal* type. The use of a high fat, or ketogenic, diet improves the condition when taken in early childhood and may be followed by a normal diet. The greatest need seems to be a better understanding upon the part of the child himself as well as by his parents that *petit mal* is something which may continue and that they must learn how to adjust to it.

2. *Minor motor seizures.* This type of seizure may begin with nearly the same symptoms as for *petit mal* attacks but such seizures seem to be arrested at an early stage. There may be slight rhythmical activity of facial muscles with only a partial clouding of consciousness. After such attacks there is drowsiness, confusion, and headache, whereas in *petit mal* the individual immediately returns to normal functioning. Although *petit mal* is not helped by dilantin, the minor motor seizure is benefited by it.

3. *Akinetic seizures.* In this type of seizure there is no type of convulsion or spasm but there is a sudden relaxation so that the person falls to the floor and immediately arises without realizing why he fell. Lennox believes that whatever localization exists is far below the surface of the cortex. Since these cases may fall forward it is known as a "salaam" seizure, suggesting a Mohammedan gesture. The electroencephalograph readings of three per second with or without spikes are characteristic of akinetic seizures.

4. *Other subminor seizures.* Myoclonic seizures may affect a single set of muscles which are mainly peripheral. If the condition becomes

progressively worse the individual becomes completely incapacitated
It is comparatively rare and in a survey of 742 children in the Epilepsy
Clinic at Johns Hopkins Hospital only one case was found. Another
rare type is the startle seizure in which a sudden unexpected loud
noise or a bright light sets up seizures whose real cause is not known.
These cases may regress into more serious types of convulsions. There
is a large list of other minor manifestations such as *psychic equivalents*
which may have no relationship to any type of seizure but which
should be carefully diagnosed and appropriate action taken.

While the number of *grand mal* cases is relatively small the entire
field of major and minor seizures constitutes a large and important
group. Many of these people go through childhood undiagnosed except that some "peculiar" mannerisms are noted. Their conditions
emphasize the need for more thoroughgoing examinations, diagnosis,
treatment, and optimum educational provisions.

### Vocational Conditions

Except for a few extreme and greatly deteriorated epileptics there
are possibilities of employment in sedentary positions. Medication
may reduce the number of seizures and an understanding of problems
by employers and by fellow employees is very helpful. During the
extreme labor shortage in World War II many epileptics were gainfully and happily employed. Vocational rehabilitation agencies supported by federal and state funds are helpful in dealing with epileptics
as well as with all types of handicapped youth and adults.

### Organizations

The general plight of epileptics is gradually receiving more recognition. Social agencies, health agencies and associations, rehabilitation
activities and epileptics themselves are joined in local, state, and national efforts. The National Epilepsy League with headquarters at
130 N. Wells St., Chicago 6, is the center for its many branches in
various states and localities. A typical unit is the Michigan Epilepsy
Center and Association which has a budget of over $100,000 annually,
a large portion of which is received from the Michigan United Fund

Allocation. In addition to the staff at the center in Detroit there is a mobile unit which has visited fifty-four of Michigan's eighty-three counties since 1951. Nearly two thousand physicians have been contacted and nine hundred patients have been seen in some eight thousand miles of mobile unit travel.

## Questions and Topics for Discussion

1. Describe the symptoms and general characteristics of an epileptic that you have known.
2. Consult Pintner, Eisenson, and Stanton, *Psychology of the Physically Handicapped*, for further references on characteristics of epileptics.
3. Review in more detail the historical account by Courville in Frampton and Gall, *Special Education for the Exceptional*, Vol. III.
4. Visit the local unit or epilepsy center in your area and learn the extent of its program and activities.
5. Witness the operation of an electroencephalograph machine and study the interpretation of results.
6. Make a list of occupations suitable and unsuitable for epileptics.
7. Discuss the latest developments in medical treatments for epileptics

Note: Consult reference material at the end of Chapter 11.

# CHAPTER 9

## Cerebral Palsy

IN THE PRECEDING CHAPTER an area of nerve impairments was discussed under the classification of convulsive disorders. Another area of nerve impairment is cerebral palsy. Cerebral palsy is paralysis of one or more portions of the cerebrum. Symptoms include poor muscular coordination and an awkward gait giving an impression of inability to complete projected actions. Surprisingly, completion is effected.

### Definitions

Those who deal with the cerebral palsied prefer a classification separate from the orthopedically handicapped. In the latter there is complete inactivity of certain muscles as in poliomyelitis, but this is not generally true of the cerebral palsied. Some severely handicapped cerebral palsied are housed with the orthopedically handicapped for practical purposes of school transportation, although technically not included in that general classification. Cerebral palsy is amenable to some therapy and to training but it is not curable in the sense that some orthopedics are capable of improvement. The orthopedically handicapped have weaknesses of muscular action, the cerebral palsied have excess strength in them.

Cerebral palsy is a condition and also a disease, although the cerebral palsied themselves, their parents, and others prefer referring to it as a condition. As a neuro-physical and neuro-psychological deviation it is basically classified as a disease according to Cruickshank and Raus[1] who review several additional definitions by Denhoff, Perlstein,

[1] W.M. Cruickshank and G.M. Raus, *Cerebral Palsy*, Syracuse University Press, Syracuse, N. Y., 1955, pp. 1-3.

138

and others. These various handicaps include psychological dysfunction, emotional disturbances, neuromuscular activity, and special sensory and peripheral handicap, caused by absent or damaged brain structures. Cruickshank and Raus point out that the term *spastic paralysis*, which occurs very frequently in the literature and discussions, is actually inappropriate since it does not cover all forms of cerebral palsy.

## Types

The complexity of cerebral palsy is disclosed in the various types which have been identified. There are many subdivisions within each type.

*Athetosis.* This condition is characterized chiefly by uncontrolled or involuntary movements of various muscles or portions of the body. The voluntary movements become distorted by the supplementary action of involuntary movements. These movements may be constant or intermittent and it is impossible to predict their occurrence. Hill[1] notes that athetosis is caused by injury to the basal ganglia of the mid-brain. It accounts for about forty per cent of all cerebral palsies. There are many varieties of athetosis; Phelps[2] identifies at least twelve of them. They include: tension, in which the principal motion is blocked in attempting to stabilize the extremity as a whole; nontension by absence of motion; tremor; rotary; shudder; dystonic and others. Each individual has his particular type and area of affliction which is his unique characteristic.

*Spasticity.* Spasticity involves an exaggeration of deep reflexes in which the stretch reflex is always present. If the arm is tensed and then passively moved through its full range of motion to the completely relaxed position, it is designated as spastic if a jerk or kick back occurs at any point in the change. Opposing muscles are thrown out of balance and become weaker so that the spastic muscle has been made

---

[1] A.S. Hill, "The Cerebral Palsied Child," Frampton and Gall, *Special Education for the Exceptional*, Vol. III, Porter Sargent Publisher, Boston, 1956, pp. 78-100.
[2] W.M. Phelps, "Description and Differentiation of Types in Cerebral Palsy," *The Nervous Child*, 1949, 8, p. 117.

stronger by its greater number of contractions. Nearly one-half of all cerebral palsies are in the area of spasticity. The spastic individual tends to move slowly so that the jerk does not occur, but this deliberation becomes so great that it is quite impractical, yet he hesitates for fear of spastic reaction.

Muscle involvement may affect one or more of the extremities. Quadriplegia affects all four extremities in triplegia three extremities are affected. When only one extremity is affected, the condition is known as monoplegia. The term "hemiplegia" is used when only one side of the body is affected. These terms which describe afflictions in various parts of the body illustrate how diverse and complex cerebral palsy may be.

*Ataxia.* Another form of cerebral palsy is ataxia, in which the various area of muscle involvements of the preceding paragraph are to be found. The sense of balance is impaired so that in walking or in other movements the person has difficulty in proceeding where he wishes to go and, if there is such deviation, he has a further problem of slow and inaccurate readjustment to compensate. Additional problems arise when muscles respond too rapidly or too slowly or not at all.

*Rigidity.* The condition described as rigidity occurs when there is complete or nearly complete resistance to any muscle movement. Tremor is an opposite condition in which involuntary movements are largely continuous.

## Causes

Brain and nerve impairment are the principal causes of cerebral palsy. This simple statement does not do justice to the many subclassifications of nerve impairment or to the causes of nerve impairment themselves. In the two preceding chapters the anatomy and physiology of the nervous system and some types of disease or impairment were discussed. These etiological or causal factors may be conveniently arranged according to the individual's longitudinal development.

*Prenatal causes.* Defect or disease in one or both parents may cause cerebral palsy. If the mother is chronically ill or malnourished during pregnancy various types of maldevelopment may result in the child. Insufficient oxygen in the mother's blood stream causes impairment or destruction of nerve cells which may also suffer further injury during and after birth delivery. Some of these conditions in addition to causing cerebral palsy produce other types of nerve disease and brain damage. Premature birth cases must be saved by the use of additional oxygen, the amount of which must be carefully governed or the optic nerve will be destroyed.

*Causes at birth.* The physical conditions of delivery may be such that nerves are impaired. Long and difficult labor shuts off the supply of oxygen to the baby with further nerve destruction or impairment. This is known as cerebral anoxia. There is some evidence of a fairly high correspondence between the use of anaesthetics to ease the mother's pain and discomfort and some harmful effects on the baby's mental condition according to studies by Schreiber.[1] When there is actual injury to the skull and to the adjacent portion of the brain, a blood clot may form which soon develops into an infection. A subdural puncture relieves this condition as mentioned in the discussion of epilepsy. Research on blood composition has yielded information about certain antibodies which are dangerous when found in the newly-born infant's blood. It is now possible to save a large percentage of lives which were formerly lost by substituting the compatible type in the circulatory system of the newly-born babies.

*Postnatal causes.* Since the nervous system is an exceedingly delicate structure, there are many conditions after birth which cause cerebral palsy and other nerve impairments. Severe accidents may crush or greatly injure the skull and the brain. Abnormally high temperatures of from four to five degress above normal from measles, whooping cough, sleeping sickness, influenza, pneumonia, typhoid, and scarlet fever reduce the breathing and oxygen intake by at least 50 per cent. The introduction of the oxygen tent in recent years helps to neutralize oxygen deficiency. The many types of cerebral palsy are matched or exceeded in number by its many kinds of causes.

[1] F. Schreiber, "Mental Deficiency from Paranatal Asphyxia," *Proceedings,* American Association on Mental Deficiency, 1939, 44, pp. 95-106.

## Characteristics

Cerebral palsied children develop a complex system of handicaps which makes their plight much more ominous than that of most other handicapped individuals. While the grand mal epileptic is seized with a paroxysm of motion, it is of short duration whereas the cerebral palsied continues in his unusual, involuntary movements. Some other types of brain-injured children are very active physically but they are the only other group whose excessive physical movements equal or surpass that of the cerebral palsied. The orthopedically handicapped, the blind, and the deaf have some physical characteristics which may attract more attention than the nonhandicapped, but theirs is a more static and stable condition. The speech handicapped share certain physical activity status with the cerebral palsied since the palsy is a cause of some speech impairments. Obviously the physical status of the cerebral palsied has implications for social adjustment which has a reciprocal effect upon the development of personality.

The cerebral palsied child may have such diverse neurological impairments that sensory areas may be affected. Wishik[1] estimated that approximately one-half of them have some degree of visual impairment and one-fourth have complete or partial loss of hearing. These secondary defects are more prevalent in some types of cerebral palsy than in others, particularly in the various plegia areas. Combinations of two defects probably square rather than double the total disability of any individual which multiplies his difficulties of adjustment.

*Personality adjustments.* From what has just been stated about the physical activity of the cerebral palsied there is cause to expect that personality adjustments would be affected in many ways. Some portions of the personality characteristics are probably derived from within the individual himself who is aware that his status and reactions differ in manner and degree from the nonhandicapped. Other portions of personality differences stem from the attitudes of oversolicitation, protection, sympathy, and parental concern, which the cerebral palsied child experiences throughout his entire childhood and adolescence.

[1] S.M. Wishik, *Planning Community Programs for the Cerebral Palsied,* United Cerebral Palsy Association, New York, 1953.

Cruickshank[1] and Bice comment on conflicting and unconfirmed characteristics as follows:

> Personality characteristics involving specific emotions such as fear, affection, or rage, which in and of themselves are difficult to identify as single psychological traits, seldom are found to be generic in nature. Emotions are the product of specific learning situations. It would be unusual to find members of one entire medical classification, who on the basis of different learning situations, developed common emotional reactions. This is a problem which needs much more research before definitive statements can be made with assurance.

The cerebral palsied child is caught on two prongs of a social and emotional dilemma. If he is seriously impaired, he gradually realizes that he is living in social isolation since his siblings go about their daily activities in ways which he cannot. Each activity in which he cannot participate drives him further into social isolation, which he may eventually accept by giving up all hope of normal social contacts. In a life of fantasy and wishful thinking he may regress from reality and take along all purpose and all motivation for actual accomplishment. By contrast he may determine that he will not accept social isolation. He strives to equal his peers but the great exertion puts a terrific strain upon his already weakened stamina which causes him to wonder if it is worth the effort. Nevertheless, he goes on with hope of social acceptance. At this stage he finds that the attitudes of his associates begin to have their frustrating effects upon him. He is not certain whether his acceptance is a genuine and mutually equal relationship or whether it is based on charitable motives of tolerance and sympathy. He may even distrust his own parents in this relationship and such suspicion may easily extend to siblings, teachers, and incidental associates. These patterns of adjustment and of rejection are also characteristic of children or adults with handicaps other than cerebral palsy.

Since many areas of the body may be affected, it is difficult to generalize about the personality characteristics of the cerebral palsied. Frustrations may arouse feelings of anger and self-pity and cause de-

[1] W.M. Cruickshank and G.M. Raus (eds.), *Cerebral Palsy*, Syracuse University Press, Syracuse, N.Y., 1955, p. 116.

viations in will power. Irritability is a common characteristic of the cerebral palsied and personalities become highly individualized.

*Psychological qualities.* Cruckshank[1] and Bice made extensive investigations of psychological qualities in various types of cerebral palsy with the Bender-Gestalt Drawings. They found no conclusive relationship between types of errors and the medical classifications of children. They believe that there is evidence of some relationship between the level of intelligence quotient and the types of errors made on the drawings but their evidence is not conclusive. The cerebral palsied and some other types of brain-injured children do not grasp an over-all perception of a figure-background in the same way that nonhandicapped children do. In the nonhandicapped, the principal figures are filled in from imagination with the ground and other background being left as indistinct and nonessential in meaning, whereas the cerebral palsied may put equal emphasis upon both, or otherwise shift the normal emphasis. Some of these characteristics are apparently related to a higher degree of distractibility and to shorter spans of attention. Many of these characteristics should be examined and known about each individual child as a basis for better approaches to psychological therapy and to educational procedures.

*General intelligence.* Any type of nerve impairment such as cerebral palsy naturally reflects some impairment in the general intelligence as well as in special mental abilities if such can be specifically identified. In many of the earlier studies the cerebral palsied were included with the orthopedically handicapped children in the gross results and reported median intelligence quotients in the middle and upper eighties. In a study of 619 orthopedically handicapped children in Detroit's Oakman School for Crippled Children, John J. Lee reported a median intelligence quotient of 89 for all types, but in this number there were 158 "spastic" cases with a median intelligence quotient of 83 which was lower than the median of all orthopedic types. The most comprehensive survey was summarized for the cerebral palsied in New Jersey by Hopkins, Bice, and Colton[2] and showed a median intelli-

[1] W.M. Cruickshank and G.M. Raus (eds.), *Cerebral Palsy,* Syracuse University Press, Syracuse, N.Y., 1955, pp. 134-165.

[2] T.W. Hopkins, H.V. Bice, and K.C. Colton, *Evaluation and Education of the Cerebral Palsied Child,* International Council for Exceptional Children, Washington, D.C., 1954, 114 pp.

gence quotient of approximately seventy points but there was a wide range of points. There were 157 cases who were at 100 or above and 284 below 50. No significant sex differences in intelligence were noted between the 600 boys and the 400 girls. In the four major classifications, the athetoids had the highest median intelligence quotients; the spastics were second; the rigidity types were third; and the ataxias were fourth. These median ranges were from 72.6 to 54.96. Within the spastic group the subgroups ranked from high to low as follows: left hemiplegia, paraplegia, right hemiplegia, triplegia, and quadriplegia, with median intelligence quotients from 79.73, to 57.39. These latter data show some positive correspondence between multiplicity of nerve impairment and intelligence. Cruickshank and Bice conclude after comparisons of New Jersey, Buffalo, and Birmingham, England surveys that the trends shown in the New Jersey report are approximately near the real mental status of the cerebral palsied.

In most of the investigations the Stanford-Binet 1937 scale was used. Certain items involving spatial relationships and orientation are more likely to be failed than items primarily concerned with verbal content. The Wechsler Intelligence Scale for Children can be adapted although some of the performance type items are not completely satisfactory. Some of the nineteen subtests of the Detroit Tests of Learning Aptitude are suitable for testing the cerebral palsied. In all testing procedures maximum time allowances are generally needed. Any deviations from the standard procedure must be evaluated carefully to determine if it is a bona fide equivalence.

The general trend of mental abilities for the cerebral palsied is toward the negative side and approximates that of the mentally retarded. Since they have the second handicap of a nerve impairment and bodily disorder, their true handicap may be greater than for the mentally retarded who have no such complications. The personality characteristics which were discussed above are intensified by the complication of limited intelligence.

### The Number of Cases

As in other disorders there is always a question of the incidence. The number in any community is of interest to the medical profession, to preschool education, and to other services before school entrance. Educators need to know what school facilities are required and, in cooperation with rehabilitation and counseling, the extent of facilities and personnel in those areas. Agencies which deal with the adult cerebral palsied should be informed since their numbers are known to be comparatively large due to low death rates in the earlier years. The problem of numbers is complicated by the varying degrees of affliction from complete incapacitation to types so mild that they escape detection. Surveys such as were formerly conducted in connection with the Federal decennial census for the blind were abandoned because of unsatisfactory criteria, reluctance of families to report, and, in the case of cerebral palsy, such a survey by lay investigators would be even more unsatisfactory. In the face of such difficulties various citizen's groups and the press frequently expect that some agency, such as the school systems, should be able to give them an accurate count upon a moment's notice.

Early estimates of numbers were more conservative than current surveys show. Winthrop M. Phelps was the first to make an estimate in the late 1930's of seven cases to every hundred thousand population. The number of draft rejections because of cerebral palsy tended to bring the problem into a new focus with parents organizing at local, state, and national levels. In 1948 the New York State legislature authorized a survey of cerebral palsy in Schenectady County and found 152 in each 100,000 of the general population. The largest concentration was in ages five to nine, with ten to fourteen years in second order, and less than one-twentieth as many of age thirty-five and older. At the school age level there would be approximately six to each 1,000 of the school population. A Connecticut survey in 1950 placed the number at three per one thousand. The United Cerebral Palsy Association has accepted a rate of from three to three and one-half per thousand of school age. At this rate there are well over 100,000 cerebral palsied children of school age in the United States. The New York State 1948 survey estimated approximately 10,000 of school age in that state alone. This number ranks cerebral palsy much above several other types of handicapped and exceptional children.

## History

The fate of the cerebral palsied undoubtedly paralleled that of the otherwise crippled in the early centuries of history. They went through eras in which they were the subjects of scorn, contempt, and rejection. Some were probably shown in pageants before tyrants and despots and vengeance was wreaked on them. In the ancient art of Egypt there are figures of crippled individuals. Many were probably hidden away by families because of shame and their general treatment is an obscure page of history. Some references appear in the Bible about the halt and the lame with St. Luke, the physician, making such a description.

An English physician, W.J. Little, began calling medical attention to the cerebral palsied in 1853. He described some of the causes which are known today and his influence was so great in this field that for many years what is now known as cerebral palsy was called Little's disease. Educational provisions for those who could attend any school were usually joined with the orthopedically handicapped. Schools and classes began to appear about 1920.

Because the problems of the cerebral palsied are somewhat unique, they tended to draw the afflicted and their parents together for mutual study and for whatever educational, medical, and vocational help they could find. Local and state organizations were formed and in recent years have joined together in the United Cerebral Palsy Associations, Inc., in New York City. This pattern of development is similar to the organizational plan for epileptics reported in the preceding chapter.

### Physical Therapy

One of the greatest needs for the cerebral palsied is an adequate program of physical therapy. This program has grown both in extent and importance. It is found in hospitals and in special schools which also house the orthopedics where instruction is being extended to parents as well as to the children themselves. The physical therapist is a comparatively recent type of trained individual and there is a great demand for them which is largely unfilled.

The physical therapy program is also a "team" project in which the medical specialist, the nurse, the physical therapist, the social worker, the psychologist, the teacher, and parents take part. All of these team members contribute their knowledge and suggestions in the unique problems of each individual case. A thorough examination in the physical, educational, psychological, and other areas is prerequisite to the program of physical therapy. In the physical examination the child is placed in many positions to note what movements are restricted or are completely absent. The four basic types of spastic, athetoid, ataxic, and rigidity should be thoroughly evaluated and for the spastic the various combinations such as triplegia or paraplegia should be surveyed.

The therapy must be carried on in several places such as special units in hospitals, in schools, in cerebral palsy centers, and in limited ways in homes. Many types of equipment such as playthings which call for the use of certain muscles are included. Some of the equipment found in the gymnasium, some stairs, and a treatment table are needed. The National Society for Crippled Children and Adults, Inc., published a useful *Manual of Cerebral Palsy Equipment* with liberal suggestions. The general purpose of physical therapy is to establish use of the disabled members of the body within the limits of practical possibility. Walking with or without permanent braces, use of arms and fingers, and general bodily movements are included in the program. The spirit of play and making a game of it rather than a painful task requires special personal qualities in the therapist. With older children, adolescents, and adults a real desire to improve must be developed and maintained, but within a framework of accepting the fact of a handicap which is to be remedied as far as possible.

If the condition is such that the child is able to live at home rather than in the hospital, parents should be instructed on how they may carry on some of the practical steps since short periods of therapy with the professional therapist might well be supplemented throughout the day, weekends, and during vacations. Such a program is not as easy as it sounds in theory because of the human element, family attitudes, limitations of equipment, adequate time, and desire.

Snell[1] gives helpful and practical suggestions on the many aspects of physical therapy.

## Education

The problems of cerebral palsy education are as wide as can be imagined. In terms of mental ability the range of intelligence includes the great majority at or near the level of extreme retardation but a small minority is at or much above average ability. The standard curriculum must be adapted to these levels and implemented as effectively as possible within the limits of restricted physical activity as well. For example, handwriting may become a very difficult, if not impossible, subject. Language is often limited and cannot adequately serve as a practical vehicle of communication and instruction.

In the extremely handicapped, instruction is limited to the simplest measures, if any, in the institution for permanent custodial care. Above this level is a group of home-bound children for whom some home teaching may be provided; many of the cerebral palsied are in this category. Some less severe types are transported to such schools as those for the orthopedically handicapped where instruction may proceed much more effectively in the social setting of the group. Those with mild forms of this impairment are able to proceed at their own rate in regular classes.

The educational plight of the cerebral palsied is unfortunate, since many are afflicted with a combination of multiple handicaps which include: the condition itself; limited mental ability; impaired hearing or vision; speech impediment; and others. Financial aid from states to local communities is frequently restricted for financing teachers of the home-bound for the palsied mentally handicapped. The natural result has been organizations of parents at local, state, and national levels united to bring the strength of numbers into action.

## Occupational Training

For the lesser handicapped there are many possibilities of training by the vocational rehabilitation financed by Federal-State authoriza-

[1] E.E. Snell, "Physical Therapy," in W.M. Cruickshank, and G.M. Raus (eds.), *Cerebral Palsy*, Syracuse University Press, Syracuse, N.Y., 1955, pp. 257-293.

tion. More than 70 per cent of 881 cerebral palsied clients in vocational rehabilitation were successfully employed in clerical, skilled, semiskilled, or professional occupations.[1] Since this organization exists in every state with branches in many localities the vocational training and placement opportunities for the cerebral palsied as well as for all other handicapped types have been greatly increased.

## Questions and Topics for Discussion

1. Report on the status of the cerebral palsied in your city or community.
2. Relate the nerve impairments of the cerebral palsied to the general information about the nervous system in a preceding chapter.
3. Make a detailed report of parents' functions with the cerebral palsied as reported in Cruickshank and Raus, Cerebral Palsy, or in Special Education for the Exceptional, Vol. III, by Frampton and Gall.
4. Observe the physical therapy activity in your local school or hospital.
5. Interview the local unit of parents interested in the cerebral palsied.
6. Report on the educational provisions for the cerebral palsied in your community.

Note: Consult reference material at end of Chapter 11.

1 Office of Vocational Rehabilitation, Persons with Cerebral Palsy Rehabilitated in Fiscal Year, 1951, Facts in Brief, 1952, Rehabilitation Service Series, No. 208, Supplement 7.

# CHAPTER 10

## The Brain-Injured

ALTHOUGH THIS CHAPTER is entitled The Brain-Injured, it is not the first discussion of this general classification. The chapters on Epilepsy and Convulsive Disorders presented conditions of brain injury and physiological change which resulted in certain characteristic types of deviant behavior. Cerebral palsy, typified by bodily movements beyond the usual scope of nerve control, has just been discussed. These defects are not mutually exclusive of other brain-injured types to be presented in this chapter. Separations or distinctions are made for the sake of clearer understanding and not to imply that they are separate entities.

### Definitions

The term "brain-injured" is self-explanatory but the effects of brain injury are not so simply explained. There are so many areas of the brain which may be injured and so many different means of injury that there is no simple or easy way to define this handicap. Some authorities use *damage*, others use *injury*, as the qualifying adjective. They are generally synonymous terms. Since there are certain types of unacceptable deviant behavior which accompany brain-injury conditions, the term has gained an unearned and undeserved reputation as the principal cause of all deviant behavior. There are many other causes of unacceptable behavior as noted in earlier chapters.

151

## Causes

The types of actual impairment and the times of their occurrence operate to produce many kinds of brain-injury causes. There are different psychological developments and reactions which take place when an injury is prenatal as opposed to postnatal. Impairments may occur in adulthood and senescence as well as in adolescence and early childhood. Many of them may also take place at birth and in prenatal or uterine periods. The more profound disturbances and impairments are closely related to the earlier developmental periods.

*Types of causes.* Toxic conditions in the mother during pregnancy is one of the earliest causes. If the mother's syphilis is not cured before the fourth month of pregnancy the child will carry a congenital infection which eventually may impair or destroy various tissues of the body. It has particular affinity for the nervous system. These effects may appear at an early age or are also known to bring nerve deterioration in middle age or later. Rubella, or German measles affecting the mother, may result in impairment of the child's sensory nervous system and particularly the auditory nerve. Incompatibility of parents' blood in the Rh factor has been mentioned previously, but this condition may be arrested if the suitable type of blood is substituted, if necessary, immediately after birth.

Premature birth, delayed birth, anoxia, injuries to the skull and brain in difficult birth are abnormal conditions which injure the actual structure of the brain. Anoxia destroys or impairs the nerve cells which require vital oxygen for survival. Modern medical knowledge and practice have greatly reduced injuries and fatalities among babies. The Detroit Department of Health reported 1,552 infant deaths in 59,200 babies born in Detroit in 1955, or 26.2 per 1,000 of live births. The fatalities for the first twenty-seven days after birth amounted to 539 of the 1,230 births or 43.8 per cent, with various forms of asphyxia and lung failures accounting for 311 or 25.3 per cent of the total. There were 322 babies who died after the first twenty-seven days after birth but within the first year. The principal causes in this group were pneumonia, congenital malformations, and accidents.

In childhood and thereafter, causes of brain injury are mainly of a different character. Encephalitis is a general term for fevers which affect the central nervous system. There are many forms such as typhoid, scarlet fever, pneumonia, and influenza which cause unusually high temperatures of five or more degrees above normal. Measles, mumps, chickenpox and other childhood diseases also carry high temperatures. Fortunately many of them are of short duration and have less opportunity to impair nerve cells from reduced oxygen supply.

*Encephalitis lethargica* or sleeping sickness has had outbreaks among children and adults and its spread to Europe and America seems to have followed the military migrations of World War I. Webster[1] lists nine types of virus which produce some form of encephalitis: rabies, poliomyelitis, St. Louis encephalitis, Japanese B encephalitis, louping ill, X disease, equine encephalomuelitis, lymphocytic choriomeningitis, and "B" virus. Several of these are transmitted to man from animals, including rabies mainly from dogs; several are from insects including the Japanese B, and equine encephalomuelitis which is transmitted by horses. "B" virus is probably native to monkeys, lymphocytic choriomeningitis is transferred to man from mice, louping ill affects sheep in Scotland, probably originating from insects. The St. Louis encephalitis is the type common in man and appears in the midwestern area during the summer. Its mode of transmission is unknown. Tumors of the brain are another cause of nerve impairment. Reference should be made to the causes of convulsive disorders and cerebral palsy in preceding chapters. These many causes and times of occurrence do not exhaust the potential list of brain injuries.

## Characteristics

Certain psychological characteristics of brain-injured children reflect unique behavior responses. It has been generally demonstrated that an injury to any portion of the brain produces disturb-

[1] L.T. Webster, "Classification of Primary Encephalitides of Man According to Virus Etiology," *Journal of the American Medical Association*, 1941, 116, pp. 2840-2841.

ances in the entire central nervous system and is not merely localized in a specific area. This condition may be better understood by reference to the many neural interconnections which were described in the chapter on the Nervous System. In general, the earlier the injury the more profound are the impairments. There are several specific impairments which will be presented.

*Disorders of perception.* Although vision may be normal, the brain-injured child does not successfully fuse his impressions into a meaningful entity. Since he cannot bring them together he cannot form complete judgments of distance and of spatial relations which soon become automatic to the noninjured child. Strauss[1] and Kephart offer the following characterization:

Gestalt psychology has emphasized the fact that a whole is not merely the sum of its parts but that there are characteristics of the whole which are different from those of the parts. Spatial perception, as indeed all perception, develops from this unique contribution of the whole which is different from the parts or any merely summative combinaton of parts. It is these various integrations among basic sensory data which it is so important to develop. It is these which convert perceptions from a unitary series of meaningless impressions into information regarding the world on the basis of which we can predict, can sort out the relevant from the irrelevant, and can mold behavior so that the needs and desires of the organism can be efficiently and adequately met.

The brain-injured child finds difficulties in many practical situations. He seems to observe the four sides of a square but does not recognize the entire figure as a unit. He has difficulty in observing the main features of a scene because he is unable to relegate the ground and borderline incidentals to their less important positions. His problems are multiplied when he tries to coordinate three-dimensional situations. Another of his problems is to interpret a proper perspective such as the actual size of objects at different distances in which imagination must play some part. It is easy to understand that if he cannot get unified meaning out of his perceptions he may respond in many bizarre ways to situations which the noninjured accept as a matter of course.

1 A.A. Strauss and N.C. Kephart, *Psychopathology and Education of the Brain-Injured Child*, Vol. II, Grune and Stratton, Inc., New York, 1955, p. 64.

*Anxiety.* The brain-injured child is an anxious child. He realizes that he differs in some ways from others who seem to get intelligent meaning out of life. His experiences are disturbing and arouse fears which lead to anxiety. He leans on his parents, his siblings, his nurse and maid, and his teacher. He always seeks reassurance in much the same manner as any child who is upset by an occasional episode will except that his needs are continuous. He senses not only an external disorganization but internal as well since his inner senses and his own body image are out of focus. His close associates weary of continual demands and great love is not enough to make them play their part. Rejection and ridicule intensify anxiety which may become progressively worse as the environment expands in the preschool years. Upon entering school the brain-injured child immediately seeks out the teacher to relieve his added anxieties but, with the entire class needing her principal attention, he finds further frustration. If perchance a little additional attention is given he becomes "teacher's pet" with all of the usual consequences to himself.

*Motor impulsiveness.* The impairment and disorganization of the nervous system produces greater motor impulsiveness. In his anxiety for acceptance he becomes impulsive in actions. He rushes into projects so rapidly that he spoils materials, interferes with orderly attempts of classmates to carry on their activities, and seldom finishes any task satisfactorily either to himself or others. In the more severe forms it is impossible for a teacher of a regular class to place him under sufficient control to carry on with the program for the entire group. Likewise the brain-injured child disorganizes the family life, his neighborhood play group, or his Sunday school class. Most of these activities are beyond his voluntary control.

*Miscellaneous types.* A few types of individuals who have deviations of size and growth also have some impaired neural conditions. Their growth deviations are discussed in a later chapter and their intelligence is described in the chapters devoted to that topic. Hydrocephalism is characterized by an abnormally large head and is caused by excess cerebrospinal fluid which exerts pressure on the skull. Infectious diseases develop with hemorrhages. Wallin reports that fully one-half of them are caused by congenital syphilis. Microcephalism is a condition in which the skull and the brain do not develop to normal size. Some portions of the brain do not develop, leading to sclerosis and possible degeneration. In both of these types there is much feeblemindedness, although the hydrocephalics may develop normal or superior intelligence.

Another type with mental retardation is Mongolism. There is evidence of imperfect nerve cells, deficiency in association tracts, and general lack of sufficient oxygen. Since Mongoloid individuals are deficient in muscular coordination the outlook for simple vocational tasks is not favorable. Cretinism may have a multiplicity of causes such as sclerosis and general nerve impairment, although the principal cause is malfunction of the thyroid gland, with enlargement of the pituitary gland. While all four of these types have some nerve impairment and deviations in size, our principal interest is in the development of intelligence.

*Intelligence.* Since both general and specialized phases of intelligence are affected by impairments in the central nervous system deviations in them may logically be expected. While the general level of the intelligence is important the success or failure on special items or types of test material are probably of more diagnostic value. Because of these gaps in the intellect, the testing may have to proceed over a wider range of items and with more unevenness of success and failure than in the non-injured children. It is true that there is "scatter" on intelligence tests by some noninjured children as well, but it seems to be found more frequently in the brain-injured children.

In the descriptions of impaired perception certain characteristics of form such as corners of squares were overlooked. It has been noted that they have difficulty in connecting the corners in drawing a diamond. Many experiments have been tried by requiring brain-injured children to reproduce various geometrical forms after brief viewing, but there has been little statistical proof that the responses definitely differentiate them from normal or noninjured children. Strauss and Kephart[1] discuss results of many other tests such as

[1] A.A. Strauss and N.C. Kephart, *Psychopathology and Education of the Brain-Injured Child*, Vol. II, Grune and Stratton, Inc., New York, 1955, pp. 152-164.

The Marble Board Test, Kohs Block Designs Porteus Maze Test, Goodenough Draw-A-Man Test, and sorting tests, some of which hold more promise of having diagnostic value than others. Their presentations are of greater interest to the clinical psychologist than to the educator, although their diagnostic findings give helpful clues to parents and teachers in training and teaching.

### Problems of Education and Training

The brain-injured child is often believed to be a normal child with no handicap and hence is expected to conform to the general rules of discipline and behavior. Unfortunately, such is not the case. Even though his impairment does not show some obvious external sign, such as an orthopedic handicap, nevertheless his problem is a real one. Attempts to treat him and expect him to conform to the normal patterns put him under undue strain, aggravate his conditions, and fill him with greater anxiety. Too often by the time he has reached school age, his condition is quite advanced and doubly difficult. Although the more extreme cases are seldom able to make a satisfactory adjustment in a regular class, information should be available about the kind of special educational provisions which may be effective.

One of the early experimental programs grew out of the treatment of postencephalitic children following the epidemic which accompanied World War I. The Franklin special school was established in connection with the hospital at the University of Pennsylvania. Reports of the experiment have been made by Bond and Appel[1] in *The Treatment of Behavior Disorders Following Encephalitis* and in various articles. In their initial experiment sixty-two children twelve years of age or younger were selected for study. Fourteen of this number had many of the same behaviors and symptoms, but had never had encephalitis. They served as a "control" group during the first study of the main encephalitic group. The entire program of twenty-four hours a day was given to a careful study of the medical, social,

[1] E.D. Bond and K.E. Appel, *The Treatment of Behavior Disorders Following Encephalitis*, The Commonwealth Fund, New York, 1931, 163 pp.

psychological, and educational factors. A quiet regime was always the rule and in the absence of undue strain and excitement these children made very satisfactory progress. Some of them had been at home for various lengths of time after the encephalitic period and before admission to the school. Their behavior had become progressively worse in most instances, but it improved under the more ideal conditions of the Franklin School.

Of twenty cases eventually discharged to their homes, nine made a good adjustment, five were doubtful, and six were poor. In a report by Appel[1] some years later, in 1935, he noted that about one-third of the children were able to return home and make satisfactory adjustments. In the school program emphasis was gradually changed from that of a hospital regime to play techniques, to child analysis, and to relationship therapy. Appel also concluded that there are many psychological factors to be taken into account as well as organic pathological factors in the rehabilitation program.

*Current adjustments.* Many types of educational adjustments are in current use. With almost superhuman efforts a very resourceful teacher manages to get along with not more than one such child in a regular class. The number of good teachers who have left their profession because of them is unknown. Some parents put pressure on teachers to do with such a child in a class what they had been unable to do with him alone at home before school entrance. There are some private schools which take brain-injured children for day or full-time care and education, but the cost must necessarily be heavy because of limited class size and with custodial care.

In some communities special classes have been established for maladjusted children. Such a class may be composed of brain-injured, socially maladjusted, and, too frequently, also the educationally retarded and the mentally retarded, mixed in with those who have sensory handicaps such as impaired hearing. Such a combination of handicaps can scarcely do justice to any of these children and poses as well an impossible task for a teacher with or without specialized training. In some larger communities classes and schools have been

---

[1] K.E. Appel, "Encephalitis in Children," *Journal of Pediatrics,* 1935, 7, p. 478 ff.

established for pupils whose behavior is not acceptable in regular classes. Since brain-injured children often show erratic behavior, not motivated by malice, they are placed in these classes in which are enrolled the socially delinquent. Although they have similar causes for admission, their problems are entirely different, both in regard to the motivation of their deviant behavior and in respect to suitable remedial programs. The brain-injured children have anxieties which are accentuated by actual fear of the socially delinquent. The latter are more worldly wise and tend to torture and threaten the brain-injured with mental and physical harm. Separation of these two types into different classes is necessary. Most of the present classes enroll boys only although some cities, such as Chicago, also have schools for girls.

The crux of the problem is not special segregation as contrasted with continuing in regular grades, but rather in finding their real needs and in providing training and education to meet them. Much of the basic research in these areas has been carried on in children's hospitals with the "team" approach consisting of teacher, psychologist, psychiatrist, psychiatric social worker, parent, and others. The research studies of Strauss and Kephart and their summaries of other investigators noted above provide a basis for precedure in diagnostic and remedial activities. The irregularities of the psychological profile are taken into account with deficiencies in various specialized areas such as visual perception. Because of their greater distractibility, study desks are provided with paneled front and sides extending high enough for privacy. Special techniques are being incorporated into the smaller classrooms with encouraging results. The individual attention and reassurance which they receive, as well as their realization of progress, all combine to raise their potentialities to the positive, rather than to the negative side. Much more basic research will undoubtedly disclose further characteristics and methods of rehabilitation.

In time school systems will be able to incorporate the elements of this program within their organization. In smaller communities and in rural areas the diagnostic facilities may necessarily be centralized in some central clinic or diagnostic agency such as a hospital.

The actual instruction for all except the most extreme could be carried on with a minimum of supplies and equipment by an itinerant teacher under the same general plan as is being found effective in the education of blind children. Parents should have some instruction in the principal training needs and supplement the special education program effectively.

## Research Problems and Needs

Although there has been much progress in the past two or three decades on the basic psychology, the personality patterns, and educational procedures, there has been limited research which is currenty being extended. Comprehensive surveys have not been made to establish the number of brain-injured children so that the extent of the problem has not been determined. The larger school systems are finding them in sufficient numbers to plan for special classes and more extensive diagnostic facilities. Some of the more severely brain-injured are hospitalized for indefinite periods of time with possibility of permanent custodial care. In the Visiting Teacher Division of the Psychological Clinic of the Detroit public schools a considerable number have been sent on for hospitalization after long and patient efforts have not succeeded in the school setting. On the more promising side a limited number who have been acepted by the various research facilities such as the Hawthorn Clinic under the direction of Dr. Ralph Rabinovitch have made marked improvement.

Since the nature of brain-injured impairments has not been known until recently, there is little history about them or their treatment. Undoubtedly many brain-injured individuals have been described in terms of anti-social or deviant behavior, peculiar personalities, and other negative characteristics.

Although there are specialized curriculums for the training of teachers for such handicaps as blindness, deafness, and mental retardation, little has been done about equivalent programs for teachers of brain-injured children. Teachers who have been trained in teaching the epileptics, the orthopedically handicapped, and the speech handicapped find that some areas of their preparation are suitable for teaching brain-injured children. Special curriculums could well incorporate the findings of Bender, Strauss, and others who have contributed to the basic knowledge in this field. The brain-injured are becoming recognized as a specialized group whose rehabilitation and treatment merit facilities suitable to their handicap.

## Questions and Topics for Discussion

1. Discuss various phases of satisfactory definitions of brain-injured conditions.
2. Make a report on the incidence of syphilis and health measures for its control and prevention.
3. Report on Bond and Appel, *The Treatment of Behavior Disorders Following Encephalitis.*
4. Report on testing techniques for brain-injured children.
5. Describe some brain-injured child you have known.
6. Outline a training curriculum of thirty credit hours for teachers of brain-injured children.

Note: Consult reference material at end of Chapter 11.

# CHAPTER 11

*Mental Disorders*

*and Diseases*

MENTAL DISORDERS and diseases have been the biggest mystery of human nature. At one and the same time they have been avoided in fear, yet observed through curiosity. Since human action is mainly guided and determined by logic and by reason, when these fail, all life seems to have failed also. A major obstacle to understanding is fear and shame. Mental aberrations are concealed from relatives and associates until extreme states have been reached. Early recognition and medical treatment is a better way. The treatment history of mental disorders and diseases has been grim and explains in part some misconceptions which prevail today.

### Significance

Aside from the medical and educational aspects of mental illness, society has brought to the fore a new urgency in this area. Up to a few years ago murderers were generally put to death or given life terms without questioning their sanity. Today the emphasis has shifted toward mental illness as the underlying cause. Legal procedures now can decide between prison or mental hospital. Mental illness is suddenly socially and legally important. Attention is being turned to children's mental conditions and their relationships to this important problem.

## History

From the earliest days of recorded history there have been references and illusions to mental disturbances. Punishment to drive out evil spirits, isolation, and neglect are examples of treatments which are now recognized as futile. In some ancient races where transmigration of the soul was a common belief any "seizures" were supposed to be the result of the murderer's soul seeking a new haven. As early as the fifth century B.C. the Greek physician, Hippocrates, believed that mental illness was a disease of, or injury to, the brain. He described with surprising accuracy some mental diseases as they exist today. It took many centuries for the medical profession to grasp the significance of his theories.

Whenever cures were attempted they were truly bizarre. Hutt[1] and Gibby report the following:

These ranged from the prescriptions inherited from the Hellenic period to new and astounding panaceas. Some of the latter included: the liver of a vulture drunk for nine days (for epilepsy); hurling the most vile epithets at the insane; crab's eyes; powder made from dogs' lice; St. John's-wort; three human skulls of unburied men, dried, pulverized, and given in a liquid.

Religious beliefs experienced a dark period during the Reformation as late as four centuries ago in the treatment of mental disease. At that time Luther and his associates were bringing about a great Reformation which set Protestant against Catholic although both believed that the mentally diseased were possessed of witches. Their text was taken from Exodus XII:18 "Thou shalt not suffer a witch to live." In a period of two hundred years from the middle of the fifteenth century to the middle of the seventeenth century it was estimated that 100,000 people were executed as witches. A famous historical town in New England had its last grim witch execution in 1648 and Great Britain had its last in 1722. The Halloween witch riding on her broomstick has not entirely passed from modern tradition.

[1] M.L. Hutt and R.G. Gibby, *Patterns of Abnormal Behavior*, Allyn and Bacon, Boston, 1957, 452 pp.

Phillipe Pinel was in charge of some hospitals in France at the time of the French Revolution. He introduced some more humane practices with the insane by removing their chains, by trying to treat them kindly and sympathetically, and by finding out something about them from their histories. Following his new line of treatment many American states established hospitals for the mentally diseased in the early years of the nineteenth century. Some of the older practices of cruelty were not entirely eliminated because of ill-trained and inefficient attendants as well as persistent ideas from centuries of tradition.

A major change in the study and treatment of mental disease resulted from the experiences of Clifford Beers[1] who was hospitalized for three years with a manic-depressive psychosis. He also suffered from brutal and inhumane treatment. Legislative bodies and citizens' commissions made wholesale investigations of conditions in mental hospitals which resulted in lasting changes to more humane and scientific care of the mentally ill. Through Beers' tireless efforts the First International Congress of Mental Hygiene was held in Washington, D.C., May 5th to 10th, 1930. It was this author's privilege to attend this Congress and to hear the leaders of a new movement discuss a wide range of related subjects such as prevention, care, and treatment; clinical and social research in the field of mental hygiene; care and treatment of mental patients outside of institutions; and many others.

Three other men made notable contributions to the knowledge of mental illness at the beginning of the twentieth century. Emil Kraepelin proposed a classification of a symptom-complex or *syndrome* to describe manic-depressive insanity and dementia praecox, which Adolph Meyer adopted at the Worcester State Hospital. Sigmund Freud studied mental patients and noted their reactions to hypnosis when in hysterical conditions. Freud developed and expounded his theory of unconscious motivation and of psychosexual development as the basis of his personality theory.

*Mental diseases in children.* The preceding paragraphs outlined some trends in the treatment of mental disorders and disease but they

---

[1] C.W. Beers, A *Mind that Found Itself*, Doubleday, Doran and Co., Garden City, N.Y., 1945, 402 pp. (original publication by Longmans Green and Company in 1908).

were centered mainly on adults whose conditions were so extreme that something had to be done. Undoubtedly many children had been similarly afflicted but aside from the Children's Crusade in 1212 A.D., which never reached the Holy Land, history makes little mention of their activities and characteristics. Kanner[1] summarizes the increased interests in children in the first four decades of the twentieth century: (1) in the first decade the rise of the juvenile court, mental testing, and the mental hygiene movement; (2) in the second decade probation, foster home placement and special education; (3) child guidance clinics, and visiting teachers in the third; and (4) agencies working with the children themselves. Although some of these projects were not specifically pointed toward mental disorders in children they did broaden the base of child study.

### The Nature of Mental Disorder and Disease

The history gives some clues about the nature of mental disorders and disease. Impaired mental perspective and loss of reality are important features. These conditions are relative in character and may not have very definite boundaries or "cutoff" points between the normal and the abnormal. A marginal condition may continue within the realm of the normal if the environmental conditions are favorable. The same condition may lapse into abnormal function under the pressure of unfavorable circumstances. The milder forms are commonly known as *neuroses* or *psychoneuroses* while the more extreme conditions or diseases are known as *psychoses*. The latter term has medicolegal complications which permit the individual to be committed by legal means upon the findings and recommendations of physicians known as psychiatrists to mental hospitals and institutions.

### Structural and Functional Causes

Within both neuroses and psychoses structural and functional causes may be found. There may also be combinations of structural and functional causes. The structural causes are based on some physiological defect, disorder, or impairment of the body and particularly

[1] L. Kanner, *Child Psychiatry* (2nd ed.), Charles C Thomas Publisher, Springfield, Ill., 1955, pp. 3-16.

of the nervous system. The functional causes imply no structural impairment but are conditions which exist in the mind or imagination only. Extreme schools of thought might deny any combinations of structural and functional causes but they are not the general trend of belief. Structural impairments may or may not have some functional phases although psychosomatic medicine provides convincing evidence of their coexistence. Individuals who have started with functional disorders have been known to develop structural impairments. Some functional cases may believe so firmly that they have structural impairments, such as a weakened heart, that they limit their activities according to that possibility and any specific proof to the contrary does not convince them otherwise.

### Classifications

Kraepelin proposed a complexity of factors such as manic-depressive and dementia praecox with the latter modified later to schizophrenic reactions. Many attempts have been made to provide satisfactory and comprehensive lists or classifications. The American Psychiatric Association[1] issued its official classification in 1952.

Classification of Psychiatric Disorders
I. Disorders Caused by or Associated with Impairment of Brain Tissue Function
   A. Acute brain disorders
      1. Disorders due to or associated with infection:
         Acute brain syndrome associated with intracranial infection
         Acute brain syndrome associated with systemic infection
      2. Disorders due to or associated with intoxication:
         Acute brain syndrome, drug or poison intoxication
         Acute brain syndrome, alcohol intoxication
         Acute hallucinosis
         Delirium tremens
      3. Disorders due to or associated with tumors
   B. Chronic brain disorders
      1. Disorders due to or associated with infection:
         Chronic brain syndrome associated with central nervous system syphilis

---

[1] American Psychiatric Association, *Diagnostic and Statistical Manual: Mental Disorders*, The Association, Washington, D. C., 1952. (Quoted by special permission.)

2. Disorders associated with circulatory disturbance:
   Chronic brain syndrome associated with cerebral arteriosclerosis
3. Disorders associated with innervation or of psychic control:
   Chronic brain disorder associated with convulsive disorder (epilepsy)
4. Disorders associated with disturbance of metabolism, growth, or nutrition:
   Chronic brain syndrome associated with senile brain disease
   Chronic brain syndrome associated with other disturbance of metabolism, growth, or nutrition (includes presenile mental disorders and those associated with pellagra and with endocrine diseases)
5. Disorders associated with new growth:
   Chronic brain syndrome associated with intracranial neoplasm
6. Disorders associated with unknown or uncertain cause:
   Includes brain syndrome associated with Huntington's chorea, Pick's disease, and other diseases of hereditary nature

II. Mental Deficiency
III. Disorders of Psychogenic Origin or without Clearly Defined Physical Cause or Structural Change in the Brain
   A. Psychotic disorders
      1. Disorders due to disturbances of metabolism, growth, nutrition, or endocrine function
         Involutional psychotic reaction
      2. Disorders of psychogenic origin or without clearly defined tangible cause or structural change:
         Affective reactions
            Manic-depressive reaction, manic type
            Manic-depressive reaction, depressive type
            Psychotic depressive reaction
         Schizophrenic reactions
            Schizophrenic reaction, simple type
            Schizophrenic reaction, hebephrenic type
            Schizophrenic reaction, catatonic type
            Schizophrenic reaction, paranoid type
         Paranoid reaction
            Paranoia
            Paranoid state
   B. Psychophysiologic autonomic and visceral disorders
      Psychosomatic disorders
   C. Psychoneurotic disorders

Anxiety reaction
Dissociative reaction
Conversion reaction
Phobic reaction
Obsessive compulsive reaction
D. Personality disorders
Personality pattern disturbance
Personality trait disturbance
Sociopathic personality disturbance
Addiction

From the earlier classification of twenty-four types the present classification presents only three major divisions with only six minor divisions and eleven subdivisions. The first major division includes disorders caused by or associated with impairment of brain tissue function. The third major division includes disorders of psychogenic origin.

Cameron[1] reports upon a modification of the classification adopted by the United States Army in which there is no clear-cut distinction between neuroses and psychoses. He outlines eight main clinical syndromes:

Hypochondriacal disorders
Fatigue syndromes
Anxiety disorders
Compulsive disorders
Hysterical inactivity and hysterical autonomy
Paranoid disorders
Schizophrenic disorders
Manic and depressive disorders

These terms use adjective modifiers which are mainly self-explanatory, and by the use of "disorders" the distinctions between neuroses and psychoses are intentionally obscured. Likewise the distinction between structural and functional has been lessened. These several kinds of classifications illustrate some evolutions in psychiatric thought.

[1] N. Cameron, *The Psychology of the Behavior Disorders*, Houghton Mifflin Co., Boston, 1947, 622 pp.

## Child and Adult Mental Disorders

The principal interests in mental disorders, as noted in the sections above, have been mainly as they concerned adults. It was necessarily so since until very recent years little research or investigations had been conducted in mental disorders of children. Since it is entirely probable that many mental disorders of adults had their etiology in obvious or latent conditions in their childhood or adolescence, the investigations of children's mental disorders became doubly significant.

The classifications and reactions of children are different in some respects from adults but similar in others. Lack of ready speech with which to formulate their attitudes and to clarify their vague ideas is a serious impediment to childhood communication. Some techniques for releasing expressions by deed or by word have been outlined in discussions of diagnosis and prevention of deviant behavior in Chapter 6, including projective activities and play therapy. By sheer force of training and of habit, many routines of everyday living become more or less automatic, and hence are assumed to be normal. But within this exterior the mental health may be only a hollow shell.

At a very early age in infancy autistic behavior is observed. It has been found in some of the less effective foundling homes where, because of inadequately trained and manned staffs, the emphasis was upon physical care lacking in the love and protection by motherhood. Infants of a few months were observed to sit and sway without paying any attention to surroundings or to people. Autism is characterized by a morbid concentration upon self with no alternative. Fear and withdrawal from all associations in later childhood years becomes the natural sequel. Other causes date back into prenatal conditions. Lauretta Bender[1] describes childhood schizophrenia in part as:

Childhood schizophrenia involves a maturational lag at the embryonic level characterized by a primitive plasticity in all areas from which subsequent behavior develops. It is genetically determined and activated

[1] L. Bender, "Childhood Schizophrenia," *American Journal of Orthopsychiatry*, 1956, 26, pp. 499-506.

by a physiological crisis such as birth. Anxiety is both the organismic and psychological response calling forth defense mechanisms.

She recognizes three principal types. The first is the autistic child who is a pseudodefective type, incorrectly diagnosed as mentally retarded. His physical homeostasis is inadequate and motor behavior remains immature. The second type is pseudoneurotic with anxieties, phobias, disturbed orientation in time and space, and indefinite as to body boundaries. The third or pseudopsychopathic types have compulsive and obsessional patterns in which they lack insight and have no feelings of guilt or anxiety. Bender traces the history of the same cases from infancy through adolescence with hopeful improvements in some cases under intensive treatment.

In the field of child psychiatry Drs. Dubo and Rabinovitch[1] review the findings in childhood schizophrenia to the effect that there is a continuum of the schizophrenic psychotic process from childhood to adulthood and hence it should be studied intensively in the childhood stages.

Both structural and functional causes of mental disorder and disease have been noted. In the structural area various types of brain injuries have been discussed in the preceding chapter. The erratic behavior over which the brain-injured seem to have little control reaches out into their social contacts and adds more difficulties because of severe and restraining discipline imposed on them. The anxieties and pressures which develop in their parents create a neurotic home atmosphere. When one parent is psychotic or neurotic, some normal children have functional reactions, and in disturbed children the condition may be worsened. A great sense of insecurity develops during childhood and in adolescence there is worry about inherited conditions which may eventually overtake them as well. The usual buoyancy of childhood fades prematurely. Domestic discord in otherwise normal homes becomes a functional cause of anxiety and unrest so that the door may be opened to more serious maladjustments in children.

In personal conference, Dr. Ralph Rabinovitch, medical superin-

[1] S. Dubo and R.D. Rabinovitch, "Child Psychiatry," *Progress in Neurology and Psychiatry*, 1956, 11, pp. 315-326.

tendent of the Hawthorn Center for disturbed children at North-ville, Mich., outlined seven criteria to be noted in the character-istics of such children: (1) the extent of neurological integration, which is related to the total anatomy and physiology of the nervous system; (2) the "intellectual" potential or possible functioning of the intellectual abilities; (3) the clarity of end boundaries or knowledge of where the individual ends his domain and where others begin; (4) the capacity for depth relationships, such as are illustrated in autistic children; (5) acculturation or the ability to adopt customs of others or of other groups; (6) anxieties of an endogenous nature or coming from within; and (7) anxieties of an exogenous nature coming from outside the individual.

In an earlier chapter the patterns of childhood and adolescent con-flicts were described. The childhood conflicts between satisfaction of self and social participation assume many forms and no adequate solutions can be reached. When the problem is too severe, complete blocking is sometimes escaped by flights into fantasy. It is actually a better mental health solution to break through one of the blocked avenues of the conflict with risk of punishment than to resort to fantasy. The adolescent conflict has the same general frame but the issues center around being restrained into continuing in childhood or achieving some adult goals. The temptation to fantasy is very great because the complicated problems of satisfactory adult adjustment are legion. Temptation to fantasy, as contrasted with grim realities of adult life, is a common denominator of neurotic conditions or of some psychotic diseases.

### The Challenge to Teachers

It is unnecessary to elaborate further upon the many causes and conditions of mental disorders and diseases since most of them are beyond the training and scope of the classroom teacher. However that same teacher must face daily experiences with such a child who actually needs complete individual attention but who fails to get it. The teacher's major attention is necessarily on the entire class. In extreme cases this experience serves no useful purpose for the pupil himself and at the same time it sets up disturbance in the class as well as driving the teacher to distraction. Parents expect the school to do what could not be accomplished at home. Such a child is expected to attend school so as to relieve the home if for no other reason. Extreme pressure is placed upon school administrators to keep such children in school even if it becomes necessary to isolate them in one corner or in the waiting room of the school's office. In these more enlightened days such conditions should no longer be necessary. Medical diagnosis and hospitalization of the more extreme cases is better for parent, for teacher, and for the child himself. Less severe cases may be segregated in small special classes for such pupils where teamwork with parent, teacher, psychiatrist, psychologist, and school social worker produces some measure of success.

## Hospitalization and Remedial Programs

Mental hospitals for adults have been pressured to admit a few mentally ill children. Often there are no special facilities nor schools for them. Some hospitals in connection with universities and medical schools are establishing units for mentally disordered children and adolescents. Most of them accept only a very limited number because of the greater cost and because their units were designed for research and staff training. There is an extreme shortage of hospital facilities for mentally disturbed adults whose care seems to be more urgent than for children. Attempts are being made to provide out-patient service for some of the less severe cases who are considered not to be dangerous to themselves or to others.

There are some promising signs that special medication will lessen the severity, if not actually cure, some mental disorders. Shock therapies of various kinds have been introduced with careful checking to determine which kinds of cases might benefit. The chemistry of the brain and the entire body is being studied in relation to new antibiotics. Since costs are excessive, it will be a great financial saving if remedies and preventions can be developed and used without the necessity of long hospitalization.

## The Number of Cases

Fortunately the number of extremely mentally ill children is not large. Many teachers are never faced with them. As noted above, the hospitalization facilities are as yet very limited and the pressures to accept more than their facilities can accommodate is a real problem. The number of adults who are afflicted with some type and degree of mental disorder is either on the increase or better means of diagnosis and identification have brought more to light. Approximately one out of every ten or fifteen adults at some time has gone through some phase of mental disorder or is dangerously near to it. With sharpened instruments of diagnosis more potential cases of children are steadily coming to light. If they can be treated and helped in childhood there is hope that the number of adults so afflicted may be reduced.

The great majority of teachers and parents should not become unduly alarmed about mental disorders in childhood or believe that every child with some deviant behavior disorder such as discussed in Chapter 5 is a potential case. Present-day society is going through one of its special phases in which there is publicity and concentration upon some particular type of condition or handicap. The current trend is mental disorder, which superseded mental retardation with the Binet test as the "only" instrument of diagnosis. Soon, it will be something else. Presently the world clamors for psychiatric service but the supply is very short of the demand. The services of the school social worker, the school psychologist, the trained counselor, and better-trained teachers can screen the more extreme cases for the psychiatrist and prepare case histories which saves him valuable time. The psychiatrist performs an important service in dealing directly with a limited number of cases, outlining methods of procedure for the follow-up by other staff members, and through lectures and printed materials offering suggestions for general improvement in the mental hygiene practices which underlie better mental health.

## Questions and Topics for Discussion

1. Discuss any type of psychotic individual with whom you have been acquainted and describe his history.

2. If possible visit a mental hospital and have a demonstration of the various types of cases.
3. Discuss the provisions of your local community for extreme mental disorders in children.
4. Report in more detail about the Children's Crusade and its young leaders.
5. Discuss in more detail the eight clinical syndromes of mental disorder adopted by the United States Army.
6. Report more completely upon investigations by Bender on childhood schizophrenia.

## A. Organizations

1. American Academy for Cerebral Palsy, Inc., 4743 N. Drake Ave., Chicago 25.
2. American Medical Association, 535 N. Dearborn St., Chicago 10.
3. American Neurological Association, 710 W. 168th St., New York 32.
4. American Psychiatric Association, Inc., 1270 Avenue of the Americas, New York 20.
5. Council for Exceptional Children, 1201 16th St., N. W., Washington 6, D.C.
6. National Epilepsy League, Inc., 130 N. Wells St., Chicago 6.
7. National Multiple Sclerosis Society, 270 Park Ave., New York 17.
8. National Society for Crippled Children and Adults, Inc., 11 S. LaSalle St., Chicago 3.
9. National Society for Medical Research, 208 N. Wells St., Chicago 6.
10. Shut-In Society, 221 Lexington Ave., New York 16.
11. United Cerebral Palsy, Inc., 50 W. 57th St., New York 19.

## B. Periodicals

1. A. M. A. *Archives of Neurology and Psychiatry* (quarterly), American Medical Association.
2. *American Journal of Psychiatry* (monthly), American Psychiatric Association.
3. *Cerebral Palsy Review* (monthly), 2400 Jardine Drive, Wichita 14, Kansas.
4. *The Crippled Child* (monthly), National Society for Crippled Children and Adults, Chicago.
5. *Digest of Neurology and Psychiatry*, 200 Retreat Ave., Hartford 2, Conn.
6. *Epilepsia*, Journal of the International League Against Epilepsy, 150 S. Huntington Ave., Boston.

7. *Journal of Abnormal and Social Psychology* (quarterly), American Psychological Association.
8. *Journal of Nervous and Mental Diseases* (monthly), 79 Pine St., New York 5.
9. *Journal of Speech and Hearing Disorders* (bimonthly), Wayne State University, Detroit 2.
10. *Mental Hygiene* (quarterly), by the National Association for Mental Health, 1790 Broadway, New York 19.
11. *The Nervous Child* (quarterly), 30 W. 58th St., New York 19.
12. *Psychiatry* (quarterly), 1711 Rhode Island Ave., Washington 6, D.C.

## C. Books

### Section I. Nervous System (Chapter 7)

1. Bard, P. (ed.), *Patterns of Organization in the Central Nervous System*, Williams and Wilkins, Baltimore, Md., 1952, 581 pp.
2. Brain, R., *Diseases of the Nervous System* (5th ed.), Oxford University Press, New York, 1955, 996 pp.
3. DeJong, R.H., *The Neurologic Examination*, P. B. Hoeber, New York, 1950, 1,079 pp.
4. Elliott, H.C., *Textbook of the Nervous System* (2nd ed.), J.B. Lippincott Co., Philadelphia, 1954, 437 pp.
5. Fulton, J.F., *Physiology of the Nervous System* (3rd ed.), Oxford University Press, New York, 1949, 667 pp.
6. Grinker, R.R., and P.C. Bucy, *Neurology* (4th ed.), Charles C Thomas Publisher, Springfield, Ill., 1949, 1138 pp.
7. Kreig, W.J.S., *Brain Mechanisms in Diachrome* (2nd ed.), Brain Books, Evanston, Ill., 1955, 188 pp.
8. ———, *Functional Neuroanatomy* (2nd ed.), McGraw-Hill Book Co., Inc., New York, 1953, 659 pp.
9. Larsell, O., *Anatomy of the Nervous System* (2nd ed.), Appleton-Century-Crofts, Inc., New York, 1951, 520 pp.
10. Penfield, W., and T. Rasmussen. *The Cerebral Cortex in Man*, The Macmillan Co., New York, 1950, 248 pp.
11. Ranson, S.W., and S.L. Clark, *Anatomy of the Nervous System* (9th ed.), W.B. Saunders Co., Philadelphia, 1953, 581 pp.

### Section II. The Convulsive Disorders (Chapter 8)

1. Bridge, E.M., *Epilepsy and Convulsive Disorders in Children*, McGraw-Hill Book Co., Inc., New York, 1949, 670 pp.
2. Gibbs, F.A., and E.L. Gibbs, *Atlas of Electroencephalography*, F.A. Gibbs, Boston, City Hospital, 1941, 221 pp.

3. Green, J.R., and H.F. Steelman (eds.), *Epileptic Seizures*, Williams and Wilkins, Baltimore, Md., 1956, 177 pp.
4. Hoch, P.H., and R.P. Knight (eds.), *Epilepsy*, Grune and Stratton, Inc., New York, 1947, 214 pp.
5. Lennox, W.G., *Science and Seizures; New Light on Epilepsy and Migraine*, Harper & Brothers, New York, 1941, 258 pp.
6. Penfield, W., and T.C. Erickson, *Epilepsy and Cerebral Localization*, Charles C Thomas Publisher, Springfield, Ill., 1941, 623 pp.
7. ———, and H. Jasper, *Epilepsy and the Functional Anatomy of the Brain*, Little Brown and Company, Boston, 1954, 896 pp.
8. Schwab, R.S., *Electroencephalography in Clinical Practice*, W.B. Saunders Co., Philadelphia, 1951, 195 pp.

## Section III. Cerebral Palsy (Chapter 9)

1. Benda, C.E., *Developmental Disorders of Mentation and Cerebral Palsies*, Grune and Stratton, Inc., New York, 1952, 565 pp.
2. Cardwell, V.E. (ed.), *The Cerebral Palsied Child and His Care in the Home*, Association for the Aid of Crippled Children, New York, 1947, 196 pp.
3. Cass, M., *Speech Rehabilitation in Cerebral Palsy*, Columbia University Press, New York, 1951, 212 pp.
4. Cruickshank, W.M., and G.M. Raus, *Cerebral Palsy* (eds.), Syracuse University Press, Syracuse, N.Y., 1955, 560 pp.
5. Egel, P.F., *Technique of Treatment for the Cerebral Palsy Child*, C.V. Mosby Co., St. Louis, Mo., 1948, 203 pp.
6. Hopkins, T.W., H.V. Bice, and K.C. Colton, *Evaluation and Education of the Cerebral Palsied Child: New Jersey Study*, International Council for Exceptional Children, Washington, D.C., 1954, 114 pp.
7. Pohl, J.F., *Cerebral Palsy*, Bruce Publishing Co., Milwaukee, Wis., 1950, 244 pp.
8. Schonell, F.E., *Educating Spastic Children*, Philosophical Library, New York, 1956, 242 pp.

## Section IV. The Brain-Injured (Chapter 10)

1. Bender, L., *Psychopathology of Children with Organic Brain Disorders*, Charles C Thomas Publisher, Springfield, Ill., 1956, 151 pp.
2. Hood, O.E., *Your Child or Mine; the Brain-Injured Child and his Hope*, Harper & Brothers, New York, 1957, 180 pp.
3. Lewis, R.S., A.A. Strauss, and L.E. Lehtinen, *The Other Child: The Brain-Injured Child*, Grune and Stratton, Inc., New York, 1951, 108 pp.

*Courtesy of Department of Special Education, Fort Worth public schools.*

**Cerebral palsy pupil supported by chair straps at cut-out sand table, Fort Worth public schools.**

Case conference, Cincinnati, Ohio public schools.

4. Strauss, A.A., and L.E. Lehtinen, *Psychopathology and Education of the Brain-Injured Child*, Grune and Stratton, Inc., New York, 1947, 206 pp.
5. Strauss, A.A., and N.C. Kephart, *Psychopathology and Education of the Brain-Injured Child*, Vol. II, Grune and Stratton, Inc., 1955, 266 pp.

Section V. Mental Disorders and Diseases (Chapter 11)

1. Aldrich, C.K., *Psychiatry for the Family Physician*, McGraw-Hill Book Co., Inc., New York, 1955, 276 pp.
2. Allen, F.H., *Psychotherapy with Children*, W.W. Norton and Co. Inc., New York, 1942, 311 pp.
3. Bender, L., *A Dynamic Psychopathology of Childhood*, Charles C Thomas Publisher, Springfield, Ill., 1954, 275 pp.
4. ———, *Child Psychiatric Techniques*, Charles C Thomas Publisher, Springfield, Ill., 1952, 335 pp.
5. Biddle, W.E., and M. Van Sickel, *Introduction to Psychiatry*, W.B. Saunders Co., Philadelphia, 1943, 358 pp.
6. Bradley, C., *Schizophrenia in Childhood*, The Macmillan Co., New York, 1941, 152 pp.
7. English, O.S., and S.M. Finch, *Introduction to Psychiatry*, W.W. Norton Co., Inc., New York, 1954, 621 pp.
8. Kanner, L., *Child Psychiatry* (2nd ed.), Charles C Thomas Publisher, Springfield, Ill., 1950, 752 pp.
9. Kaplan, O.J. (ed.), *Mental Disorders in Later Life*, Stanford University Press, Stanford University, Calif., 1956, 508 pp.
10. Masserman, J.H., *The Practice of Dynamic Psychiatry*, W.B. Saunders Co., Philadelphia, 1955, 790 pp.
11. Menninger, W.C., *Psychiatry in a Troubled World*, The Macmillan Co., New York, 1948, 636 pp.
12. Moore, T.V., *The Nature and Treatment of Mental Disorders* (2nd ed.) Grune and Stratton, Inc., New York, 1951, 362 pp.
13. Olkon, D.M., *Essentials of Neuro Psychiatry*, Lea and Febiger, Philadelphia, 1945, 310 pp.
14. Sadler, W.S., *Practice of Psychiatry*, C.V. Mosby Co., St. Louis, Mo., 1953, 1183 pp.
15. Strecker, E.A., *Basic Psychiatry*, Random House, New York, 1952, 473 pp.
16. ———, *Fundamentals of Psychiatry* (2nd ed.), J.B. Lippincott Co., Philadelphia, 1944, 219 pp.
17. Sullivan, H.S., *Clinical Studies in Psychiatry*, W.W. Norton and Co. Inc., New York, 1956, 386 pp.

18. Weiss, E., and O.S. English, *Psychosomatic Medicine*, W.B. Saunders Co., Philadelphia, 1943, 687 pp.

## D. Films and Filmstrips

1. *Breakdown,* 40 minutes, sound. Illness and treatment of young woman with severe emotional difficulty. National Film Board of Canada.

2. *Chorea,* 16 minutes, silent. Three groups of degenerative chorea. New York University Film Library.

3. *Convulsive and Allied Conditions,* 18 minutes, silent. Illustrates many convulsive conditions. New York University Film Library.

4. *Diagnosis of Childhood Schizophrenia,* 35 minutes, sound. Outlines the various steps and illustrates teamwork approach. New York University Film Library.

5. *Epidemic Encephalitis,* 31 minutes, silent. Sequential histories over a period of years, with some bizarre entities. New York University Film Library.

6. *Maternal Deprivation in Young Children.* 30 minutes, sound. Psychotherapy techniques and their effect after maternal deprivation. Illustrates mental disorders. New York University Film Library.

7. *Nervous System,* 11 minutes, sound. Structure of the nervous system, and general description. Encyclopaedia Britannica Films.

8. *Paranoid Conditions,* 13 minutes, sound. Two cases of extreme delusions. McGraw-Hill Text-Film Department.

9. *Psychoneuroses,* 23 minutes, silent. Patients with signs and symptoms of seemingly psychogenic nature. New York University Film Library.

# PART 4

## Deviations in Abilities
## and Aptitudes

# CHAPTER 12

## The Nature of Abilities
## and Aptitudes

TESTS OF ABILITIES, aptitudes, and intelligence have probably attracted more attention in the past three or four decades than all other topics in education taken collectively. The intelligence quotient became a byword everywhere and its significance was elevated to the absurd position of being the principal cause of all human action. As noted in the preceding chapter, emphasis on it is presently being replaced by the study of mental disorders. In the meantime qualified psychologists continue to make careful and thorough investigations to determine its rightful place in human affairs.

The nomenclature of intelligence needs some clarification. The term "intelligence" formerly meant information, such as the attorney's intelligence about legal matters, or the teacher's intelligence about English literature. The meaning has gradually changed to the potential ability to acquire this information rather than the information itself. Intelligence, or ability to acquire mastery in some field, is not necessarily synonymous with the former meaning of the term. An individual may have high potential ability for learning dentistry but because of his lack of training and experience he does not have adequate "intelligence" about it according to the former meaning of the term. Since there continues to be some use of the former meaning, care must be exercised to establish what is actually being discussed.

The term "aptitude" implies a potential for learning or mastery in some particular or general area. When applied to aptitude for general learning, it is largely synonymous with the modern meaning of "intelligence." However, aptitude has taken on a large number of other specialized meanings such as musical aptitude, mechanical aptitude, and artistic aptitude. The term "aptitudes" is also applied to various specialized phases of general intelligence such as linguistic aptitude, and auditory and visual spans of attention for specific materials. The Detroit Tests of Learning Aptitudes is an illustration of such use. For purposes of practical discussion the modern use of "intelligence" will cover abilities and aptitudes.

Intelligence constitutes one of the three basic ingredients of the personality structure as noted in Chapter 4. It takes its place together with the unlearned needs and drives, and with the bodily attributes, as part of the basic foundation upon which personality is built. It gives some direction to other elements of personality such as the will. It is not all powerful since the feelings and emotions may overwhelm the intellect so that unreasoned action may occur. When it balances with the feelings and emotions, logic and reason go hand in hand with warmth of personality.

The evaluation of intelligence has been helpful in the general diagnosis and interpretation of all types of handicapped and exceptional children. There is some mention of it in practically all types of the handicapped. For example, the blind child who is slow of mind poses different educational problems than the bright blind child. Measurements of intelligence form a convenient base in such evaluations. However it is a hopeful sign that characterizations in terms of other personality factors in these various handicapped types are becoming more frequent and meaningful. The methodology of measuring intelligence has served a useful purpose in illustrating how measurement and evaluation may be applied to other elements of personality.

### Faulty Concepts About Intelligence

Every individual is a self-styled psychologist when he tries to make others understand him, when he tries to understand others, and less often when he tries to understand himself. He evaluates the ability of others to understand him. His ability in these contacts, or his basis of judgment, may be very faulty; in other cases, remarkably, it may be accurate. A few common faulty concepts about intelligence will be mentioned.

Except in extreme cases, intelligence cannot be estimated from the general appearance of facial characteristics. Some good-looking individuals are found among the inmates of an institution for the custodial feebleminded, whereas some very inadequate- and insignificant-looking individuals are observed among scientific men. Such irregularities as unusual shape of the nose, or spacing of the eyes, and asymmetrical shape of the lower jaw occur a little more often among the lower levels of intelligence, but since they are noted at higher mental levels also they are not safe criteria in judging intelligence. Size of the head is not an index of intelligence, although, as a group, mental defectives have heads smaller than the average. At the other extreme, there are hydrocephalics with very large heads, who are usually feeble-minded.

Certain mannerisms and deviant behavior are not reliable indicators of intelligence. A pose of concentration, such as knitting the forehead, may be an earnest attempt at mental activity, although there may not be much real ability behind it. Ability to do one or two simple tasks repeatedly is of little value in estimating intelligence. For example, the ability to rearrange the upturned corner of a rug is indicative of intelligence only when it is accompanied by successful adaptations to many other commonplace occurrences.

Speed of physical movement is not very helpful although accuracy may be a little more significant. A mere flutter of exciting activity without a real purpose is likely to indicate mental inferiority rather than mental superiority. Another source of error is judging ability from rapid speech without an analysis of the reasoning or the vocabulary in which thoughts are couched. Since logical and reasoned actions and thoughts are more reliable indications of intelligence, judgments upon external physical symptoms and simple habits are obviously of much less value. Unless opportunities are available to evaluate these more meaningful evidences of ability, the trained and experienced psychologist is reluctant to judge abilities from physical, external characteristics or from brief contacts. Little is to be gained from further consideration of inadequate and unreliable ways of guessing at intelligence.

## The Foundations of Intellect

There are two important positive approaches in the understanding of intellectual abilities: (1) the neural basis which is inherent in the human body; and (2) the potential opportunities for ways of expressing them.

*The neural basis.* Intellectual abilities have a neural basis in the central nervous system as described in Chapter 7. The direction and control of bodily systems are vested in the nervous system with both voluntary and involuntary nerve activations. All of these principal reactions are channelled through the intellectual activities of the brain. Synapses are delicate points of connection between nerves through which the nerve impulse must pass. The potential force of the nerve impulse is probably based in part upon nerve strength and vitality. The difficulty or ease with which the impulse passes through the synapse seems to depend to some degree upon the actual texture or quality of synaptic tissue. The quality and quantity of intellectual abilities rest largely upon the physical constitution of the body. If so, change of intellectual status depends more or less directly upon changes in bodily constitution.

The nature of neural activity has been one of the mysteries of science. Many theories have been proposed. Some form of electrical or electro-chemical energy is present in the nerve cells and is transmitted along the nervous system. As mentioned in Chapter 7 there may well be some combination of electro-chemical reaction which has not yet been discovered. In the modern era of fission, harnessing and unleashing of seemingly unlimited power, newer discoveries about the nature of nervous impulses are by no means impossible. For the present the fact of nerve conduction may be accepted and its applications utilized in guiding human affairs.

*Potential opportunities.* The practical expression of intelligence also arises from opportunities to use it functionally. The Savage of

Aveyron had lacked the opportunity for association with people and hence did not develop speech and language. He must have possessed some intelligence in order to have survived in his natural state. Individuals living in practical isolation would ordinarily have developed a lesser range of intellectual interests than those living in rich social and cultural environments. Since intelligence tests usually include items which are drawn from the environment, the socially deprived might logically be expected to perform at some disadvantage. Lack of equal opportunity produces some differences but possibly not as much as would ordinarily be expected. Some of the current intelligence tests have introduced items which are claimed to be "culture-free" so as to take such differences into account.

*Definitions.* Satisfactory definitions of intelligence are difficult to formulate. Intelligence includes many complex factors and is capable of being expressed in many different ways. Binet defined it as the ability to take and to maintain a definite direction, to adapt it to new situations, and to check it for accuracy. Woodworth had a somewhat similar concept in retentivity, or the ability to use facts and activities already acquired, by ready adaptability to novel situations, by curiosity, by interest in, and by desire to know about things; and by persistence, or the trait of sticking to what is begun. These definitions emphasize adaptability to life situations, which include school learning, and practical adjustment as to neighborhood and social customs.

Dr. Edward Thorndike proposed three areas of intelligence: (1) the abstract, or the ability to understand and manage ideas and symbols such as words, numbers, scientific principles, and similar factors; (2) mechanical intelligence or the ability to learn, to understand, and to manage things and mechanisms; and (3) social intelligence or the ability to manage people and to act wisely in human relations. Dr. Terman emphasized verbal or linguistic aptitude as one of the principal vehicles of intelligence, since thoughts and ideas are expressed mainly in language.

### Test Construction

There has been too much lay exploitation of the nature of, the construction of, and the interpretation of intelligence tests. Professional standards for these procedures have been established by members of the American Psychological Association who have specialized in test construction. These psychologists are thoroughly versed in the nature of intelligence and other aptitudes and in the principles of test construction and standardization. Items which satisfy criteria proposed by Binet, Terman, and others are administered to a large number of children at successive ages until an age is found where approximately one-half of the children are successful. There should be a steep rise in the percentages who fail in successive years.

There are many kinds of test items which satisfy the criteria of intelligence. Some are relatively complex and demand resourceful reasoning for their solution. Other items evaluate the span or number of items capable of immediate or delayed recall in order to evaluate the level where efficient learning takes place. All items, or series of items, should satisfactorily meet other known criteria of intelligence. The psychologists' judgment about valid and satisfactory items takes precedence over lay opinions and impressions.

### Terminology of Test Results

Although there are many kinds of intelligence tests, such as individual or group, in the majority of them mental age norms are established. For each child tested it is possible to divide the mental age by the chronological or life age to determine a ratio which is usually known as the intelligence quotient. This number or ratio was devised by Dr. Lewis M. Terman in connection with the 1916 form of the Stanford-Binet test. The intelligence quotient has been subjected to many uses and abuses. On the abuse side qualified psychologists have vainly tried to emphasize that it is an approximation with a standard error of a few points in either direction, and not as scientifically absolute as is the case with some precise physical measurements. Since the measure seemed to be quite definite and gave considerable ready information about the individual, there was a tendency upon the part of educators and others not thoroughly trained in intelligence measurement to put too much dependence upon it by ignoring many other qualities of character in evaluating the over-all abilities of children which were not so easily measured.

On the positive side the intelligence quotient was found to be an approximate ratio which tended to maintain itself with relatively little variation from year to year and hence it was valuable in educational and vocational planning. Since it was an approximate but numerical indication it could serve as a pivot or anchor in studying the other less definitely measurable qualities of human nature. Another important use was found in the great range of abilities illustrated in the Diagram on the Distribution of Intelligence. Educational planning for the mentally retarded, for the mentally gifted, for the slow-learning, and the rapid-learning was greatly advanced through knowledge of these differences.

## THE DISTRIBUTION OF INTELLIGENCE

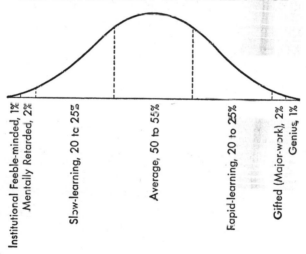

**DIAGRAM III**

Another method of reporting results is by the use of letter ratings which correspond to certain "cutoff" points on the range of intelligence quotients for large groups of children at each particular age. On the various Detroit Group Intelligence tests a system of letters ratings is used as follows: (1) the highest 8 or 10 per cent with intelligence quotients of approximately 118 to 120 or higher rated A; (2) the next

12 per cent from 110 to 118 rated B; (3) the next 18 per cent rated C+, 105 to 109; (4) C ratings for about one-fourth of all near 100; (5) C— in the low nineties; (6) D ratings in the eighties; and (7) E ratings for the lowest 8 to 10 per cent from the low eighties and lower. The purpose of the letter ratings is to convey the idea that the group intelligence rating is an *approximation* rather than a specific number. When very specific numbers are needed percentile or one-hundred-step scores could be computed. It is also possible to approximate by grouping the percentiles into ten decile groups, or five quintile groups. Other types of reporting are PLR (probable learning rate) and ratings expressed as sigmas so that three sigma plus would be only a very select group of individuals with extremely high ability.

As noted elsewhere the quality of intellect is equally if not more important than the quantity as expressed in mental age and intelligence quotient. Two children with the same mental age of ten years are quite different in their abilities and the quality of intellect if one is eight years in actual age with an intelligence quotient of 125 and the other fifteen years in actual age with an intelligence quotient of 67.

### General Versus Specific Abilities

One of the most perplexing problems in the analysis of intelligence centers around the question of whether or not intelligence is a general factor or a series of specific factors relatively independent of each other. Although certain statistical methods, known as factor analysis, have been applied to test results, there are still differences of opinion about the constitution of abilities. Freeman[1] summarized these points of view under three heads: (1) Thomson and Thorndike consider general intelligence to be a composite of a large number of highly popularized abilities; (2) Kelley and Thurstone consider intelligence to be composed of a limited number of primary mental abilities, each relatively independent of the others with the sum of all being general intelligence; and (3) the views of Spearman and Hol-

1 F. N. Freeman, "Intelligence: Its Nature and Nurture," *Thirty-Ninth Yearbook, Part I*, National Society for the Study of Education, University of Chicago Press, Chicago, 1940, pp. 19-20.

zinger that there is one general factor, a limited number of group factors running through many operations, and a large number of very specialized factors, but there is some question whether or not the general factor should be considered as general intelligence.

A better understanding of intelligence may be realized if the content of some individual intelligence tests are briefly outlined. The Stanford-Binet test of 1937[1] has a great variety of items or problems with six at each age. Immediate recall of sentences and of number spans read orally by the examiner, picture absurdities, and information tests such as the number of fingers, or the days of the week. All the items passed successfully over a range of a few years are totalled to make a general mental age. In making an interpretation the general mental age is presented, but comments are made on the lowest items failed and the highest items passed. Both the general and the specific factors are discussed.

The Wechsler Test for Children[2] is divided into two principal parts with five verbal tests and five performance tests. Each of the ten and the two alternate parts have a series of items and a scaled score is determined for each; for the verbal series; for the performance series; and for the entire series. Intelligence quotients may be determined for the verbal, the performance, and the full scale. The full scale represents general intelligence and the two subparts, special phases of intelligence.

The Detroit Tests of Learning Aptitude[3] consists of a series of nineteen subtests with mental age norms for each. Some subtests are suitable for young children and others for older youth and adults; only about one-half of them are usually administered to any individual although a greater number may be used. A variety of special abilities includes spans of visual attentive ability, auditory attentive ability, motor speed and precision, orientation, verbal knowledge, free association, assembling disarranged pictures, reproduction of geometric

[1] L.M. Terman and M.A. Merrill, *Measuring Intelligence*, Houghton Mifflin Co., Boston, 1937, 461 pp.
[2] D. Wechsler, *Wechsler, Intelligence Scale for Children*, Ages 8-15, The Psychological Corp., New York, 1949, 113 pp.
[3] H.J. Baker and B. Leland, *Detroit Tests of Learning Aptitude*, C.A. Gregory Co., Cincinnati, Ohio, 1935, 157 pp.

designs, social adjustments, detection of pictorial or verbal absurdities. A sample profile of results on the accompanying diagram shows a range of mental age from thirteen years, six months, on auditory attention span for syllables to six years, six months, on visual attention span for objects. Near the midpoint six of the thirteen subtests extend over a range of only two years which indicates the approximate gen-

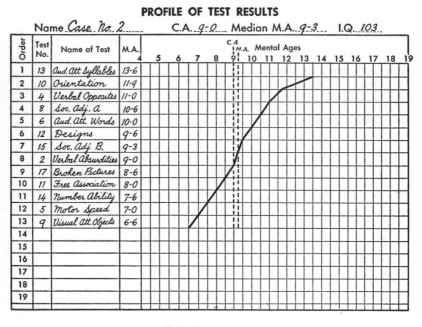

**PROFILE OF TEST RESULTS**

Name _Case No. 2_     C.A. _9-0_ Median M.A. _9-3_ I.Q. _103_

| Order | Test No. | Name of Test | M.A. | 4 | 5 | 6 | 7 | 8 | 9 | 10 | 11 | 12 | 13 | 14 | 15 | 16 | 17 | 18 | 19 |
|---|---|---|---|---|---|---|---|---|---|---|---|---|---|---|---|---|---|---|---|
| 1 | 13 | Aud. Att. Syllables | 13-6 | | | | | | | | | | | | | | | | |
| 2 | 10 | Orientation | 11-9 | | | | | | | | | | | | | | | | |
| 3 | 4 | Verbal Opposites | 11-0 | | | | | | | | | | | | | | | | |
| 4 | 8 | Soc. Adj. a | 10-6 | | | | | | | | | | | | | | | | |
| 5 | 6 | Aud. Att. Words | 10-0 | | | | | | | | | | | | | | | | |
| 6 | 12 | Designs | 9-6 | | | | | | | | | | | | | | | | |
| 7 | 15 | Soc. Adj. B. | 9-3 | | | | | | | | | | | | | | | | |
| 8 | 2 | Verbal Absurdities | 9-0 | | | | | | | | | | | | | | | | |
| 9 | 17 | Broken Pictures | 8-6 | | | | | | | | | | | | | | | | |
| 10 | 11 | Free Association | 8-0 | | | | | | | | | | | | | | | | |
| 11 | 14 | Number Ability | 7-6 | | | | | | | | | | | | | | | | |
| 12 | 5 | Motor Speed | 7-0 | | | | | | | | | | | | | | | | |
| 13 | 9 | Visual Att. Objects | 6-6 | | | | | | | | | | | | | | | | |
| 14 | | | | | | | | | | | | | | | | | | | |
| 15 | | | | | | | | | | | | | | | | | | | |
| 16 | | | | | | | | | | | | | | | | | | | |
| 17 | | | | | | | | | | | | | | | | | | | |
| 18 | | | | | | | | | | | | | | | | | | | |
| 19 | | | | | | | | | | | | | | | | | | | |

**DIAGRAM IV**

eral median mental age computed as nine years, three months. While the subparts have less comprehensive meaning than the median of all subparts, nevertheless they give some clues about strong and weak points in the individual's mental constitution.

In all of these intelligence tests there is an attempt to determine a general mental age or level and to make finer descriptions of phases or parts. The process is similar to getting a general view of a mountain peak from a distance and upon moving closer to observe it from various directions and to view its specific terrain in more detail.

## History

The measurement of intellectual abilities and of allied aptitudes is one of the major fields of psychology. This portion of psychology is much younger than the general field of psychology itself. The forerunner of psychology was philosophy which sought for certain universal truths and the logic by which they had been discovered. Philosophers pondered over truths but also turned to a study of the mind itself as the principal instrument for deductions about the truth. This special group of philosophers who devoted their attention to the mental processes and to the mechanisms of thought became known as psychologists. Gradually psychology became classified as a science and ceased being a branch of philosophy. When the American Psychological Association was first organized in 1892 its annual meetings were held concurrently with the American Philosophical Association. After a few years it began meeting alternately with the philosophical association and with The American Association for the Advancement of Science, which was in the field of science as its title indicates. Psychology began to grow by leaps and bounds and to expand into many areas so that it soon began to hold its annual conventions separate from any other organizations.

At the present time the American Psychological Association has eighteen divisions grouped under a variety of titles such as clinical psychology, evaluation and measurement, personality and social psychology, industrial and business psychology, military psychology, educational psychology, and school psychologists. There are also many state and local associations. The American Psychological Association publishes eleven journals, monographs, or bulletins on a regular schedule.

*Psychological testing.* The modern period of psychological testing was begun in a modest way by Dr. J. McKeen Cattell in Wundt's laboratory in 1879. He discovered that individuals had different rates of reaction time. In the period from 1890 to 1900 Cattell examined students at Teachers College, Columbia University, with tests of special aptitudes but found comparatively little relationship between test results and scholarship. The range of abilities among his college students was limited and the tests were of such a simple psychological nature that much less was probably to be expected of them than from the more comprehensive test batteries which are in current use.

At about the same time the French psychologist, Alfred Binet, was having somewhat similar and relatively unsatisfactory experiences with simple psychological tests. In 1901 he had been commissioned to discover and to diagnose the mentally retarded pupils in the public school system of Paris and needed some practical method of mental measurement. By 1905 he devised tests of a more complex nature which began to be much more satisfactory for his practical needs. He published a second edition of his tests in 1908 and a third in 1911 shortly before his untimely death. He also discovered the use of age standards which made his tests much more practical and specific than any previous projects.

At about the same time Whipple[1] in 1910 compiled a book of psychological tests with a second edition of two volumes in 1914 and 1915 under the title of *Manual of Mental and Physical Tests*. These books proved very useful and served as a great stimulus to the expansion of testing programs. Whipple believed that the mental constitution had many dimensions and that its more thorough testing would disclose many high and low spots which might not come to light on a single test. Such an experiment was conducted by the present author using a series of psychological tests which required a full eight hours of testing time for each of twenty-five high school and twenty-five college students. The profiles of two high school students are shown on the accompanying diagram with case No. 1 averaging at the 78th percentile and ranging from 99th to the 35th percentile. Case No. 9 at the 31st percentile ranged from the 82nd to the 1st percentile.[2] This testing plan was followed with another series of tests and a shorter testing time in the Detroit Tests of Learning Aptitude discussed elsewhere in this chapter.

[1] G.M. Whipple, *Manual of Mental and Physical Tests*, Warwick and York, Baltimore, Md., 1910, 690 pp.
[1] H.J. Baker, "Mental Tests as an Aid in the Analysis of Mental Constitution," *The Journal of Applied Psychology*, 1922, 6, pp. 349-377 (abstract of doctoral thesis).

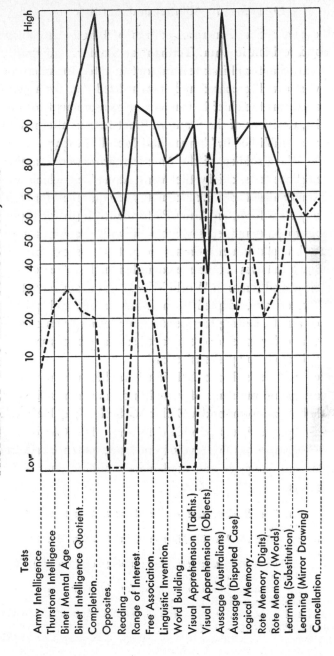

PROFILES OF TWO HIGH SCHOOL SUBJECTS

Tests

Army Intelligence
Thurstone Intelligence
Binet Mental Age
Binet Intelligence Quotient
Completion
Opposites
Reading
Range of Interest
Free Association
Linguistic Invention
Word Building
Visual Apprehension (Tachis.)
Visual Apprehension (Objects)
Aussage (Australians)
Aussage (Disputed Case)
Logical Memory
Rote Memory (Digits)
Rote Memory (Words)
Learning (Substitution)
Learning (Mirror Drawing)
Cancellation

Low    10    20    30    40    50    60    70    80    90    High

———— Case 1        – – – Case 9

DIAGRAM V

193

Goddard prepared an American edition of Binet's tests known as the Vineland revision in 1911. Terman[1] at Stanford University produced the first Stanford-Binet test in 1916 adapted to American use. This test was so well prepared and standardized that for a period of twenty years it was the chief instrument of measurement for intellectual abilities. Revisions of the Stanford-Binet tests in alternate forms, L and M, were published by Terman and Merrill[2] in 1937.

In World War I soldiers of the American army were examined by group intelligence tests, chiefly the Army Alpha Test which was prepared and standardized with five alternate and equivalent forms. There was an Army Beta form, an Army Performance form for those who were unable to be examined satisfactorily with the Alpha form. In case of very low performance on all group tests a short form of the Stanford-Binet test was administered individually. The testing program for the armed forces in World War II was again activated with a new battery of tests, adapted to machine scoring, and quick interpretation of results. During this period many other types of aptitude testing were also developed and employed so that diagnosis was placed upon a much more comprehensive basis.

Wechsler[3] has devised two individual intelligence tests, each of which give separate measures of verbal and nonverbal abilities. The Adult Scale has two forms and a Children's Scale.[4] The Detroit Tests of Learning Aptitude[5] was published in 1935. The California Test of Mental Maturity[6] has five levels from kindergarten to adulthood. It is divided into language and nonlanguage abilities and is divided into five factors.

[1] L.M. Terman, *The Measurement of Intelligence*, Houghton Mifflin Co., Boston, 1916, 362 pp.
[2] L.M. Terman and M.A. Merrill, *Measuring Intelligence*, Houghton Mifflin Co., 1937, 461 pp.
[3] D. Wechsler, *The Measurement of Adult Intelligence* (3rd ed.), Williams and Wilkins, Baltimore, Md., 1944, 258 pp.
[4] D. Wechsler, *Wechsler Intelligence Scale for Children*, Ages 5-15. The Psychological Corp., New York, 1949, 113 pp.
[5] H.J. Baker and B. Leland, *Detroit Tests of Learning Aptitude*, C.A. Gregory Co., Cincinnati, Ohio, 1935, 157 pp.
[6] E.T. Sullivan, W.W. Clark, and E.W. Tiegs, *California Test of Mental Maturity*, California Test Bureau, Los Angeles, 1946.

## Other Types of Intelligence Tests

Most of the discussion up to this point has been concerned with tests standardized and used on an individual basis. In such testing the psychologist not only records the numerical results but he is able to observe the manner and reactions of the individual being tested. If he feels that full effort is not being put forth because of exhaustion, emotional blocking, language difficulty, or impaired vision or hearing he discounts his results accordingly. His clinical observations as well as numerical results are taken into account and are expected of him because of his training and his experience. Since individual testing is a time-consuming process, the numbers tested must be limited.

*Group intelligence tests.* Practical situations demanded that some other means of intelligence testing be devised. Shortly before World War I various psychologists including Otis were experimenting with such ideas. The first wide use of group tests came in World War I as noted in a preceding section. Shortly after the war many psychologists who had been in military testing returned to civilian positions where they began devising group intelligence tests for children. Eventually testing reached down as low as entrance to the first grade as in the Detroit Beginning First Grade Intelligence Test.[1] There are many group intelligence tests for various grades and ages such as the Detroit series above the first grade by the Public School Publishing Company of Cincinnati and the Pintner and the Terman-McNemar tests by the World Book Company.

Group intelligence tests usually have eight or more pages of materials, some verbal and some nonverbal in character. Time limits range from thirty minutes to more than an hour. Methods of reporting results have already been discussed. Young children should be tested in very small groups but older students may be tested in large classes or in study halls. Some school systems use their own radio stations to test an entire grade with an experienced psychologist as the announcer and each class having its own teacher as monitor. Since there is a minimum of personal observation low scores may be due to some

[1] H.J. Baker and A.M. Engel, *The Detroit Beginning First Grade Intelligence Test,* World Book Co., Yonkers, N.Y. (original edition, 1921).

of the impairing conditions mentioned in connection with individual testing. Such results should be rechecked and reexaminations made by individual methods. With these safeguards and proper perspective group tests are great time savers and have much value in the general classification of all children.

The individual testing techniques have been extended to children with various sensory and physical defects and are discussed in chapters devoted to those handicaps. Group testing techniques have been extended to various specialized aptitudes such as mechanical aptitude, clerical, artistic, musical, and many others. Individual and group testing techniques have been adapted to tests for personality evaluations and were discussed in Chapter 6 in the general area of mental health and mental hygiene.

Another significant type of test is the Vineland Social Maturity Scale[1]. As the title indicates the items are based on observation and information on habits and practices which indicate social maturity. Age norms range from one year of age to mature adulthood.

### Testing Programs Outside of School Systems

While there are millions of psychological tests of many kinds used annually in school systems there is also extensive use in industry, business, and the military services. These other uses actually preceded much of the school testing and results were found to be so valuable that demands for such services were made upon the schools to have test results available on graduates and dropouts as a quick means of evaluation. The Industrial and Business Psychology section of the American Psychological Association has a large membership with many of its group occupying important positions in personnel management and employee relationships.

### The Profession of Psychologist

In the few decades since World War 1 there has been a great expansion of opportunities and services for psychologists. These op-

[1] E.A. Doll, The Vineland Social Maturity Scale, Educational Test Bureau, Minneapolis, Minn., 1946.

portunities extend far beyond the administration and interpretation of psychological tests. In the field of clinical psychology, in test construction, standardization, and allied activities ethical standards and practices have been developed and strictly observed. Commercial publishers of psychological tests observe certain standards in that only individuals who seem authorized by training or position are able to secure such materials for their use. High standards of training for psychologists have been adopted by universities in the granting of doctoral degrees. Many state departments of public instruction have established requirements up to thirty of forty hours of graduate credit for positions as school psychologists. These illustrations are a few of the many factors which has made psychology a true profession.

The following three chapters illustrate differences in intelligence and what adaptations school systems are making for them.

### Questions and Topics for Discussion

1. Discuss your own experiences in taking psychological tests.
2. Elaborate on definitions of various terms such as intelligence, aptitude, etc.
3. List other faulty concepts about the nature of intelligence.
4. Report on the professional training requirements for psychologists.
5. Discuss verbal and nonverbal intelligence tests.
6. Discuss contrast between values of individual and group intelligence tests.

Note: Consult reference material at the end of Chapter 15.

# CHAPTER 13

## *The Mentally Retarded*

THE MENTALLY RETARDED constitute an important type of exceptional children. Uninformed observers use the term too liberally, and, in many cases, incorrectly. Popular opinion frequently ascribes most acts of delinquency to the mentally retarded which is not the case. They have suffered from more undeserved slander and name-calling than almost all other exceptional types combined. While it would be considered cruel, tactless, and devoid of sympathy to ridicule the blind or the crippled there is less restraint in such attitudes toward the mentally retarded. However their handicaps are equally valid although not so physically evident. In the great complexities of present-day living, the mentally retarded find it increasingly difficult to make reasonably successful adjustments.

### *Identification*

Changes in the complexity of society as well as in the methods of examination and diagnosis have confused the identification of the mentally retarded. Before the era of compulsory education school systems were not generally aware of their existence. Schooling was for a select few who trained for teaching or other professions such as medicine. These requirements immediately excluded the mentally retarded. In the quiet surroundings of rural living, the mentally retarded were able to protect themselves from common dangers and could be trained for the few simple tasks necessary for the life. Aside from the family and a few outstanding physicians, society took little serious account of the mentally retarded as recently as early in the twentieth century.

## History

The treatment of the mentally retarded has been one of the most grim chapters in human history. In savage tribes in the early eras of civilization the low-grade feeble-minded were often cast out to perish as being unworthy members of the human race. The Spartans destroyed them ruthlessly lest their nation become degenerate. During the most enlightened days of Greek civilization the mentally retarded did not fare any better. The Greek word *idios* described striking individuals, possessed of demons, and frequently left to themselves, which generally meant to perish. In the Christian era in Rome a spirit of greater compassion was shown toward all types of deviates including the mentally retarded. In royal courts many of the jesters and court fools were recruited from these ranks, although it is difficult to believe that their antics could have been very entertaining. At times they were supposed to have the power of oracles or were believed to be possessed of evil spirits. In the medieval ages after the fall of Rome, there was a long period of superstitious reverence for the mentally retarded during which they were allowed to roam and beg with surprisingly good returns in some instances. As "Children of the Great Spirit" many tribes of American Indians allowed them to roam about freely.

During the reformation period of European history there was much persecution of the mentally retarded which was also shared by the mentally ill as noted in Chapter 11. Because of confused or limited reason any individuals unable to understand or to accept the teachings of Catholicism or of Protestantism were ruthlessly persecuted. Without doubt some of the 100,000 witches killed in a two-century period included the mentally retarded.

There were some notable exceptions to these conditions. As early as the beginning of the seventeenth century, a chateau to shelter unfortunates, including the feeble-minded, was begun by Saint Vincent de Paul (1576-1660). There were many orders of priesthoods which provided shelter and protection for unfortunates. Locke (1632-1704) in his *Conduct of the Understanding* had argued that learning came through the senses and that it should be accompanied by pleasurable sensations. He was followed by Rousseau, who believed that education must be based on a child's native instincts and capacities. These scholars began to direct attention to children's potentialities. The most significant event in the training of the mentally retarded occurred in 1798. A wild, unclad boy was found living in the woods of southern France and was brought to Paris where his training excited great speculation. Under the auspices of the Academy of Science in Paris, Jean Itard began his systematic training while working under the impression that his subject was merely wild and untaught, but otherwise normal. Itard worked patiently and made some progress but at the end of one year he secretly concluded that the boy was defective as well as untaught, and by the end of four or five years he was forced to give up completely when a "wild storm of passion" made him so unmanagable that he was probably institutionalized. However, during the training period he learned some simple forms of language, to read a little, and to comprehend the meaning of words and objects. Although Itard felt disgraced by his probable mistake in diagnosis and his relative failure in training the boy to be a normal, civilized individual, the Academy of Science recognized that he had actually made a great contribution to human understanding and encouraged him to write the classic book, *The Wild Boy of Aveyron.*

The discoveries of Itard continued to have their beneficial effects in the contributions of Edward Seguin who founded a school for the mentally retarded in Paris in 1837. He had been a pupil of Jean Esquirol who had tried to distinguish the difference between mental disorder and mental retardation. He believed that mental ability was improvable by physiological methods which would be able to remedy imperfect sensory organs. Training should also progress in moral, literary, and other intellectual dimensions. Among his materials he perfected the Seguin Form Board consisting of cutout blocks such as a circle, square, triangle, and several others which were to be placed into the correct spaces. Although some slight improvement was made by extended practice, the basic comprehension was usually beyond the range of the low-grade types of the mentally retarded. Eventually the form board became accepted as a part of intellectual test batteries with norms of development rather than continued in use as a training device. Seguin migrated to the United States in 1848 where he was associated with several state institutions and became the practical founder of the modern era in the study of the feeble-minded. He studied the needs of each child and although some of his sensory methods were not very successful his versatile ideas and his scientific approach laid the modern foundation. He published two books: *Idiocy and Its Treatment by the Physiological Method;* and *The Moral Treatment, Hygiene, and Education of Idiots and Other Backward Children.*

The nineteenth century witnessed the establishment and expansion of state schools and institutions for the feeble-minded. Massachusetts opened the first school in 1848 which was incorporated in 1850 as the Massachusetts School for Idiotic and Feeble-minded Youth and is now known as the Walter E. Fernald State School at Waverley. All but two of the less populated states have state schools and these make provision for their small number in other suitable quarters. The first bona fide classes in public schools for the mentally retarded were established in Providence in 1896 and in Springfield, Mass., in 1897 with many other cities following shortly thereafter. The history of psychological testing as one of the principal means of discovery by Alfred Binet was discussed in the preceding chapter. He needed some practical diagnostic method of identifying the mentally retarded for the Paris Schools at the start of the twentieth century.

### Nomenclature and Classification

The preceding section noted many uncomplimentary and unjustified ways of defining the mentally retarded, with the *idiot* term applied in the ancient Greek culture. In more recent times before the use of intelligence tests, definitions were made chiefly in terms of social adjustment. This practice had much to commend it since it involved observations of the practical adaptability of children and adults to social living. The Mental Deficiency Act of 1913 in England was stated along these lines as follows:

The *feeble-minded* are persons in whose case there exists from birth or from an early age mental defectiveness not amounting to imbecility, yet so pronounced that they require care, supervision and control for their own protection and for the protection of others; or, in the case of children, that they by reason of such defectiveness appear to be permanently incapable of receiving proper instruction in ordinary schools.

*Imbeciles* are persons in whose case there exists from birth or from an early age mental defectiveness not amounting to idiocy, yet so pronounced that they are incapable of managing themselves or their affairs, or in the case of children, of being taught to do so.

*Idiots* are persons so deeply defective in mind from birth or from an early age as to be unable to guard themselves against common physical danger.

A similar classification was adopted in America but the term *moron*, originated by Goddard, was substituted for the English *feeble-minded*, since the latter term was beginning to be adopted to include all levels or types. In 1931 England's new classification included three groups in terms of mental-age retardation: *mental defective* or those with mental ages below half of the chronological age which corresponded roughly to their earlier classifications of imbeciles and idiots; the *more retarded*, from one-half to seven-tenths of their chronological age which corresponded to their earlier classification of feeble-minded; and a group known as *less-retarded* just above the latter.

Various attempts to classify the mentally retarded solely by numerical limits of intelligence quotients have been deplored by psychologists and educators alike, since such a classification entirely discounts other important factors such as social adjustment and slow rates of maturation. Ingram[1] notes that certain states do not define the intelligence quotient limits but place the responsibility for the selection of candidates with a qualified psychologist who is certified by the state board of education. Attempts at designating names for special classes were also troublesome. For many years the classes in Cleveland were known as Moron classes. In Detroit the classes for the younger pupils are designated as Special A and classes for older pupils as Special B. Pre-Special A class are for trainable but not educable

[1] C.P. Ingram, *Education of the Slow-learning Child*, Ronald Press Company, N.Y., 1953, p. 6.

children. An intermediary type of class known as Junior Special B is being developed as well as Special Preparatory for the more advanced mentally retarded older pupils.

A practical and comprehensive classification of the mentally handicapped was proposed by the Public Instruction Department[1] for Illinois: (1) the totally dependent mentally handicapped child; (2) the trainable mentally handicapped child; and (3) the educable mentally handicapped child. This classification is similar in type and description to the 1913 English plan except that it adds some qualifications regarding educational achievement in the two higher types.

The most recent and authentic classification of mental retardation has been recommended by the Committee on Nomenclature of the American Association on Mental Deficiency.[2] This broad classification includes three groups: (1) inadequate social adjustment; (2) reduced learning capacity; and (3) slow rate of maturation.

Mental Retardation is a generic term incorporating all that has been meant in the past by such terms as mental deficiency, feeble-mindedness, idiocy, imbecility, and moronity, etc.

The committee recommends nineteen subclassifications such as cerebral birth trauma, cerebral maldevelopment, psychogenic, familial, and many others which are discussed in various chapters of this book under sections on impaired neurological conditions. The present specific nomenclature recommended by this committee will greatly improve the identification and classification of mental retardation and make census data more definite and understandable. It should have wide circulation and distribution to school systems as well as to Home and Training Schools.

## Methods of Diagnosis

The various types of mentally retarded which have just been listed furnish a basis of classification. There has been some abuse in setting arbitrary limits with cutoff points by the intelligence quotient which

---

[1] Issued by V.L. Nickell, Superintendent, Public Instruction: *Report on Study Project for Trainable Mentally Handicapped Child,* Department of Public Instruction, Springfield, Ill., 1954, pp. 3-4.

[2] Committee on Nomenclature, *Etiological Classification,* American Association on Mental Deficiency, Willimantic, Conn., 1957, pp. 9-16.

is only one factor of many which should be taken into account. Similarly, there is no definite limit between the educable mentally retarded child and the lower limit of normal children. The uniqueness of every individual must be taken into account with his many factors as previously discussed in Chapter 4 on the organization of the personality structure.

Among these factors the intellectual status should be evaluated. Several well-known and well-standardized individual psychological examinations yield reasonably accurate measurements if administered by competently trained clinical psychologists. There is a small zone of probable error of a few points in intelligence quotient which comes to light upon examinations repeated within short intervals so that a determined intelligence quotient of 50 or 75 may actually be a few points above or below. As a general standard the mentally retarded who are eligible for special instruction range from approximately one-half to three-fourths of their chronological age in their mental age. At the chronological age of six years the approximate limits would be from three years to four-and-one half years in mental age. At the chronological age of twelve years the approximate limits would be from six years to nine years in mental age. Although this fact is well known by the psychologists, there are school administrators, state regulations, and even legislative bodies who use such limits with a finality which is not warranted. The standards of acceptable psychological examinations have been outlined in the preceding chapter.

The physical examination should be taken in account. Usually it should have been done previously. The sensory examinations of vision and hearing are especially important since impairments in either or both affect possible school learning. In case of possible doubt a complete neurological examination should be made. Any mentally retarded child's placement should be graded upward or downward to some degree depending upon his physical status. The descriptions given in the twelve chapters of Parts 6 and 7 should be kept in mind when evaluating the effects of physical and sensory impairments.

A thorough case history is a minimum essential in the diagnosis of mental retardation as well as for all other types of the handicapped

and exceptional. Family status in regard to employment, home ownership, economic status, health of parents, and general home atmosphere is evaluated to determine possible effects upon children's attitudes. Favorable environments make considerable difference in the
success and outlook of mentally retarded children. Under favorable
circumstances a child may be classified as at the minimum of educationally trainable, whereas unfavorable circumstances may easily place
him in a totally dependent classification. His developmental history
including prenatal conditions, birth conditions, age of walking and
talking, his childhood diseases, and early childhood history furnish
valuable clues about his present mental status. Parents often do not
realize that these factors are causative but use them to explain reasons
for retardation. The description of the child's physical appearance
and his social reactions and relationships with his peers influence his
status in social adjustment. The preparation and interpretation of a
case history are as time-consuming and fully as important as the formal examination.

If there has been any previous school attendance, the impressions
of the teacher are particularly valuable. The adjustment to classmates,
the power of attention to tasks appropriate for the grade, and the
actual achievement are good illustrations of children in action. Actual
ability may be concealed in shyness or in personality impairment, but
well-trained and observant teachers are able to distinguish the real
effective status. Poor scholarship and many school failures are significant evidence of retardation if the nonintellectual factors are duly
taken into account.

In ideal conditions of diagnosis a case conference should be arranged with psychologist, teacher, social worker, physician, and family
in attendance. Joint agreement should provide a workable and effective diagnosis and plan for future action.

### The Totally Dependent Mentally Handicapped Child

The plight of the totally dependent mentally handicapped child is
a most unhappy one. He is incapable of attending school or, if he
is brought there, his condition is so evident that the school refuses

admittance since no constructive good can be gained. Frequently his condition includes some extreme physical disability which confines him in bed. In any event, his physical care, requiring assistance in eating, dressing, and toilet habits, extends his period of helpless babyhood month after month and year after year. The normal social life of a family is completely disrupted and the expected perspective toward a normal child is not able to materialize. Mothers who have this extraordinary responsibility and care live in vain hope that normality will eventually come. They are likely to resist any suggestions that care for such cases should be arranged within the private or public institution although modern governments recognize that they have a responsibility in such cases. All but a very few who may be in extremely favorable financial circumstances and able to employ sufficient help find it necessary after many futile years to send the severely handicapped child to the appropriate institution. Legal commitment is usually necessary and such procedure is an unfamiliar experience which is to be avoided as long as possible. The author[1] has prepared a brief statement designed to be helpful to parents of a backward child. Although schools may not have any direct contact with such extreme cases they should stand ready to assist them in any legal or civic action which seems necessary. In many states such cases come to the attention of school systems when they have reached the age of compulsory education and are brought to light by the annual census conducted by the census departments of school systems. Examinations and official exclusions from school attendance complete the record as it concerns the school systems. In the Detroit public schools approximately one hundred such new young cases are discovered annually.

### The Trainable Mentally Handicapped Child

The trainable mentally handicapped child is a type slightly higher than the totally dependent mentally handicapped child. Many school systems do not make any provisions for them since they are below the usual level of the educable mentally retarded. These children are

[1] H.J. Baker, *Suggestions to the Parents of a Backward Child*, C.A. Gregory Co., Cincinnati, Ohio, 1957, 2 pp.

capable of caring for their simple bodily needs, but they are unable to learn the academic skills of reading and arithmetic. They are limited in language ability but learn how to make simple social adjustments to their classmates. They may be successfully instructed in safety measures in their local neighborhoods. Those who are the less effective in adjustment may belong almost equally well in the totally dependent group while the more effective ones are able to join the educable mentally handicapped. These conditions show that any arbitrary classification with definite cutoff points on the scale of intelligence quotients is fallacious.

In school systems where there is no provision for any types of mentally retarded such children pose many problems to regular teachers. The least effective have usually been excused from attendance at any school or they may be unable to adjust in the class for the educable mentally handicapped. Because they show a little promise parents have objected to exclusion from school and demand some type of educational service. They have formed associations of parents of retarded children with local, state and national organization. In some instances they have succeeded in having school systems organize and conduct classes for their children or have organized centers of activity in which they themselves staff and conduct programs. Since the services which such children require are more nearly social service rather than formal education, school systems have questioned their own responsibility and are fearful that if the programs become established they will also be forced into preschool classes for all three and four-year-old children which would mount school costs and overtax present facilities already facing a shortage of trained teachers.

Unless conditions are very favorable these children may also be institutionalized. Quite often the change of parental attitude must be very slow and will not take effect until the child has grown into adolescence and his problems are becoming very acute. His brothers and sisters feel that he disrupts the home and tends to cast a shadow of some possible mental taint upon them. When maladjustments in the neighborhood become very severe and younger children become afraid some action must finally be taken.

### The Educable Mentally Handicapped Child

This third and highest type of mentally handicapped child has some possibilities of formal education; hence the title which has been selected. The most retarded in this classification are able to do at least second grade work while the more advanced can progress into the upper elementary grade levels. These goals are accomplished by specially trained teachers with classes small enough for much individual attention, and with materials of instruction gauged to limited learning abilities. Most of these pupils have from two-thirds to three-fourths normal intelligence and hence they have some fair possibilities in prognosis. Their vocational outlook is fair in unskilled and semi-skilled labor for which they are usually trained with more emphasis and clarity of goals than is true of the slow-learning regular grade pupils.

In the Detroit public schools single classes housed in regular buildings with one teacher having up to twenty-two per class are known as Special A classes. Boys and girls up to about twelve years of age are enrolled. Beyond this age separate centers for boys and girls have been established. Here there are larger groups and more teachers and the students are provided with suitable vocational training in addition to the traditional subjects. These groups are known as Special B classes. There is a new type of class known as Junior Special B, in which boys and girls eleven and twelve years old continue in mixed classes which are housed in junior high school buildings. This arrangement provides these children some opportunity to mingle and share some classes with pupils of their own chronological age. The older Special B pupils continue in special centers and, wherever possible, in junior or senior high school buildings. The most advanced Special B pupils are promoted to Special Preparatory classes with some classes housed in senior high schools so as to gain many of the advantages offered to high school students.

Some attention is being given to the educable mentally handicapped pupil in smaller communities where there are not enough of these cases to warrant a special class. In Michigan the State Department of Public Instruction has authorized a type C program in which

Mentally retarded pupils, Rockwood school, Winnipeg, Manitoba.

Courtesy of Department of Special Education, Detroit public schools.

Handwork activities, mentally retarded girls, Logan school, Detroit.

a special teacher, known as a counselor, may be appointed for one or more districts to work with the regular teacher in interpretation and methods for the individual pupil in her class. This plan is similar in some respects to the program of the itinerant teacher which is being used successfully with blind children.

## The Number of Cases

The number of the mentally retarded is mainly a matter of estimates. It is generally believed that about two or three per cent of the population falls into the three classifications with fewest in the totally dependent group. In the Detroit school system approximately 1,000 out of a school enrollment of nearly 300,000 are excused or excluded from school because of low-grade status; this amounts to approximately one-third of one per cent. A survey by the American Association on Mental Deficiency in 1954 disclosed that there were 338,129 mentally retarded children enrolled in public schools and 134,189 persons in homes and schools for the mentally retarded in 1950.

## Causes of Mental Retardation

There are many possible causes of mental retardation. Various investigators such as Strauss divide them into two general classes of endogenous and exogenous. The endogenous type is caused mainly by hereditary conditions and may account for about one-third of all cases. It has long been believed that mental retardation is a recessive rather than a dominant trait and hence tends to be reduced except in families where both parents are markedly retarded. Normal variation, such as occurs in the adult height of a large family of children and which seems to be a well-understood and expected situation, probably occur by the same logic as mental retardation or mental acceleration.

The exogenous causes are multiple in character and some have been described in Chapter 10 on brain-injured children. Chief causes are venereal diseases. Brain fever of various types not only results in mental instability but in mental retardation in many instances.

Brain injury at birth and various forms of anoxia add their quota to the long list of causes. Social isolation resulting in autism has been mentioned in Chapter 11 on mental disorders and for practical purposes many such cases are functionally mentally retarded.

Certain cases of mental retardation have characteristic physical abnormalities which are related in some way to the general mental imperfection. Mongolism is a condition in which the facial features seem to resemble some Oriental patterns. Toxic conditions in older mothers during pregnancy are common characteristics. Cretinism is a second condition which is caused by hypothyroidism and if allowed to go untreated produces a dwarfed bodily condition with short legs and deformed hands and feet. Early detection and medication have probably reduced the number which formerly occurred. In hydrocephaly an excess of cerebrospinal fluid produces a greatly enlarged skull and usually results in a totally dependent child whose life span is usually short. The microcephalic condition is the opposite condition whose cause is not definitely known but is probably related to some defect in germ cells. There are a few other miscellaneous physical types described in Chapter 28 who are also usually mentally retarded. While there are physical stigmata in many of the mentally retarded such characteristics are not very reliable means of diagnosis and should never be considered a single determining factor. Any attempts to make diagnosis from external physical symptoms are extremely hazardous and highly unreliable.

In the endogeous cases a defect in the central nervous system seems to have some causal relationship. There is a theory that the synaptic connections from one nerve to another offer more resistance in the mentally retarded so that impressions do not pass across nerve tracts as readily as for normal or superior minds. There may be a weaker nerve potential inherent in the physiological constitution. The entire nervous system may be defective. Further studies of the chemistry of the brain and electroencephalographic phenomena may ultimately throw more light on the conditions basic to intellectual abilities and aptitudes.

## The Prevention of Mental Retardation

The various causes of mental retardation give hope that a more comprehensive program of prevention is not far away. An encouraging report on prevention has just been prepared by Richard Masland[1] in a survey sponsored by the National Association for Retarded Children, Inc. He reports that progress is being made with considerable accuracy on genetic maldevelopment, prenatal development arrest, and prenatal destructive processes. Statistics are being kept in many centers on familiar conditions which are throwing light on causes. In the area of postnatal causes the various types of encephalitis are among the chief factors. Masland's report summarizes many conditions from numerous research studies which will result in the reduction of mental retardation if the various medical and social causes can be reduced.

### Vocational Possibilities

The totally dependent child becomes a burden which society must carry since the great majority of them are in mental homes or institutions. The trainable mentally handicapped have only a slightly better vocational outlook. They must be placed under carefully supervised and guarded conditions for the maximum results with unskilled or simple forms of semiskilled labor. The educable mentally retarded have much better chances of vocational success, although automation is rapidly reducing the number of jobs in which hand operations are necessary.

Several centers, including Wayne State University in Detroit and the Wayne County Training School, are making follow-up studies of mentally retarded. Unfortunately, no results are available at this writing. A few years ago the Federal Rehabilitation Service, which was originally designed to assist physically handicapped individuals, was extended to mental and emotional types. Staffs are gradually being trained in this newer type of placement activity and in knowledge of opportunities which industry and business may provide for the mentally retarded.

[1] R.L. Masland, "The Prevention of Mental Retardation," A.M.A. *Journal of Diseases of Children*, 1958, 95, No. 1, Part II, 111 pp.

## Questions and Topics for Discussion

1. Describe some type of extreme mental defective whom you have known.
2. Report on the *Wild Savage of Aveyron*.
3. Describe the teaching methods of Seguin.
4. Discuss the various ways in which the mentally retarded are classified.
5. Report on the educational provisions for the mentally retarded in your community.
6. Report on the branch association of parents of retarded children in your community.
7. What causes of mental retardation are most significant?
8. What vocational opportunities for the mentally retarded are available in your community?

Note: Consult reference material at the end of Chapter 15.

# CHAPTER 14

## The Gifted

IN NEARLY ALL CHAPTERS of this book descriptions are given of handicapped children. This chapter on the gifted and a portion of the following one on the rapid-learning are the principal exceptions. In a very broad sense these two types might also be considered as handicapped since they are not always provided with maximum educational programs suited to their needs. The term "exceptional" might more properly be applied to them as well as to all others that deviate from the average or nonhandicapped child in some respect. When the term "exceptional" is used there is a popular but erroneous impression that only the gifted are being discussed. Regardless of these considerations, the gifted as well as the rapid-learning deserve their rightful place among those who deviate from average, normal children in some respect, since they have problems of adjustment which presently fall far short of being satisfactorily treated.

### Definitions

Definitions of the gifted are always troublesome since there are many different interpretations, as illustrated by "genius," "special talents," "intelligence quotients of 200 or higher," "the highest one or two per cent," etc. Special talents are a particularly troublesome problem since the popular impression is that the individual so endowed in music, art, or other specialities must be a very ordinary individual in general, including all his other attributes. While there are probably a few instances in which this is true, it is usually the case that there is a generally high level of all abilities and talents to accompany some

213

very outstanding talent. True specialized ability in music requires knowledge of the basic principles upon which music is founded, such as harmony, counterpoint, and interpretation of mood that cannot be fully appreciated by average or slow minds. The ability to rapidly pound out some simple theme repetitiously on the piano can scarely be classified as real musical talent, and almost all other fields of special talent yield the same result when carefully analyzed for their real component parts and phases.

The author prefers to designate the gifted as having high general level of ability and trusts that, in addition, one or more special talents will stand out in a very exceptional way beyond this high level. Interpretation of "gifted" in terms of a high intelligence quotient only does not completely satisfy the gifted description, since reference should always be made to the many factors in the personality structure enumerated in Chapter 4. A high level of intellect alone may produce a certain degree of efficiency, but it does not meet satisfactorily the specifications for a happy, well-adjusted individual. Fortunately high levels of ability are usually accompanied by well-rounded personalities although the occasional exception has set the popular impression in the opposite direction. Studies of gifted children by Terman and the experience of many school systems ably disprove this idea. However, there is an educational challenge to cultivate the best of the nonintellectual factors in the exceptions to the general rule. It is also important to discover motivations so that all gifted children will achieve in accordance with their potential abilities.

In considering this general field, Dr. Samuel Brownell, superintendent of the Detroit public schools, prefers the terms "special abilities" so as not to categorize gifted children into one general type, capable of being "labeled" in some manner. In the heterogeneity of special abilities of a large group with high abilities, the democratic setting is still preserved.

### The Bases of Identification

The *bases* of identification is a plural rather than a singular term. This principle was followed by the author and by a committee of school personnel in a plan of selection of elementary school pupils of high abilities in 1938 for four Detroit elementary schools. Ten factors were used as follows:

1. General behavior
2. Effort as related to ability
3. Group intelligence rating
4. Rating of age for grade
5. Height ratio for age
6. Weight ratio for age
7. Rating for comprehension in reading
8. Rating on recent scholastic marks
9. Rating on number of permanently erupted teeth
10. Rating for participation in school activities

Each of the ten items was arranged on a five-point scale from very poor to very good on approximately 2,500 pupils.[1] It was decided to make a first rough selection of the upper 5 per cent in total score for some major-work classes. In the four schools the minimum total cutoff score for this selection ranged from 37 to 39 out of a possible 50 points. Individual cases slightly below these points were considered and a few were accepted for trial. In general, all-round abilities were represented in this process of selection, and no undue emphasis was placed upon intelligence which became only one factor of ten in the scale. As the work progressed, various children with high intelligence quotients but with unstable and antisocial personalities who did not qualify at first were gradually assimilated into the classes.

An individual psychological examination should be one of the standard factors in the identification of the gifted. In the major-work classes in Cleveland, such examination is required and an intelligence quotient of 125 or higher is part of the qualifying data. A high performance on an intelligence examination is usually a bona fide indication, since it is very difficult if not practically impossible, to achieve such a result by accident, whereas low results may be caused by various factors and conditions such as described in Chapter 12. In the early primary grades of any school system the actual scholastic record, as well as the recommendation of the teacher or teachers should be taken

[1] For details of this rating plan, see *Appendix*.

into account. From time to time there are gifted children whose school achievement does not measure up to expectation but when such achievement is actually of high standard it should be a helpful and significant factor.

### Types of Educational Adjustment

Gifted pupils are usually limited to 1 or 2 per cent of the most able in general as well as having one or more specialized abilities. There are many types of educational adjustment possible for them and probably there is no one plan superior to all others since each has its merits and many factors should be taken into account.

*Segregation.* Except for a few large cities, there is no large scale segregation of gifted children into special classes. Cleveland has one of the best organized systems of gifted classes which has functioned successfully for about forty years. It has been Cleveland's experience that most of the theoretical arguments against such classes do not materialize in actual practice. Their pupils find many advantages from associating with classmates of similar mental and social interests in an atmosphere of freedom which is much more difficult to develop in a heterogeneous class. When such pupils are segregated, they tend to maintain higher academic standards since they have competition on their own level, whereas in the absence of such a standard it is easier to meet or to excel, by a little, the standard of the heterogeneous class. In addition to having similar intelligence quotients, their mental ages are much above those of average pupils. For example, if a school system has a semester system of classification, the gifted pupils of the beginning and the advanced first grade classes with chronological ages of six years, and six years and six months respectively have mental ages of seven years, six months, and eight years and one month respectively. These mental ages are only seven months apart whereas they are seventeen or eighteen months above the average mental age for their chronological age, which is fully three times as great a difference as the mental ages of the gifted pupils of the two half grades. This difference of only seven or eight months in mental age between half grades continues through the higher grades but at these levels the difference between these mental ages and that of average pupils becomes five or six times as great.

In case of such segregation these pupils do not become particularly aware that they are superior to other children but rather they are humbled to find that their classmates are fully as capable as they are. There are two arguments against such segregation which have considerable merit. One important point has social implications in that gifted pupils should not be deprived of associating with other types of minds, abilities, and interests which is an actuality in adult life. The second point of consideration is that the average pupils and others of lesser ability miss the stimulation and competition of these more able pupils. Specific evidence is needed to prove or disprove the merits of these considerations. In a narrow interpretation of equality all pupils should be given exactly the same educational programs, but in a more meaningful interpretation equality of opportunity should be provided in accordance with aptitudes or with impairments. There are some further adjustments which are not literal as implied in such statements. The major-work pupils in the Cleveland schools have opportunities to mingle with the regular-grade pupils in various activities so that segregation is not absolute.

*Acceleration.* If no special provision is made for gifted children, they are likely to be double promoted or to enter school at an earlier age so that they become accelerated ahead of children of their own age. If no other provision is made, acceleration takes place as a natural phenomenon. There is some danger that gifted pupils who are accelerated will absorb only the intellectual phases of subject matter without much realization of their social, political, and economic values. Terman and Oden[1] divided the gifted children of their study into two groups according to acceleration and nonacceleration. The fact was disclosed that in most respects the accelerated group showed slight excellence over the nonaccelerated group. They concluded that the risks of moderate acceleration were not as great as commonly believed.

Since gifted pupils easily master the basic skills of beginning reading and number concepts, skipping one or more of the early primary

[1] L.M. Terman and M.H. Oden, *The Gifted Child Grows Up*, Stanford University Press, Stanford University, Calif., 1947, 448 pp.

grades does not bring gaps in the learning and mastery sequence particularly if the school offers considerable latitude in individual progress. In the upper elementary grades and at the secondary level many gifted pupils become accelerated by attending summer school. Since many of them attend college and professional curriculums which require extended schooling, a moderate amount of acceleration shortens the total preparation period and is a real advantage.

A special kind of acceleration may be provided without actually completing the high school course ahead of time. In some of the gifted sections, subjects such as algebra, world history, and a foreign language may have two semester's work covered in one semester. In this plan some advanced courses in mathematics and other subjects may be offered in high school with advanced credit given in college. In the course of events this plan may result in acceleration of college graduation.

*Enrichment.* A third adjustment plan for gifted pupils is to provide enrichment in curriculum and in variety of subjects at all grade levels. For instance in beginning reading several primers may be read rather than one. All subjects of the curriculum have such enrichment materials so that great opportunities are available without acceleration and can be made available without special segregation. Various school systems, including Detroit's, provide an enriched type of program for all pupils including the elementary schools. The Detroit plan provides not only for the fundamental subjects but there are also regularly scheduled courses in art, music, science, nature study, library, health, and physical education. Gifted pupils with special abilities are able to take advantage of offerings in all of these areas and hence benefit from enrichment without the need of acceleration or segregation. Further evidence of this plan will be presented later in the chapter. Combinations of these three types of adjustments are possible and are practiced in many different ways in various school systems. It is doubtful if any one plan is universally superior to all others and local conditions, size of school buildings, availability of curriculum materials, and tradition of communities affect what may be done for gifted pupils.

A fourth possible type of adjustment would be the services of an itinerant teacher to work with the regular teacher one or more times per week. As noted in other chapters this plan is meeting with considerable success in filling the needs of the mentally retarded, the blind, and the partially seeing in small communities and may be extended to crowded school systems where no rooms are available for special classes.

### History and Status of Detroit's Projects

The history and status of projects for gifted pupils in the Detroit schools throw light on the many departments concerned with a cooperative program. The first experimental class was for seventh and eighth graders in an elementary school in September, 1915. Principals selected the pupils. Latin and Algebra were added to the regular subjects so that advanced high school credits were possible. Within the next two or three years similar centers were established in three other elementary schools. Selection by principals was replaced by group intelligence tests and achievement tests. By 1925 several junior high schools were built and many seventh and eighth grade classes were placed in them. With the large number of pupils in each grade it was possible to have several class sections with the highest sections being actually gifted pupils. Enrichment in the curriculum replaced the earlier elementary classes. In this evolution the change in school organization was the chief factor.

In 1928-29 a class for gifted pupils in grades one to three was established in one elementary school. Although the teacher in this self-contained room tried to provide many enrichment projects she was unable to provide all of the opportunities which the Detroit elementary plan was furnishing to all the pupils in the regular classes. It seemed impossible to place this self-contained class as a distinct class in the Detroit plan to take advantage of the enrichment possibilities and hence the class as such was discontinued in order that the more complete enrichment opportunities could be shared in classes with average pupils.

In 1928-1930 an extensive individualization experiment was undertaken using pairs of elementary schools in the Dalton plan, the Winnetka plan, mass instruction plan, the regular Detroit plan, and a plan of "vertical" organization. The vertical plan was so named because it provided sections or classes consisting of the above-average pupils of two adjacent half-grades known to be more homogenous than when placed with all mental types in the same class. There were some sections of below-average pupils and each home-room teacher also had one of her two classes of average pupils so that a proper perspective might be maintained. In the vertical plan instruction and curriculum materials were adjusted as nearly as possible to the known abilities of pupils and all teachers voted highly in favor of it. All projects were discontinued at the end of the two-year period.

In 1938 the author was appointed chairman of a committee to plan some pilot projects for gifted pupils in elementary schools. The ten-point plan, listed in the section on bases of classification, was used to provide a wide foundation for selection. Four elementary schools from different types of neighborhoods were selected for study. One school was in a neighborhood with first and second generation of southeastern Europeans who were somewhat reluctant at first to accept more than the familiar three R's. Music and art were added and some special club activities were arranged for a small group of the more able students. The school building soon had additional capacity with shops, auditorium, music, art, science, and the more able pupils found enrichment opportunities which were not available before.

Administrative problems affected two other schools after a few years. In one of them an additional teacher of great resourcefulness had the complete use of a two-room portable building into which certain selected pupils were allowed to come one or more times per week from their regular classes in order to pursue special projects of their own choosing. This activity ended abruptly when the teacher took personal leave to be with her husband on military duty and the two room portable was moved to another location where it was badly needed. The momentum of this project carried it on in the regular building so that the more able pupils found ways of continuing enrichment in the great variety of offerings. Another building continued successfully for some time with special groups meeting for lessons in Spanish, some commercial subjects, and other activities of their choice. In a period of about three years there were different principals assigned as part of a rotation plan in promotion affecting all school buildings. Each new principal naturally needed a period of orientation to become acquainted with the regular teaching staffs and with general problems inevitable to a new position. As a result the formal program was no longer feasible. In the fourth building the pupils were mainly from homes of professional and successful business men. Approximately one-third of the entire school was gifted pupils and several of the class sections were composed exclusively of them. This plan continued for a few years, but with increasing parental pressure to put all pupils in such class sections and when tensions of both parents and pupils began to get out of control, the class sections were reorganized on a strictly alphabetical basis within grades. These results all came about in the natural course of events but illustrated the difficulties of providing for gifted pupils without special segregated classes somewhat removed from and independent of the regular organization.

In the meantime many cases came to light in which unusual talent had been noted in pupils in the various specialized subjects of the Detroit elementary organization. The supervisors of the various fields of curriculum prepared supplementary assignments which were appreciated by the more able pupils. These materials appeared in regular text books or were suggested in teachers' guides. Throughout this period special instrumental music classes were organized and met after regular hours or on Saturday mornings. Similar activities were carried on in art and in creative writing, while the school system's radio and television stations attracted many pupils talented in dramatics and in public speaking and other production projects. A plan was formulated to extend the offerings in grades four to twelve for after school and Saturdays by districts in mathematics, science, creative writing, children's theatre, foreign language, social studies, and literature with a total of one hundred classes early in 1958. Through this plan gifted pupils will have opportunity to explore their special abilities and receive enrichment while remaining enrolled in their regular classes.

As a starting point only, for identification, group intelligence tests have been regularly administered to all kindergarten pupils ready to enter the first grade, reexamination at the end of the fourth grade, in the early semester of the eighth grade, and of the twelfth grade. A series of letter ratings, rather than intelligence quotients are used to report results to teachers. Norms are based on chronological age with scores advancing a few points for the various letter ratings as chronological age advances. The plan of these letter ratings is that the highest 8 to 10 per cent in numerical score for any chronological age group are rated A. This general plan was described in Chapter 12. The A ratings correspond approximately to intelligence quotients of 118 or higher; B ratings from 110 to 117, etc., with E ratings of 82 or less. In order to make more specific designation of the most able of the A ratings, a rating of A** was set up for the highest 1 per cent, and A* for the second 1 per cent within each chronological age group through the various tests up through the eighth grade. An E* was also given for the lowest 1 per cent to help identify potential candidates for classes for the mentally retarded. In studies of educational adjustment various other factors, such as achievement tests are included to be taken into account in selecting pupils for special projects.

A *first-grade survey.* In the first semester of 1956-1957 502 beginning first-grade pupils out of a total of 25,000 were rated either A** or A* or 2 per cent of them. At the end of the semester in January a questionnaire was filled out by the classroom teachers on these pupils so as to learn what results and impressions had occurred. Transfers to schools outside of Detroit or to parochial schools removed one hundred twenty-four pupils so that the summarized findings were based on three hundred seventy-eight pupils. A one-page questionnaire was submitted for each pupil and was made up largely as a checklist to save the teacher's time. Girls outnumbered boys in the ratio of three to two.

The attendance record was 5 per cent better than the entire first-grade classes, and only twenty-six pupils were tardy one or more times. Their health record was better than for the entire class; thirty-two had children's diseases; sixteen had defective speech; twenty-two had some visual defects; forty-three had miscellaneous conditions such as rheumatic fever, allergies, and eczema.

Several items were arranged on a five-point scale with descriptive terms which the teacher could check. In grooming and general neatness none were rated as unkempt and unattractive but seven were rated poor and showed little evidence of self-pride. In emotional balance thirty pupils were considered poor, or, one out of twelve. A few others were quite stolid and revealed little emotional tone. These young children with high mental potentialities should profit by visiting-teacher service. A few whose emotional balance was judged to be poor by their teachers seem to be frustrated by their associations with pupils of average or below average ability. They were puzzled by the difficulties which these less able pupils had in learning to read. They did not seem to fit very satisfactorily into heterogeneous classes where they were usually the only one with their unique abilities.

Seven per cent were rated as poor or very poor in self-direction, which may have been related to too much parental guidance. By contrast two-thirds of them seemed to be keeping a reasonable balance between their high potential abilities and their many possible activities. Twenty-two pupils could have developed more special interests and activities and two were already considered as being in too many activities. There could be profitable use of counseling for a few deviates in some activities either by special counselors or by their own teachers in time reserved for it.

Comments had been requested on unusually high special talents or abilities in one or more fields, and 79 per cent of the pupils were so described by teachers, with an average of one and three tenths such citations per pupil. These items included art and drawing, expressive arts in which they appeared on television and radio shows, liberal use of their own library cards from branch public libraries, and much supplementary reading at home. Independent work, leadership, sense of humor, fertile imagination, phenomenal memories, and reasoning ability were occasionally mentioned. It is a fine art to teach and to rear such children even below school age and, because of their great independence, to guide them successfully without "breaking their spirit."

After the tabulations were made and summaries completed, the original questionnaires were returned to the individual schools to become part of permanent record. Each school was advised to keep a similar record of the next several first-grade classes and from time to time call them all together for a small unit of resourcefulness and enrichment in many fields. As a preliminary survey this minimum method, starting with the special intelligence ratings, plus the study and observation by teachers and principals provided considerable stimulation for young children with high abilities but did not require much expense in money or in time.

*Secondary school special science and arts curriculum.* Within the past year a special Science and Arts Curriculum has been set up at Cass Technical High School. It was patterned somewhat along the lines of four science and art schools in New York City, including the Bronx High School of Science, Brooklyn Technical High School, the High School of Music and Art, and Stuyvesant High School. A rare degree of intelligence, a keen desire to learn, and a willingness to work provide necessary background in addition to more formal requirements, which include a group mental rating of A, two or more years of achievement age beyond their grade on the Iowa Multi-Level Achievement Test, satisfactory scholarship in the eighth grade, recommendation by the school, and willingness by parent and pupil. The Detroit Alpha Adjustment Inventory[1] was administered to candidates for the second class and disclosed only a few pupils with some physical, social, or emotional problems in need of attention. As a group they proved to be well-adjusted individuals, and the few doubtful cases will be serviced by the visiting teacher at the Cass School.

Slightly more than two hundred ninth graders started the first class in September, 1957. Two semester's work in one is provided in algebra, world history, and French but only two of the three subjects are allowed per pupil. The third course may be elected at the usual pace in some other regular section or class of the school. This form of acceleration is not designed for earlier graduation, but to provide for advanced courses in mathematics, science, and others which may yield college credit, and to provide opportunity for election from a wide variety of courses offered in this school beyond those in the regular high schools. The current general interest in mathematics and science

1 Available from C.A. Gregory Co., Cincinnati, Ohio.

has chanced to coincide with this project and has given unexpected support.

## Other Historical Records

History is filled with the names of men gifted in different lines— government, sciences, literature, the arts, and all other fields of worthy endeavor. History is largely a recital of their achievements and in it more emphasis should be placed upon the influences which they have had upon the world of their day and later generations. In *Genetic Studies of Genius, Vol. II*, Cox[1] gives very illuminating accounts of the early mental traits of three hundred geniuses, from which psychologists attempted to establish their intelligence quotients by evaluating the available data. Eminent men in many fields were discussed and generally were shown to have had high abilities in early childhood. Many musicians composed creditable music in early childhood, and likewise some very fine literature and art were produced in childhood years. Among these exceptional individuals were Mozart, Beethoven, Rembrandt, Michelangelo, Tennyson, Emerson, Sir Walter Scott, and others.

From an educational point of view the selection of gifted individuals has attracted the attention of great leaders. In Ancient Greece, Plato advocated the use of a series of tests to discover the talented of his country and to train them in accordance with their superior abilities. They were to be trained in science, philosophy, and metaphysics so as to become future leaders of the state. He believed that Greece would continue only as long as such a course was followed. At a later time noted teachers from enslaved Greece were used as tutors for the sons of Roman nobility.

The most marked example of selecting gifted and superior individuals for government positions was the system used by Suleiman, the Magnificent, ruler of the Ottoman empire in the sixteen century. At regular intervals he sent emissaries throughout all parts of the empire, not only among the Turks, but among the conquered peoples as well,

[1] C. Cox, "The Early Mental Traits of Three Hundred Geniuses," *Genetic Studies of Genius, Vol. II*, Stanford University Press, Stanford University, Calif., 1926, 842 pp.

and selected the most promising youths. They were trained in the Mohammedan faith and were developed as leaders in war, religion, art, and science. During his reign Suleiman threatened to conquer all the world and for centuries afterward his empire continued as a great power. There is plenty of evidence that the twentieth century is having similar experiences.

*The development of classes.* There were many efforts to provide some special educational opportunities during the latter part of the nineteenth century. In 1867, William T. Harris, Superintendent of Education in St. Louis, introduced a more flexible plan of advancement, giving promotions at the end of five-week periods instead of annually. The Elizabeth plan, the Cambridge plan, the Santa Barbara plan, and those of Batavia, San Francisco, and other cities provided for more flexible grading resulting mainly in the rapid acceleration of gifted pupils through the grades. The first gifted class was a kind of "preparatory school" in Worcester, Mass., in 1901. Children in grades 7 to 9 who were in good health and of high scholastic standing were allowed to take some high school subjects such as algebra and foreign languages. These classes have been in continuous operation since that time and several hundred children are usually enrolled. Whipple[1] reported on some experimental classes under his direction while he was teaching educational psychology at the University of Illinois.

Bruner[2] organized classes for the gifted, the rapid-learning, and the slow-learning in 1918 in Okmulgee. The modern period began about 1920 with programs in Cleveland, Los Angeles, Rochester, New York, and Detroit. In Canada the first special classes were held in London, Ontario, in 1928, and Saskatoon in 1932. Hunter College in New York has specialized in the training of teachers for the gifted and has promoted the program in many ways. In the United States Office of Education report of 1947-1948 there were fewer than 21,000 in special classes for the gifted and over ninety per cent were in and about New York City.

[1] G.M. Whipple, *Classes for Gifted Children*, Public School Publishing Co., Cincinnati, Ohio, 1919, 151 pp.
[2] H.B. Bruner, *The Junior High School at Work*, Teachers College Contributions to Education, No. 177, Columbia University, New York, 1925, 111 pp.

## Follow-Up Studies

The history of attitudes toward the gifted in the past century has been marked by misconceptions and criticisms of many kinds. The dangers of generalizing from a few exceptions to the presently known facts are amply illustrated, yet the false impressions continue. One might hazard a theory that those of lesser abilities have subconscious jealousies and wishful thinking that compensation in the form of personality disturbances and economic failures should overtake those with superior intellects. This theory seems to work in some families where the interpersonal relationships are unwholesome. In any event there were a few cases whose names were well known in the early decades of the twentieth century and who were supposed to represent the general trend. Those who resist changes or new discoveries too often try to put them on the defensive. Programs for gifted children seem to be no exception.

Sumption[1] made a thoroughly illuminating study of results of Cleveland's major-work classes. He compared a control group of sixty-five adults of equally high intelligence who had not had the major-work program with a group who had spent from one to three years in major-work, and a third group who had spent from four to twelve years in this program. In each of three groups there were 34 women and 31 men. A questionnaire of 59 questions was returned by all of these adults, and approximately one-third of the 1,120 major-work graduates who could be located cooperated by sending in similar information.

Some very marked results in favor of the major-work program were reported when results by groups were summarized. The major-work program developed a greater sense of social responsibility and its members held more positions of leadership. They had received more scholarships, awards, and citations. They had had more opportunity to develop their individual aptitudes and a wide range of self-expression. Critical thinking was developed in a larger measure, as well as a

[1] M.R. Sumption, *Three Hundred Gifted Children*, World Book Co., Yonkers, N.Y., 1941, 235 pp.

more ambitious attitude with regard to their vocational careers. In leisure-time activities the major-work groups did more reading of nonfiction books and professional and technical magazines, and more of them went to college. In spite of greater emphasis upon many phases of enrichment in various fields, the major-work program did not sacrifice the acquisition of fundamental knowledges and skills. There were no important differences in health between the groups and the major-work program did not harm the health nor impair the eyesight of pupils.

*The Stanford Study.* The Stanford study of gifted children was initiated in 1921 by Dr. Lewis M. Terman who has made a regular study of the same individuals from time to time over a period of twenty-five years. The reports of the early examinations and of the characteristics of 1,500 children were described in Volumes I and III of *Genetic Studies of Genius* by the Stanford University Press.

The initial high level of intelligence quotients, ranging from 135 to 200, with an average of 152, was maintained in the majority of cases in adulthood, which showed that intellectually superior children became intellectually superior adults. Superiority in mental abilities was generally found but varied in amount depending upon the type of testing materials. Excellence was also shown in traits of originality and in behavior which are closely related to intelligence. It is a sad commentary upon educational procedures that while in elementary school, gifted children on the average were kept at school tasks fully two or three full grades below the level of achievement that they had attained on standardized educational achievement tests.

Although these gifted children were not placed at the proper level of grading, they continued into higher education with almost 90 per cent entering college and almost 70 per cent graduating, which, in both instances, is about eight times more than the corresponding figure for the general population of their time. It was noted that some who did not attend college were prevented by ill health, but many others did not attend because of lack of good guidance and encouragement by their high schools.

The great majority of the entire group were found to be in the professions or in the higher business occupations, with only four per cent in the four lower occupational classes, as measured by the

Minnesota Occupational Scale, in which more than half of the general population are to be found. They maintained their general superiority in marriage rate, in good marital adjustments, and in all-round social adjustments as well. The incidence of delinquency was very low and mortality rate was only four-fifths of the normal expectation. The superiority of these gifted individuals was demonstrated in practically all of the many areas which were studied and reviewed. Brumbaugh[1] and Lorge[2] have recently reviewed additional studies with similar results.

## The Conservation of Talent

There has been a recent period of history in the Western Hemisphere when material prosperity came easily and without too much effort. Times are gradually changing, a series of global wars have forced new perspectives in many fields and particularly in the various fields of science. Shortages of some natural resources are beginning to force new sources of power, materials, and foods. The race for control of outer space and for exploration of ocean beds are some of the principal problems which up to yesterday were only dreams.

In this new orientation the utilization of human abilities is assuming a new importance. While some simple phases of discoveries may have been by accident, the great majority have come and will be coming through the inventive genius of gifted minds. Not one single gifted mind should be allowed to go untrained and be lost in mediocre achievement because of indifference or by lack of educational opportunity.

The talents of the gifted should not be directed toward science alone. Affairs of business, politics, government, and social culture need resourceful guidance. Reduction or elimination of crime and delinquency would be a real boon. The cure and prevention of the many disorders described in this book is a challenge which needs to be more seriously considered. In all of these matters the conservation of talent is the paramount problem of today.

[1] F.N. Brumbaugh, "Intellectually Gifted Children," and
[2] I. Lorge, "Social Gains in the Special Education of the Gifted," in Frampton and Gall, eds., *Special Education for the Exceptional*, Vol. III, Porter Sargent Publisher, Boston, 1956, pp. 2-14 and 24-28.

## Questions and Topics for Discussion

1. Discuss the merits of various definitions.
2. Describe the most talented child you have ever known.
3. Which educational plans for the gifted seem most desirable?
4. What further steps need to be taken in refuting present conceptions on outcomes of the gifted?
5. Visit a class for the gifted and give your impressions.
6. What provisions is your community making for gifted children?

Note: Consult reference material at the end of Chapter 15.

# CHAPTER 15

## The Slow Learning and
## the Rapid Learning

TYPES OF EXTREME mental deviations were discussed in the two preceding chapters. In both the mentally retarded and the mentally
accelerated only approximately 2 or 3 per cent were being considered. It was noted that both groups deviated quite markedly from
the average and hence special educational facilities or adjustments
have been shown to be necessary for them.

Differences between types do not exist in sealed-tight compartments and hence average children do not all fall into a fully
homogeneous and identical group markedly different from either
of the extremes. Within the average group and immediately adjacent
to the extremes are a few children who differ from them only by a
very imperceptible amount. A little nearer to the average there are
several more who resemble the extremes to a lesser degree, but who
deviate from the typically average pupil. Although all of these varying
degrees of averageness are enrolled as regular pupils, they offer problems to teachers in curriculum adjustments and in methods of
teaching. In a certain practical sense they are handicapped and exceptional children and hence merit special attention.

Each of these two groups constitute about 20 per cent of all
children. The slow-learning group is generally identified by finding
it difficult to keep up with the average and the rapid-learning. By contrast the rapid-learning find it easy to set the standard or to be
above it and hence are not necessarily working up to their capacity.

There are several ways in which average, slow-learning, and rapid-learning pupils differ from each other. The problems of the slow-learning should not seem to be an entirely strange and unexplored field, since the problems of the mentally retarded who fall below them have been thoroughly investigated with the result that their needs and their characteristics are well understood. It would seem logical to strike some balance between the average pupil and the mentally retarded pupil to approximate the characteristics of the slow-learning pupil. Likewise, the rapid-learning pupil may well be an approximate medium between the average pupil and the gifted whose characteristics have also been described.

## Quantitative Mental Differences

There are quantitative mental differences between the slow-learning, the average, and the rapid-learning. These differences may be expressed as mental age or the level of mental development. Since mental age is known to be one of the important determining factors in school achievement, the accompanying table is significant.

The mental age is based on a median intelligence quotient of 83 for the slow-learning, 100 for the average, and 117 for the rapid-learning groups. The ratio or intelligence quotient of 83 for the slow-learning indicates five-sixths normal progress or five months of mental age for six months of chronological age. The ratio of 117 for the rapid-learning indicates seven-sixths normal progress or seven months of mental age for each six months of chronological age.

This table merits careful study. It starts from birth and extends through fifteen years of age so as to illustrate that mental growth rates begin to deviate at that time rather than when children are first enrolled in school. The cumulative effect of different mental-growth rates results in mental age of only five years by the chronological age of six years; of ten years at the age of twelve; and of twelve and one-half years in mental age at fifteen years of age. The cumulative effect produces this gap of one year at the age of six years which seems to be a real difference. It gives the false impression that the slow-learning pupil is making no progress at all, since he is not fully

## TABLE XII

Chronological age and mental age of the Slow-Learning
the Average, and the Rapid-Learning

| Chronological Age | | Slow-Learning | | Mental Age Average | | Rapid-Learning | |
|---|---|---|---|---|---|---|---|
| Years | Months | Years | Months | Years | Months | Years | Months |
| 0 | 6 | 0 | 5 | 0 | 6 | 0 | 7 |
| 1 | 0 | 0 | 10 | 1 | 0 | 1 | 2 |
| 1 | 6 | 1 | 3 | 1 | 6 | 1 | 9 |
| 2 | 0 | 1 | 8 | 2 | 0 | 2 | 4 |
| 2 | 6 | 2 | 1 | 2 | 6 | 2 | 11 |
| 3 | 0 | 2 | 6 | 3 | 0 | 3 | 6 |
| 3 | 6 | 2 | 11 | 3 | 6 | 4 | 1 |
| 4 | 0 | 3 | 4 | 4 | 0 | 4 | 8 |
| 4 | 6 | 3 | 9 | 4 | 6 | 5 | 3 |
| 5 | 0 | 4 | 2 | 5 | 0 | 5 | 10 |
| 5 | 6 | 4 | 7 | 5 | 6 | 6 | 5 |
| 6 | 0 | 5 | 0 | 6 | 0 | 7 | 0 |
| 6 | 6 | 5 | 5 | 6 | 6 | 7 | 7 |
| 7 | 0 | 5 | 10 | 7 | 0 | 8 | 2 |
| 7 | 6 | 6 | 3 | 7 | 6 | 8 | 9 |
| 8 | 0 | 6 | 8 | 8 | 0 | 9 | 4 |
| 8 | 6 | 7 | 1 | 8 | 6 | 9 | 11 |
| 9 | 0 | 7 | 6 | 9 | 0 | 10 | 6 |
| 9 | 6 | 7 | 11 | 9 | 6 | 11 | 1 |
| 10 | 0 | 8 | 4 | 10 | 0 | 11 | 8 |
| 10 | 6 | 8 | 9 | 10 | 6 | 12 | 3 |
| 11 | 0 | 9 | 2 | 11 | 0 | 12 | 10 |
| 11 | 6 | 9 | 7 | 11 | 6 | 13 | 5 |
| 12 | 0 | 10 | 0 | 12 | 0 | 14 | 0 |
| 12 | 6 | 10 | 5 | 12 | 6 | 14 | 7 |
| 13 | 0 | 10 | 10 | 13 | 0 | 15 | 2 |
| 13 | 6 | 11 | 3 | 13 | 6 | 15 | 9 |
| 14 | 0 | 11 | 8 | 14 | 0 | 16 | 4 |
| 14 | 6 | 12 | 1 | 14 | 6 | 16 | 11 |
| 15 | 0 | 12 | 6 | 15 | 0 | 17 | 6 |

ready to learn reading, and is barely ready for the start of the kindergarten. Actually his rate of progress is at the ratio of 83 or at five-sixths the normal rate. However, and regardless of theories of five-sixths normal progress, classroom teachers are faced with a practical question of how to proceed in teaching these slow-learning pupils.

The rapid-learning present conditions in the opposite manner. Their rate of mental growth averages seven-sixths the normal rate from birth and has accumulated a year of excess mental age by six years of age. With this qualification they are fully ready for first-grade reading and many of them have already learned to read. They continue on the positive side with larger and larger differences developing between mental and chronological age. In many respects they become a challenge as to what teaching procedures and materials should be provided for them. In both the rapid-learning and the slow-learning the mental-age status is an important determining factor in optimum educational offerings.

### Qualitative Differences in Intelligence

In addition to quantitative differences there are qualitative differences in the intellectual processes between the slow-learning, the average, and the rapid-learning. These various types of minds have unique characteristics which should be understood and utilized in the teaching process. Experienced psychologists in evaluating the psychological constitution of their examinees are familiar with qualitative characteristics of different levels of brightness or dullness. One of the foremost observers was Dr. Lewis M. Terman in his interpretations of reactions and of manners of response to problems on intelligence tests. A thorough acquaintance with such observations makes it possible for the experienced psychologist to determine the approximate type of mind as high, average, or below average without having to compute a mental age, divide by the chronological age, and judge the quality of brightness from the intelligence quotient alone. Knowledge of these qualitative characteristics throw light on the educational processes of the rapid-learning and the slow-learning. In more extreme forms they also characterize the gifted at the positive end, and the mentally retarded at the negative end of the intellectual scale.

*Independent procedure.* In whatever is to be done the less able minds appear to need more help and stimulation, whereas the more able minds tend to work with greater independence. Some of this difference is related to the ease or difficulty of tasks which are often beyond the abilities of the slow-learning, and below the abilities of the rapid-learning. In some experimental research the mentally retarded could do some independent study and procedure only when their mental age was fully one year above that required for normal average pupils. More specifically, certain learning processes, comprehended by average pupils at six years in mental age could be covered with some independence by the mentally retarded only when they had advanced to at least seven years in mental age. The teacher of the slow-learning must constantly give more direction and encouragement, but offer it in lesser degree to the rapid-learning who will otherwise set up a subtle yet effective revolt, the nature of which the teacher does not readily understand. Slow-learning pupils who do not have such help are frustrated by too much responsibility and hence they develop feelings of insecurity. The great independence of very capable and gifted minds was discussed in the preceding chapter.

*Associative learning.* Differences exist in the powers of associative learning. Able minds find more than one way to learn by association of related elements. If it becomes important to remember an individual's name the mere repetition of it may not suffice, but he may resemble some one with a similar name, or wear a suit similar in some respect, or is met in company with another whose mannerism is similar, the chances of correct recall are much greater. More able minds naturally utilize these associative techniques in their learning processes, whereas the less able become confused if too many associative elements are brought into play. They may profit from the use of a very few assists, otherwise they are likely to be at a complete loss when simple recall is the only method. There are unlimited opportunities for investigation of how education may utilize the knowledge about the number and use of associations in the learning processes.

*Concrete versus abstract learning.* The ability to proceed in learning from the concrete to the abstract or to the general is an ideal goal in education. The more able minds are capable of easy and workable transitions, whereas the less able have greater difficulty. The more able may even prefer to start at once with the abstract, since they may look upon the concrete as a necessary evil. When they grasp the general principles of algebra, the entire process of learning becomes such an art that it releases time for more advanced thinking and for the development of greater abstractions. The less able are likely to be swamped in the details of the concrete and unable to rise to the abstract rules which can bring order out of chaos. In desperation they often guess or choose at random. The learning process must necessarily be reduced to terms simple enough so that they are able to gain some mastery of the abstract. Frequently the less able learn abstract rules so that they may repeat them with facility, but this should not be confused with actual understanding or application.

*Verbal versus nonverbal learning.* There is a common and universal misconception that the less able amply compensate in nonverbal learning for deficiences in verbal learning. The compensation is not in actual performance but in the greater *interest* which they have in these areas over that of the more able. Mere production of simple shop projects in quantity is not a principal goal of education. The manipulative process in any subject needs to be related logically to the theory of its use, and the principles of its construction. Able minds become interested in nonverbal projects if they can find theories in the verbal areas to bring meaningful associations to them. A class of the rapid-learning took a renewed interest in handwriting when they developed with it a historical scrapbook of handwriting throughout the ages. Woodshop took on a new meaning when the history of the available woods and their characteristics were also subjects of study. The slow-learning should have enough of the reasons for nonverbal manipulative projects so that they will provide some worthwhile motivations in their activities.

*Coordination and long-time planning.* There seems to be considerable difference between the slow-learning and the rapid-learning in long-time planning and coordination of various related projects. Part of the difficulty for the slow-learning may be in their immature mental age for the projects which they are expected to undertake. However it comes to light in trying to do reading in supplementary sources on a basic topic, or in planning the coordination of materials for a specific project. The rapid-learning are able to carry out such projects with comparative ease and enjoy greater returns from the longer investments. Teachers attempting to coordinate activities of pupils who attend their several classes find it comparatively easy for the rapid-learning, but difficult for the slow-learning.

These various qualitative differences are by no means absolute characterizations of all pupils but are *trends* from which exceptions can be found. Since there is presently more attention to the mental health of all school pupils and a better adjustment of teaching methods and of curriculum materials, some of the difficulties of the slow-learning may gradually be eased.

### General Abilities and Special Abilities

The discussion in Chapter 12 emphasized that abilities were both general and special and that there is a positive relationship between them. The sample profile from the Detroit Tests of Learning Aptitude in that chapter showed a range of mental ages from thirteen years, six months, in auditory attention span for related syllables to six years, six months, for visual attention span for objects, but a clustering of submental ages near the median of nine years, three months. Scatter of test results is also noted in tests by other authors. There are four special cases or categories of relationships between general abilities and special abilities which throw more light upon the specific learning characteristics of slow-learning and rapid-learning pupils.

The slow-learning pupil with a special disability below his general ability is especially handicapped whenever this particular aptitude, such as an auditory retention span, is called into action. Such a pupil finds himself no stronger than the weakest link in his mental chain. He lacks resourcefulness sufficient to bypass it by utilizing other mental abilities. In contrast is the slow-learning pupil with a special ability which he is tempted to exploit on all possible occasions to the deteriment of his general mental resourcefulness.

The rapid-learning pupil with a special disability in some portion of his mental constitution is able, because of general mental resourcefulness, to short-circuit his disability and to proceed with only a minor delay. The rapid-learning pupil with a special ability does not exploit his talent extravagently but uses it wisely as a reserve of power and as a tonic to all of his mental activities.

### Other Differences

It is unfortunately true that the differences between the slow-learning and the rapid-learning do not end with the mental characteristics but extend in some degree to other important factors. The health of the slow-learning is generally not up to the par of the rapid-learning; they have more children's diseases, they are absent more frequently from school, and often they come from less favored social and economic conditions. While no one of these factors is extremely significant, the total effect of several minor handicaps in combination may result in cumulative ineffectiveness. The problems of the slow-learning must be faced in a more realistic manner once the multiple nature of their problems becomes better known.

### Curriculum Adjustments

Curriculum adjustments for the rapid-learning seem to be a simpler problem than for the slow-learning. It is obvious from the table of mental ages, earlier in this chapter that the rapid-learning are already advanced one year in mental age by school age and this advantage increases still further throughout school life. It is important that rapid-learning pupils be challenged to do the best which their superior abilities warrant. The various plans of acceleration, enrichment, segregation, or combinations of them discussed for the gifted, also apply to lesser degree for them. Enrichment may begin in the early primary grades when several primers and readers may be read with profit. All of the fundamental subjects offer opportunities for enrichment and suggestions are being inserted in modern text books and in teachers' guides. Many of the more capable become accelerated. In an Age-Grade-Progress report for the Detroit elementary schools the average of all pupils rated "A" with approximate intelligence quotients of 118 or higher on group intelligence tests were accelerated one semester or half year by the end of the sixth grade. The pupils "B" had made normal progress, but all below that point had had one or more semesters of retardation because of extended illness or for other reasons.

Curriculum adjustments for the slow-learning are a much more complicated and difficult matter. The first problem arises at the very beginning of school when the mental retardation of one year has already occurred. Various investigations have proved that it is very difficult for a pupil only five years in mental age to proceed satisfactorily in learning to read. The problem is being met, in part, with programs of reading readiness and in other situations which provide experiences preliminary to reading. It is no unsolved mystery why slow-learning pupils are likely to fail to repeat one or more grades, so that they become overaged and retarded. This retardation is not in accord with present educational philosophy which recommends that all pupils should progress as nearly as possible with those of the same chronological age. It implies that the slow-learning should advance into high school and benefit from the opportunities which it offers by way of general educational and vocational preparation. However, if there is some delay at the very beginning, it is difficult to make up any time, particularly since the rate of mental growth is slow and the mental age continues to fall further behind. After some of the fundamentals have been mastered as well as possible in the early primary grades, the curriculum should be couched in easy units so that the later subjects may be understood in simple terms. There is a grave and very heavy responsibility upon the shoulders of curriculum and text book writers to meet these restrictions and qualifications and for teachers to be adequately trained to utilize them wisely.

Classroom teachers are well aware of the challenge which they find every day they enter their classrooms. Some years ago five hundred Detroit elementary school teachers wrote short essays on how they could best adapt curriculum and methods of teaching for slow-learning and for rapid-learning pupils in the various subjects of very diversified programs of regular and special subjects. The author[1] was asked to summarize these reports in a monograph entitled *Characteristic Differences in Bright and Dull Pupils* which has furnished many clues to solutions of problems in these two types of pupils.

### The Grouping of Pupils

The correct and optimum grouping of pupils for instruction is not a new problem in modern educational practice. As early as 1936 it had created so much interest that the author was a member of a committee for the National Society for the Study of Education which prepared Part I of the Thirty-fifth Yearbook[2] on this topic. Many diverse opinions came to light as might be expected. The principal issue centered around whether any kinds of grouping were in conflict with principles of true democracy. Even the most theoretical proponents of some segregation for reasons other than democratic participation did not take the extreme view that segregation should be final and complete. The purpose of any segregation was not for the segregation itself, but rather to achieve goals which could not be obtained otherwise. There was some agreement that when educational processes were highly specialized segregation was efficient, necessary, and desirable, such as a school orchestra meeting together at regular rehearsals. Various shops and vocational subjects segregated pupils because of equipment. Within these groupings classes might be composed of all levels of abilities of the same grade.

When it came to understanding the curriculum needs and the learning characteristics of the slow-learning as compared with the rapid-learning there was much less appreciation of the real nature of the differences. Some argued that it was easier and more democratic to keep them all grouped together and to let the teacher struggle along as best she could with three curriculum adjustments and three

---

[1] H.J. Baker, *Characteristic Differences in Bright and Dull Pupils*, C.A. Gregory Co., Cincinnati, Ohio, 1927, 118 pp.

[2] National Society for the Study of Education, *Thirty-fifth Yearbook, Part I, The Grouping of Pupils*, University of Chicago Press, Chicago, 1936, 319 pp.

Class discussion, major-work group, Cleveland public schools.

French lesson, gifted pupils, Indianapolis public schools.

different types of learning processes. The chief point of failure in grouping consisted of giving it publicity and attaching a name to whatever was being done. A more desirable attitude would have been to consider any groupings, either segregated or nonsegregated, as merely internal adjustments for the sake of better instruction. Unfavorable publicity wrecked many worthwhile attempts. Grouping according to the alphabetical listing of last names proved to be the safe haven.

In a summarizing chapter Cornell[1] reported that tests were not given over long enough intervals to be valid; slow changes in work habits; administrative difficulties; and, no general agreement on criteria for grouping, for procedure, or for evaluating results. Where thorough and long-time trials had been made there was definite evidence that homogeneous groups had produced better achievement than heterogeneous groups. The modern practice is as yet in a state of flux and the current emphasis upon better social understanding indicates that some forms of heterogeneous mingling are desirable. It should be accompanied by some interpretation of different points of view and how to deal with them, otherwise the mingling enhances rather than abates the conflicts over differences. A little training in these areas is as necessary as is training in appreciation of art and music if much real enjoyment is to be realized.

## The Challenge

Knowledge of individual differences has placed a new orientation upon the needs of pupils. Teaching methods must vary to fit the pattern and it is obviously difficult to shift continuously from one to another in a short lesson period. There is a greater problem of building up a curriculum, or curriculums, which give adequate education to slow-learning, to average, and to rapid-learning pupils. While five-sixths normal progress does not seem to be a serious handicap, its cumulative effect from birth has resulted in a lag by six years of age. The seven-sixths rate for the rapid-learning should be capitalized more completely and effectively than at present. Finally,

[1] E. Cornell, "Effects of Ability Grouping Determinable from Published Studies," *Thirty-fifth Yearbook, Part I*, p. 304.

while it may be said that the slow-learning and the rapid-learning do not fall into the general classifications of handicapped and exceptional children, they offer problems which are worthy of special consideration.

## Questions and Topics for Discussion

1. Discuss the administrative groupings of pupils in your school system.
2. What factors in addition to intelligence tests should be taken into account in groupings?
3. Discuss some subject-matter adaptations which have been made.
4. Report on the implications of the mental-age table in the text.
5. Discuss the optimum terminal education for the slow-learning in regard to grade reached, subjects offered, etc.

## A. Organizations

1. American Association for Gifted Children, Gramercy Park, New York 3.
2. National Association for Retarded Children, 129 E. 52nd St., New York 22.
3. The American Association on Mental Deficiency, Willimantic, Conn.
4. The National Association for Gifted Children, 409 Clifton Springs Ave., Cincinnati 17, Ohio.

## B. Periodicals

1. *American Journal of Mental Deficiency* (quarterly), American Association on Mental Deficiency, Willimantic, Conn.
2. *The Gifted Child* (monthly), American Association for Gifted Children, New York.

Note: Many educational and psychological journals frequently publish articles in these fields.

## C. Books

### Section I. Intellectual Abilities (Chapter 12)

1. Baker, H.J., and B. Leland, *Detroit Tests of Learning Aptitude* (rev. ed), Public School Publishing Co., Cincinnati, Ohio, 1939, 157 pp.
2. Buros, O.K. (ed.), *The Fourth Mental Measurements Yearbook*, The Gryphon Press, Highland Park, N. J., 1953, 1,163 pp.

3. Carmichael, L. (ed.), *Manual of Child Psychology* (2nd ed.), John Wiley and Sons, Inc., New York, 1954, 1,295 pp.

4. Cronbach, L.J., *Essentials of Psychological Testing*, Harper & Brothers, New York, 1949, 475 pp.

5. Eells, K., A. Davis, R.J. Havighurst, V.E. Herrick, and R. Tyler, *Intelligence and Cultural Differences*, University of Chicago Press, Chicago, 1951, 388 pp.

6. Guilford, J.P., *Psychometric Methods*, McGraw-Hill Book Co., Inc., New York, 1954, 597 pp.

7. Gulliksen, H., *Theory of Mental Tests*, John Wiley and Sons, Inc., New York, 1950, 486 pp.

8. Hildreth, G.H., A *Bibliography of Mental Tests and Rating Scales*, The Psychological Corp. New York, 1946, 86 pp.

9. Mursell, J.L., *Psychological Testing*, Longmans Green and Co., New York, 1947, 449 pp.

10. Peterson, J., *Early Conceptions and Tests of Intelligence*, World Book Co., Yonkers, N.Y., 1926, 320 pp.

11. Rapaport, D., *Diagnostic Psychological Testing*, Vol. I, 1945, 573 pp.; Vol. II, 1946, 516 pp., The Yearbook Publishers, Inc., Chicago.

12. Review of Educational Research, *Educational and Psychological Testing*, American Educational Research Association, Washington, D.C., 1956, 110 pp.

13. Rubinstein, E.A., and M. Lorr, *Survey of Clinical Practice in Psychology*, International Universities Press, New York, 1954, 363 pp.

14. Sarason, S.B., *Psychological Problems in Mental Deficiency*, Harper & Brothers, New York, 1949, 366 pp.

15. Schafer, R., *The Clinical Application of Psychological Tests*, International Universities Press, New York, 1948, 346 pp.

16. Spearman, C., and LL. W. Jones, *Human Ability*, The Macmillan Co., New York, 1950, 198 pp.

17. Stoddard, G. D., *The Meaning of Intelligence*, The Macmillan Co., New York, 1943, 504 pp.

18. Terman, L.M., and M.A. Merrill, *Measuring Intelligence*, Houghton Mifflin Co., Boston, 1937, 461 pp.

19. Thorndike, E.L., *The Measurement of Intelligence*, Teachers College, Columbia University, New York, 1927, 616 pp.

20. Wechsler, D., *The Measurement of Adult Intelligence* (3rd ed.), Williams and Wilkins Co., Baltimore, Md., 1944, 258 pp.

21. ———, *Wechsler Intelligence Scale for Children*, The Psychological Corp., New York, 1949, 113 pp.

Note: Consult the list of test publishers at the end of Chapter 2.

## Section II. Mentally Retarded (Chapter 13)

1. Baker, H.J., *Suggestions to the Parents of a Backward Child*, Public School Publishing Co., Cincinnati, Ohio, 1958, 2 pp.
2. Birch, J.W. and G.D. Stevens, *Reaching the Mentally Retarded*, The Public School Publishing Co., Cincinnati, Ohio, 1955, 44 pp.
3. Burt, C., *The Causes and Treatment of Backwardness*, Philosophical Library, New York, 1953, 128 pp.
4. Channing, A., *Employment of Mentally Deficient Boys and Girls*, United States Children's Bureau, Government Printing Office, Washington, D. C., 1932, 107 pp.
5. Heiser, C.F., *Our Backward Children*, W.W. Norton and Co., Inc., New York, 1955, 240 pp.
6. Ingram, C.P., *Education of the Slow-Learning Child* (rev. ed.), Ronald Press Co., New York, 1953, 359 pp.
7. Kirk, S.A., and R.L. Erdman, *Education of Mentally Retarded Children*, University of Illinois, Urbana, Ill., 1948, 46 pp.
8. ———, and G.O. Johnson, *Educating the Retarded Child*, Houghton Mifflin Co., Boston, 1951, 434 pp.
9. ———, M.B. Karnes, and W.D. Kirk, *You and Your Retarded Child*, The Macmillan Co., New York, 1955, 184 pp.
10. Kugelmass, I.N., *The Management of Mental Deficiency in Children*, Grune and Stratton, Inc., New York, 1954, 312 pp.
11. Levinson, A., *The Mentally Retarded Child*, John Day Co., New York, 1952, 190 pp.
12. Loewy, H., *Training the Backward Child*, Philosophical Library, New York, 1956, 166 pp.
13. Masland, R.L., "The Prevention of Mental Retardation," A.M.A. *Journal of Diseases of Children*, 95, Part II January, 1958, pp. 1-109.
14. Sarason, S.B. *Psychological Problems in Mental Deficiency*, Harper & Brothers, New York, 1949, 366 pp.
15. Tredgold, A.F., and R.F. Tredgold, *A Textbook of Mental Deficiency* (8th ed.), Williams and Wilkins, Baltimore, Md., 1952, 545 pp.
16. Tucker, C. D., *Betty Lee; Care of Handicapped Children*, The Macmillan Co., 1954, 168 pp.
17. Wallin, J.E.W., *Children with Mental and Physical Handicaps*, Prentice-Hall, Inc., Englewood Cliffs, N. J., 1949, 549 pp.
18. ———, *Education of Mentally Handicapped Children*, Harper & Brothers, New York, 1955, 485 pp.

## Section III. The Gifted (Chapter 14)

1. Birch, J.W., and E.M. McWilliams, *Challenging Gifted Children*, Public School Publishing Co., Cincinnati, Ohio, 1955, 49 pp.

2. Burks, B.S., D.W. Jensen, L.M. Terman, and others, *The Promise of Youth*, Genetic Studies of Genius, Vol. 3, Stanford University Press, Stanford University, Calif., 1930, 508 pp.
3. Carroll, H.A., *Genius in the Making*, McGraw-Hill Book Co., Inc., New York, 1940, 307 pp.
4. Cox, C. M., and others, *The Early Mental Traits of Three Hundred Geniuses*, Genetic Studies of Genius, Vol. 2, Stanford University Press, Stanford University, Calif., 1926, 815 pp.
5. Cutts, N.E., and N. Moseley, *Bright Children: A Guide for Parents*, G. P. Putnam's Sons, New York, 1953, 238 pp.
6. DeHann, R.F., and R.J. Havighurst, *Educating Gifted Children*, University of Chicago Press, Chicago, 1957, 276 pp.
7. Educational Policies Commission, *Education of the Gifted*, National Education Association, Washington 6, D.C., 1950, 88 pp.
8. Galton, F., *Hereditary Genius*, Horizon Press, New York, 1952, 379 pp.
9. Goddard, H.H., *School Training of Gifted Children*, World Book Co., Yonkers, N. Y., 1928, 226 pp.
10. Hall, T., *Gifted Children: The Cleveland Story*, World Publishing Co., Cleveland, Ohio., 1956, 91 pp.
11. Hildreth, G., *Educating Gifted Children*, Harper & Brothers, New York, 1952, 272 pp.
12. Laycock, S.R., *Gifted Children*, The Copp Clark Publishing Co., Toronto, Canada, 1957, 180 pp.
13. National Society for the Study of Education, *Education for the Gifted*, Fifty-seventh Yearbook, Part II, University of Chicago Press, Chicago, 1958, 420 pp.
14. Passow, A.H. et al., *Planning for Talented Youth*, Bureau of Publications, Columbia University, New York, 1955, 84 pp.
15. Sumption, M.R., *Three Hundred Gifted Children*, World Book Co., Yonkers, N. Y., 1941, 235 pp.
16. Terman, L.M., and others, *Mental and Physical Traits of a Thousand Gifted Children*, Genetic Studies of Genius, Vol. I, Stanford University Press, Stanford, University, Calif., 1926, 641 pp.
17. ———, and M.H. Oden, *The Gifted Child Grows Up*, Genetic Studies of Genius, Vol. 4, Stanford University Press, Stanford University, Calif., 1947, 448 pp.
18. Witty, P.A. (ed.), *The Gifted Child*, D.C. Heath and Co., Boston, 1951, 338 pp.

### Section IV. Slow-Learning and Rapid-Learning (Chapter 15)

1. Baker, H.J., *Characteristic Differences in Bright and Dull Pupils*, Public School Publishing Co., Cincinnati, Ohio, 1927, 118 pp.

2.  Lightfoot, G.F., *Personality Characteristics of Bright and Dull Chil-dren*, Teachers College, Contributions to Education, No. 969, Columbia University Press, New York, 1951, 136 pp.
3.  Smith, M.F., and A.J. Burks, *Teaching the Slow-Learning Child*, Harper & Brothers, New York, 1954, 175 pp.

Note: Many educational and psychological journals frequently publish articles in these fields.

## D. Films and Filmstrips

1.  *Development of Individual Differences.* No two individuals alike resulting from same heredity and environment. McGraw-Hill Text-Film Department.
2.  *Individual Differences.* 23 minutes, sound. Members of the same families are not replicas of one another. McGraw-Hill Text-Film Department.
3.  *The Challenge of the Gifted Child.* Available for sale only through that department. McGraw-Hill Text-Film Department.

# PART 5

## Deviations in Educational Achievement

# CHAPTER 16

## The Educationally Retarded

EVERY CHILD with any type of impairment or disability deserves to have his problems diagnosed, and remedial procedures put into effect. The child who is retarded in reading or any other school subject should be given special attention according to his needs just as the child who is deaf, blind, mentally retarded, or mentally gifted. It is not necessary for enrollment in a completely segregated class to qualify for equal opportunity along with other handicapped and exceptional children. Special education is not something separate and apart from regular education. It includes children with mild defects who can be aided with a minimum of special care in the regular grade to the bedridden child confined to hospital or at home. The educationally retarded qualify for such consideration.

### Definitions

It is probably within the personal experience of everyone to have had some school subjects which were more difficult than others. Straight "A" records are the exception. These irregularities in educational achievement may have occurred in the primary grades, in the secondary schools, or at the college level. In the great majority of individuals they were probably minor variations from general scholarship averages. There are individuals who have experienced very marked disability in some particular school subject. Educational retardation does not necessarily have defined numerical limits. Some extreme cases are those whose reading achievement is two or more years below their mental age and pupils in primary grades who have not mastered one primer. In a practical remedial program a beginning should be made with the more marked cases and proceed as far as possible with the less severe cases.

## Significance

Educational retardation may occur in any school subject and in any grade. Retardation in reading seems to be the most serious problem of all, since reading becomes a tool for other subjects. When reading is a failure most of the entire educational process breaks down. Retardation in arithmetic may cause serious errors in computation, in measurements, and in handling money. Mistakes in arithmetic have serious consequences for the individual and for those dealing with him. Spelling may be of less importance as to consequences from errors themselves, but it is often a source of social embarrassment. Good handwriting is a decided asset even in these days of typewriters and printing, whereas poor handwriting is excused many times when it might easily have been improved. Other school subjects with extreme retardation may sometimes be avoided by choice of electives. It is the educational birthright of every individual to achieve success in all required school subjects in accordance with his ability. In addition to educational inefficiency there are some grave effects upon the individual with the educational retardation. A few of them will be briefly sketched.

*Puzzled state of mind.* A puzzled state of mind may accompany extreme educational retardation. As early as in learning to read in the first grade the six-year-old cannot understand why he does not progress with classmates who seem to do it so easily. He goes through all the motions and activities used by the others but with little or no effective result. There are valid causes which an experienced reading diagnostician is able to recognize, but without such help the child does not know what to do. Such a child is off to a very bad start with his puzzled state of mind.

*Feelings of Inferiority.* In addition to being puzzled the child who cannot read soon begins to have feelings of inferiority since he cannot compete successfully and on equal terms with his classmates. Rather than putting more effort into reading he turns his attention to other accomplishments mostly in after-school hours. He has a better chance for success in the opinion of his friends. These feelings of inferiority may easily have a profound effect upon all of his schoolwork. Such feelings may also become a part of his general attitude toward success in any activity in adult life. Once the pattern of inferiority has become established in a school subject it takes unusual success in remedial measures for a long time to neutralize it. Evidence has been presented in Chapter 6 that attitudes in children are slightly more difficult to change than are those of adults. This fact should be an ominous sign in any educational process which leads to feelings of inferiority.

*Compensatory reactions.* Although a pupil may have extreme retardation in one or more school subjects it is difficult for his regular teacher to give him individual assistance even though she may be aware of his difficulties. He begins to feel neglected and overlooked by everyone and no longer feels a part of the social picture. Since he cannot get attention for worthy achievements he is likely to resort to deviant behavior which will gain him immediate attention. He is willing to risk such possible consequences for the satisfaction of getting attention. Whatever punishment he may receive he attributes indirectly to his educational retardation and his bitterness toward it increases.

*Feelings of frustration.* If adults could be subjected to long and repeated failure in one line of important activity they might more clearly appreciate the frustrations felt by children who continue to fail. Laws require that they must attend school and repeatedly face the same subjects and the same causes of failure. A state of deep indifference may descend upon them. Their situation is similar to the autistic behavior of babies who are deprived of maternal care. It may be considered as a form of "brainwashing" with some possible escapes into deviant behavior. In its more aggressive forms, children hate school. Agencies and diagnosticians who deal with them are beginning to coin and use the term "school-phobia." It is high time that steps be taken so that such implications are not possible.

*Parental attitudes.* While parents are theoretically interested in efficient schools, they have a more personal interest in the education of their own children. No matter what the reasons may be, their child's failure is a threat to themselves and an injustice to their children. They do not understand the child's difficulties and blame the school either secretly or openly. The child may be comforted at home or he may even be punished which adds insult to his injury. He faces difficulties from all sides.

These various unfavorable attitudes which exist in some degree would disappear or would have been prevented if the need for remedial education had been recognized before the damage had been done. Specialists in many fields allied to or part of education have joined their efforts so that educational retardation could be greatly reduced if remedial teachers were available and if facilities were provided.

### Delimiting Causes of Educational Retardation

There are many causes for children not progressing satisfactorily from grade to grade. This list of causes is related to the many kinds of handicapped and exceptional children discussed in this book. Reference to these handicaps will help to set more definite limits to the real field of educational retardation.

*Impaired vision.* If a child is unable to see reasonably well he does not grasp the printed page. There are many such children whose impairments range as far as the extreme of blindness. Parents and teachers sometimes overlook serious visual impairments unless a thorough vision examination has been given. Inadequate visual perception in connection with normal vision may be a cause of educational retardation. Individuals with this defect seem unable to associate any meaning with symbols which are usually recognized as letters or words. Their experiences are similar to what any uninstructed individual would get from a casual glance at a page of oriental characters.

*Impaired hearing.* Full educational adjustments for children with greatly impaired hearing or with total deafness should make it possible for them to avoid becoming educationally retarded. However, there are children whose inadequate auditory perception or whose incomplete neural connections produce aphasic conditions so that learning does not function. Such cases may need the coordinated services of the remedial teacher and of the speech correctionist.

*Generally impaired health.* There are a few children whose generally impaired health cause them to have very irregular school attendance records. Unless home or hospital teaching is provided they are liable to fall behind their grades. If their general abilities are average or better they make up for lost time very quickly.

*Level of mental development.* Within broad limits mental age is one of the important determiners of educational progress. Unless the mental status of a mentally retarded child is known, he is often considered to be educationally retarded. Whenever his educational achievement is in line with his mental age he is not educationally retarded in the true meaning of the term. Such qualifying conditions are true of all levels of mental age and educational achievement. By contrast, a highly intelligent child, with poor educational achievement may be considered as educationally retarded.

*Personality maladjustments.* Children with severe emotional and personality maladjustments should be discovered and serviced by the school social worker, or visiting teacher, early enough so that educational retardation does not develop. If it has already occurred, there is need for cooperative action with the remedial teacher. The implications in this area were discussed in Part 2.

### Types and Degrees of Educational Retardation

From the various conditions which have just been cited, it is evident that there are varying degrees as well as many causes of educational retardation. Educational retardation follows the same general pattern which has been discovered in many other types of defects and disabilities: (1) a relatively large group with mild degrees for which simple corrective measures are quite effective; (2) a smaller group whose defects are more serious, but who respond well to treatment if specialized teachers coordinate their corrective and remedial measures with programs by regular class teachers; and (3) a small number with very extreme disabilities whose specialized needs must be met wholly or in part outside of the regular classroom. There are no absolute limits separating these groups from each other. The first two types are able to have a high rate of restoration if proper corrective or preventive measures are instituted. The third type often has extreme conditions and causes which are not completely understood. It is encouraging that many centers for intensive research have recently been established. The several chapters of Part 3 on neurological disorders and diseases throw light upon the nature of such educational disability.

### Causes of Educational Retardation

Many causes of educational retardation have been discovered. Along with the causes the actual experiences of such retardation produce a whole series of undesirable by-products. In some instances these by-products also become causes. By the time the educational retardate is discovered he generally has a mixture of causes and effects or of causes and results which are difficult to untangle. While separation of causes and effects are important, the chief goal is to consider the plight of the whole child who is the product of several factors operating singly or in combination. Since a start must be made somewhere, any one of several factors may serve.

*Lack of educational readiness.* A basic principle in the psychology of learning is readiness. Recently a great amount of instructional material has appeared on reading readiness. Experiences preparatory to reading should be provided such as trips outdoors, stories about domestic animals, and pleasurable events with the family. They provide a practical vocabulary of meaningful words which are soon to be recognized and utilized in reading. Physical activity develops verbs while number, color, and other meaningful terms become a part of vocabulary preliminary to reading itself. Unless such experiences with meaning are provided, learning to read about unfamiliar things and events becomes a highly theoretical and uninteresting activity. Learning the meaning of numbers in practical situations is a helpful preliminary to arithmetic instruction. Actually seeing two things joined with two more in a meaningful unit is much more interesting than learning the abstract fact that two plus two equals four. After the values of specifics have been grasped, the reasons for some abstractions will be better understood. In learning a foreign language, unless a large percentage of the vocabulary has been learned the unfamiliar words cannot be safely judged from the context. In learning to read and in arithmetic young children are in much the same predicament. The unfamiliar or the unknown should be explained and understood in advance, otherwise guessing may become habitual and may have serious implications throughout school and adult experiences. Making an inventory of what is actually known, unknown, or guessed, is one of the first tasks when dealing with the educationally retarded.

*Physical and sensory disabilities.* A few extreme physical and sensory disabilities have been mentioned. A very specialized type of education has been provided for the blind, the deaf, and for many other types so that educational retardation has not developed. The marginal cases of such defects may be unrecognized but yet be severe enough to block effective learning. They continue throughout all school experience. The freshman class of Dartmouth College in one year of extensive ocular examination showed that more than one third of the class had not had adequate visual examination and correction, according to a report by Bear.[1] In addition to needs in correction for accommodation in regard to distance, other types of vision difficulty are equally or possibly more important. Some of them are as follows: unequal size of visual images from the two eyes, known as aniseikonia; double vision from other causes; general inability to fuse two images; incoordination of the two eyes from muscle imbalance; and inability to achieve depth perception. Learning by auditory methods may not be effective from lack of biaural fusion from the two ears. Many of these conditions are discussed in later chapters of Part 6.

*Lateral dominance.* There has been much speculation and considerable research about the relationship of lateral dominance to edu-

---

[1] R.M. Bear, "The Dartmouth Program for Diagnostic and Remedial Reading with Special Reference to Visual Factors," *Educational Record Supplement*, 1939, 20, p. 76.

cational retardation, particularly with regard to learning to read. Handedness has always attracted teacher attention since in many situations the left-handed child presents certain problems in physical adjustment, such as in handwriting. It has been easy to theorize that disturbances in handedness or in other types of dominance have caused reading disability. The fact remains that a large majority of left-handed children have no difficulty in reading or in other subjects. More attention is directed to those who have had forced changing of handedness but it may well be that any educational retardation in their case was due to the emotional difficulties with parents or teachers rather than from the physical change itself. Ambidexterity which results in lack of lateral dominance may be more responsible for directional confusion in reading than change of handedness or left-handedness itself. Fernald[1] reports that of fifty cases of total reading disability twenty-nine had right-handed and right eye dominance; eleven had left-handed and left eye dominance; five with left-handed and right eye; one with the opposite condition; and four were ambidextrous.

*Methods of teaching.* There are many ways in which children learn and hence not all of them can be poured into the same mold. An experienced teacher must be able to make adaptations. Woolf and Woolf[2] comment on this problem as follows:

If teacher and pupil are to communicate satisfactorily with each other, each must have some idea of how each reading situation appears to the other. The pupil with less experience and with less maturity cannot comprehend exactly how the teacher perceives, so it is the responsibility of the teacher to try to understand as nearly as possible how the pupil perceives a situation, a story, a phrase, a word, an experience, an idea. If learning is really a function of the whole personality, the child puts into a given act of learning his interpretations of physical sensations, memories, and feelings. He may see threats or rewards not clearly visible to the teacher.

*Personality, emotional, and other factors.* Personality, emotional, and other factors are causes, or causes intermingled with results. The

[1] G.M. Fernald, *Remedial Techniques in Basic School Subjects*, McGraw-Hill Book Co., Inc., New York, 1943, p. 150.
[2] M.D. Woolf and J.A. Woolf, *Remedial Reading*, McGraw-Hill Book Co., Inc., New York, 1957, p. 11.

author[1] published in 1929 results of remedial teaching on sixty cases of nine-year-old pupils. On estimates of general personality adjustments by the remedial teachers, thirteen were very poor, twenty poor, nineteen average, three superior, and five had excellent personalities. Fifty-three of the cases had a total of seventy citations of physical aggressiveness, or lacking in aggressiveness, and other miscellaneous conditions. The remedial teachers soon discovered that although the pupils had been selected on the basis of failing marks in basic subjects the personality factors were of equal if not greater significance in educational retardation.

Ephron[2] reports on several cases where the emotional factors were discovered to be strongly causative in reading retardation in individuals from secondary schools and colleges. Some of them traced very hidden attitudes through psychoanalytic treatment. Her discussions illustrated that educational retardation may have very complex and interwoven factors and much beyond the fact that reading retardation was measurable on achievement tests.

## Methods of Diagnosis

Many causes which just have been cited suggest some methods of diagnosis. More specific details and suggestions are necessary for an adequate diagnosis. A few of the diagnostic factors will be outlined briefly.

*Teacher observations.* The regular classroom teacher is able to furnish first-hand information about the general status of educational achievement. It is reflected directly in the scholastic grades which she puts on report cards to parents and enters on the permanent school records. In many instances she lists how many sight words he has mastered, what words he misspells, what number combinations are incorrect, and what letters he reverses in his writing. She is able to report on personality and social characteristics and adaptability to the class as a unit. She may have some evidence of physical and

[1] H.J. Baker, *Educational Disability and Case Studies in Remedial Teaching*, Public School Publishing Co., Cincinnati, Ohio, 1929, pp. 19-30 (out of print).
[2] B.K. Ephron, *Emotional Difficulties in Reading*, The Julian Press, New York, 1953, 289 pp.

sensory handicaps and be aware of, but puzzled by, many less obvious disabilities. Her opinions and observations should have high priority in a diagnostic schedule.

*Achievement tests.* There is a rich and varied inventory of achievement tests which extend from the first grade through the secondary school. Some are for general surveys but others probe into fine details of educational difficulties. Publishers' catalogues list so many useful educational diagnostic tests that college survey courses are necessary to make suitable selections for specific conditions, as mentioned in Chapter 2. The remedial teacher specializes in the selection and administration of achievement tests as part of her activities.

*Tests of intelligence.* A qualified clinical psychologist should administer batteries of individual intelligence tests which include not only measures of general ability but a series of special aptitudes as well. A profile of strengths and weaknesses provides one of the most useful inventories for the remedial teacher. Such factors as verbal and nonverbal abilities and profiles that were described for the Detroit Tests of Learning Aptitude in Chapter 12 give many clues to difficulties in the psychology of learning.

*Personality inventories and case backgrounds.* Personality inventories disclose many areas of motivation or lack of motivation which add to causes of educational retardation. The child who feels neglected or left out may try to compensate for such limitations by excellent scholarship or he may regress in his studies. A thorough case history discloses the general culture and attitudes of the home which influence his attitudes toward school. Further elaboration of values from case histories and adjustment inventories was given in Chapter 6.

*Physical and sensory examinations.* In addition to general physical examinations which should be conducted for all children certain specialized techniques should be added for the educationally retarded. Testing for handedness is important. Betts[1] suggests: (1) tapping tests with several trials by paper and pencils with alternating hands; (2) trying to write with first one hand, then the other; (3) throwing, hammering, and equivalent operations; (4) using scissors; and (5)

[1] E.A. Betts, *The Prevention and Correction of Reading Difficulties*, Row, Peterson and Co., New York, 1936, pp. 121-124.

strength of grip. Betts also suggests peeping through a half-inch hole in a sheet of paper held at arm's length to show which eye is the preferred one for seeing. The Telebinocular Test[1] gives valuable evidence on depth perception, visual coordination, and other unusual conditions of seeing which affect recognizing symbols in reading. In certain types of brain-injured children it has previously been noted that some of them cannot form normal perception of objects and perspectives, which would also interfere with learning to read, spell, and write.

In cooperation with one large elementary school in a community of low economical and social status the author and the principal of the building hastily scanned without any formal tests the eyes of sixteen six-year-old pupils selected by their teachers from a total of one hundred fifty in the first grades. Without exception by this informal method the selected pupils obviously had severe visual impairments, and as yet none of them had had glasses or been given thorough visual examinations. Undoubtedly there were many others in the large group in need of visual correction. These various types of examinations are some of the principal techniques necessary in the diagnosis of educational retardation. The complexity of the disability must be matched by a complexity of diagnostic techniques.

Wherever school systems conduct special classes for pupils whose problems are primarily deviant behavior the great majority of such pupils are also educationally retarded. There is evidence that educational retardation may be a strongly motivating cause of deviant behavior. Nearly all large cities have such classes or special schools such as the Montefiore School for Boys in Chicago or the Moore School for Boys in Detroit. In these schools remedial education is an important part of the corrective program. In a personal interview, Edward Stullken, principal of the Montefiore School, stated that confirmed truants are more likely to return willingly the second day after enrolling in his school if a lesson in remedial education was immediately started on the first day.

Other places where educationally retarded children are found in numbers are detention homes affiliated with juvenile courts and in a large group who are on probation to such courts. This trend also

---

[1] Available from the Keystone View Co., Meadville, Pa.

continues into the area of adult offenders as well. It is a disturbing implication concerning deficiencies in education.

Although the numbers are not large, the pupil populations of hospitals and centers for mentally and emotionally disturbed children contain many children with educational retardation. Neurological impairments may have been logical causes for such retardation. Such centers are surprisingly successful in their special techniques of remedial education.

## The Number of Cases

Since the limits of what may be considered to be educational retardation are not too clearly defined, the number of cases is indefinite. In young children the absolute deficit of achievement below expectation from mental age may be much less than for older children. Traxler[1] reported ranges from 10 to 25 per cent of pupils by the end of the elementary grades as retarded two or more years beyond expectation in reading. In a survey of nine-year-olds in seven Detroit elementary schools the author[2] found 7 per cent with failing marks in one or more of four basic subjects at the end of the semester preceding the program of remedial correction. From these two statements it would appear that if educational retardation is not checked, a greater number of pupils is affected the further they progress through school. Traxler's report was on reading only. Waite[3] reported 1.7 per cent of 2,212 third-grade pupils in Omaha public schools with reading proficiency one and one-half or more grades below that level, and 28.5 per cent retarded between one-half and one and one-half grades.

## Organization of Programs

Several types of remedial programs exist in different school systems. All of them have merit in that pupils improve with some individual

[1] A.E. Traxler, "Research in Reading in the United States," *Journal of Educational Research*, 1949, 42, p. 496.

[2] H.J. Baker, *Educational Disability and Case Studies in Remedial Teaching*, Public School Publishing Co., Cincinnati, Ohio, 1929, 172 pp. (out of print).

[3] W.H. Waite, "The Improvement of Reading in Omaha Public Schools," *Elementary School Journal*, 1948, 48, pp. 305-311.

attention and with methods of learning suited to their needs. Some of them are organized more effectively than others.

*The itinerant teacher.* Where the school enrollments are small an itinerant teacher may confer at stated intervals with the regular teacher and offer suggestions. The regular teacher has the principal responsibility of finding time for giving individual attention to such a pupil. Such a method has limitations in the amount which the regular teacher can do and how much special materials and training she has available for remedial work. Such help would be much more effective if some free time were provided for the regular teacher.

*Placement in other special education classes.* Where there are special classes for the mentally retarded, for the deviant behavior, for health conservation, and for other types, a few cases of the educationally retarded are sometimes enrolled. To the extent that the entire class profits from methods of remedial education the educationally retarded share in its benefits. If the class is only a mixture of many types of handicaps, an undesirable practice, the educationally retarded do not get their full share of attention!

*Help from other pupils.* Help from other pupils of the same grade or from higher grades is a common practice. It has some good and some less desirable features. If the relationships between them are satisfactory, the educationally retarded child feels comfortable. If the other pupil merely reads to him or does his problems for him, he becomes more dependent. If the coaching pupil is impatient and takes the assignments in poor grace, the results are unfortunate. Parents sometimes complain that their children are sent to school to learn and not to teach others. On the favorable side the coaching pupils may get genuine satisfaction from the improvements which accrue and thus strengthen their decision to become teachers themselves. Some cases of extreme educational disability do not profit from this program of unskilled and untrained coaching.

*After-school classes.* Some school systems are experimenting with a plan of having educationally retarded pupils coached after regular school hours. The teachers for these classes are given additional pay for this service and when there is a general shortage of teachers for regular classes this plan provides additional service without reducing the general supply of teachers. Unless pupils appreciate the benefits of this plan they are likely to feel that staying after school is an unnecessary punishment. In theory they are entitled to remedial programs in their school day by the same logic that a blind child gets his education during regular school hours.

*Parallel organization of classes.* Within some large school buildings a plan is sometimes put into effect in which all classes in reading, or in arithmetic meet at the same class period. For each particular subject the classes are regrouped according to the grade level results on educational tests so that the educationally retarded in reading from several regular grades are brought together and the advanced ones also have the benefit of enrichment and advanced study. This plan has considerable merit but it does not necessarily give the most retarded readers the benefit of the specialized teaching techniques which they may need with teachers trained in such methods.

*The special segregated class.* Another method of remedial adjustment is to enroll a class of pupils recruited from several grades and keep them under one teacher in the same manner as any other class. The pupils may miss association with other children who are of their same age and grade and who are succeeding in all of their subjects. This type of special class may enroll a smaller number than the regular class and hence is more expensive. There is some likelihood that the class will gradually be filled with the mentally retarded, or with cases of deviant behavior and fail to fulfill the original purpose for which it was established.

*The special remedial teacher.* One of the most effective programs is to assign a special remedial teacher to one or more schools on a weekly schedule basis. The pattern of this plan is similar to that for the speech correction teacher. She has a room with special equipment, books, and supplies to which remedial cases report for two different periods per week. Several pupils with similar remedial problems report in small groups to each of the three or more sessions held in each half day. In a typical program the teacher visits large school, A, on Mondays and Thursdays, alternating the morning and afternoon sessions so that the pupils do not miss the same classes twice weekly. On Tuesdays and Fridays she has smaller schools, B and C, where she spends a half day in each, alternating the morning and afternoon classes. Wednesdays are reserved for records, coordination, visiting her pupils in regular classes and conferring with those teachers and with parents. By this method it is possible to service between fifty and one hundred different pupils twice weekly. The turnover of pupils is much more rapid, since their specific problems are discovered and treated almost individually in small groups. Of all the methods noted above this plan seems to be the most effective because it handles the greatest numbers and removes them from their regular classes only two short periods weekly.

### A Combination of Factors

Pupils with educational disability and retardation illustrate very clearly the effects of combinations of factors. Any one of the various elements taken by itself may not appear very grave, but when several are combined in one individual the cumulative results are serious indeed. To the parent such pupils do not appear to be handicapped physically or intellectually. When learning does not take place they are apt to blame the school. The return in good, improved scholarship with remedial programs is one of the best examples of good public relations which a school system is able to offer to its public.

### Questions and Topics for Discussion

1. Describe a case of very severe educational retardation which you have known.
2. What were the causes and what was done?
3. Report on what your school system does for the educationally retarded.
4. Add to the list of causes of educational retardation.
5. Elaborate on Fernald's technique of remedial education.
6. Discuss advantages and disadvantages of various plans for remedial education.

Note: Consult reference material at the end of Chapter 17.

# CHAPTER 17

## Programs in
## Remedial Education

THE COMPLEXITY of causes of educational retardation has been outlined in the preceding chapter. Programs of remedial education in the
various subjects will now be discussed. They rank in difficulty starting with the teaching of the blind or the totally deaf who need special
training and preparation, although that fact is not generally recognized.

### Methods of General Reading Instruction

There have been several methods of teaching reading and sooner or
later each of them has been blamed as the cause of retardation or of
failure in reading. Actually, in some of the more extreme cases any or
all methods of teaching would have failed. However, a brief review
of reading methods throws some light on the problem. The standard
method known to the present older generation was learning by the
alphabet. Learning the letters by rote was a difficult and generally
uninteresting exercise. Although the letters were presented a few at
a time, it required a feat of memorization known to be much beyond
the abilities of first graders. Painfully the letters were put together to
form a few simple words. It had the virtue of definiteness and later
assisted in locating words in the dictionary. In current practice the
alphabet is generally taught near the end of the first grade or in
the second grade. A second method started with learning a few words

from sight in much the same manner as a face may be recognized or the make of an automobile. Except that there was more interest, the more unfavorable features of this method compared with learning the letters as a series of unrelated units. Interest developed shortly after the words were combined into meaningful sentences. A third general method was the use of phonics in which letters and combinations of letters were learned by sound so that a word could be analyzed and pronounced. Combinations of the phonic and the word recognition methods have produced better and more interesting results than the alphabet method. In some extreme cases of phonic analysis pupils became so interested in the mechanics of pronunciation of words that they lost the meaning of the word. Psychologically it seems difficult to keep two different ideas or purposes in mind concurrently.

Another problem in learning to read is the present emphasis upon silent rather than oral reading. When silent reading is started early, the errors which pupils make may go undetected. Reading for comprehension by following directions in handwork may disclose this deficiency. Silent reading is much more rapid than oral reading, but in the case of slow-learning pupils the rate of oral reading is sufficient for most practical purposes.

### Fundamental Reading Abilities and Skills

The modern approach to reading involves the development of fundamental reading abilities and skills. The author is indebted to Dr. Gertrude Whipple, supervisor of reading, and to Mrs. Dorothy Cooper, principal of the McLean School of the Detroit public schools for their summary in these areas, which include: (1) word recognition skills; (2) skills in obtaining word meanings; (3) comprehension and interpretation skills; (4) skill in reading silently at suitable speed; (5) oral reading skills; and (6) skills in the use of books. In their list of reading skills the first grade includes such items as development of a sight vocabulary, interpretation of pictures accompanying reading matter; in the second grade, the ability to follow directions in reading material; recognizing hyphenated words in the third grade; reading for the main idea of a passage in the fourth grade; grasping the organization and structure of paragraphs in the fifth grades; and in the sixth grade adjusting speed of reading to the purpose. From these few random illustrations it is evident that reading implies many skills beyond mere recognition of the printed word.

### Corrective and Remedial Procedures in Reading

Many causes of retarded reading were outlined in the preceding chapter. Some corrective and remedial procedures are suggested to parallel these difficulties. The first factor to be considered is the feeling and emotional attitude which the pupil has already developed. It would have been fortunate if preventive measures had been put into operation in the beginning stage of reading readiness so that this condition would not have occurred. If attitudes deteriorate to an extreme degree, it is good practice to omit all reading for a short period and replace it with interesting experimental background materials. The logic of this practice should be as evident as the omission of certain foods which produce disturbing allergies. The professional opinion of the clinical psychologist or other specialized personnel should be taken into account.

*Physical and sensory causes.* In many other chapters already presented, as well as in others to follow, physical and sensory impairments are shown to be significant causes of reading retardation. It has been noted even after satisfactory correction has been made that visual or auditory sensations may not function effectively because of nerve impairment or of inadequate sensations reaching the central nervous system. The number of such extreme cases is comparatively small in comparison with many more obvious causes of reading retardation. Complete neurological examinations are necessary in such cases.

*Lateral dominance.* Lateral dominance has been widely proclaimed as a cause of confusion particularly in learning to move the eyes along the reading line from left to right. Some of the investigators lacked definite information about the extent of changed handedness or of ambidexterity, but when seeking causes it is easy to jump to conclusions about these interrelationships. Fernald[1] has done extensive and successful work with kinesthetic methods in which the forms of letters and words are traced with the finger and later combined with looking at and saying them. She notes that early Greek scholars advocated some of these combined methods which avoided exclusive dependence upon one avenue of learning such as visual impressions only. There are many methods by which learning may be strengthened.

*Motivation.* Unless there are some extreme causes of disability, progress in reading may be advanced by improved motivation. Exciting action stories of adventure encourage pupils to learn what happens at the end. Books which do not have specific labels of "first" reader printed conspicuously may entice an older retarded reader to become interested at that level. Books with social interests geared to chronological age but couched in easy and readable vocabulary are valuable aids. Incidental reading of signs in the environment have practical meaning for reading. A more important motivation is the realization that reading is the basis of practically all other school subjects.

*Individual attention.* In addition to the specific help which the remedial teacher gives in reading or in other subjects, the very fact of individual attention adds some subtle motivation which is difficult to define but which is a real asset. It assures the pupil that the school considers his problems important and gives him a new evaluation of his own importance and raises his own self-esteem. This restoration of morale is reflected in renewed hope in his parents which gives him further support. These personal and social qualities may be further enhanced if the visiting teacher becomes a member of the team and aids the pupil and his parents in these more positive and constructive attitudes.

*The process of remedial teaching.* The process of remedial teaching is an expression which should not be used in the singular because in reality there are as many processes as there are individual pupils in need of such services. The remedial teacher develops a folder contain-

---

[1] G.M. Fernald, *Remedial Techniques in Basic School Subjects*, McGraw-Hill Book Co., Inc., New York, 1943, 349 pp.

ing material pertinent to each individual pupil with such items as: (1) his initial survey of difficulties; (2) his physical or sensory defects; (3) his attitudes; (4) the analysis of his psychological profile such as illustrated in the Detroit Tests of Learning Aptitude; (5) the specific problem such as reversals, word calling, guessing, and many others. Progress entries should be kept up to date in regard to books read, processes improved, and any details pertinent to each individual. After a short period of exploration small groups of pupils with somewhat similar difficulties may be grouped together. This procedure economizes time and sight is not lost of the individual case.

Reading is a very complex process. Whenever there is partial or total failure an entire series of cause and effect relationships is put into operation. The threads of complexity may be traced one at a time but they lead into so many areas that it is impossible to state just what improvements have taken place. Any improvements spread slowly to other portions of the disability as was well illustrated in one of the author's earlier pilot studies. At the end of one semester little progress was reflected in scholastic grades issued by the regular teachers, but in a followup study two years later, these reading grades were much improved.

### Corrective and Remedial Measures in Spelling

Spelling ranks close to reading in importance, since words must be spelled accurately if reading is to be correct. Spelling utilizes the twenty-six letters of the alphabet, which seems to be very definite and specific. However, the English language has many silent letters in certain words, it has many different pronunciations of the same letter, and some of the phonetic soundings may be interpreted quite differently than the correct spelling indicates.

The methods of teaching spelling have gone through many changes but none of them are complete panaceas for correct spelling. In the days of the alphabet method in reading spelling was very formalized and there were liberal amounts of rote drill on words which were not necessarily those used in reading. The lists of words in the upper elementary grade spellers were among the most difficult in the dictionary and their meanings were far beyond the needs of those grade levels. Spelling was such an abstract and uninteresting subject any success was a pleasant surprise.

Changes in reading methods brought a new focus on spelling. The same words were developed in both reading and spelling. When phonics were taught they were applied to both subjects. This coordinated plan worked so well that the teaching of spelling tended to degenerate into an incidental by-product of reading. Spelling books began to disappear from classrooms. The phonic sounds of words created temptation to spell merely as words sounded. This, of course, added to lax standards. Adults with little formal education make some amazing spellings by this practice and words with different meanings result, such as the farmer's sign "No hunting aloud." Another subject combination came when writing and spelling were combined into a single activity. The ability to give equal attention to the correct spelling and to the quality of handwriting is generally beyond the powers of young children. This difficulty was increased when the exercises were dictated orally at too rapid a rate and with units too long for pupils with poor auditory attention spans to follow. Modernized spelling books are again coming into use with words suited to grade levels and to age interests. Specific time allotments are made for spelling instruction.

*Causes of poor spelling.* Many of the same factors which result in retardation in reading also operate for spelling. The emotional factors, discouragement, and trends toward reversals have been mentioned in earlier discussions. To this list may be added the temptation toward phonetic spelling. Poor visual memory for words is a common cause of misspelling and poor auditory memory contributes its quota as well. There seems to be less urgent need for correcting the errors in spelling than in other subjects. If spelling is nearly correct the pupil may rationalize that others will know what word it is. This temptation to approximate does not function as effectively in arithmetic in which the exact total makes a difference in money and in the amount of goods. Once an error is made in spelling the process of relearning seems to require unusual concentration and much more effort than did the original learning.

*Diagnostic procedures.* The various causes of misspelling suggest some diagnostic procedures. Brueckner and Melby[1] cite a list of twenty-four difficulties encountered by 275 pupils in a school system. They list the most frequent as "Has not mastered the steps in learning to spell a word," 88 times, and an equal number of "Writes poorly"; 78 cannot pronounce the words being studied, 71 had bad attitudes toward spelling, 49 did not associate the sound of the letters or the syllables with the spelling of the word, and so on. Gates[2] listed twenty-two specific causes under five general headings as follows: defects or deficiencies of training; unfavorable behavior; defects of sensory mechanisms; defects of motor mechanism; and defects or deficiencies of connecting mechanisms.

*Remedial procedures.* Because of the many difficulties cited above, it is evident that spelling is not the simple, easy, and definite process which too often it is assumed to be. Spelling should be correct the first time a word is to be spelled. Enough practice should be given to auditory, visual, and motor learning, together with the meaning and use of the word so that all phases of spelling are taken in account. Remedial teachers should be provided with profiles of the psychological constitution of each pupil to determine how much utilization of the various avenues of learning is possible so as to put less emphasis upon weak portions of that constitution. High ideals of correct spelling must be established and maintained although this is a difficult task in the case of young pupils. Older pupils frequently hear that chances of employment are much better if letters of application are spelled correctly. It would be of assistance toward a better psychology of spelling if adults who actually spell very well would not discount themselves by claiming to be poor spellers. In many instances such individuals perform on standardized spelling lists at a very high level yet continue to color the whole impression by chronically misspelling one or two words only. Actually they are good spellers but their negative psychology, based on incorrect data, tends to discourage children and young people from setting a high standard.

[1] L.J. Brueckner and E.O. Melby, *Diagnostic and Remedial Teaching*, Houghton Mifflin Co., Boston, 1931, pp. 396-399.
[2] A.I. Gates, *The Psychology of Reading and Spelling*, Teachers College, Columbia University Press, New York, 1922, p. 89.

## Handwriting

Handwriting is the third of four basic subjects in which errors and faulty standards are self-evident. The general effectiveness of schools is judged by the quality of handwriting. There is no single panacea for poor handwriting.

In the past few years the teaching of handwriting in the early primary grades has been encouraging the use of manuscript handwriting rather than the traditional cursive style of writing. The letters are made up of straight lines which resemble printing. Young pupils are able to master it more readily because of its greater simplicity. After about two years a change is generally made to cursive writing, although some school systems continue or allow individuals to continue with the manuscript method. In adult affairs practically all documents give specific instruction to print or to typewrite one's name and other information, which is a wide-open admission of handwriting illiteracy. Stenographers usually type the signer's name with a space left above it for the actual signature, which is count number two against handwriting.

There has also been a tradition that the brighter the individual the poorer his handwriting is supposed to be. This idea was fostered by the belief that handwriting was a purely mechanical process requiring no mental attention and that all interest was focused on the content rather than on the framework in which it was couched. Another factor interfering with good handwriting has been combining the teaching of handwriting with spelling. Both subjects suffered. When attention was directed principally to the correct spelling, attention to the quality of handwriting sank to a low ebb and vice versa.

### Causes of Handwriting Deficiency

*Inappropriate subject matter.* Certain old types of copybooks are now known to have had glaring pedagogical faults. The pupils were required to copy several lines of a simple sentence such as "The dog runs after the cat." The dog running after the cat once tells a story, but holds little interest after the first running has been understood. The purpose of handwriting to impart useful information has been realized after writing such a sentence once. This type of simple learning appealed more effectively to slow-learning rather than to rapid-learning minds. An upper elementary class of rapid learners found their own handwriting more interesting when they prepared an historical scrapbook of writing throughout the ages.

*Inappropriate materials.* In that same era writing with a traditional type of sharp pointed pen, dipped too frequently in ink, and catching liberal quantities of lint and other accessory materials from a cheap grade of paper was not conducive to good penmanship. It was the standard as early as in the third grade. What was written became quite incidental to the mechanical distractions in the writing itself.

*Unsupervised formal drills.* Since handwriting could be conducted individually and silently the teacher found time to tend to the other mechanics of daily schedules and hence paid little or no attention to how the writing was actually done. Bad habits of incorrect posture, placement of paper, and other details were easily overlooked. Young children cannot correctly proceed without teacher stimulation and direction.

*Individual differences.* There are individual differences in many kinds of mental factors which are utilized in handwriting. Motor or kinesthetic skill and speed in rhythm and timing are among the principal components of good handwriting. When these abilities are immature, young children's readiness for handwriting suffers. Formal drills to develop such skills add discouragement and makes further trial a greater effort. Individual differences exist in the size of the handwriting itself. Expecting uniform size of writing for all members of a class is as unrealistic as requiring them to be the same physical size. In some earlier investigations the author noted a correspondence between deficiency in gross orientation for the general environment and the miniature orientation of knowing the correct direction when starting to write any specific letter. Uncertainty and aimless wandering on the page may be noted when the direction must change from up to down, or from left to right.

*Other causes.* Poor eyesight, faulty hearing, general nervous debility,

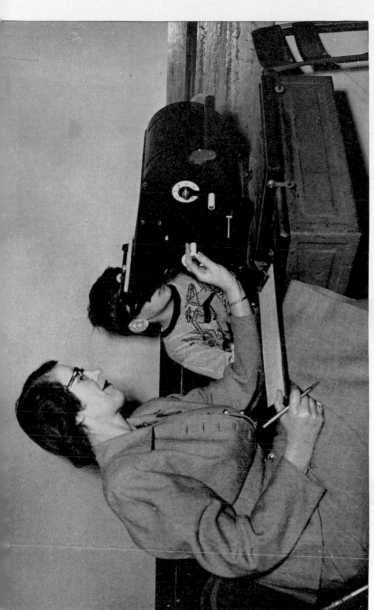

Visual screening test with the Ortho-Rater, Department of Education, University of Chicago.

Finding reading levels at the Reading Clinic, Department of Psychology, Temple University, Philadelphia.

*Courtesy of the Reading Clinic, Temple University.*

and various personality traits are among the causes of poor handwriting. The great majority of left-handed pupils develop bizarre methods of holding paper and pencil unless there is early detection. If the pupil is to write with his left hand the pencil should be held far enough out in front of the hand so that the writing may be seen in process. Many other specific causes contribute to poor handwriting.

Quality should be a first consideration, after which speed should be regulated so that quality is not sacrificed. A rapid rate with acceptable quality is a valuable asset throughout school and even with the modern conveniences of typewriters and shorthand, the majority of pupils must do great amounts of handwriting. The instruction in handwriting should be varied in accordance with actual conditions met in the course of events. Learning to write for short periods with only a notebook being held in one hand, writing with paper held against a vertical surface, writing on hard surfaces or on soft ones, writing on the sands of a beach, and writing when one must hurry, add interest to a grossly neglected topic which merits a much better place in the program of elementary education.

### Arithmetic

Arithmetic has undergone significant changes in the past few decades. The rote phases of learning number combinations have become less important than a well-defined number sense which is fundamental to arithmetic. What adding really means is probably more significant than the fact that two plus three equals five. When its value is understood there is more interest in finding out that this sum is five, rather than four. From the very beginning the meaning of numbers should be the first consideration. Their meaning needs to be specific and concrete in the early stages but eventually they may be carried up into very abstract and generalized concepts. Numbers and mathematics become the basis of most other sciences.

In the early stages of developing number sense it seems necessary for pupils to visualize small numbers in terms of actual quantity. Unless the pupil is able to see four men walking together when two men plus two men are mentioned, learning the abstract concept that two plus two equals four is of little value. Nevertheless, many pupils learn whatever arithmetic they know only by the knowledge of number combinations. Learning the multiplication tables one set at a time is much easier if the pupil senses and appreciates how these numbers increase by multiplication. When the pupil understands these meanings he will appreciate the need of mastering many combinations and having them readily at hand so that he does not have to stop to look them up repeatedly.

### Causes of Retardation in Arithmetic

There are many causes of retardation in arithmetic. The actual errors may be noted but why they occur is not always easy to discover. Errors may occur in each of the four fundamental processes, as well as in common and decimal fractions, percentages, and in problem solving. The concept of zero is one of the most confusing questions of all. If properly taught, it should cause much less trouble. Unless the pupil understands the meaning of multiplication by two-place numbers or by higher ones, performing the operation by following a previous example is of little real value. Estimates of the actual value of numbers and of reasonable answers is usually foreign to the training in arithmetic. This deficiency is particularly true in the correct placement of decimals.

Vocabulary difficulties have been a chief cause of failure in problem solving, although the modern arithmetic texts have usually been checked for difficulty of words by standardized lists. Extraneous numbers in problems such as dates of events often are incorporated in some incongruous manner into incorrect solutions. The slow-learning pupils have particular difficulty with the selection of the correct process in problem solving.

It is comparatively easy to score the results of an arithmetic test and rate the pupil according to his grade level. The value is lost unless the teacher uses the pupil's work sheets or test materials to discover his particular difficulties and to assist him in correcting his errors. If this is not done, he becomes more confused. A similar process should be used on his written or oral work if effective learning is to take place.

Arithmetic is an exact science. It should be understood correctly in order to add to the feeling of confidence and definite accomplishment. Although the theory of formal discipline in which tasks learned in one subject have values which may be transferred to other subjects has been largely discredited, the fact of success may provide some momentum for success in other subjects as well.

## Results of Remedial Programs

Since the causes of educational retardation are known to be complex and have interrelationships with many fields, it is difficult to isolate specific factors or evidences to prove the beneficial effects of remedial programs. The opinion of the remedial teacher should have high priority, especially if substantiated by the results of standardized achievement tests. In general practice the regular teacher usually determines the report-card marks which may continue to be at variance with the judgment of the remedial teacher. This difference of opinion may have logical causes if the remedial teacher has spent most of her time on developmental materials whereas the regular teacher must judge progress on subjects she is currently teaching and in which the pupil is continuing to have difficulty.

In some of the remedial programs in which the problems are deep-seated the results do not begin to show immediately, but come to light some time later. In a two-year follow-up of the author's 1924-1925 pilot program many pupils were making much better relative progress than was noted at the immediate end of the program. At the time of the remedial program all 60 pupils were nine years of age and mostly in the third and fourth grades.

Since the two-year report showed encouraging results further follow-up was made. Nine years after the pilot program this author chanced to meet one of the girl students who was being graduated from high school. Upon questioning she readily recalled the remedial program and enthusiastically stated that she had received lasting help from the remedial teacher who had taken a personal interest in her.

The services of a graduate student were available to make a follow-up study of all 60 pupils when they were eighteen years old or older. With regard to the grade eventually reached, nine of the sixty finally left school when enrolled in the eighth grade or lower, twenty-three were in grades nine to eleven, and twenty-seven were in the twelfth grade or in college. Only one could not be located within a year or two after the program had closed. Nearly one-half of the total reached the twelfth grade or college which is higher than the proportion of the general pupil population of that time. It is evident that coaching must have been a very practical aid to them when they were failing and discouraged at an early age and many years before they were ready to finish school.

There were some interesting relationships between the final grade reached and the early characteristics. Intelligence had some mild correlation with progress, since the eighth-grade group or lower had a median intelligence quotient of 88, the nine-to-eleven grade group 92, and the higher group 95. There was a trend toward arrested mental development in the lower group with four of the nine cases having second individual examinations and with intelligence quotients falling from ten to fifteen points from the first examination. In the group reaching the highest grade, three of them had higher intelligence quotients of group intelligence tests than on the earlier individual tests.

The influence of the nonintellectual factors was probably more important than the mental ratings in helping to determine eventual school progress. Of the lower group all nine had been characterized at the time of the program as "poor" or "very poor" in traits of character and personality, eight of the nine had homes which were uncooperative with the school, and the ninth's home was described as neutral in attitude. Among these nine cases there were many physical disabilities and other unfavorable circumstances, described as general bodily weakness, nervous, dirty, ragged, sleepy, shiftless, tardy, poor vision, paranoid tendencies and similar characterizations. These unfortunate cases are among the best illustrations available of mild defects operating in combination which nullify efforts of schools. None of these cases qualified for any of the usual types of classes for physically or mentally handicapped children.

A vivid example of a case complicated by neurological disorder whose real nature was not too readily recognized at the time came to light in the subsequent history. The boy was described as lacking in self-control, continually removing his glasses, tying his shoe laces, fixing his hose, and playing with various small toys which he always carried in his pockets. He interrupted all regular classes and coaching activities to pick up books and other materials which he had forgotten or misplaced. At the age of fourteen he died of spinal meningitis.

The characterizations of the higher twenty-seven cases presented a much more favorable picture. Only five of the home attitudes were uncooperative, three were poor or very poor in home status, while the personality and physical deviations were of a much more minor nature. Among these difficult cases were overstimulated children who were constantly admonished at home to hurry so as to do better schoolwork, including two who were babyish and immature, and three who had speech defects. As a group, they were more nearly free from non-intellectual factors than the other groups which failed to progress as far in school.

A different type of result was reported by Powell[1] on a group of two-hundred fifty cases who had remedial assistance as contrasted with a control group of the same size who needed such special assistance which was not available. The latter group received only whatever incidental help the regular program was able to offer. Powell's study was not directed at the educational results but at the social and personality adjustments of the two groups. He checked all available sources of evidence such as referral to and study by visiting teachers, placement in special classes for socially maladjusted pupils, police and juvenile records, and further study by psychological clinics and other adjustment agencies. The experimental group showed only four per cent of cases with such records, whereas the control group showed 20 per cent with evidences of maladjustment. While this report has been mentioned in Chapter 6 on Diagnostic and Remedial Programs in Deviant Behavior it takes on added significance in the field of educational retardation.

It was also noted in that chapter that only a very small percentage of pupils who had been suspended from school for serious malbehavior

[1] H.F. Powell, "Social Adjustments as Related to Reading Disability," master's thesis, University of Michigan, Ann Arbor, Mich., 1943.

had been serviced previously by the visiting teachers whose general remedial services apparently have very favorable results when available. Programs of remedial education are known to be as necessary as those for blind, deaf, or other types of handicaps. They occupy a marginal position between special education for the exceptional and regular education. They should enjoy the services of the "team" approach by the remedial teacher, the regular teacher, the special supervisor of subject matter, the visiting teacher, and the school psychologist. The returns for remedial education are high when a comprehensive program is put into effect and are measured not only in actual educational improvement but in changed home and community attitudes and in personal and social adjustment of the pupils themselves.

### Questions and Topics for Discussion

1. Visit a class of remedial education.
2. Report on what your local school system is doing in remedial education.
3. Discuss remedial education and its relationship to delinquency and deviant behavior.
4. Discuss the training necessary for a remedial teacher.

### A. Organizations

1. American Educational Research Association, Washington, D.C.
2. Association for Supervision and Curriculum Development, Washington, D.C.
3. National Conference for Measurements Used in Education, R.D. North, Secretary-Treasurer, 21 Audubon Ave., New York 32.

Note: See also the list of Educational Test Publishers at the end of Chapter 2.

### B. Periodicals

1. *Education* (monthly September to May), The Palmer Co., Hingham, Mass.
2. *Educational Administration and Supervision* (monthly October to May), 10 E. Centre St., Baltimore 2, Md.

3. *Educational and Psychological Measurement* (quarterly), College Station, Durham, N.C.
4. *Elementary School Journal* (monthly September to May), University of Chicago, Chicago 37.
5. *Journal of Educational Psychology* (monthly October to May), Columbia University, New York.
6. *Journal of Educational Research* (monthly September to May), Dembar Publications, Madison 6, Wis.
7. *School Review* (monthly September to May), University of Chicago, Chicago.

## C. Books

1. Adams, F., L. Gray, and D. Reese, *Teaching Children to Read*, Ronald Press Co., New York, 1949, 525 pp.
2. Baker, H.J., *Educational Disability and Case Studies in Remedial Teaching*, Public School Publishing Co., Cincinnati, Ohio, 1929, 172 pp. (out of print).
3. ———, and B. Leland, *In Behalf of Non-Readers*, C.A. Gregory Co., Cincinnati, Ohio, 1940, 40 pp.
4. Betts, E.A., *Foundations of Reading Instruction*, American Book Co., New York, 1946, 757 pp.
5. ———, *The Prevention and Correction of Reading Difficulties*, Row, Peterson and Company, Evanston, Ill., 1936, 402 pp.
6. Blair, G.M., *Diagnostic and Remedial Teaching* (rev. ed.), The Macmillan Co., New York, 1957, 409 pp.
7. Bond, G.L., and E.B. Wagner, *Teaching the Child to Read* (rev. ed.), The Macmillan Co., New York, 1950, 467 pp.
8. ———, *The Auditory and Speech Characteristics of Poor Readers*, Teachers College Contributions to Education, No. 657, Columbia University Press, New York, 1935, 48 pp.
9. Broom, M.E., M.A.A. Duncan, D. Emig, and J. Stueber, *Effective Reading Instruction* (2nd ed.), McGraw-Hill Book Co., Inc., New York, 1951, 499 pp.
10. Brueckner, L.J., and E.O. Melby, *Diagnostic and Remedial Teaching*, Houghton Mifflin Co., Boston, 1931, 598 pp.
11. Buckingham, B.R., *Elementary Arithmetic*, Ginn and Co., Boston, 1953, 750 pp.
12. Carmichael, L., and W.F. Dearborn, *Reading and Visual Fatigue*, Houghton Mifflin Co., Boston, 1947, 483 pp.
13. Durrell, D.D., *Improvement of Basic Reading Abilities*, World Book Co., Yonkers, N.Y., 1940, 407 pp.

14. Ephron, B.K., *Emotional Difficulties in Reading*, The Julian Press, New York, 1953, 289 pp.

15. Fernald, B., *Remedial Techniques in Basic School Subjects*, McGraw-Hill Book Co., Inc., New York, 1943, 349 pp.

16. Fitzgerald, J.A., *The Teaching of Spelling*, Bruce Publishing Co., Milwaukee, Wis., 1951, 233 pp.

17. Gates, A.I., *The Improvement of Reading* (rev. ed.), The Macmillan Co., New York, 1947, 657 pp.

18. ———, *Spelling Difficulties in 3,876 Words*, Bureau of Publications, Columbia University, New York, 1937, 166 pp.

19. Greene, H.A., A.N. Jorgensen, and J.R. Gerberich, *Measurement and Evaluation in the Elementary School* (2nd ed.), Longmans Green and Co., New York, 1953, 617 pp.

20. Harris, A.J., *How to Increase Reading Ability*, Longmans Green and Company, New York, 1947, 582 pp.

21. Lennes, N.J., *The Teaching of Arithmetic*, The Macmillan Co., New York, 1924, 486 pp.

22. Morton, R.L., *Teaching Children Arithmetic*, Silver Burdett Company, New York, 1953, 566 pp.

23. National Society for the Study of Education, *The Teaching of Arithmetic*, Fiftieth Yearbook, Part II, National Society for the Study of Education, University of Chicago Press, Chicago, 1952, 302 pp.

24. ———, *Reading in the Elementary School*, Forty-eighth Yearbook, Part II, National Society for the Study of Education, University of Chicago Press, Chicago, 1949, 343 pp.

25. Rinsland, H.R., *A Basic Vocabulary of Elementary School Children*, The Macmillan Co., New York, 1950, 636 pp.

26. Robinson, H.M., *Why Pupils Fail in Reading*, University of Chicago Press, Chicago, 1946, 257 pp.

27. Spencer, P.L., and M. Brydegaard, *Building Mathematical Concepts*, Henry Holt and Co., Inc., New York, 1952, 372 pp.

28. Spitzer, H.F., *The Teaching of Arithmetic*, Houghton Mifflin Co., Boston, 1948, 397 pp.

29. Wheat, H.G., *How to Teach Arithmetic*, Row, Peterson and Company, Evanston, Ill., 1951, 438 pp.

30. Witty, P., *Helping Children Read Better*, Science Research Associates, Chicago, 1950, 49 pp.

31. Wilson, G.M., *Teaching the New Arithmetic* (2nd ed.), McGraw-Hill Book Co., Inc., New York, 1951, 483 pp.

32. Woolf, M.D., and J.A. Woolf, *Remedial Reading*, McGraw-Hill Book Co., Inc., New York, 1957, 424 pp.

# PART 6

*Sensory Disorders
and Defects*

# CHAPTER 18

## The Anatomy and
## Physiology of Vision

IT HAS BEEN SAID that the eyes are the windows of the soul. As we exchange greetings the sparkle and radiance of our eyes often reveal more real feeling than do spoken words. The searching gaze of the tiny child seeks to discover our moods and attitudes. They form their judgments accordingly and puzzle us with their understanding when they have passed over our words. We failed to note the language which came through their eyes rather than through ears. Even domestic and wild animals are keen observers of human behavior.

Correctly or incorrectly one's intelligence is often judged by the brightness or sparkle of the eyes. Likewise beauty of women and handsomeness of men are universally measured by that standard. The blind who lack the luster of normal eyes must compensate through other signs of bodily beauty and by lovely traits of personality.

Seeing is one of the most important of the five senses. The great majority of all impressions come through the eyes in a seeing person. The blind cultivate the other senses, particularly hearing, when getting about. Their keen sense of smell provides an unusual awareness of objects missed by those who see. The fine tactile sense of their delicate fingers enables them to fly over the Braille letters as a substitute for seeing the printed word. But even with these clever substitutions vision is overwhelmingly preferred to blindness.

As is the case in many other human qualities vision is usually functioning at much less than maximum capacity. This statement does

283

not imply that concentration to greatest capacity should be practiced one hundred per cent of the time. However, training in better visual observation may bring much richer meanings to life. The world of nature has unlimited possibilities for observation. Through concentration the details of distant objects may be multiplied over what a casual look may reveal. Likewise, the form and substance of tiny plants, animals, and insects may be observed by closer attention. Shades of color vary by infinitesimal degrees which become more meaningful through patient practice in taking better notice.

Keen vision is a valuable asset in many kinds of occupations, and in hunting the sharp eye is a basic requirement. When going about in daily routines, it is possible to see much or to see little. Some thought and attention to what may be seen can easily develop into a useful habit. In the case of deafness, keenness of vision is cultivated beginning with very young children in order to compensate in part for lack of hearing. The deaf must be very keen observers of others' lips if they are to be successful in lip reading. Visitors to deaf schools and classes marvel at the visual attention which is given to teachers and to classmates. The deaf not only see more, but they learn to note finer shades of feelings and emotions. Parents and teachers of normal children can be very helpful in training children to observe. Discretion must always be used toward the few whose eyes are weak or defective, lest such training be harmful rather than beneficial.

In addition to the great majority of school children who see reasonably well, there is a smaller number who have great difficulty in seeing. Among these are a group who benefit by special care and training in the use of their eyes. A much smaller group do not have effective or practical use of their eyes and are considered blind. In order that the problems of the partially-seeing and of the blind may be better understood, the present chapter describes the anatomy and the physiology of the eye and the mechanics of vision. Methods of examination are also included as preliminary explanation.

### The Mechanisms of Vision

When reduced to its lowest terms, seeing is based on a simple principle of mechanics. Rays of light enter the eye via the pupil, and in passing through the crystalline lens they are bent to a focus on the retina at the rear of the eyeball. The optic nerve embedded in the retina transmits the visual impression to the brain where meaning is given to it. Major or minor variations in the structure of the eye produce some type and degree of a typical vision. Gross deviations in structure or diseases of the eye may cause blindness.

The accompanying diagram of the human eye is helpful in understanding the seeing process. The most external portion is the transparent cornea. The upper eyelids cover it instantaneously by reflex action for protection from flying objects. The constant winking washes

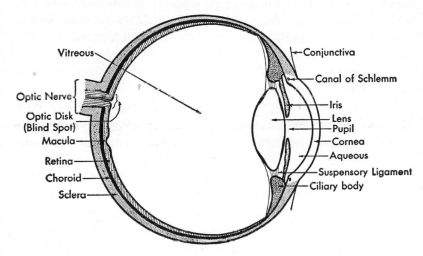

*Courtesy of National Society for the Prevention of Blindness, New York.*

**The human eye.**

away any dirt with an antiseptic fluid supplied by the tear glands. Just behind the cornea is a small chamber of aqueous liquid through which the rays of light pass to the crystalline lens.

The pupil of the eye is the black opening surrounded by the colored iris which gives the characteristic color or pigment to the eyes. The iris is capable of expanding or contracting so as to regulate the amount or intensity of light which may enter the lens. Special automatic nerve centers make this adjustment which is supplemented by voluntary or involuntary partial closing of the eyelids. Immediately behind the pupil and the iris is the crystalline lens, which is the important adjustment mechanism for focusing the rays of light upon the retina. The lens is suspended and held in place by a ciliary body whose ligaments control its adjustments for flattening or widening to bend the light rays. The ciliary body also operates the expansion and contraction of the iris so that the pupil of the eye varies in size as noted above.

When the lens is relatively more flattened the rays of light are bent or deflected in lesser degree, but when the lens is widened or becomes thicker the deflection is greater. It can adjust to many shapes to accommodate for focusing images on the retina. The lens also serves as a kind of color filter which reduces the blue and violet tints which accompany the shorter light waves. In older persons the lens gradually darkens so that these colors are noticed less and less. The lens becomes less flexible in middle life so that glasses are generally needed in order to compensate for this loss, a condition known as presbyopia.

*Variations of focusing.* There are many kinds and degrees of variations in focusing. Perfect vision, known as emmetropia, is believed to occur in not more than two per cent of the population. From this ideal condition there are almost imperceptible degrees of defects and diseases extending into total blindness. Hyperopia or farsightedness occurs when the lens is not sufficiently convex to bring the focus on the retina but after it has been reached. Glasses with convex lens are needed. Myopia or shortsightedness is the opposite condition and requires convex lens to delay the focus until the retina is reached. When the cornea or external window of the eye has imperfections in its curved surface, blurred images occur in a condition known as astigmatism. Glasses with compensating corrections are needed. The imperfections which cause hyperopia or myopia may be due to the distortions of the lens or to the relative length of the eyeball or to both conditions. The lens is the principal organ in deflecting the rays of light. Some deflection is caused in passing through the cornea, in passing through the aqueous liquid between the cornea and the lens, and in passing through the vitreous liquid in the main portion of the eyeball. In later paragraphs the methods of examination will be discussed.

*Variations in fusion of vision.* In the interest of simplicity, the description of focusing seemed to apply to one eye, but actually the process applies to both eyes. The existence of two eyes rather than merely one, adds further complexity to the process of seeing. Each eye produces separate visual images, but in normal vision these images should blend so that they appear as one, although this is not always the case. Double vision, astigmatism, or blurred vision in one eye, and two visual images of different sizes are some of the varieties of poor fusion. Whenever there is imperfect fusion headaches from visual strain often occur, and may be accompanied by general loss of interest in reading and other schoolwork. The causes are many, but chiefly result from the two eyeballs not being focused on objects with perfect coordination. In the ideal condition the two images coordinate almost exactly, but with enough slight difference at the margins so that depth perception occurs. Depth perception is not possible in using one eye only, except as the mind *imagines* it. Vision is much more meaningful when perfect bifocal vision with depth perception is present. The crossing of optic nerves from the two eyes and leading to the brain may also be related to depth perception.

A typical fusion produces squinting or straining of one eye in attempting to match the image from the other. The squint may be convergent when the eyes converge or turn inward, divergent when they turn outward and the angle of vision of one eye is higher or lower than the other. Properly fitted glasses may remedy some of these divergences. Qualified examiners sometimes recommend bandaging the stronger eye so that the weaker eye may gain strength through forced use.

*The eyeball and the optic nerve.* In the preceding paragraphs brief descriptions were made of normal and abnormal mechanics which affect focusing the visual images on the retina where the optic nerve is located. The eyeball consists of three coats, each with its unique and specific function. The outer coat, or sclera, is composed of a tough substance which keeps the eyeball in shape and protects the delicate structures within. The portion which is visible appears as a white area surrounding the iris and pupil of the eye. Since it is comparatively thin in childhood, the whites of the eyes seem to be bluish because the middle coat shows through. The sclera has few nerves and acts primarily as a protection. Filling the eyeball is the vitreous liquid. The middle layer, known as the choroid, is heavily enlaced with tiny blood vessels, both arteries and veins. Since the eye is a very active organ of the body it needs abundant nourishment and replenishment of life processes. The inner coat is the retina and contains the endings of the optic nerve. It may be more accurately described as being nerve tissue rather than any other substance with its structure originating from the brain.

The retina extends over most of the inner surface of the eyeball so that light rays may be perceived from various directions. However, there is one point of most minute vision known as the macula directly in line from a point straight ahead of the pupil and where most of the visual images fall. The optic nerve endings in the retina are in microscopic rods or cones. The rods are estimated to be 130,000,000 in number and are primarily sensitive to low-level illumination. They give impressions primarily of outlines in shades of gray. There are about 7,000,000 cone-shaped cells which yield color impressions of red, green, and blue-violet light. Although much has been said about color blindness, all but a few persons can distinguish between red and green. Quite near the macula the optic nerve leads from the retina to the brain, and at that tiny spot there are no receptive rods or cones, which produces a tiny blind spot. It is so small that it seldom interferes with normal vision.

It is as yet a mystery just what takes place when vision functions. Some type of chemical or electro-chemical reaction operates to stimulate the optic nerve or some tiny portion of it. This impulse is transmitted to the brain where it is magnified many thousand times. On their journey, the optic nerves from each eye cross over to the other side of the body. Some type of electrical or chemical induction from the adjacent optic nerves when crossing may produce or enhance three-dimensional vision or depth perception which may also be caused by the slightly irregular spacing of the eyes. From all of these microscopic phenomena more than 85 per cent of all our impressions from the world outside ourselves are obtained.

## The Examination of Vision

Hundreds of thousands of school children have been examined for defects of vision. A small number are blind; a slightly larger number have very poor vision; a much larger number have vision corrected by wearing glasses; a yet larger number have mild defects which should probably be corrected; only a small number have perfect vision. The majority of young children have a tendency to be farsighted. Learning to read or to do other close work at a desk is much more taxing than looking at distant scenes or across a schoolroom. Periods of close work should be short and mixed with tasks using more distant vision.

*Pre-natal conditions.* Any venereal condition in the mother during pregnancy should be treated medically. Farrell[1] reports that if all venereally infected prospective mothers could be given a Wasserman test and treatment administered before the fourth month of pregnancy that the venereal disease problem affecting newborn babies would be solved.

*Testing of newborn infants.* The vision examination of babies should start immediately after birth and it should be the responsibility of the physician in charge. In a report issued by the National Society for the Prevention of Blindness[2] three physicians from the Boston area have cooperated in constructing an apparatus containing a nine-inch-wide, sixteen-foot-long strip of striped paper reeled before an infant's eyes on two spools. This reel contains stripes of black and white of varying thickness to attract the infant's eye. Nearly all of the infants responded, and those who did not were found to be blind or had very defective vision.

*Testing of preschool children.* The physician should make use of the ophthalmoscope in young children if there is the slightest evidence of visual defect. Two- or three-year olds may be asked to name small familiar objects placed at varying distances. Further methods of testing for four-year-olds are also suggested by Dr. Walter Fink[3] who

[1] T.H. Farrell, "Some Causes of Blindness," *The Sight-Saving Review*, 1935, 5, pp. 108-115.

[2] National Society for the Prevention of Blindness, "Vision Test for Newborn Infants," *The Sight-Saving Review*, 1957, 27, pp. 22-24.

[3] W.H. Fink, "Ocular Defects in Preschool Children," *The Sight-Saving Review*, 1954, 24, pp. 196-200.

recommends drawing a hand or other familiar figure on a circular card which may be rotated at different angles. The child indicates using first one eye, then the other, the direction of the hand or object, and finally both eyes are tested together.

*Testing of school-age children.* For testing children of school age, three methods or types of examinations will be described: (1) screening by the Snellen Letter Chart or by the "E" Symbol Chart; (2) informal observations by parents and teachers; and (3) examinations by eye specialists.

*The Snellen Letter Chart and "E" Symbol Chart.* Two of the most practical methods of visual screening used by teachers and school nurses, are the Snellen Letter Chart and the "E" Symbol Chart, shown in the accompanying illustrations. The recommended distance is 20 feet from the eye, which is the usual distance for vision without accommodation to focus on the retina. For young children the Symbol "E" chart is the most practical since the pupil does not have to read the letter, but, by pointing with the arms or fingers, can indicate the direction of the shafts of the "E." The largest symbol on both kinds of charts is normally seen at a distance of 200 feet and should ordinarily be seen with ease at 20 feet. The others are arranged in descending size for distances of 100, 70, 50, 40, 30, 20, 15, and 10 feet respectively. The pupil or teacher holds a card in front of one eye while the other is being tested. If a hand is held instead of a card, care should be taken not to press it on to the eye, so that the vision will be blurred when that eye is to be tested. The cards upon which the symbols are printed should be kept clean and white and should be well lighted.[1]

In testing, the examiner usually starts with one of the larger symbols and gradually decreases to the smaller sizes. It is possible to cover the symbols singly with a frame, or in the case of the "E" symbols to cut the card up so that only one of each size is made up into a pack. The examiner may use the one "E" of each size several times, removing it from view and rotating it to a different axis. This procedure helps to make a game of the test so that children are

---

[1] At a nominal cost there is available from the National Society for the Prevention of Blindness, 1790 Broadway, New York 19, *A Guide for Eye Inspection and Testing Visual Acuity.*

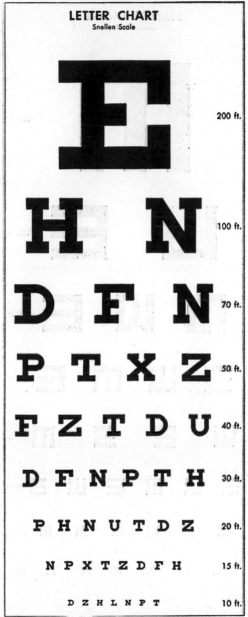

Courtesy of National Society for the Prevention
of Blindness, New York.

Snellen Letter Chart.

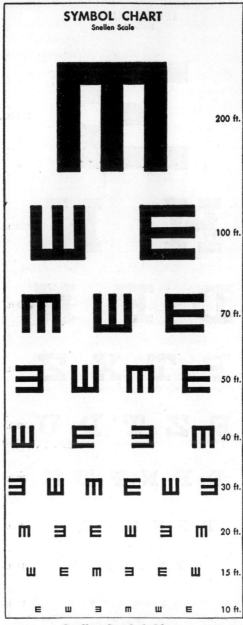

Snellen Symbol Chart.

pleased. It is also more convenient to handle if the examiner carries it to different locations. The right eye is usually tested first. The examiner may eventually reach a line or size which may be seen correctly but the next smaller size is seen with great difficulty and with much guessing. He then returns to the line above and considers it to be the distance of practical vision of that eye. If the pupil can see only at the line of 50 feet, the notation is made of 20/50, which means that what he sees at a distance of 20 feet he should be able to see at 50 feet. This notation is not a fraction in the usual meaning and does *not* denote 40 per cent vision. According to equivalent percentages mathematically worked out for the American Medical Association, 20/50 is 76.5 per cent of perfect vision; 20/200 is 20 per cent, and not 10 per cent, of perfect vision. The left eye is tested and recorded in the same manner. The degree of acuity may not be the same for the two eyes.

*Wheel chart tests for astigmatism.* In astigmatism the visual image may be blurred in certain portions, but clear in others. The astigmatism may also produce hyperopia or myopia in certain areas of the vision field. The chart for astigmatism consists of lines radiating from the center and intersecting a series of concentric circles of increasing sizes. Children with no astigmatism see the chart as being of about equal darkness or lightness in all portions, but individuals with astigmatism believe there are definite shades of difference in various portions.

*The Massachusetts Vision Test.* This test is somewhat more elaborate than the "E" chart since it makes use of the Betts' "telebinocular" with a series of slides which give stereographic vision. It detects astigmatism, errors of refraction, and inadequate fusion of the image from the two eyes functioning as a team. This test requires more elaborate and expensive apparatus than the Snellen "E," but discovers more minute and complex visual defects. As a simple device the "E" chart does remarkably well, although the rate of detection is lower according to a study conducted in St. Louis, Mo., in 1948-1949.[1]

*Observations by teachers and parents.* One of the limitations of

[1] F.M. Foote and M.M. Crane, "An Evaluation of Vision Screening," *Exceptional Children*, 20, 1954, pp. 153-161 and 180.

testing by the methods just noted is that the child may strain his eyes to some degree so as to test approximately normal which is not the true state of his vision. Observation by parents and teachers may give additional and more meaningful clues to possible diseases of the eyes as well as to defects of accommodation and fusion.

The pupil may hold his books or other materials much too close to his eyes. In a few instances this condition may have become a habit without visual meaning, but if it occurs with all kinds of materials and in many situations it is probably a symptom of myopia. In converse manner there may be an unusual interest in objects very far away and a tendency to avoid any kind of close work. It may indicate hyperopia. Myopic vision is more likely to attract attention because it is shown by little or no interest in outdoor games of ball and by tripping or stumbling over small objects. Shutting or covering one eye, holding the head at some unusual angle, and brushing away blur may be indications of astigmatism or of lack of fusion. If the eyes are weak they may shed tears too easily or be too sensitive to bright lights.

Bloodshot eyes are a cause for concern. Eyes that seem listless and with no sparkle of childhood or youth may indicate some defect or disease or they may reflect a generally weakened physical state. Conjunctivitis is an inflammation of the connecting tissue or conjunctiva. One of the more common forms in childhood is "pinkeye" which is a contagious condition, often becoming epidemic in school, where many children are in close personal contact. Pus discharge and rubbing of the eyes easily spreads the infection. In chronic epidemics strict medical inspection may be necessary to remove some general source of infection. Sties are infections of the roots of eyelashes and usually run their course within a period of a day or two but sometimes they are chronic and become prevalent in an entire neighborhood. Sties and pinkeye are temporary conditions and ordinarily have no permanent effect upon vision. However, they may lead to serious damage unless checked.

Accidents may cause serious injury to the eyes. In playing ball the eyes are sometimes hit. Children may fall on sticks or be hit with other sharp objects and injure their eyes. When he was only five years old, Louis Braille cut one eye with his father's knife. An infection spread to the other eye and soon he was blind in both eyes. Burns also take their toll of vision. All of these accidents should have the prompt and expert medical care of specialists in visual conditions and diseases. Other conditions of the eyes may not affect vision. Puffy eyelids, when accompanied by general changes in bodily status or condition should serve as a symptom of need for medical care. Eyelids sometimes become swollen so that children find it difficult to open them in the morning. Such sticking, if chronic, should have medical attention; this is also true of children with dark circles under their eyes. In extreme cases the beauty of the features may be permanently marred.

Albinism is a condition which affects vision. There is a lack of pigment which is noticeable in the hair as well as in the iris and in the choroid coat of the eye. The iris has a pinkish appearance which is probably caused by reflection from the blood vessels in the interior of the eye. The eyes of the albino are very sensitive to light since the pigment is lacking. While albinism is not very common, with only one case in every twenty thousand of the population, it is an hereditary condition.

*Eye specialists.* The examinations by the Snellen methods and observations by parents and teachers are very important as screening devices and their continued use is strongly recommended. Whenever any unusual condition is discovered, referral to eye specialists should be made. Special attention should be given to the terms oculist, ophthalmologist, optometrist, and optician since there are important distinctions between the types of services which they are qualified to give. The terms "oculist" and "ophthalmologist" may be used interchangeably, since both titles refer to registered physicians. They are qualified to examine for general medical conditions of the eyes as well as for refraction and for visual accommodation. While they are properly addressed as "Dr.," they seldom write it in front of their names or put it on their office doors or on their stationery, but have it appear as M.D. after their names.

The term "optometrist" applies to a doctor of optometry who is qualified to examine for refraction and for accommodation of vision but not for diseases of vision. Frequently the optometrist may be associated with the offices of the ophthalmologist where he carries on his professional services. If he has a bona fide degree in optometry he may be properly addressed as "Dr." but he also writes his professional degree of M.D. after his name and omits the "Dr." before it.

Any of these three specialists may write prescriptions for glasses which are to be filled by the optician who is a technician for making or dealing in glasses or in filling prescriptions. Unless he has a medical or optometric degree the term "Dr." would give an erroneous impression. He deals with highly calibrated optical instruments designed to correspond to the measuring instruments used by the optometrist or ophthalmologist in their recommendations and prescriptions, and is familiar with their methods of examination.

The number of ophthalomologists and optometrists is much too limited for the services which are needed and are found mainly in the larger cities. All physicians have some training in the field of vision as part of their over-all medical curriculum. Many family doctors examine for errors of refraction when specialists are not available. Unfortunately glasses are manufactured in large quantities with varying degrees of refraction, and in forty-three of the states they may be purchased over the counter without a medical or optometrical prescription. Such practices are far from ideal and certainly should not be used for children. Anyone who selects glasses in this manner probably tries various pairs until one seems to give better vision. Whether it is proper for his eyes, too strong or too weak appears to be beside the point.

*Testing by eye specialists.* Testing by the bona fide specialists noted above is a very thorough and exact examination. At the beginning some of the simpler Snellen or equivalent methods are used and give a rough estimate of the visual condition. It is followed by setting into a spectacle frame a whole series of lenses which range from extreme myopia to extreme hyperopia. In many cases some drops of a solution are previously placed in the eyes which relaxes the muscles and tendons of adjustment so that the true state of visual accommodation is certain to be tested. The trial lenses include some which test astigmatism by rotating them with areas of differing curvature. Other equipment such as the Betts' telebinocular examines for fusion and for depth perception. The amount or range of peripheral vision is measured by naming objects which come into view gradually when brought from the side.

Instruments which reflect light through the pupil of the eye give a first-hand view of the retina, of the optic nerve entrance, of the blood vessels, and of the general condition of the rear portion of the interior. In 1851 the great German scientist, Hermann Helmholtz, invented the ophthalmoscope which showed the interior of the eye by reflecting light into it and by providing a small aperture in the reflector through which the observer might view this illuminated interior. Improvements in this field resulted in the invention of the retinoscope, which uses the same theory of observing the interior of the eye but adds a rotation of the illuminating light and its surrounding shadow. The state of refraction can be determined by this process. The ophthalmologist also examines for any structural defects and for any diseases of the eye which need treatment, all of which are technical matters of medicine.

### Number with Defective Vision

From careful surveys and estimates by the White House Conference of Child Health and Protection[1] it was stated that 20 per cent of all children have eye defects. This number means that one child out of every five has some sort of visual defect and obviously is many times more than first impressions would indicate. These figures may be stated in more practical and meaningful terms as follows: In every 10,000 children 8,000 have reasonably normal vision; of the remaining 2,000 children, 1,975 have some type and degree of vision defect which could be corrected; of the remaining twenty-five, after maximum correction has been obtained, four out of every 2,000 are classified as partially-seeing and in need of some type of special education known as classes with that name or their equivalent; and one of every 2,000 is a blind child. These numbers vary between portions of countries and between countries of the world. The number of the blind in the entire world has been estimated at 330 in each 100,000,

[1] White House Conference, *Special Education: The Handicapped and the Gifted*, D. Appleton-Century Co., Inc., New York, 1931, pp. 126-127.

which is more than six times greater than in the United States. This latter figure was obtained from a survey made by the Department of Social Affairs of the United Nations. In the St. Louis survey of 1,215 school children, 327 or 27 per cent were found to be in need of eye care.

### Plans of Action

Thus far in this chapter many of the pertinent facts about normal and defective vision have been presented. The crucial test of effectiveness is in what is accomplished because of this information. Ideally parents should have had vision examinations for their children during infancy or in early childhood. In any case, the vision should have been tested preliminary to school entrance. Whether done before entrance to school or immediately thereafter, the vision of every child should be tested. There should be periodic rexaminations at least once a year.

It has been noted that 20 per cent of all children have some degree or type of visual defect or disease. For the great majority of these cases some type of glasses, prescribed by a competent and qualified examiner, would provide sufficient correction. The big problem is to have the corrections made rather than finding the need for corrections. While this responsibility lies with the parents, it becomes the problem and duty of the school to encourage and urge parents to get correction. Teachers should be alert to possible defects in their daily activities with children.

In the category of greater visual handicaps are the four children in every 2,000 who need some type of special education service commonly known as sight-saving classes. While there is provision in several of the larger population centers in many localities, these pupils continue to be enrolled in regular grades. A new type of itinerant teacher service to assist the regular class teacher is being organized in some localities and will be considered at greater length in the following chapter.

A similar plan of itinerant teachers is being used for blind children in some communities where there are too few for special classes. More details of this plan will be discussed in the chapter on the blind. In both instances the teachers of regular classes receive additional suggestions and information about how to handle the blind as well as the sight-saving pupils.

The education of pupils with lowered vision or blindness requires close and effective cooperation between teacher, parent, the eye specialist, and many others for effective action.

## Questions and Topics for Discussion

1. Describe the system and program of vision examinations used in your school system.
2. Cite examples which you may have known where glasses have not been procured and give probable reasons.
3. Relate any experiences which you may have had with the use of the Snellen charts and list the advantages and limitations of results.
4. Describe the Massachusetts Vision Test and demonstrate its use if available.
5. Describe the medical facilities available in your community for vision examinations.

Note: Consult reference material at the end of Chapter 20.

# CHAPTER 19

## The Partially - Seeing

IN THE PRECEDING CHAPTER there was a general introduction to problems arising from defective vision. The present chapter discusses a smaller but very important group known as the partially-seeing.

### Types

There are three principal types of partially-seeing cases. The first has impairment in the acuity of vision. Former specific limits of distance have been replaced by the judgment of the eye specialist in each individual case. The second type has noncommunicable diseases of the eye including myopia. In this type are also included cases in which diseases have affected the vision and for whom vision conservation is vital. The third type includes miscellaneous cases of chronic eye weaknesses, and injuries to the eyes which may require close supervision.

### Causes

There are many causes of partial vision which might be logically expected since the human eye is a complex structure. Any affection in any one or more of its portions is likely to cause defective vision or even loss of vision.

The most comprehensive survey of visual handicaps was made from a census of classes for the partially-seeing in the spring of 1951. The survey was conducted by the National Society for the Prevention of

300

Blindness and aided by a grant from the New York Community Trust from the late Mildred Anna Williams estate. Replies were received from 600 out of 675 special classes for the partially-seeing in 37 states, in the Territory of Hawaii, and the District of Columbia. The replies contained reports on 4,179 boys and 3,131 girls with a grand total of 7,310 pupils. The summary by C. Edith Kerby[1] who is associate in statistics and analysis for the National Society for the Prevention of Blindness appeared in *Exceptional Children*.

*Refractive errors.* The largest group of causes was refractive errors comprising 3,562 or 48.7 per cent of the total. Within this subgroup myopia including myopic and mixed astigmatism were 2,599 cases or more than one-third of the grand total. Hyperopia including hyperopic astigmatism was found in 12.8 per cent of all cases and thirty cases of refractive errors were listed as "type unknown." In recent years many ophthalmologists recommend that certain myopic children who have good vision with glasses be retained in regular grades if the condition is believed to be hereditary. Kerby believes that hyperopics probably have more difficulty with close work in regular classes than is ordinarily believed, since more than one pupil out of every eight in classes for the partially-seeing have this type of defect.

*Developmental anomalies of structure.* There is a common but erroneous impression that cataracts are conditions affecting chiefly adults, particularly the aged. Cataracts or some form of lens dislocation was found in 11.3 per cent of the partially-seeing. Albinism occurred in nearly 300 cases. Several less well-known anomalies are in this grouping. Amblyopia is dimness of vision without any apparent diseases or defect of the eye. Buphthalmos or megalophthalmus is an unusual enlargement of the eyeball caused by infantile glaucoma and microthalmos describes an abnormally small eyeball in all of its meridians. Coloboma is a congenital cleft caused by failure of some portion to develop normally and aniridia is congenital absence of the iris. Retrolental fibroplasia is a blinding disease which may occur in premature babies who are much below normal weight. In it a growth

---

[1] C.E. Kerby, "A Report on Visual Handicaps of Partially-Seeing Children," *Exceptional Children*, 1952, 18, pp. 137-142.

of fibrous tissue takes place in the interior of the eyeball which blocks the rays of light and the retina becomes detached. Some recent discoveries will be discussed in a later section. In addition to these somewhat unusual conditions there are also multiple anomalies involving combinations which lower vision or destroy it.

*Defects of muscle function.* The muscles which control the movements of the eyes may fail to function properly or to coordinate perfectly for the two eyes which should operate as the two members of a harmonious unit. One child out of every five in classes for the partially-seeing falls into this muscle-defect group. There are two principal types, strabismus and nystagmus. Strabismus is failure of the two eyes to direct their gaze at the same object. It is also known as squint because of the fact that in trying to coordinate the eyes the person is likely to partially or completely close one eye. The technical medical term is heterotropia. Two subconditions often occur, esotropia and exotropia. In the former the two eyes turn or converge inward and is commonly known as cross-eyes. Exotropia is the opposite condition. Nystagmus is an involuntary, rapid movement of the eyeball. The movement may be circular, vertical, lateral, or a mixture. There is a possibility that nervous tension, undue weariness, or lowered vitality may aggravate nystagmus. When it occurs the person suffers from an interruption while reading or in other tasks which require steady attention and concentration. Cases of nystagmus often have a general reduction of vision from other causes which tend to aggravate the entire visual process.

*Diseases and defects of the eyes.* One pupil out of every ten in the classes for the partially-seeing is afflicted with some disease or defect of the eye. Most of the diseases of the eye are a result of infection of one or more of its parts. For example, infection of the iris is known as iritis. Uveitis may extend to the entire uveal tract which includes the iris, the ciliary muscles, and the choroid coat of the eyeball. Interstitial keratitis is a disease of the cornea which causes it to develop a haziness so that the iris and pupil of the eye are hidden from view. Ophthalmia neonatorum is an inflammation of the eye which involves the conjunctiva and is an infection arising from a parental gonorrheal infection. Several other types of infections of the eyes are known to the ophthalmologists.

Injuries to the eyes are more common in adults than in children because of industrial accidents. However children are also victims of traffic accidents, injuries in play, and laxness in general safety precautions at home and elsewhere. Because of their active outdoor play boys have three times as many visual injuries as girls.

After all of the varied causes listed above have been taken into account Kerby's report showed that 98 of the 7,310 cases had undetermined causes. Although there are certain standards for the amount of effective vision present in the better eye after correction the classes for the partially-seeing have many who do not fall within these limits. Many factors in addition to the amount of minimum vision must be taken into account in deciding that a pupil would benefit more effectively in the class for the partially-seeing than in the regular classroom. At the more extreme end of the scale there were 20 per cent of all cases very close to functional blindness. In case there were no classes available for the blind this placement in the class for the partially-seeing was possibly a better adjustment than leaving them in the regular classrooms.

### The Number of the Partially-Seeing

In any field of the handicapped, including the partially-seeing, the exact number is a relative matter. There are almost imperceptible shades of difference between those who are just marginally blind and those whose seeing is at the extreme end of the partially seeing scale. The same is true of those whose vision is somewhat impaired but who are just slightly better than the least impaired in the partially-seeing classification. At best, numbers are an approximation but a necessity for any group if it is to be given due consideration.

In the preceding chapter it was stated that approximately four out of every 2,000 children would qualify for training as partially-seeing pupils, or one in every 500. In a personal letter Dr. Franklin Foote estimated that there are approximately 70,000 partially-seeing children in the United States. At present there are only 8,000 such children enrolled in the more than 600 classes or other facilities for the partially-seeing. Only one pupil out of every nine has a suitable educational program.

The ratio of one partially-seeing child in every 500 produces some startling facts when applied to school populations of various cities. If a class for the partially-seeing has an enrollment of only eight members, which is the minimum standard in some states, it would mean that any community with a school population of four thousand pupils would have a possible eight members for the class. General enrollment figures indicate that any community tends to average about one-fifth of its total population in school. In a city of twenty thousand general population with a school population of four thousand, there should be one partially-seeing class of eight members. There are hundreds of cities with populations of twenty thousand or more which do not make any provision for the partially-seeing, or, as a matter of fact, for any other types of exceptional children. On the other hand, there are a few cities of less than twenty thousand population which combine their educational facilities with the smaller towns and rural areas to conduct at least one class for the partially-seeing. Unfortunately, it is not merely a matter of numbers, but rather of inadequate knowledge about such needs which keeps the numbers down to the present figure.

Formerly it was believed that severe cases of myopia or nearsightedness became progressively worse from strain in trying to see. The present trend, based on careful observations by ophthalmologists, does not seem to indicate such an extreme position. When fitted with proper lenses some of these pupils may get along satisfactorily in regular grades. The gradual removal of some myopes from the classes for the partially-seeing has tended to keep the enrollment figures from advancing but there are obviously many with other types of visual impairment who should take their place.

Visual defects are not limited to those of school-entrance age. Some children are born blind, others have such defective vision that it is evident without detailed examination in the first few weeks or days of life. The experience with retrolental fibroplasia in premature babies, discussed in another section, is a case in point. Dr. Walter H. Fink,[1] an experienced oculist, reports on serious visual defects of several types in one hundred children of preschool age. Referrals had

[1] W.H. Fink, "Ocular Defects in Preschool Children," *The Sight-Saving Review*, 1954, pp. 196-200.

Courtesy of Department of Special Education, Detroit public schools.

Partially-seeing pupil using Projection Magnifier, American Optical Company.

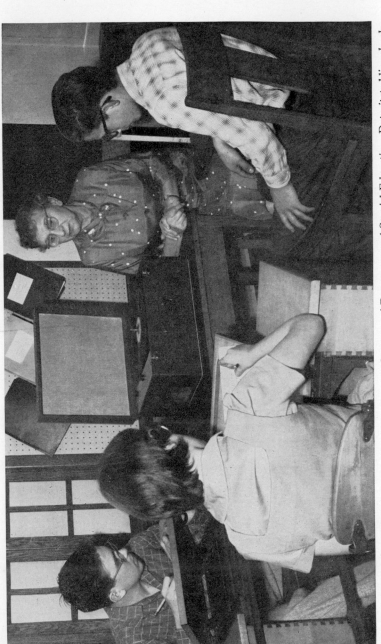

*Courtesy of Department of Special Education, Detroit public schools.*

**Partially-seeing pupils, Post school, Detroit public schools.**

been made by school nurses, by family physicians, by parents, and by the oculist himself who had noted a hereditary tendency in some families.

As in the case of the blind there is a greater percentage of partially-seeing in the southern states. But since the northeastern part of the country is heavily industrialized it might be expected that more male adults would have vision impairment from accidents than in other sections of the country. Boys exceed girls in number with impaired vision, since they play with more dangerous toys and engage in sports and other outdoor activities.

### Characteristics

There are two extreme and diametrically opposed positions or points of view, with varying degrees between, which may be taken with regard to the characteristics of partially-seeing children. The one view holds that the partially-seeing have all the human emotional and social characteristics. They are not different from those with normal vision. According to this theory, partially-seeing children, their parents, their teachers, and other associates discount or ignore any possible differences except that vision is limited. There is considerable merit to the positive sociological and psychological aspects of such a position. The other extreme view would hold that a physical or sensory handicap such as very defective vision has a marked effect upon the personality and general outlook of the partially-seeing. In recent years there has been a growing belief in the intimate relationship between mind and body which is expressed as somatopsychology or psycho-somatic medicine. This theory would place great emphasis upon the fact that the somatic or bodily handicap of impaired vision would have profound effects upon the mind. It could easily set the partially-seeing apart as a separate and distinctly different group of individuals.

The true status lies somewhere between these extremes. There are many variables which affect the final adjustment. One of the least understood of these is the fact that two children with identical type and degree of visual impairment react entirely differently to practically identical environments. It is possible to venture a generalization that if the parents of partially-seeing children are themselves emotionally disturbed and over-solicitous that their partially-seeing children will show more apprehension and disturbed states of mind than if the parents were of an opposite type. While there is probably some evidence to support such a theory there are well-adjusted children among the partially-seeing who have the first type of parents noted above and vice versa. There are many personality factors in unique combinations within each individual which determine the adjustment he makes to his particular environment. Teachers of the partially-seeing encounter much the same variety of personalities, reactions, and other human qualities among their pupils as are noted by teachers of regular-grade pupils.

Whenever suitable vision correction and learning materials are not available to a partially-seeing pupil in the regular classroom he may react in an obviously atypical manner. The contributing factors include unusual eye strain, inability to see, to read, or to learn as readily as other children, and feelings of being overlooked or neglected. It would not be surprising if such traits of personality and character would get out of focus. Any judgments or generalizations about unusual characteristics of the partially-seeing may have been derived from such cases rather than from those who have had the benefit of suitable facilities for their care and education.

*Surveys of intelligence.* Those who look for ways in which the partially-seeing might be different may try to find them in the intelligence. Since it is estimated that fully 85 per cent of all impressions tend to be received through the eyes and since the vision of the partially-seeing is limited to some degree it would seem to be a logical deduction that intelligence might also be limited to some degree. Further limitation might also be expected since many of the visual items of intelligence tests either must be omitted, or presented in some form of enlargement which may not be as satisfactory as in its true size and form. As in the case of personality traits there are superior and gifted minds among the partially-seeing. The median intelligence quotient of the partially-seeing lies at about 90 rather than at the average of 100 as for the regular-grade pupils. Psychologists interpret the intelligence quotient of 90 as near the lower limit of average intelligence. In the White House Conference on Child Health and Protection,[1] Myers found in a summary of intelligence tests results on 970 partially-seeing children from several cities that the median intelligence quotient was slightly below 90, with nearly 10 per cent under 70 but approximately 3 per cent 120 or higher. In the three-year period of 1939-1942 the Psychological Clinic of the Detroit Public Schools tested 190 partially-seeing pupils with a median intelligence quotient of 93. In the school year 1955-1956 the same clinic examined 100 partially-seeing pupils with a median intelligence quotient of 86; with 14 per cent under 70; and with 3 per cent at 120 or higher. Since there seems to be a tendency toward the lower levels of intelligence it is doubly important that optimum educational facilities should be provided for the partially-seeing lest their double handicap prove very detrimental to their complete education.

## History

*Famous individuals.* From the earliest accounts of history there have been many famous men who were partially blind, blind in one eye, or had suffered from some type of eye disease which made their seeing very difficult.[2] In the book of Genesis is found, "And it came to pass that when Isaac was old, his eyes were dim, so that he could not see." In Grecian days, Philip of Macedon, father of Alexander the Great, lost an eye from an arrow wound about 353 B.C. Rome also had its eye casualties: Hannibal lost one eye in the Second Punic War, and Horace lost one in 507 B.C. He also sustained a second physical injury when he permanently disabled one hip while jumping into the Tiber River in a battle to defend Rome. The orator, Cicero, had a type of recurrent eye disease over a period of years. The very myopic Nero used to view gladiatorial combats through some kind of concave emerald which probably improved his vision, but not his mental perspective.

[1] White House Conference on Child Health and Protection, *Special Education, The Handicapped and the Gifted,* D. Appleton-Century Co., Inc., New York, 1931, p. 205.
[2] C.A. Bahn, "The Eyes of Some Famous Historical Characters, I. Little Journeys in Ophthalmology," *The American Journal of Ophthalmology,* 1933, 16, pp. 425-429.

Records of later periods also give evidence of the existence of eye defects. On a tombstone in a Florentine Chapel is the following inscription: "Here lies Salvino D'Armati, a native of Florence, the inventor of spectacles. May God forgive him his sins. Died in the year of our Lord, 1317." Apparently D'Armati's work bore some fruit, for more than a century later Leonardo da Vinci, the famous painter and engineer, wore glasses with extreme refraction. Gustavus Adolphus, king of the Swedes and military leader of the Protestants, was killed in the battle of Lutzen in 1532 when his myopic vision betrayed him into the hands of the Germans as he strayed from his followers.

Although color blindness is not a qualifying classification of the partially-seeing nevertheless it has always been a topic of great popular interest. Daltonism was a name frequently given to color blindness because of the famous John Dalton, who wrote the first great work on color vision. He was also the father of the atomic theory. He is said to have worn color combinations which were the marvel and amazement of his age. The poet Schiller and the musician Beethoven were both very myopic; the poet Milton had some type of myopia which eventu-turned to blindness. Guy de Maupassant, the great French short-story writer, had diplopia due to paralysis of the extraocular muscles; his death resulted from the general paresis caused by it. Dr. George Gould[1] writes that many famous myopic individuals wrote or created many gloomy and pessimistic masterpieces including the works of Nietzsche, the two Carlyles, George Eliot, and Schopenhauer. Whittier, Elizabeth Barrett Browning, Darwin, Coleridge, and others avoided the myopic tendency by giving up close work and resorting to walking or to other outdoor exercise to relieve eye strain.

The vigorous Teddy Roosevelt had very astigmatic vision, and lost one eye from an injury in a friendly boxing contest while residing in the White House. President Wilson became blind in one eye from a retinal hemorrhage. The portraits of Lincoln show that his eyes probably had a very hyperopic condition.

*Education.* Although there has always been a great interest in the

---

[1] G. Gould, *Biographic Clinics*, The Blakiston Co., Philadelphia, 1900-1906, 3, 72 pp.

education of the blind, the partially-seeing were mainly neglected or ignored. Most of them were usually found in the regular grades, but a few of the more seriously handicapped were in schools for the blind, which were recognized as unsuitable placements. Methods of educating the totally blind and the partially-seeing are entirely different, and wherever the partially-seeing have been placed with the blind where Braille methods usually prevail, this has been to the detriment of the partially-seeing. More than one hundred years ago, Franz von Gaheis of Austria recognized that the partially-seeing should not be educated with the blind because the latter used them as "eyes" thus robbing themselves of the independence which was considered desirable for them. The partially-seeing tended to develop superiority complexes and became spoiled children who failed to learn their own true place in the world.

In England the evils of mixing the two groups became recognized strongly enough so that in 1908 separate classes were started for the partially-seeing, but were limited strictly to myopic cases. This policy tended to persist in that country. Shortly afterward, Robert Irwin started a class for the blind in Cleveland in 1909, and some partially-seeing children were also admitted. After some unsatisfactory experiences, by the fall of 1913 he organized a separate class for them which was the first such class in America. In the same year classes were established in Boston, Roxbury, Newark and Jersey City. Cincinnati followed in 1914, Detroit in 1915, and New York City in 1916.

### Patterns of Education

There are several patterns or plans for the education of the partially-seeing. From this fact it may well be that the most optimum plan has not yet been determined. The various plans will be presented.

*Placement in schools for the blind.* Some of the partially-seeing are placed in the residential schools for the blind. Although there are many disadvantages both for the partially-seeing and for the blind the number of such classes has increased in recent years. Such placement is contrary to the recommendation of the Committee on Education of Partially-Seeing Children of the National Society for the

Prevention of Blindness.[1] The Committee pointed out that the methods of teaching the blind are not suitable for them; that institutional living is not good preparation for living in regular society; that the blind are placed in an inferior position by the partially-seeing; and that local school systems are able to dodge their responsibility by not providing for pupils who rightfully belong in their schools.

*Placement in special day schools.* Some school systems have built special schools to house all types of the physically handicapped. The need for such placement was supposed to arise from needs common to the blind, the deaf, the orthopedic, and other groups. Most of them do not need special transportation, occupational therapy, or hearing amplification which are provided for some other types. Their needs are more nearly identical with regular children than with the other physically handicapped.

*Placement in the special segregated class.* Many of the larger school systems have provided special segregated classes in regular school buildings. They are not recommended if the segregation is total and complete. If completely segregated they tend to feel and to become stigmatized and are denied association with regular-class children.

*Cooperative placement plans.* Some special classes are established when there is close cooperation with regular-class children. The partially-seeing do their close eye work in the special class under a specially trained teacher but join the normally-seeing for several periods daily to benefit from this natural association. In a somewhat similar plan the partially-seeing are enrolled with the regular-class children but go to the special teacher for the close eye work preparation and any other special services which they might need. In this manner they are considered to be normal children.

*Service by the itinerant teacher.* In some communities, where the numbers of the partially-seeing are small, an itinerant teacher trained in the methods for the partially-seeing has a regular schedule of visits to the various classrooms or schools where the partially-seeing are enrolled in regular classes. This teacher orients and advises regular teachers about the special needs of the partially-seeing child. She

---

[1] The Committee on Education of Partially-Seeing Children, "Education of Partially-Seeing Children," *The Sight-Saving Review*, 1952, 22, pp. 2-6.

also needs a small special room[1] provided with large-type typewriters and other supplies and equipment, with suitable storage space. The number of visits to each child depends upon his individual needs, with some needing one per week while others may require two or three. Bryan reports that the teacher can work satisfactorily and individually with as many as 30 children. The itinerant teacher plan is feasible in large school systems, and is effective in small communities and in rural areas.

*Partially-seeing children in regular classrooms.* Eight out of every nine partially-seeing children do not have any special educational facilities provided for them either in special classes or by an itinerant teacher. The first duty of any teacher of regular grades is to note one or more of the symptoms listed below as possible signs of severe visual impairment. This report was prepared by the Advisory Committee on Education of Partially-Seeing Children of the National Society for the Prevention of Blindness.[2]

Attempts to brush away blur; rubs eyes excessively; frowns.

Shuts or covers one eye, tilts head or thrusts head forward when looking at near or distant objects.

Has difficulty in reading or in other work requiring close use of the eyes.

Blinks more than usual, cries often, or is irritable when doing close work.

Stumbles or trips over small objects.

Holds books or small objects close to eyes.

Is unable to participate in games requiring distance vision.

Is unduly sensitive to light.

Other signs of eye trouble to be noted are: red-rimmed, encrusted, or swollen eyelids; recurring sties; inflamed or watery eyes; crossed eyes; complaints that the child cannot see well, that he experiences dizziness, headaches, or nausea following close eye work, that he has blurred or double vision. Some times a visual defect may manifest itself in restlessness, lack of interest in sports or in reading, or other activities requiring close use of the eyes. The classroom teacher should be alert to these reactions and record them.

[1] D. Bryan, "The Itinerant Teacher Plan for the Education of Partially-Seeing Children in Illinois," *The Sight-Saving Review*, 1953, 23, pp. 218-222.

[2] *The Sight-Saving Review*, 1953, 22, pp. 95-99. Quoted by permission of the National Society for the Prevention of Blindness.

The committee recommends further that adjustable furniture be placed according to the needs of each partially-seeing pupil, and that some of the 18- or 24-point type printed books be available. With a little friendly assistance from the seeing children fairly good progress may be made.

### Classrooms

The classroom for the partially-seeing should be fully as large as for any regular class although the number of pupils is much less. Several grades are usually represented and are equipped with typewriters, dictating and recording equipment, and large storage space for the Clear-Type books. The desks should be movable and turned so that no pupil faces the direct outside light. The finish of desks and other furniture should be in a neutral color so as not to reflect light from outside or inside illumination. Dr. Franklin M. Foote,[1] who is executive director of the National Society for the Prevention of Blindness, also recommends that contrasts between light and dark be kept at a minimum such as 85 per cent reflectances for window frames and walls adjacent to windows. Many of his practical suggestions could well be adopted for regular classrooms in the interests of better illumination and comfort.

### Equipment and Educational Supplies

The equipment and educational supplies of classrooms for partially-seeing children are quite different from regular classrooms. There should be a liberal supply of large-type books in 18-point or 24-point size and since they are bulky and quite heavy special book racks should be provided to hold them while in use. Suitable cupboard space for storage is a minimum essential. Typewriters with special desks and chairs need ample space for optimum placement for light and effective use. It is somewhat beyond the scope of this book to give detailed descriptions but only to apprise teachers of regular

[1] F.M. Foote, "Classrooms for Partially-Seeing Children," *Exceptional Children*, 1956, 22, pp. 318-320, 341, and 342.

grades and prospective teachers of the partially-seeing of the unique character of their education. Hathaway[1] gives many detailed descriptions in the third edition of her informative book.

## Teacher Training

Because of the nature of their visual handicap it is evident that partially-seeing children present problems in their education which are different in certain respects from those of regular pupils. Teachers of partially-seeing children must have some type of special training in addition to and beyond that of regular teachers. A minimum basic practicum of 120 clock hours of specialization is recommended, including 30 hours of lectures and discussions on the organization and administration of facilities for the partially-seeing, including buildings and equipment; 30 hours on the programs for different grade levels; observation for 30 hours in a recognized demonstration school; and 30 hours of lectures and discussion on the anatomy, physiology, and hygiene of the eye and the principles of vision. However in order to qualify for state aid in many states 24 semester hours of specialization are necessary including some in other fields of special education, in mental hygiene, arts and crafts, and typewriting.[2] In addition to these training qualifications the teacher of partially-seeing children must be a very socially mature and well-adjusted individual who is able to maintain wholesome and effective relationships with teachers of regular grades, with parents, with the medical specialists, and with the general public. Some states pay an additional salary differential to induce teachers to take the additional training for the partially-seeing.

## Questions and Topics for Discussion

1. Report in further detail on Kerby's survey.
2. Describe your observations of some acquaintance with quite defective vision.

[1] W. Hathaway, *Education and Health of the Partially Seeing Child* (3rd ed.), Columbia University Press, New York, 1954, 227 pp.
[2] M.A.C. Young, "Certification of Teachers of Partially Seeing Children," *Exceptional Children*, 1952, 18, pp. 207-215.

3. Visit a class for the partially-seeing and observe the many important phases of the program.
4. If possible visit the office of an ophthalmologist and have him explain and demonstrate the equipment.
5. Make a report on the itinerant teacher plan.
6. Discuss Hathaway's *Education and Health of the Partially Seeing Child.*
7. Make a survey of one year's numbers of the *Sight-Saving Review* and comment on its general nature.

Note: Consult reference material at the end of Chapter 20.

# CHAPTER 20

## The Blind

THE EXTREME GRAVITY of blindness has stirred mankind throughout the ages to most notable endeavors in behalf of those unable to see. As a class the blind do not want sympathy. It is an interesting and gripping experience to assemble even in sketchy outline the story of the blind. It is filled with the deeds of countless pioneers whose collective efforts have brought the education of the blind slowly up to its present state of comparative perfection. These pioneers delved into many phases of blindness, including methods of teaching, into the physiology and psychology of the blind, into the establishment of schools, and into legal and financial provisions for their care and protection.

### Definitions of Blindness

At first thought the definition of blindness seems very simple and final. However, this is not the case since there are many kinds and degrees of blindness. Frampton (et al.)[1] comments "In considering definitions of blindness it is important to remember that these must be formulated in terms of the purpose which they are expected to serve. Functional definitions are necessary and should include consideration of the educational program required, vocational possibilities, and economic prognosis."

In terms of pupil education the White House Conference on Child Health and Education in 1930 defined blindness as "A blind

---

[1] M.E. Frampton and E.D. Gall eds., *Special Education for the Exceptional,* Vol. II, Porter Sargent Publisher, Boston, 1955, p. 3.

person is one who cannot use his eyes for education."[1] In terms of visual acuity a person is considered blind if his vision is not practically functional in the better eye after maximum visual correction. Another criterion for blindness is that although the person may have enough vision to distinguish lights and shadows of some forms he cannot make practical use of such vision. Finally there is the person with absolute blindness or inability to perceive light.

Primarily in the case of adults the term "economic blindness" implies inability to do any kind of work in which sight is essential. Vocational blindness includes persons who are unable because of their blindness to earn a living. A special case of vocational blindness develops when there is some vision but the field of vision is so restricted that the widest diameter of seeing subtends an angular distance of not more than twenty degrees. In other words the person can see only a very narrow space immediately ahead whereas the vision of the normally seeing person extends out to somewhere between 90 and 180 degrees. Drivers of some cars apparently have a lesser degree of width or peripheral vision than others. In any case blindness is not merely absolute absence of light.

### Characteristics of the Blind

There has been a great amount of speculation about the characteristics of the blind. Because of their visual limitations some believe that the blind are different in many ways, but this conclusion is that of seeing persons. On the other hand the blind themselves and those who know them well and associate with them all the time tend to minimize their differences. Because of so many variables it is difficult to draw simple and definite conclusions about the characteristics of the blind. However some evidence concerning characteristics will be considered.

Lowenfeld[2] observes that there are three psychological aspects of blindness: cognitive functions, mobility, and personality and social

---

[1] White House Conference on Child Health and Protection, *The Handicapped Child*, D. Appleton-Century Co., Inc., New York, 1933, p. 1.

[2] B. Lowenfeld, *Psychology of Exceptional Children and Youth*, W.M. Cruickshank, ed., Prentice-Hall, Inc., Englewood Cliffs, N.J., 1955, pp. 214-283.

factors. In cognitive functions the person must depend upon senses other than vision for the recognition of objects. Lowenfeld concludes that while other senses such as hearing are probably practiced to a greater degree than is true of seeing persons, the actual or innate ability in hearing is probably no greater. Mobility tends to be a handicap of the blind although many blind adults have made such amazing adjustments as being able to get about by themselves in the traffic of large cities. Lowenfeld asserts that in the matter of personality and social factors there are no fundamental differences between the blind and the seeing, and that any deviations are unique to individuals and result from situations similar to those faced by seeing persons.

One of the interesting characteristics of the blind is the lack of visual imagery which is usually strong in seeing persons. Those who became blind after some years of seeing gradually lose their visual imagery. The blind tend to live in a world of temporal sequences rather than in the spatial sequences of seeing persons. The seeing person plans his day in terms of the visual surroundings accompanying each activity or event. The blind person plans mainly that he does first one task, then a second, and a third, in whatever order they come. His associations are largely kinesthetic and auditory rather than visual.

Among the environmental factors which complicate satisfactory adjustments for the blind are parental attitudes both toward themselves and their blind children. Attitudes range from acceptance and determination to play a wholesome role to the other extreme of rejection and feelings of guilt and denial. Parents are known to play such roles in the case of seeing children and with much the same reactions as occur in blind children.

*Personality tests.* Many types of personality tests have been administered to blind children and adolescents. Some testing has been done by an examiner reading aloud the problem and its suggested answers from which one response was selected. Scholl[1] had the testing materials and responses transcribed on a tape recorder for the Bell

[1] G. Scholl, "Some Notes on the Use of Two Personality Tests with Visually Handicapped Students," *New Outlook for the Blind,* 1953, 47, pp. 187-295.

Adjustment Inventory and the Bernreuter Personality Inventory. She reports that this method seems to work quite well, although results of the two tests were contradictory in some areas. Girls generally showed better adjustments than boys in many areas which is also true of the seeing.

*Intelligence of the blind.* The most extensive reports on the intelligence of the blind have been made by Samuel P. Hayes. He collaborated with Robert Irwin in a Binet Scale for the Blind in 1923 and with Terman in 1930 on the Stanford-Binet with an edition for the blind. An Interim edition was prepared upon the 1937 edition of the Stanford-Revision.

Hayes' summaries of testing results on over 2,000 blind children found a mean intelligence quotient of 98.8 which is just below the average intelligence quotient of 100. His various summaries show a wider scatter of intelligence quotients than for seeing children with more at the superior and also more at the slow and retarded end of the scale. Frampton[1] comments about the larger number of lower mentality cases among the blind, "Blindness and feeblemindedness are often associated as concomitant effects of some underlying constitutional defect. Blindness due to specific eye diseases and accidental causes is being reduced by prevention efforts, leaving a large proportion of blindness due to systemic and degenerative diseases with which feeble-mindedness is often also associated."

Komisar and MacDonnell[2] report a mean gain of 6.3 points in intelligence quotient on 89 students at the Oak Hill School with an average time between tests of 37.8 months. In most cases the Hayes Interim test was the first examination and the second was the Weschsler Intelligence Scale for Children. The mean intelligence quotients were 97.8 and 104.1. Pupils with initial intelligence quotients below 90 made the greatest gains of 11.4 points whereas those above 110 gained only 2.33 points. The authors suggest that the initial retardation may have been brought about by inadequate contacts

[1] M.E. Frampton et al., *Special Education for the Exceptional*, Vol. II, Porter Sargent Publisher, Boston, 1955, p. 15.
[2] D. Komisar and M. MacDonnell, "Gains in I.Q. for Students Attending a School for the Blind," *Exceptional Children*, 1955, 21, pp. 127-129.

with their environment. They conclude that caution is necessary in the prediction of achievement on the basis of the initial examination.

### The Number of the Blind

Reliable figures about the number of the blind are very difficult to obtain. This fact was so apparent that after including a special count of the blind in the United States census each ten-year period from 1830 to 1930 the practice was abandoned. The variations in the number in the various ten-year periods illustrate the problem. In the first four enumerations from 1830 to 1860 the number averaged a little over 400 in each million of the population. In the latter part of the nineteenth century it rose to more than twice as much and then declined in the early twentieth century to 517 for each million in the census enumeration in 1930. It is very doubtful that there was actually such fluctuation during this span of a century. In more recent years other organizations and agencies entered the picture with better methods of survey and population sampling.

As an example of such discrepancies, the 1920 census listed 52,567 whereas shortly thereafter a survey made by the American Foundation for the Blind, Inc., reported 56,566 blind in only 17 of the 48 states, comprising about one-half of the population of the country. The United States Public Health Service conducted a nationwide survey in 1935-1936 and placed the number of the blind at 117,000.[1] More recently programs of Federal Aid including an additional income tax personal exemption and Social Security provisions have encouraged bringing the actual number of the blind out into the open. Blinded veterans from World Wars I and II have added to the total number of the blind.

After careful study of government and other agency data such as available by the American Foundation for the Blind, Inc., Ralph G. Hurlin[2] estimated the number of the blind in the United States at

[1] *Blindness—Amount, Cause and Relation to Certain Social Factors, National Health Survey*, 1935-1936, U.S. Public Health Service, Washington, D.C., 1938.
[2] R.G. Hurlin, "Estimated Prevalence of Blindness in the United States," *Social Security Bulletin*, March 1945-September 1950.

308,000. This recent number is almost three times as many as in the survey of twenty years earlier.

*Number of preschool blind.* In recent years it became evident that the number of blind preschool children was on the increase. Much of this blindness occurred during fetal life or in the first year of life. The National Society for the Prevention of Blindness cooperated with the health agencies, ophthalmologists, and many other sources to make a survey of blind children under seven years of age as of December 31, 1950. A comparison was made in 1943 and showed that most blindness resulting from various causes actually decreased, but that in the case of retrolental fibroplasia there was a marked increase. Kerby[1] estimated the number of preschool blind from all causes as 5,500. In later sections of this chapter on causes, remedies, and preventions the more hopeful treatment of this condition will be presented.

*Number of school-age blind.* Upon the basis of one blind child for every 2,000 children there are probably upwards of at least 20,000 blind children of school age in the United States. Lowenfeld[2] reported that from 1943 to 1953 the number of blind children in special schools or classes in the United States increased from 6,067 to 6,538. The American Printing House for the Blind reported over 7,000 blind children in such classes in 1954. At best special classes are provided for about one child out of every three who are blind. However these figures do not by any means indicate that no schooling at all is provided for the other two-thirds. New types of programs of itinerant teachers for the blind will be discussed. There are probably many other blind children who attend regular classes and, with or without special methods for their instruction, they may be profiting to some degree from this experience. This statement does not imply that these arrangements are the best that should be provided.

*Number of adult blind.* While there are many blind children the number of adult blind is much greater. Diseases of adulthood and

---

[1] C.E. Kerby, "Blindness in Preschool Children," *The Sight-Saving Review*, 1954, 24, pp. 15-29.
[2] B. Lowenfeld, "California: Educational Facilities for the Increasing Number of Blind Children," *New Outlook for the Blind*, 1953, 47, pp. 221-225.

old age take their heavy toll of vision. Frampton[1] reports that two-thirds of the entire increase in the number of blind during the decade 1940-1950 was in the group sixty years of age or older. He summarizes further that there are at least fourteen million blind in the world. Farrell[2] gives a much more conservative world estimate from data furnished by the Department of Social Affairs of the United Nations. Upon a ratio of 330 per 100,000 there might be 6,700,000 blind persons in the world. This number is a more hopeful estimate than that of Frampton since it is less than one-half of his figure. But regardless of who is more nearly correct, blindness is one of the great scourges of the world.

## Causes, Remedies, and Preventions

There are many causes of blindness. They fall into two general classes in a Standard Classification of Causes of Blindness, 1957 revision, by the Committee on Statistics of the Blind.[2] The first classification lists them according to site and type of affection into eight areas: eyeball in general; cornea; crystalline lens; uveal tract; retina; optic nerve, nerve pathway, and cortical visual centers; vitreous; and not specified. In these areas there may be congenital defects of structure, with accidents or disease causing disorder or destruction. The second classification lists them by etiology or underlying cause. There are eight areas of such causes: infectious diseases such as syphilis; trauma or accidental injury; poisonings; neoplasms or tumorous growth; diseases not elsewhere specified; pre-natal influence not elsewhere specified; etiology undetermined or not specified; and supplementary classification for cases resulting from trauma or poisoning or by type of activity at time of injury such as in play or sport. For the general public the etiological causes are of greater significance while the locational or topographical causes are primarily a matter of medical concern, often related to surgery with delicate and involved

[1] M.E. Frampton et al., *Special Education for the Exceptional*, Vol. II, Porter Sargent Publisher, Boston, 1955, p. 8.
[2] G. Farrell, *The Story of Blindness*, Harvard University Press, Cambridge, Mass., 1956, p. 219.
[3] Committee on Statistics of the Blind, "Revision of the Standard Classification of the Causes of Blindness," *The Sight-Saving Review*, 1957, 27, pp. 112-115.

operations. Since there are so many possible causes of blindness it is remarkable that there is so little rather than so much blindness.

*Preschool children.* There was an alarming increase in blindness beginning about 1940-1945 in children under seven years of age. Most of it could be traced back to the prenatal period or to the first year of life. What had been included in undetermined or unknown to science became identified as retrolental fibroplasia. The most encouraging report about the cause and prevention of this disease was reported by Yankauer, Jacobziner, and Schneider[1] in 1956. Their investigations were carried on in New York State beginning in 1954 in close cooperation with the New York State Commission for the Blind. In that state the number of such cases had risen from 24 in 1947 to 181 in 1953. A relationship was discovered between the volume of oxygen therapy for premature infants and blindness. As a result of their findings it was recommended that volumes of oxygen should be kept below 40 per cent and should be administered only under physician's orders. They also recommended that oxygen concentrations in incubators should be checked periodically and that an ophthalmologist should examine all premature infants upon discharge from the nursery and at three months of age. The number of blind cases from this cause dropped from 181 in 1954 to 93 in 1955.

*Other causes.* A survey reported by Kerby[2] summarizes the causes of blindness in 2,412 cases in 16 states as follows: 47.0 per cent were mainly retrolental fibroplasia as noted above; 37.5 per cent to prenatal influence with most of the causes not specified; 5.5 per cent with etiology undetermined or not specified; 4.1 per cent from infectious diseases such as German measles, meningitis, and ophthalmia neonatorum; 2.8 per cent mainly birth injuries; 2.7 per cent from tumors; and 0.3 per cent from general diseases. As to topographical causes, over one-half involved the choroid and retina; approximately 20.0 per cent resulted from structural anomalies of the eyeball; 11.1 per cent involved the optic nerve, visual pathway, and cortical visual centers; and 9.8 per cent were located in the crystalline lens.

---

[1] A. Yankhauer, H. Jacobziner, and D. Schneider, "The Rise and Fall of Retrolental Fibroplasia in New York State," *The Sight-Saving Review*, 1956, 26, pp. 86-91.
[2] C.E. Kerby, "Blindness in Preschool Children," *The Sight-Saving Review*, 1954, 24, pp. 15-29.

*School-age children.* The figures which have just been cited carry on with some modifications into children of school age. If the same success is secured country wide in the prevention of retrolental fibroplasia as was found in New York State, there will be a few years in which this disease will stand out as the largest single cause of blindness after which it will decline. In the meantime accidents begin to rise as one of the chief causes. In general, accidents cause five times as much blindness among males as females. Explosions and flying objects exact a heavy toll among boys and men, whereas girls and women have blindness resulting from falls, burns, and cutting instruments. Since many more women are working in factories than before World War II, their causes of blindness may gradually approximate that of men. In the case of children and young people explosives from Independence Day celebrations have taken such a heavy toll that they are prohibited in many localities and in some states such as Michigan and New York. When the great toll of blindness was added up it was obvious that the spirit of the Fourth of July should be expressed in less dangerous ways.

Modern methods of sanitation hold promise of reducing blindness, such as trachoma which is caused from infections. Blindness may result from the various fevers, from measles, smallpox, diphtheria, and meningitis, but all of these diseases are on the decline in the more enlightened areas of the world. Although cataracts are rather common in children, they are much more prevalent among people beyond middle age and this is also true of glaucoma. Since the number of older people is on the increase the number of the blind may also increase from these causes.

*The adult blind.* Mention has been made of some causes of blindness among adults as contrasted with causes among children. With the great increase in automobile travel individuals of all ages are becoming blinded from car accidents. The numbers would probably be much larger if safety glass had not become mandatory. The use of heavy goggles with shatterproof glass and with various colored lenses to reduce glare from chemicals and furnaces are hopeful signs. Farrell[1] comments that there has been a 40 per cent decrease in industrial

---

[1] G. Farrell, *The Story of Blindness*, Harvard University Press, Cambridge, Mass., 1956, p. 233.

eye accidents although there is an estimated number of 300,000 eye accidents annually. The Wise Owl Club was established in 1947 and admits to membership only those whose sight has been saved by wearing safety glasses. The efforts of the National Society for the Prevention of Blindness have been well repaid in promotion of this movement in industrial plants since over 7,000 men and women have qualified for membership.

### History of the Blind

Since the dawn of history the treatment of the blind has reflected the entire range of human emotions from that of having supernatural powers to complete care and protection because of their handicap. They have been exploited as beggars and they have been used in China to learn and to transmit history by word of mouth before permanent written records were available. During the Middle Ages the blind were placed under the care and supervision of monasteries as a result of more humanitarian treatment during the early Christian era. The Duke of Bavaria established a home for the blind in 1178 A.D., and attempted some kind of instruction. In 1254 A.D., a refuge for blind Crusaders, known as the *Hotel des Quinze-Vingts*, was established in Paris. During the next five hundred years various brotherhoods founded many other institutions for the blind throughout western Europe. Eventually these efforts led to the establishment of schools for the blind.

*Famous blind persons.* Blindness has not been accepted as a handicap by many famous blind persons. They have followed the basic principle of utilizing whatever talents they may have and their talents have proved to be many and very great. The *Iliad* and the *Odyssey* have been masterpieces of literature throughout the ages and were written by the blind Greek poet, Homer, some two thousand years ago. Didymus of Alexandria who became blind at about five years of age developed a system of letters which gave him the ability to read and helped to make him a famous teacher and theologian in the fourth century of the Christian era. Prospero Fagnini became blind at about forty-four years of age but after he had received a good education at the University of Perugia. He had always been interested in canon law and particularly in the many inconsistencies which had crept into its interpretation. Coon[1] reports that Fagnini presented his views in the form of five books which went through several editions before his death in 1678 A.D. at about ninety years of age. He always emphasized that reasonableness should be an important principle in rulings and in all decisions.

Nicholas Sanderson, born in 1682, rose above his handicap of blindness to become a mathematician and professor at Cambridge University. Soon afterward the blind John Metcalfe became a successful engineer interested in and builder of improved roads. The blind Milton also lived and wrote in the same century. The Braille system of raised letters was devised by Louis Braille (1809-1852) who was blinded at five years of age in an accident with a knife. Many more very interesting blind persons are described in Farrell's[2] book.

*Recent and contemporary blind persons.* Not all famous blind persons existed in the distant past. Many of them lived in recent years or are living and active today. Dr. Robert Irwin (1883-1951) was one of these. He became supervisor of classes for the blind in Cleveland and in 1913 he organized the first cooperative plan of sight-saving in this country. In 1920 he established the Clear Type Publishing Company to produce and distribute books in 24-point print for use in sight-saving classes. He served as executive director of the American Foundation for the Blind, Inc., from 1929 to 1949. He organized the World Conference on Work for the Blind held in New York in 1931, which was typical of many other projects which he instituted in behalf of the blind. There are several blind members of the board of trustees of the American Foundation for the Blind, Inc., including the executive director and Helen Keller, who is both blind and deaf. Peter J. Salmon has completed forty years of service at the Industrial Home for the Blind, Brooklyn, after serving since 1945 as its executive director.

*Establishment of schools for the blind.* The blind Maria Theresia

---

[1] N. Coon, "Prospero Fagnini," *The New Outlook for the Blind,* 1955, 49, pp. 62-64.

[2] G. Farrell, *The Story of Blindness,* Harvard University Press, Cambridge, Mass., 1956, 270 pp.

von Paradis of Vienna performed so brilliantly in music that she inspired Valentin Hauy of Paris to establish a school for the blind in 1784. Shortly after several other schools were established in western Europe, greater interest in the blind spread to the United States. The blind were included on a special listing in the Federal census of 1830 which was just one year after the Massachusetts legislature authorized the establishment of the first such school in the United States. Dr. Samuel Gridly Howe was chosen to take charge, but was first sent to Europe to learn firsthand what had been accomplished by Hauy and others. In August, 1832, the school opened with six pupils and thus was started the famous Perkins Institution and Massachusetts School for the Blind. The establishment of similar schools soon got under way in other states and at the present time every state either has a school or provision for its blind in a neighboring state. Public school systems of large cities discovered that there were enough blind children in their communities to establish classes. The first was in Chicago in 1896.

*History of methods of teaching.* Although mention has been made of a system of letters devised by Didymus of Alexandria it was probably understood by him alone and not used to teach others. More than one thousand years later the blind Jacob Netra of Germany set up a system of notches cut out of small sticks for symbols in reading and eventually he assembled quite a sizable library of these materials. Hauy devised and improved a method of embossed printing of raised letters which was not too satisfactory since the sense of touch was not fine enough to distinguish their finer markings. Linear symbols developed by William Moon in England and resembling Roman letters, made out of wire and fastened to metal plates were more successful than Hauy's methods. The most successful system was developed substantially in its present form by Louis Braille and named for him. He developed a frame of six dots in two vertical rows with three dots in each row. These dots were indented in stiff paper and could also be written by the pupil with a suitable frame and stylus. Dr. Robert Irwin invited authorities on different versions of Braille in various countries and a uniform system was eventually adopted.

## Educational Programs

Several kinds of educational programs have been developed. There are state schools where the pupils are housed away from home and there are schools or nurseries for very young children. In public school systems there are special classes or schools and recently a plan of itinerent teachers has been developed in some communities by which blind pupils remain in regular classes but the itinerant teacher gives special instructions for one or more periods per week. The itinerant teacher plan saves any unusually long transportation for blind pupils and leaves them in their natural social setting of known childhood associates.

Many arguments pro and con support or weaken claims for the state school. Proponents claim that blind children are safe from traffic and other locomotion hazards, that they have better controlled living habits, and that they feel more at ease with children having similar handicaps. High school pupils from the state schools often attend the community high school where larger numbers of pupils are provided with a greater variety of curriculums than can be offered to a limited number of blind in the state school. A large majority of blind pupils attend state schools because there are so few in all but the larger cities that public schools do not provide special classes for them. The program of itinerant teachers may alter present policies.

The arguments for public school placement or for the itinerant plan include leaving blind pupils in their own homes, playing with siblings and childhood associates, and learning to get about in natural community settings where they will be likely to live as adults.

Recently there has been some lively discussion about the state school versus the public school. It was started with a 26-page mimeographed statement adopted in June, 1956, by the American Association of Instructors of the Blind, and entitled a "Proposed Statement of Policy by the American Association of Instructors of the Blind." Three well-known authorities in special education have offered[1] some

[1] E. Newland, M.R. Barnett, and W.M. Cruickshank, "Some Observations on the 1956 Statement of Policy issued by the American Association of Instructors of the Blind," *Exceptional Children*, 1957, 23, pp. 320-326, 328, and 330.

observations on the lack of sufficient recognition of individual differences and too little mention of psychological services. A second commentator observes that in addition to a statement of policy it is a combination of philosophy, policy, and procedure with no clear distinctions between them. He lists fifteen items such as standards of teacher preparation which he does not find in the statement. The third commentator notes that any possible contributions to educational progress cannot be limited to state schools and that such an assumption, stated or implied, leaves much to be desired.

### Equipment and Supplies

From what has been described about the blind thus far it is evident that educating the blind has always been a difficult and complicated task. In the past century the chief progress was made in teaching the blind to read and write Braille. Braille books which contain the usual content materials for seeing children are many times larger than the regular editions. They require special care and liberal storage space. The American Printing House for the Blind at Louisville is subsidized by the Government to allow publication of such books. Typewriters are usually provided since the older blind children can learn typing and use it in many helpful ways. Equipment also includes Talking Books, record players, wooden relief maps, arithmetic boards, and cubes.

### Teacher Training

From the description of the blind and of the materials for their instruction it is evident that teachers of the blind must have extensive specialized training. In many states the requirements are for at least 24 semester hours of specialization in the anatomy and physiology of the eye, remedial and preventive measures, the correct use of typewriters, operation of talking books and other equipment, and thorough knowledge of how to read, write, and teach Braille. The teacher must have an unusually fine personality with great patience and tact in dealing with blind children. She must also be adept in dealing with parents and regular teachers in coordinating the educational program between the activities of her special room and the participation of her pupils in the regular classes.

## Research in Programs for the Blind

Mention has already been made of Talking Books and wire and tape recorders. In a chapter in Zahl,[1] Corner reports on the activities of the Committee on Sensory Devices composed of six eminent men from the fields of physics, physiology, otological research, psychology, and embryology who outlined and undertook research in: (1) devices for reading ordinary print by the totally blind; (2) guidance devices for ranging and obstacle finding; (3) optical magnifiers to aid persons of limited visual acuity; and (4) improvement of the "Visagraph," a machine for the production of enlarged embossed images of print, diagrams, etc. Some progress has been made in all four of these areas with encouraging progress in the development of the "Optophone" designed to translate ordinary printing into sounds which might eventually supersede Braille and Talking Books.

Progress on optical magnifiers has been advanced by the invention of the megascope. This mechanical aid to those who have low vision will magnify ink print letters or other material 25 times without undue distortion, and reproduce them on a screen for convenient reading. This machine is one of the many appliances designed under the direction of the Technical Research Department of the American Foundation for the Blind (*New Outlook for the Blind*, April, 1953). Electronic travel aids are being perfected through the cooperation of U.S. Army Signal Corps at Fort Monmouth, N.J., the Polaroid Corporation of Cambridge, Mass., the General Electric Company's Lamp Development Laboratory, the Biophysical Instrument Company, and the Massachusetts Institute of Technology, with projects directed by Thomas Benham, blind physics professor at Haverford College, and Dr. Clifford M. Witcher at the Massachusetts

[1] P.A. Zahl, ed., *Blindness*, Princeton University Press, Princeton, N.J., 1950, pp. 431-442.

Institute of Technology.[1] Electronic devices are familiar to most persons in the form of "automatic" door openers in many public buildings such as hospitals and supermarkets. This principle is applied not only to detect objects immediately ahead but also has a "step-down" detection which is very important for safe walking. Dr. Witcher hopefully reports that such a device may be perfected in usable portable form within the next few years. It should prove to be a great boon to the blind.

### Financial Assistance

Costs for educating blind children are higher than for seeing children. The classes are much smaller, many teachers of the blind are paid additional bonuses, and the equipment and other materials are much more expensive. Many states provide supplementary state aid to help local school systems meet these additional costs. The Federal government subsidizes the American Printing House for the Blind to print Braille books and materials. The Post Office Department allows free postage for reading matter for the blind to encourage their cultural activities and the Library of Congress acts as a clearing-house for books for the blind.

### Problems of the Adult Blind

Although this book is primarily concerned with exceptional children, their adult adjustments are an important secondary interest and are closely related to problems of educational and vocational guidance.

The Federal government matches funds by states for rehabilitation of physically and mentally handicapped persons beyond compulsory school age. The purpose is to provide facilities for training so that the handicapped may become self-supporting. The League for the Handicapped carries on a program of vocational training and placement. In order to provide suitable guidance in the employment of the blind

[1] C.M. Witcher, "Electronic Travel Aids," *The New Outlook for the Blind,* 1955, 49, pp. 161-165.

it is often necessary to bring them together into workshops. The general public tends to regard these assemblages as charitable institutions similar to the asylums of medieval days, which is not in accord with the modern philosophy of individual self-esteem and worthiness. This modern philosophy leads away from the "Workshop" plan and delegates services and opportunities for the blind through many community agencies with greater total expense and some duplication of service. In the opposite program of centralization the expenses are less and easier to administer since the funds may be allocated to one agency. Teamwork upon the part of all agencies is the ultimate goal rather than either of these extreme positions. Barnett[1] pleads for several lines of constructive research in such matters as teacher training, vocational experimentation, and the educability of children with double handicaps such as blindness and deafness.

In the meantime the blind adult is left in a quandary. He receives an additional personal exemption on his income tax and a special social security grant up to at least forty-five dollars per month. He is torn between the thought that it is nice for public and private charity to provide for him and the idea that as a self-respecting individual he wishes to work and to pay his own way.

## Other Handicaps of the Blind

Whenever one particular disability or handicap is being discussed the emphasis is necessarily directed toward it. However one must always be aware that such a handicapped person is a human being with physical, intellectual, emotional, and social attributes as well. Taken together with blindness they constitute the blind person whose success or failure, happiness or unhappiness depends upon these total reactions.

The most remarkable and successful illustration is the life story of Helen Keller, blind and deaf from birth. There is no greater saga in the psychology of learning or in human endeavor than the story of her life. Many others with lesser secondary handicaps have also succeeded

---

[1] M.R. Barnett, *Special Education for the Exceptional*, Vol. II, Porter Sargent Publisher, Boston, 1955, pp. 80-82.

according to the measure of their determination and their opportunities. Blind children experience the usual inventory of childhood diseases, they experience the ups and downs of family living, and they respond to a multitude of situations in accordance with their intellectual abilities. Such is the composite picture of the blind.

## Organizations

There are many public and private agencies and organizations interested in the education and welfare of the blind. State legislatures took the lead with Massachusetts authorizing the establishment of a state school in 1829. It was soon followed by many others and as rapidly as states were organized and voted into statehood they soon built their own state schools.

There are several national organizations such as the American Foundation for the Blind and the National Society for the Prevention of Blindness. Many additional organizations such as the International Council for Exceptional Children have comprehensive programs featuring the blind as well as many other types of handicapped. There are teachers' organizations, Federal organizations, Leader Dog societies, and many which are concerned with the adult blind. Lions International with service clubs in thousands of communities has taken a great interest in the welfare of the blind at national, state, and local levels. In some communities other service clubs such as Kiwanis, Rotary, and Exchange have joined forces in this activity. A comprehensive list of agencies can be found in *Directory of Activities for the Blind in the United States and Canada* published by the American Foundation for the Blind, Inc.

### Questions and Topics for Discussion

1. Discuss orally or in writing any firsthand experiences which you have had with any blind persons, interpreting them in the light of problems discussed in this chapter.
2. Discuss why any arbitrary definition of blindness such as 20/200 or poorer is not a practical means of classification.
3. Describe orally or in writing how the daily experiences of a blind and a seeing person differ significantly.

4. Make a thorough, complete report on Hayes's studies of the intelligence of the blind.
5. Select some special phase of the number of the blind as discussed in Best's *Blindness and the Blind in the United States.*
6. Discuss some other famous blind people, including contemporaries, with their accomplishments.
7. Make a report on Talking books and Talking-book machines, how they operate, where they may be obtained, and their probable value.
8. Make an enlarged set of Braille characters and explain the characteristics of different grades, such as Grade 1½.
9. Make contacts with the local luncheon clubs to learn firsthand what any of them are doing for blind children in the community and report to the class.
10. Visit a state school for the blind and a Braille public school class or school.

## A. Organizations

1. American Foundation for the Blind, Inc., 15 W. 16th St., New York 11.
2. American Printing House for the Blind, Inc., 1839 Frankfort Ave., Louisville 6, Ky.
3. National Society for the Prevention of Blindness, Inc., 1790 Broadway, New York 19.

## B. Periodicals

1. *Outlook for the Blind* (monthly except July and August), American Foundation for the Blind, Inc.
2. *The Sight-Saving Review* (quarterly), National Society for the Prevention of Blindness, Inc.

## C. Books

1. Best, H.A., *Blindness and the Blind in the United States*, The Macmillan Co., New York, 1934, 714 pp.
2. Bindt, J.A., *A Handbook for the Blind*, The Macmillan Co., New York, 1952, 244 pp.
3. Brandt, H.F., *The Psychology of Seeing*, Philosophical Library, New York, 1945, 240 pp.
4. Chevigny, H., and S. Braverman, *The Adjustment of the Blind*, Yale University Press, New Haven, Conn., 1950, 320 pp.

5. Cutsforth, T.D., *The Blind in School and Society*, D. Appleton-Century Co., New York, 1933, 263 pp.
6. Farrell, G., *The Story of Blindness*, Harvard University Press, Cambridge, Mass., 1956, 270 pp.
7. Frampton, M.E., *Education of the Blind*, World Book Co., Yonkers, N.Y., 1940, 430 pp.
8. French, R.S., *From Homer to Helen Keller*, American Foundation for the Blind, Inc., New York, 1932, 298 pp.
9. Friedenwald, J.S., H.C. Wilder, A.E. Maumence, T.E. Sanders, E.L. Keyes, M.J. Hogan, W.C. Owens, and E.U. Owens, *Ophthalmic Pathology*, W.B. Saunders Co., Philadelphia, 1954, 489 pp.
10. Gesell, A., F.L. Ilg, and G. Bullis, *Vision—Its Development in Infant and Child*, R.B. Hoeber, New York, 1949, 329 pp.
11. Gowman, A.G., *The War Blind in American Social Structure*, American Foundation for the Blind, Inc., New York, 1957, 237 pp.
12. Hathaway, W., *Education and Health of the Partially Seeing Child* (3rd ed.), Columbia University Press, New York, 1954, 227 pp.
13. Hayes, S.P., *Vocational Aptitude Tests for the Blind*, Perkins Institution, Watertown, Mass., 1946, 32 pp.
14. Huxley, A., *The Art of Seeing*, Harper & Brothers, New York, 1942, 273 pp.
15. Irwin, R.B., *As I Saw It*, American Foundation for the Blind, Inc., New York, 1955, 205 pp.
16. Lende, H., *Books About the Blind*, American Foundation for the Blind, Inc., New York, 1953, 357 pp.
17. Lowenfeld, B., *Our Blind Children*, Charles C Thomas Publisher, Springfield, Ill., 1956, 205 pp.
18. Luckiesh, M., *Light, Vision, and Seeing*, Van Nostrand, New York, 1944, 323 pp.
19. Merry, R.V., *Problems in the Education of the Visually Handicapped Children*, Harvard University Press, Cambridge, Mass, 1933, 243 pp.
20. Norris, M., P.J. Spaulding, and F.H. Brodie, *Blindness in Children*, University of Chicago Press, Chicago, 1957, 173 pp.
21. Putnam, P., *Cast off the Darkness*, Harcourt Brace and Co., Inc., New York, 1957, 253 pp.
22. Rocheleau, C., and R. Mack, *Those in the Dark Silence*, The Volta Bureau, Washington, D.C., 1930, 169 pp.
23. Wilbur, L., *Vocations for the Visually Handicapped*, American Foundation for the Blind, Inc., New York, 1937, 224 pp.
24. Zahl, P.A. (ed.), *Blindness*, Princeton University Press, Princeton, N.J., 1950, 576 pp.

## D. Films and Filmstrips

1. *Johnny's New World*, 16 minutes, 16-mm., sound, color. Explains need for early detection and treatment of children's eye problems. For rental and sale price consult the National Society for the Prevention of Blindness, Inc., 1790 Broadway, New York 19.
2. *Eyes for Tomorrow*, 22 minutes, 16-mm., sound. Deals with eye health problems throughout life. Stresses relationship with general health. For rental and sale price consult the National Society for the Prevention of Blindness, Inc.
3. *Protecting Eyes at Work*, 50-frame 35-mm. filmstrip, color, silent. For students in junior and senior high schools and vocational schools. Text-Film Department, McGraw-Hill Book Company, 330 W. 42nd St., New York 36.
4. *Growing into Reading through use of Braille*, 25 minutes, color, silent. Many aspects of reading readiness for the blind through Braille means. American Foundation for the Blind, 15 W. 16th St., New York 11.

# CHAPTER 21

*The Anatomy and*
*Physiology of Hearing*

WHEN THE IMPORTANCE of vision was being discussed it was noted that the eyes are considered to be the windows of the soul. It is true that the eyes play a very important role in human affairs but in a different way the ears carry on their function also. Whereas some meanings may be judged from the gleam of the eye, what is heard in the spoken word may not be as easily mistaken or overlooked. While sounds other than speech have meanings, the spoken word and hearing it join together to be the most effective avenue of human communication. On the surface it would seem that blindness is a greater handicap than deafness, but psychologically deafness is the greater handicap. Progress has been made in bringing the speech of others to the deaf and to the hard-of-hearing as well as the development of speech in these handicapped persons themselves.

Ways to improve communication over distances beyond the reach of the human voice have always intrigued and challenged the resources of man. Signal fires were developed to a remarkable efficiency by Indians. The most modern version is said to be associated with the atomic blast which lighted up the heavens and brought a return signal advising that it was not necessary to shout. The use of couriers is carried over from the Greek civilization to the revival of the Olympic games today. Carrier pigeons played their part in wars when other means of communication often failed. The invention of the telegraph by Morse more than one hundred years ago advanced

*Courtesy of photographic services, Chicago public schools.*

Class for the blind, Bell school, Chicago.

*Courtesy of Dr. Richard G. Brill, superintendent.*

Intermediate classroom building, California School for the Deaf, Riverside.

the rate to instantaneous communication. Further advances were made by the invention of the telephone by Dr. Alexander Graham Bell about seventy-five years ago. The widespread use of the telephone into the humblest homes is evidence of its universal appeal. Incidentally, both speech and hearing, but not vision, are involved. No matter how great the distance the communication is instantaneous.

During the early decades of the twentieth century two modes of entertainment were coming into popular use. The first was the silent movie which could only be seen and the second was the radio which could only be heard. In recent years the movie added the voice and the radio added the picture to make the television which brings the talking movie into the home. These remarks about communication are not intended to detract from vision but to show that hearing is also very important in human affairs.

## The Mechanisms of Hearing

When reduced to its simplest terms, hearing is based on a simple principle of mechanics. Sound waves are transmitted to the auditory nerve in the ear and the nerve impressions are transmitted to the brain. There are various refinements in the process which are truly marvelous and which are made possible by the anatomy and structure of the ear.

The diagram of the human ear is helpful in understanding the hearing process. There are three principal parts to the ear: (1) the outer ear; (2) the middle ear; and (3) the inner ear. The outer ear, or pinna, is the most obvious portion but relatively less important. Its main function is to conduct sounds to the inner parts. Its irregular shape is designed so as to gather up the sound waves and direct them into the canal. Outer ears are of various sizes and shapes and vary in how close they lie to the head. These variations may add to, or detract from, the general facial appearance but this is not so obvious in women who generally keep theirs hidden. The ears of boxers and wrestlers are vulnerable parts of the anatomy with distortions known as "cauliflower" ears. Some deaf children have no external ears and no canal from them. In some cases this defect is hereditary.

The canal allows passage of the sound waves to the tympanic membrane. A secretion of excessive wax sometimes forms, hardens, and blocks this passage so that hearing is temporarily impaired. Children sometimes block the canal with small objects which may require medical care for removal. Small insects may get into the canal and cause much discomfort until removed.

The middle ear contains a very interesting mechanism which permits free operation of its various parts. The tympanic membrane must have free vibration which is ordinarily attained by air reaching its inner side or tympanic cavity through the Eustachian tube. This tube leads from the throat and in good health performs its function very well. Throat infections may spread up through it into the middle ear, block the passage of air, and infections destroy three tiny bones which are located there. These three bones are known as the malleus, the incus, and the stapes. The malleus is joined to the tympanic membrane in such a manner as to transmit its vibrations to the incus. The malleus has a socket type of connection with the incus similar to the hip joint. The incus is joined to the stapes so that the latter gives a direct thrust to the vestibular window leading to the inner ear. The complete mechanism gives definiteness and sharpness to the sound waves which does not prove to be of this superior quality whenever the tympanic membrane and the three bones have been destroyed and the sound waves go direct to the vestibular window. The area of the vestibular window is only about one-thirtieth as large as the tympanic membrane. Since these mechanisms of the middle ear are very delicate there are many ways in which their functioning may be impaired or destroyed.

There are two parts to the inner ear, each has its own distinctive function. The part which is concerned with hearing is the cochlea or spiral canal from whose walls the cochlear or auditory nerve extend into the cochlear liquid in some 25,000 to 30,000 tiny hair cells in each ear. The liquid vibrations set up impressions in the auditory nerve which are transmitted to the brain. In order to provide a balance a second or a cochlear window is located in the wall of the middle ear to compensate for the presure on the vestibular window. The second part of the middle ear consists of three semicircular canals posited in three different directions and designed to keep a person aware of balance. One axis detects falling forward or backward, a second detects sidewise motion, and a third detects rotation or dizziness. Special vestibular nerves lead from these canals to the brain. Nature has ingeniously planned this auxiliary function in a well-protected place and in connection with liquids which were available for a different purpose. The entire structures of the middle and inner ears are embedded deeply in the bones of the head since as a unit the ear is a very delicate organ needing maximum protection.

## The Examination of Hearing

The examination of hearing is not a simple process although a few easier methods of informal observation and testing give significant clues. Examinations may range from these simple techniques to the detailed analysis with an individual audiometer by a consultant in audiology which indicates the nature and extent of hearing or of hearing loss. This type of examination reveals the function of the ear. A second phase of examination is by the medical specialist in which two titles are noted: the aurist is a medical specialist in diseases of the ear; an otologist is a medical specialist in the science of the ear, its anatomy, functions, and diseases. The otolaryngologist specializes in these other fields as well as in diseases and disorders of the throat, in speech, and in other allied areas. The general field of examinations is analogous to vision testing in which some were qualified in acuity or refraction and others in the diseases of the eye. There are many qualities of sound each of which has its unique problems of measurement and in addition there are anomalies of anatomy and diseases of the various portions of the ear.

*Symptoms of hearing defect.* Symptoms of hearing defect fall into four general classes:

    I. *Physical Symptoms*

        Failure to respond, says "What?" constantly, cups his hand to ear, moves closer, has peculiar posture, tilts head at unusual angles to get better sound, mouth breathing, running ears, earaches, and noises in head.

II. *Speech Symptoms*

Defects in speech, peculiar voice often high pitched and without expression, avoids talking to people, lack of adequate flow of language.

III. *School Symptoms*

Poor general scholarship, poor oral work, generally slow and inaccurate in schoolwork, particularly poor in spelling where dictation methods are used, puts his own incorrect interpretation on many questions and topics as a substitute for complete hearing and understanding.

IV. *Social Symptoms*

Listless, uninterested in any group, sensitive, aloof, suspicious, hard to accept as a cordial acquaintance.

*Informal and formal testing.* Hearing is usually judged in terms of how weak or how strong the sounds must be to be heard. The whisper test consists of whispering simple numbers behind the child, first in one ear and then the other, with the numbers to be repeated by the child. The purpose of this position is to prevent him from reading the lips of the examiner. Listening to a *watch tick* or the clicking of two coins together are additional testing methods but are not very satisfactory since such tones are above the usual range of hearing for the conversational voice.

A more formal method of hearing examination is to test each ear separately with the spoken voice. The child is placed with first one ear, then the other toward the examiner who stands on a line marked off every foot up to 20 feet. A wad of cotton or a suitable plug of rubber is placed in one ear so that only one ear hears at a time. In sidewise position lip reading is not possible. The examiner speaks in an ordinary tone, asking simple everyday questions suited to the child's age and interests. The examiner starts at a distance of 20 feet and if the child does not hear he comes closer, foot by foot, until he is heard. Each ear is tested separately and results are recorded in terms of the fractional part of the 20 feet, such as 8/20, which is interpreted as hearing at 8 feet what should be heard at 20 feet.

*Group tests of hearing.* In recent years another method of hearing examination is the group use of an audiometer. Entire classrooms of pupils may be tested at a time. Early elementary school pupils may be examined successfully if limited to smaller groups. Each pupil is fitted with a pair of earphones and provided with pencil and paper. The audiometer transmits the human voice from an instrument similar to a victrola, adjusted to gradually diminishing degrees of loudness. Numbers are spoken from the audiometer first into the right ear, then the left ear, and each pupil records what he hears. The record has first a woman's voice and then a man's so that four tests are available. By scoring the papers it is possible to determine at what point the hearing is no longer functioning satisfactorily. The numbers are short so that failure should not be due to mental inability. A few pupils do not respond well because of the novelty of the task or from excitement. Whenever a pupil fails he may be reexamined a few days later and if no more successful he may be referred for individual hearing examination along with others who have made poor showings. Many school systems are conducting such surveys in certain regular grades. Some school systems have found that the individual audiometer is no more time-consuming and gives a more reliable result.

*Individual tests of hearing.* If the informal and group tests of hearing disclose some marked defect of hearing an individual examination should be made. There are several variations of the individual method. One of the earlier methods consisted of using standard tuning forks in octave frequencies of 64, 128, 256, etc., cycles per second. The estimate of hearing loss was based upon how long the pupil could continue to hear the progressively fainter vibrations. The tuning fork is currently used for a quick approximation and to detect high-tone deafness as well as testing for bone conduction. The chief weakness is variation in the intensity of the sound produced when the fork is struck. This weakness is bypassed by the use of pure-tone audiometers in which intensity and frequency of vibrations are carefully controlled by vacuum-tube circuits. The intensity is regulated by a dial usually graduated in five-decibel steps. The decibel is the standard of intensity and is the amount of difference which is barely discernible between two intensities. Head phones are used and a bone-conduction receiver may also be used and held tightly against the temporal bone just behind the ear. Three recent types of audiometers include the Western Electric 6PB, the Sonotone model 20, and the Maico D-9. From time to time new models appear and are usually designated by higher numbers or by later letters of the alphabet. The final judgment of deafness, degree of hearing defect, or diseases affecting hearing should always be made by the specialized physician known as the otolaryngologist.

### The Characteristics of Sound

There are many dimensions and meanings of sound. There is a physical meaning of sound which can be measured by some of the apparatus and in units such as decibels. They are ranked from low numbers to high according to intensity, with a faint whisper being about 15 decibels, average speech about 60 decibels, and 140 decibels for the largest air-raid siren at a distance of 100 feet. There is a psychological meaning of sound which is expressed as pleasant or unpleasant, loud or faint, and various levels of pitch. This interpretation of sound follows after the physical aspects of sound have been recorded in the ear and the auditory nerve has transmitted it to the brain. The physical source of sound which reaches the ear is from molecules of air which are set in motion when an object moves or vibrates setting up sound waves. These sound waves travel about 1,000 feet per second in air or more than 700 miles per hour. This rate is many times slower than the rate of light which is 186,000 miles per hour. The distance away of a bolt of lightning can be measured roughly by counting the seconds between seeing the flash which is practically instantaneous and the sound of the thunder which travels at approximately five seconds per mile. Great interest has been shown in recent years in the "sound barrier" or the rate at which an object must travel to exceed the speed of sound. When jet-propelled aircraft were able to attain and exceed this speed the expectation of destruction of the aircraft did not materialize, although a sound similar to a loud clap of thunder results when the barrier is broken or passed.

The physical loudness of sound is measured in decibels with the practical range from no decibel at the threshold of hearing to the threshold of pain from extremely loud noises at 140 or more decibels. The measure of pitch is in the frequency of cycles of sound waves at the low end of the range theoretically at zero to 32,000 or more per second and from thence on into the range of ultrasonics. The usual range of speech is from 250 to about 4,000 cycles. Frequencies above this range may be heard by dogs and some other animals. Very low frequencies merge into physical vibrations which may be interpreted as impressions of sound but it is difficult to distinguish their true nature. All of these qualities of sound together with the intricate anatomy and physiology of the ear combine to make hearing a very complex process.

### Number with Impaired Hearing

The great majority of children have reasonably normal hearing and a few have hearing superior to the general average. In the field of impaired hearing four groups may be recognized: (1) the largest group who have slight loss of hearing but whose educational needs are met mainly by seating near the front of the classroom; (2) a second smaller group who remain enrolled in regular grades but who would profit by one or more special sessions with an itinerant teacher using methods of lip or speech reading; (3) a third and still smaller group known as the hard-of-hearing whose hearing is so markedly impaired that special classes for full or part time are necessary and with special teachers and special equipment; and (4) special schools or classes for the totally deaf. The totally deaf represent a larger number than the hard-of hearing in educational facilities!

The number who have impaired hearing and fall into each of the four groups are based mostly on estimates although some surveys have been made. A committee on Hard-of-Hearing Children of the American Federation of Organizations for the Hard-of-Hearing reported in 1926 that 14 per cent of pupils have hearing defects, amounting to at least three million children of school age. These estimates were also quoted by the White House Committee on Child Health and Protection in 1930. The later estimates are somewhat more conservative. Ronnei[1] and Silverman[2] agree that 5 per cent is a more reasonable estimate, with from one and one-half to two million children in the United States with defective hearing. Reports of actual enrollments of the hard-of-hearing and of the deaf will be given in Chapters 22 and 23.

### Impaired-Hearing Pupils in Regular Classes

In the preceding section four types of impaired hearing were listed. For the most effective education special classes or schools should be available for the deaf and for the most extremely hard-of-hearing pupils. Supporting data will be found in the next two chapters. The mildly impaired and the lesser degrees of hard-of-hearing are usually found in regular classrooms. The regular teacher should provide all possible individual adjustments within her power, such as seating near the front of the room, speaking clearly and with emphasis when addressing such pupils and the rest of the class. If hearing aids have been procured she should see to it that they are worn and whether or not they are in perfect working order as revealed by the pupil's reactions.

Speech reading, formerly known as lip reading, is coming into general use in instruction of the hard-of-hearing and the deaf. For the hard-of-hearing pupils in regular classes some school systems are now providing special itinerant teachers trained in speech reading who take these pupils one or more periods weekly in small groups for such instruction. The regular teacher is acquainted with the general idea and procedure so that she can speak in the manner of the speech-reading teacher and thus hard-of-hearing pupils may benefit from full-time instruction more nearly suited to their needs.

[1] E.C. Ronnei, *Special Education for the Exceptional*, Vol. II, Porter Sargent Publisher, Boston, 1955, p. 261.
[2] S.R. Silverman, *Hearing and Deafness*, Rinehart Books, Inc., New York, 1951, pp. 354-355.

The following suggestions for the guidance of the regular teacher are offered in the Michigan bulletin.[1]

1. Encourage the child to make a study of speech reading (lip reading).
2. The teacher should speak distinctly to the child.
3. Stand where the child can see the movements of your lips easily.
4. Give attention to the correction of speech defects or incorrect pronunciation of words.
5. Make greater use of visual materials.
6. Provide an opportunity for the child to participate in the activities of his group in such a way that he may see the lips of the other pupils.
7. See that the child's customary seat is in the front of the room near the window.
8. Arrange for the correction of vision defects. (It is difficult to read lips with poor vision.)
9. Urge the child's parents to speak distinctly and to stand so that their lips can be seen by the child.
10. Consider with parents the feasibility of individual hearing aids for children who have serious hearing losses. Such individual hearing aids should only be purchased on the recommendation of an otologist.

## Questions and Topics for Discussion

1. Describe individuals with hearing defects whom you have known personally in regard to their symptoms and characteristics.
2. Describe any other methods of informal diagnosis with which you are familiar.
3. Which do you believe is a more serious handicap, lack of hearing or lack of vision of the same degree? State your reasons.
4. Describe any changes in your opinions about hearing handicaps from the discussion of this chapter.
5. If possible arrange for a demonstration of hearing examination with one of the individual audiometers.
6. Conduct a discussion about the intensity of incidental sounds about you in units of decibels.
7. Conduct a discussion about the pitch of various sounds, musical notes, etc.
8. What provision does your school system make for hearing surveys?

Note: Consult reference material at the end of Chapter 23.

[1] F.E. Lord, *Helping the Exceptional Child in the Regular Classroom*, Bulletin No. 315, Superintendent of Public Instruction, Lansing, Mich., 1941, p. 21.

# CHAPTER 22

## The Hard-of-Hearing

THE HARD-OF-HEARING comprise a group of persons between those mildly handicapped in hearing and the totally deaf. They are so handicapped that the regular methods of teaching do not adequately serve their needs. In spite of this fact there are thousands enrolled in regular classes with great educational loss to themselves and to society. Many suffer from the misinterpretations mentioned in the preceding chapter, being mistaken for having antisocial behavior problems or for the mentally retarded. Some of them are unaware of defects and merely assume that everyone's hearing is supposed to be at that level. Thanks to the great advances in amplification of sound, in hearing aids, in speech reading, in speech correction, and in many other ways there is new hope for the hard-of-hearing.

### Definition and Classification

For practical purposes O'Connor and Streng[1] suggest classifying children into four groups according to hearing loss. Group A has children with slight hearing loss up to 20 decibels and hence able to make a fair adjustment in regular classes if allowed special privileges in seating. Group B with 25 to 50 or 55 decibel loss in the better ear in the usual speech range show a need for help either in speech reading or possibly in the hard-of-hearing class. Since most of these pupils in Groups A and B remain in regular classrooms, the suggestions for

[1] C.D. O'Connor and A. Streng, *Teaching the Acoustically Handicapped*, in *The Education of Exceptional Children*, National Society for the Study of Education, Forty-ninth Yearbook, Part II, Chicago, 1950, pp. 152-175.

346

their care and education were discussed in the preceding chapter. Group C with 55 or 60 to 65 or 75 decibel loss may profit from hard-of-hearing classes with hearing amplification so as to take advantage of speech reading. At the more extreme end of the scale is Group D with 70 to 75 decibel loss who are unable to have practical hearing of speech and language so that they must be taught by methods applicable to deaf children.

Elwood A. Stevenson[1] states the distinction between the deaf and the hard-of-hearing as follows:

A deaf person—though many times, say six cases out of ten, possessed of some sound perception—is one who *does not react* understandingly to spoken language. A hard-of-hearing person is one who reacts to spoken language understandingly, provided the source is brought within his hearing range, either through a loud voice, through amplification of sound, or through some other mechanical device. A deaf person may have 20 per cent of sound perception, but nevertheless he does not understandingly hear spoken language. A hard-ot-hearing person may have only 5 per cent of hearing, yet nevertheless he hears understandingly.

Marginal cases at either extreme of the hard-of-hearing classification have their practical hearing dependent upon many additional factors such as their native intellectual ability, their personality characteristics, and the effects of home and parental influences.

### The Number of the Hard-of-Hearing

The number of children with some degree of impaired hearing is much greater than the hard-of-hearing and the deaf. As noted in the preceding chapter estimates of those with impaired hearing have been lowered from 14 to 5 per cent as a result of more careful methods of screening and refinements of group and individual diagnosis. The very careful hearing survey conducted for the Board of Education of New York City in 1941 found that fully 3 per cent had a hearing loss of at least nine decibels or more in either ear. Upon this basis Dr. Clarence D. O'Connor[2] estimated that there were 80,000 children of

[1] M.E. Frampton and H.G. Rowell, *Education of the Handicapped*, Vol. II, *Problems*, p. 218.

[2] C.D. O'Connor, "Children with Impaired Hearing," *The Volta Review*, 1954, 56, pp. 433-439.

school age and an additional 44,000 under school age with impaired hearing. Of the 80,000 only 25,000 have losses of more than 20 decibels. Slightly more than one-half of the severely impaired in hearing were enrolled in any special schools or classes, since it is estimated that one child in 1,000 needs such educational facilities. In October, 1952 there were 1,950 pupils enrolled in such schools in New York State with an estimated number of 2,800 in this classification.

The *American Annals of the Deaf* publishes figures in January each year on the enrollments of the deaf and the hard-of-hearing in all types of public and private schools and classes as of the preceding October 31. The report for 1956[1] lists 3,839 hard-of-hearing pupils in residential or in day-school facilities. Fifty-three per cent were in day schools or classes and forty-seven per cent were in residential schools. In these same facilities there were 18,487 deaf children, hence the hard-of-hearing comprised only 17 per cent of the total. From these figures it may be concluded that only one of the hard-of-hearing in every 5,000 pupils is now likely to be enrolled in special facilities. Obviously the greater number continue to be enrolled in regular classes where in many communities they profit from speech reading, from hearing aids, and from other remedial processes.

## Causes

The detailed description of the ear gave some clues about the many causes of impaired hearing. There are the three principal parts of the ear as well as the nerve mechanisms in the brain itself which may be affected. Any interference which arises in the outer or middle ear is classified as causing *conduction impairment* or *conduction deafness*. Abnormal production of wax in the canal may block the passage of air waves completely or distort them as they reach the tympanic membrane. Anomalies of structure of the pinna or outer ear may result in hearing impairment.

Disease and destruction of the middle ear contribute heavily to causes of hearing impairment. Throat and nose infections spread to the middle ear through the Eustachian tube. Otitis media is an

[1] *American Annals of the Deaf*, 102, 57, p. 118.

inflammation of the middle ear which can be of a tuberculous type often associated with active pulmonary tuberculosis, although it may run an independent course. The delicate mechanism of the three tiny connecting bones is easily thrown out of balance by abscesses. The stapes, or last bone of the chain, may become immobilized by otosclerosis so that the sound waves are not transmitted to the inner ear. The proper functioning of the outer and middle ear may be affected by loud explosions, by continuous high-pitched tones such as from high-powered airplanes in military duty and loud noises in manufacturing plants—all of which affects adults rather than children.

A second general area of causes is associated with the inner ear and falls under the title of *perceptive deafness*. Defects and diseases may weaken or destroy the supporting liquid in the cochlea and in the semicircular canals. Unless this transmitting medium is in good condition the wave impressisons are not perfectly received by the tiny hairlets containing the auditory nerve ends. This inner mechanism is damaged by infectious diseases such as meningitis. Head injuries from forced birth delivery add their toll to injuries but this cause should be rapidly lessened if the most modern procedures of obstetrics are used with pelvic measurements which indicate Caesarian or normal delivery. Nerve impairment results if the mother has had Rubella or German measles during the early months of pregnancy. Osteomyelitis and other diseases of the bones of the skull which surround the inner ear may result in impairment of hearing. Congenital deafness adds its number to the causes of impairment.

The causes of hearing impairment are not necessarily eliminated when the total ear is in perfect condition. Further trouble may lie in the auditory and other nerve tracts and centers of the brain, which is known as *central deafness*. Brain tumors are abnormal growths which may affect the auditory centers. Hemorrhages add their effect to the list of causes. Abnormal conditions of the brain are discovered by the electroencephalogram or by the pneumo-encephalogram which provide graphic X-ray pictures of the brain. Another cause of hearing impairment is of psychogenic origin. Hysteria and other severe emotional conditions make deafness appear to be an absolute reality although there may be no physical basis.

Many forces combine to reduce the number who have impaired

hearing. The medical profession is able to do much in preventive and remedial measures. Parents provide better health and safety conditions in homes and in general welfare. The manufacture and use of hearing aids have developed rapidly in recent years. The improvement of speech reading methods with its more extended use has brought speech communication to thousands who otherwise might be denied its extremely valuable use.

### Characteristics of the Hard-of-Hearing

Unless there is some impairment of the nervous system which may affect the auditory centers and other portions of the brain there seems to be no logical reason to expect that the personality characteristics of the hard-of-hearing would be different than those of the normal hearing persons. For those hard-of-hearing with brain damage any deviate characteristics would in theory be more nearly like other brain-damaged persons than like the normal hearing. The characteristics of such brain-damaged persons have been discussed in earlier chapters.

The hard-of-hearing have certain symptoms of their impairment which are unique to them. Regardless of what these symptoms are the very fact of their existence puts certain reactions into play since the desire to conform and not be different from classmates is a universal need. These types of behavior include physical signs such as cupping the hand to the ear and asking others to speak louder. The cupping of the ear may be observed by only one person at a time but in the course of time there are many such occasions involving many persons. Speaking louder in the classroom or within any group is likely to draw unusual attention to the hard-of-hearing person. Unless he can overcome his feelings of being conspicuous his disturbed emotions may rise to intense levels.

Since the hard-of-hearing person does not hear all that is being said around him he may become suspicious and sensitive, with a desire to withdraw from all social relationships. If his speech is not of the normal quality it leads him to become less communicative and in case of poor scholarship the cycle of withdrawal and regression is complete. None of these symptoms in themselves are basic or congenital in origin and hence in theory the hard-of-hearing are not different from the normal hearing. It is only because the conditions generated by being hard-of-hearing bring about this kind of behavior that the hard-of-hearing appear to be somewhat different in their social and personality reactions.

It is unfortunate that these social patterns begin to operate in infancy and a few years of such conditioning are operative before the young child is ready for school entrance. These early formative years have effects which cannot be remedied overnight. Such modern devices as hearing aids, and such modern methods as speech reading are bringing a new era of better adjustment for the hard-of-hearing not only in the improvement of hearing, but in the normal speech communication which ensues.

*Personality traits.* Reports of personality studies of the hard-of-hearing are comparatively few. This is probably due in part to the very few special classes where they are segregated and in part to the greater interest and experimentation in rehabilitation techniques. In a personality study Madden[1] had teachers rate hard-of-hearing and normal-hearing children who were matched in respect to intelligence, sex, age, and race. There were no differences between the two groups in attentiveness, obedience, and social attitude, but the hard-of-hearing were rated lower in leadership and definitely lower in aggressiveness and in shyness.

Pintner[2] compared over one thousand hard-of-hearing with normal-hearing children from the upper elementary grades on results with the Pupil Portraits Test. He found that the boys who were hard-of-hearing tended to rate themselves somewhat lower than the normal-hearing boys. There was only a slight difference between the two groups of girls. It was probably more significant that those with slightly defective hearing made scores practically the same as did the normal-hearing; the more extreme the handicaps, the greater the

---

[1] R. Madden, *The School Status of the Hard-of-Hearing Child*, Teachers College, Contributions to Education, No. 499, Columbia University, New York, 1931, 64 pp.
[2] R. Pintner, "An Adjustment Test with Normal and Hard-of-Hearing Children," *Journal of Genetic Psychology*, 1940, 56, pp. 367-381.

differences. The same author summarized various studies and investigations of personality and concluded that the differences between the hard-of-hearing and the normal-hearing are very slight. The hard-of-hearing are somewhat more introverted and slightly less well balanced emotionally. The younger hard-of-hearing tend to be more dominant than the normal-hearing, but as they grow older they find less satisfaction in dominant attitudes.

*Intelligence.* There are two principal types of materials in group intelligence tests: (1) verbal or language; and (2) nonlanguage. Because of limited communication the hard-of-hearing and the deaf are generally more limited in verbal or language usage than are the normal-hearing. The impaired-hearing tend to develop their visual powers to the maximum and hence are apt to make a relatively better showing on the nonlanguage test materials which feature visual content. Pintner[1] administered his Verbal or Language test to pupils with impaired hearing and found that their intelligence quotients were a few points below 100, but when he used his Non-language Mental Test the deficit disappeared. Waldman,[2] Wade, and Aretz used the National Intelligence Tests on several hundred hard-of-hearing children and found an average intelligence quotient of about 92. This test had mainly verbal or language material.

Testing of impaired-hearing pupils in the Detroit Public Schools includes various tests such as the Nebraska test by Hiskey and certain portions of the individual examination known as the Detroit Test of Learning Aptitude with omission of subtests requiring oral directions. Various regular Detroit Group Intelligence tests are used on small groups and sufficient time is devoted to giving directions for each page by pantomime or otherwise so that the nature of each part is understood. After this the regulation time limits are followed for the test items themselves.

As in the case of personality characteristics there is no reason to expect limited mentality because of impaired hearing itself unless

[1] R. Pintner, J. Eisenson, and M. Stanton, *The Psychology of the Physically Handicapped*, F. S. Crofts Co., New York, 1940, pp. 190-192.
[2] J.L. Waldman, F.A. Wade, and C.W. Aretz, *Hearing and the School Child*, The Volta Bureau, Washington, D.C., 1930.

it is coupled with some deterioriation or malfunctioning of the brain which may also occur in other handicapped or nonhandicapped children.

## History of the Hard-of-Hearing

Because the hard-of-hearing have only recently been a more clearly defined group their education and rehabilitation have been in indefinite status. Up to about 1900 they did not have recognition as a group. Those with the milder impairment were enrolled in regular classes and achieved what they could with regular methods although many individual teachers of these regular classes had made whatever adjustments they could for them. The more seriously impaired of the hard-of-hearing were placed in schools and classes for the deaf. On October 31, 1956, slightly more than one-half of the 3,839 hard-of-hearing pupils were in day schools or classes and the remainder were in residential schools.

The Detroit Day School for the Deaf was formally organized in 1900 with two classes for the deaf starting as a nucleus two years earlier. By about 1912 the administration of this school became increasingly aware that there were some pupils in the school who were not so completely deaf as the others and that some speech and meaningful interpretations were possible for them. Special study was made of them which marked the beginning of Detroit's classes for the hard-of-hearing. Many other schools for the deaf were having similar experiences at about the same time and thus the movement spread into the larger cities.

Progress in any field of special education for exceptional children does not necessarily mean an expansion of the number of special schools or classes where heads may be counted and impressive statistical summaries of enrollments may be made. Developments in the remedial and preventive programs with less need for segregation become the line of progress. Acoustic hearing aids, speech reading, and the development of speech enter the picture so that today the hard-of-hearing child may receive maximum help in one or more periods with the itinerant speech and hearing teacher while otherwise remaining in his regular classroom. Since speech reading and the development of speech are included in the chapters on speech, only a discussion of the hearing aid will be taken up here.

### Hearing Aids

Since the hard-of-hearing have some degree of hearing there is a universal urge upon their part to improve the intensity and other qualities of what hearing they have. The most time-honored method consisted in cupping the hand behind the ear and it continues to have considerable use today. The normal-hearing person may sometimes resort to it if the speaker is far away, if his voice is weak, or if there are other distracting noises. Davis[1] reports that the cupped hand may raise the intensity of sound as much as ten decibels which is the difference between a whisper and faint speech in the lower range of decibels. He also reports as follows:

The man with a mild hearing loss puts in his ear a button with a shoe-lace attached, sticks the other end of the lace into his collar, and goes on his way. His friends think he is wearing a hearing aid; and, distrustful of its effectiveness, instinctively raise their voices, and all is well.

Serving somewhat more effectively than the cupped hand is the simple ear trumpet or a speaking tube, both of which amplify the sounds but are conspicuous accessories. A metal held against the teeth may amplify bone conduction to the inner ear. There are several more recent types of hearing aids which are improvements over the cupped hand or the speaking tube. One of these is the carbon-type hearing aid which operates on the same principle as a telephone receiver. It was probably developed because many hard-of-hearing people discovered that they could hear much better over the telephone than in face-to-face conversation. The most recent advances came with the development of electronics which also made radio reception possible. Amplification of sound could be stepped up to an unbearable intensity. Headphones with adjustments for each ear to operate individually on small groups of hard-of-hearing children were installed in various schools such as the Detroit School for the Deaf. With better

[1] H. Davis, *Hearing and Deafness, A Guide for Laymen*, Rinehart Books, Inc., New York, 1951, pp. 163-164.

hearing rapid progress was possible in speech reading. Further improvements came with the invention of the tiny transistor which replaced the bulky vacuum tube. Hearing aids are going through a rapid process of refinement in size and hearing qualities. Many kinds are being manufactured and are advertised in many of the widely circulated magazines.

Although there have been remarkable improvements in modern hearing aids, it is futile to expect that perfect reception will be possible. Reception may be good at some parts of the pitch or sound frequency scale and less satisfactory in other ranges. When the intensity of sound is increased there may be difficulty in tolerance which might be illustrated in the unpleasantness for the normal-hearing person if he must listen for some minutes to someone shouting rather than speaking in ordinary tones.

Under the best conditions it is almost impossible for the hearing aid to function perfectly and users must anticipate and accept some degree of compromise. Unless a hearing aid improves the hearing by at least thirty decibels it is somewhat of a liability rather than a complete asset. Users of hearing aids should consult with their otologist about the best type suited to the individual's needs. Within these limits the hearing aid is becoming more nearly perfected and is a great boon to thousands of the hard-of-hearing. Some success has been achieved with the use of hearing aids by children two years of age. The time may come when hearing aids will be in as common use as glasses and will not be so conspicuous and will not be in danger of breaking.

### Other Remedial Measures

In addition to hearing aids many cases improve under proper and continual medical care. Modern antibiotics such as penicillin rapidly clear up infections which formerly might have run their course and destroyed various portions of the ear. Infections in the middle ear which burst the tympanic membrane or which required a surgical incision to avoid such destruction may now be usually cured without these complications and dangerous effects.

The procedures for aiding the hard-of-hearing have changed greatly in the past few years. The improvements have made it possible for many of them to hear much more nearly at a normal level so that they are becoming better integrated into regular classrooms. Some of them are serviced by itinerant teachers who assist in the development of speech and in the art of speech reading. The hard-of-hearing are becoming as self-reliant as the normal-hearing. However there is some danger in this very independence in that no one trained in their needs will be available to survey their status from time to time. Under careful direction more of them would procure hearing aids which would be checked to see that they are used and kept in good condition. There are other procedures for the hard-of-hearing which should be kept at a high level in the regular classrooms but which may gradually be overlooked. Unless an itinerant teacher is available there should be a special consultant provided to see that no phases or activities be allowed to deteriorate. If such provisions are made there is new hope for the hard-of-hearing.

## Questions and Topics for Discussion

1. Discuss orally or in writing any firsthand experiences which you may have had with any hard-of-hearing persons and interpret them in the light of problems discussed in this chapter.
2. If possible arrange to have a demonstration of group as well as of individual audiometer testing.
3. If hearing aids are available learn more about them by having them tried on you.
4. Visit a hard-of-hearing class and make firsthand observations on the procedures.
5. Observe what the itinerant teacher for the defective in speech and hard-of-hearing is able to accomplish.
6. Report how your local school system is providing for its hard-of-hearing.
7. Discuss the nature of articles in the *Volta Review* and in *Hearing News*.

Note: Consult reference material at the end of Chapter 23.

# CHAPTER 23

## The Deaf

THE MOST EXTREME TYPE of hearing defect is deafness. Understanding the deaf is a paradox. The untrained deaf adult may generally pass as a nonhandicapped person as far as external appearances are concerned. Actually he has a handicap that is more baffling in some respects than the totally blind or the physically crippled whose handicaps are immediately observable but for whom social communication is possible. The deaf person may be judged to have no handicap, yet he is grossly misjudged. It is truly a challenge for those who teach and work with the deaf to break through the barriers to communication and to neutralize the effects of the handicap.

### Definitions of Deafness

There has been so much progress in the study and treatment of the deaf that definitions which seemed to be appropriate a few years ago are rapidly going out of use. Some time ago the deaf were known as the "deaf and dumb" or "deaf-mutes" because it was not known in those days that the deaf could be taught to speak and hence their silence was dubbed "dumbness." Two definitions with somewhat different emphases have been widely quoted. The White House Conference on Child Health and Protection[1] proposed the following definition:

*The deaf* are those who were born either totally or sufficiently deaf to prevent the establishment of speech and natural language; those who became deaf in childhood before language and speech were established; or

[1] *Special Education*, p. 277.

those who became deaf in childhood so soon after the natural establishment of speech and language that the ability to speak and understand speech and language has been practically lost to them.

This definition emphasizes the onset of deafness in three possible stages from birth or in early childhood but with the same end result. This definition leaves a vague inference that speech and language will never be developed and this is not the true state of affairs.

The point of view of the Conference of Executives of American Schools for the Deaf[1] is expressed in its definition:

*The deaf.* Those in whom the sense of hearing is non-functional for the ordinary purposes of life. This general group is made up of two distinct classes, based entirely on the time of the loss of hearing; (a) *the congenitally deaf*—those who were born deaf; (b) *the adventitiously deaf*— those who were born with normal hearing but in whom the sense of hearing has become non-functional through illness or accident.

It will be noted that in both definitions there is reference to those born deaf and those who lost their hearing at a later time. The basic distinction between the deaf and the hard-of-hearing is in the practical use of hearing. It cannot be in terms of some arbitrary line on audiometer tests. In this distinction Pintner[2] makes a practical summary:

There is, of course, no sharp dividing line between these two groups of individuals. One cannot divide them into two groups by means of audiometer tests, because some of the deaf may have more sound perception than some of the hearing. Nevertheless, the difference between the two groups is psychologically clear and distinct. The deaf are those who have never learned language incidentally in the ordinary way—in the way the normal child picks it up from his environment, casually, unconsciously. The hard-of-hearing are those who, in spite of their hearing handicap, did learn language in just this unconscious casual manner like the normal hearing child. This basic difference between the two groups means that they require quite different methods of education.

[1] Conference of Executives of American Schools for the Deaf, "Report of the Conference Committee on Nomenclature," *American Annals of the Deaf,* 1938, 83, pp. 1-3.
[2] R. Pintner, J. Eisenson, and M. Stanton, *The Psychology of the Physically Handicapped,* F.S. Crofts Co., New York, 1940, pp. 101-102.

## Characteristics of the Deaf

Since social communication is one of the basic components of human understanding and development any loss or absence of it, such as in the deaf, opens up a great gap in their life and experiences. Unless modern social methods of deaf instruction are applied to children at a very early age so that speech reading can enable them to comprehend the speech of others and to develop their own speech so that they can converse in normal oral ways with others, the gap in communication exists. Unfortunately, the number of the deaf who reach this ideal goal may be too few and hence the lack of communication remains as a stark reality.

Even though social communication may be established, there are certain characteristics of deafness which are different for the normal-hearing and to a considerable degree for the hard-of-hearing. Ramsdell[1] defines them as three psychological levels or losses: (1) the symbolic level in which the hearing makes language play a highly symbolic role; (2) the signal or warning level, "which serves as a direct sign or signal of events to which we make constant adjustments in our daily living. At this level it is not the word 'bee' (which is a symbol for the actual bee itself), but the sound of its angry buzz that makes us jump"; and (3) the incidental sounds of daily living are not present to create a *background of feeling* or "affective" tone and so the deaf person *feels as if the world were dead*. Ramsdell had noted this third level in adults who had become deaf and recognized it as the symptom that deafness had become complete. He designated this condition as the primitive level.

These three levels of hearing in the normal-hearing develop a fullness of meaning to life, which characterizes it as greatly different from the meager meaning in the deaf. It is difficult to know what the real world is like if we cannot hear and interpret what is heard. Myklebust[2] summarizes it as:

---

[1] D.A. Ramsdell, "The Psychology of the Deafened Adult," in H. Davis (ed.), *Hearing and Deafness*, Rinehart Books, Inc., New York, 1951, pp. 394-396.
[2] H.R. Myklebust, "Towards a New Understanding of the Deaf Child," *American Annals of the Deaf*, 1953, 98, p. 347.

Deafness does not simply cause an inability in communication. It causes the individual to see differently, to smell differently, to use tactual and kinesthetic sensation differently. And perhaps more important than all of these, but because of them, the deaf person perceives differently. As a result of all of these shifts in functioning, his personality adjustment and behavior are also different. To say that the deaf person is like the hearing person except that he cannot hear is to oversimplify and to do an injustice to the deaf child. His deafness is not only in his ears, it pervades his entire being.

Meyerson[1] describes three patterns of adjustment made by deaf adults which throws some light on the adjustments of children: Pattern 1 is a type that tends to seek associates with similar handicaps with some advantages and some disadvantages in competing with the hearing; pattern 2 aspires to be in the world of the hearing but he does so with a great amount of effort; pattern 3 succeeds quite well in these associations and activities with the hearing. There are no sharp lines of demarcation between the characteristics in the three patterns. Doubtless there may be some trends of a similar nature in children as well as in adults.

*Intelligence of the deaf.* Many groups of deaf children have taken intelligence tests and the results show quite a range of intelligence quotient points differences even with the medians. Meyerson[2] summarizes the findings for studies using individual performance tests which may be given in pantomine and with no language, either by the examiner or subject. In ten reports of studies, the median intelligence quotient of the means reported by these investigators was 91. A similar type of compilation from studies by twelve other investigators yielded a median intelligence quotient of 100, while three other investigations found the mean intelligence quotient to be 110. The deaf populations in these studies came from many sources and undoubtedly had highly selective factors operating in some of them. He also summarized studies using group Non-Verbal and

[1] L. Meyerson, "A Psychology of Impaired Hearing," in *Psychology of Exceptional Children and Youth*, Prentice-Hall, Inc., Englewood Cliffs, N.J., 1955, pp. 150-154.
[2] L. Meyerson, "A Psychology of Impaired Hearing," in *Psychology of Exceptional Children and Youth*, Prentice-Hall, Inc., Englewood Cliffs, N.J., 1955, p. 132.

Non-Language Tests with nine of them at the intelligence quotient of 85 and four studies close to 100.

A recent comprehensive study of intelligence was made by Hiskey[1] who is the author of the Nebraska Tests of Learning Aptitude. This test has eleven subdivisions with a total of 124 individual parts. The original standardization was made on 466 deaf children, four to ten years of age. This, however, had left a question about the correspondence of norms with average-hearing children. This question was answered by giving the Nebraska test and Stanford-Binet test to 380 hearing children of chronological ages four to ten years. The mean intelligence quotients on both tests were 100, which proves that the original standardization of the Nebraska test on deaf children was set at the norm of 100. The 466 deaf children in the original standardization had a mean intelligence quotient in the mid-90's. Apparently they were penalized because of communication difficulties between examiner and examinee and by lack of vocalization which is an *assist* to hearing children. The deaf tend to excel where visual perception is of paramount importance.

*Other characteristics of the deaf.* It is unfortunate that the deaf have other disabilities in addition to deafness. Summaries by Frampton and Rowell disclose that up to 40 per cent of the deaf have defective vision. Since vision is a compensating sense, particularly helpful in speech reading, any visual impairment is a double handicap. Tests of motor control and balance disclose weaknesses which might be the natural result if the semicircular canals which provide balance are not able to function normally. In the area of social adjustment the evidence of different characteristics is confused by the fact of individual differences. There are some tendencies toward being more introverted and withdrawn and showing greater insecurity although Pintner discounts such evidence as lack of language ability in understanding test items rather than in basic differences.

*Deafness versus aphasia.* Some children who do not seem to respond to hearing and are believed to be deaf are found to be aphasic. Aphasia is an organic loss or impairment of the capacity to use words

[1] M.S. Hiskey, "A Study of the Intelligence of Deaf and Hearing Children," *American Annals of the Deaf*, 1956, 101, pp. 329-339.

as symbols of ideas which may exist without any impairment in the organs of speech or of hearing. It is caused by lesions in the cortex and in the association paths of the dominant hemisphere. The aphasiacs have a poor memory span for speech and a lack of understanding of language which causes them to profit little from the methods of instruction of the deaf. They are subject to more numerous temper tantrums and extreme negative characteristics than are the deaf. Their crying and response to incidental sounds prove that they can hear. The aphasic child has the *receptive* language, but he lacks the associations which make up *inner* language and hence has difficulty with returning ideas as *expressive* language. The deaf have difficulty with receptive language because of hearing defect, but once they have received it they do not have the aphasiac's difficulty with inner language.

## Causes, Remedies, and Preventions of Deafness

There are many causes of deafness. A look at the diagram of the human ear furnishes some convincing evidence that the ear itself is a complicated and delicate mechanism. A defect or disorder in any small portion causes hearing impairment. The description of the various portions of the ear given in Chapter 21 affords further evidence of what may happen to hearing. Hereditary or congenital malformations of the pinna and outer canal may close off hearing at the very start. Bone conduction of sound within the skull is a helpful, but not entirely satisfactory substitute for air conduction in such cases. Plastic surgery, general surgery, or other medical treatment sometimes restores anatomical disorders of these external conductors.

Descriptions of diseases, defects, and other conditions affecting the middle ear and the inner ear are sketched in the preceding chapter on the hard-of-hearing. The nature of the disability suggests potential remedies. Whenever infections occur the use of appropriate antibiotics such as penicillin has been extremely effective in clearing up many complications, which in earlier times ran their course with disastrous results. Some of the conduction disorders which cause impaired hearing or deafness in adults are not commonly found in children. Otosclerosis or excessive growth and hardening of the bones of the ear and of the adjoining skull are illustrative. Two methods of surgical operation are becoming more successful in restoring hearing. Since the tiny bones of the middle ear may become immobilized, conduction of sound to the middle ear is lost. Recent advances in surgery have been able to mobilize again the incus and especially the stapes, which restores the normal functioning, but there is some possibility of recurrence.

The fenestration operation seeks out ways of conducting sound waves to the inner ear if the stapes cannot be restored to mobilization. Some of the earlier operations removed the stapes and it was hoped that a flap of skin from the wall of the canal would heal over the vestibular window. In this case sound conduction through air in the middle ear substitutes for the mechanical sound conduction of the three bones. In very recent years, the fenestration operation now bypasses the immobilized stapes and goes direct from the outer canal to an opening made in the horizontal semicircular canal. This opening is also sealed with a flap of skin so that vibration may function and through the liquid of the semicircular canals and of the cochlea sound vibrations reach the auditory nerve endings. The cochlear window also continues to operate and may also transmit some of the sound vibrations. Studies are being made on how to keep the new opening from being healed over or further ossification blocking the passage. Since this fenestration operation provides a direct connection to the outer ear, greater precautions must be taken for injuries from loud explosions or from infections. For some time after the operation dizziness is unusually troublesome, since the horizontal canal which governs dizziness has been given a direct rather than an indirect line to the outside world. Recent reports by Shambaugh[1] and by Brockman[2] are encouraging.

The causes of deafness which originate in the auditory nerve and in the auditory centers of the brain are much more difficult to diagnose and to treat. The anatomy and physiology of the entire brain

[1] G.E. Shambaugh, "The Fenestration Operation," *The Volta Review*, 1956, 58, pp. 9-10.

[2] S.J. Brockman, "Recent Advances in Experimental Otologic Research," *The Volta Review*, 1957, 59, pp. 105-110.

and nervous system is an area of study larger in scope than that of the auditory centers and is discussed elsewhere in this book. Suffice it to comment here that various diseases and disorders affect mental response and comprehension in countless ways. Surgery is successful in such conditions as brain tumors. Medication can cure some types of brain diseases. In these instances, if restoration includes the auditory centers, hearing will be restored or improved.

## The Examination of Deafness

The characteristics of deaf children and the causes of deafness show that the examination and diagnosis of the deaf is a comprehensive task which merits the services and cooperation of many specialists. Several specialists in medicine are involved, such as the pediatrician, the neurologist, the otolaryngologists, clinical psychologists and educators, and speech pathologists and audiologists. The otolaryngologist has the primary responsibility for the medical diagnosis since many causes of deafness lie in the intricate mechanisms of the middle and inner ear. The audiologist has devised many methods and tests of auditory acuity and the areas and ranges of auditory loss and speech audiometry. Whenever the nerve mechanisms are involved, such as the auditory nerve or the various association areas of the brain, the neurologist contributes his knowledge and professional skill.

The clinical psychologist measures the general learning potential so that the teacher and her associates may be informed about what to expect in each individual case. He develops a profile of the mental constitution so that the strengths and weaknesses of the abilities are disclosed. In cooperation with the psychiatrist they develop a meaningful picture of the emotional, temperamental, and ethical qualities which play an important role in the total educational process. The speech pathologist enters the picture since modern methods of teaching the deaf usually include the development of speech. Speech is largely an automatic process for those with normal hearing. By contrast the deaf have not only potential speech disorders but inadequate language concepts as well. Language development is the larger aspect of speech pathology. Cooperation of these various specialists brings new hope for the deaf.

## The Number of the Deaf

With better methods of reporting and with improved diagnostic procedures, estimates of the number with impaired hearing has decreased in recent years from 14 per cent to about one-third as much. Conservative estimates place as deaf one pupil out of every 1,000 of school age. This percentage yields 35,000 deaf children of school age in the United States. Below the usual school age, there are between fifteen and twenty thousand and more. A few of these preschool children are in school and receiving benefits of instruction before they get conditioned against any effort to learn or to communicate intelligently.

The annual enrollment report of deaf pupils in residential and day schools of all types as of October 31, 1956,[1] listed a total of 18,487 pupils, which is approximately one-half of all deaf children. Nearly three-fourths, or 72 per cent, are in residential schools and the remainder are in day schools or classes. Only in the larger centers of population does there seem to be enough deaf pupils to warrant establishing public school facilities. There were only ten public day schools for the deaf in the 1956 report, and 190 day classes. The Detroit Day school for the Deaf is listed as one school although for several years there has also been an east-side branch. Because of small numbers in rural areas, in villages, and in small cities, deaf children are generally enrolled in state residential schools.

There remains a question of the whereabouts and school placement of the other 50 per cent of all deaf children who are not accounted for in any of the educational facilities noted in the carefully prepared annual report in the *Annals of the Deaf*. The *Annals* reports additional pupils in special facilities who are afflicted with double handicaps: seven schools for the deaf-blind with an enrollment of 63 pupils; three schools for the deaf and mentally retarded with 30 pupils; the Spaulding Schools for Crippled Children in Chicago, with fourteen

[1] *American Annals of the Deaf*, 1957, p. 102 and 118.

deaf and crippled pupils; and two schools with 9 deaf and cerebral palsied pupils. There are only 119 pupils in these four types of double-handicap classes. While these thirteen schools or centers have bravely done pioneering in the area of double handicaps in other communities, much remains to be done.

Doubly handicapped children probably exist in much greater numbers than these few enrollments would indicate. State residential schools for the mentally retarded and mental hospitals include many with the additional handicap of deafness. Public school classes for many other types of disabilities enroll some deaf children in attempting to make whatever provision they can for them, and where no special facilities for the deaf are provided. A much larger group probably continues in regular classes for the same reason and receives what benefit it can. Due to lack of information by parents or by family physicians some deaf children do not attend any school. As one considers the total problem of finding and educating the deaf, much remains yet to be done.

### History of the Deaf

The history of the deaf will be discussed under the following topics: (1) their treatment in society; (2) schools and founders of schools for the deaf; and (3) methods of teaching the deaf.

*Treatment in society.* In the chapter on the blind it was noted that throughout the early history of civilization there was much sympathy for the blind because of the obvious and visible nature of their handicap. Since the handicap of deafness was not so obvious and the deaf were able to get about without help, they did not receive the same sympathetic consideration.

Actually the deaf had a threefold handicap in those early days. There was the deafness itself, which deprived them of the usual means of communication. A highly superficial opinion might be that if the person could not hear it would be simple enough to write what was to be said and have him read it. Unless the person had been fortunate enough to have learned to read and write, which was rare, those avenues of communication did not function. The deaf had to depend chiefly upon some crude sign language, often of their own making and only their most immediate family and a small circle of associates went to the trouble to communicate with them.

The second handicap followed more or less naturally from the first. Since the deaf person seemed uncommunicative and did not respond, he was often thought to be feeble-minded. Since others judged the deaf to be incapable of understanding, they were ignored although their mental abilities may have been normal or superior. In these same historical eras the feeble-minded were also treated in many brutal and socially unacceptable ways so that the misjudged deaf got the same treatment. This confusion of two types of defects is not nesessarily historical only. The lay public may easily fall into the same error. It is not too uncommon today when diagnostic mental tests and tests of hearing are not used that children are sent to the wrong institution or training school. At the time of the White House Conference on Child Health and Protection in 1930, there was considerable discussion of this problem and need for clarification.

The third type of handicap was the fact that the deaf generally did not speak and hence were judged to be incapable of speech. The great Greek philosopher, Aristotle, came to this conclusion and believed that the deaf were uneducable. His opinion became that of the church, and it was believed so implicitly because of its seeming authority that little was done for the next two thousand years to discover the real facts. Actually the deaf tended to be without speech, not because they did not have the organs of speech, but because their very deafness deprived them of the opportunity of training in speech. Speech is generally developed by hearing others speak and by copying their speech sounds through trial and error. Fortunately those who understood the real nature of speech and its methods of development have joined forces with workers for the deaf to develop speech in the deaf. Although treated separately in this and the next two chapters it is emphasized that impaired hearing and speech development should always go hand in hand.

*Schools and founders of schools for the deaf.* In an earlier paragraph the adverse opinion of Aristotle about deafness was cited. Silverman[1]

[1] S.R. Silverman, *Hearing and Deafness*, H. Davis, ed., Murray Hill Books, New York, 1947, p. 343.

notes that in about the seventh century A.D., Bishop John of York, taught a "deaf-and-dumb" youth to speak intelligently. He adds:

This accomplishment, however, is chronicled in the nature of a miracle, and the educational method is left to our imaginations. Nevertheless, the mere recording of the incident is a first, admittedly feeble, attempt, conscious or otherwise, to dispel the fog of misunderstanding in which deafness was enshrouded.

In Rome the deaf Q. Pedious of the family of the orator, Messala, became very proficient in the art of painting.[1] The Spanish Titian, Juan Fernandez Navarette, won fame by painting portraits of many members of the court of King Philip II.

In the sixteenth and seventeenth centuries three famous Spaniards, Pedro Ponce de Leon, Bonet, and Ramires de Carrion, achieved fame in successfully educating many of their countrymen who were of noble birth. This suggests a hereditary strain of deafness within the group. Many of their pupils were so successful that they were admitted to Mass and eventually the long held theories of Aristotle that the deaf could not be taught were broken.

In the period of brilliant French history in the eighteenth century, two great teachers of the deaf are to be found: Abbé de l'Épée; and his pupil, Abbé Sicard. The former taught by a combination of oral and manual methods, although he believed that the oral method would eventually be the most practical. Sicard laid more emphasis upon the manual method and used writing as a basis of teaching. Contemporary with these men was the German Samuel Heinicke who established a school for the deaf in Leipzig in 1778. He was a strong advocate of the oral methods of teaching. The oral method was monopolized in England by the Braidwood family and did not have much general usefulness during their time.

Thomas Hopkins Gallaudet (1785-1851) was the American pioneer in teaching the deaf. Today the Gallaudet College for the Deaf in Washington, D.C., is a lasting memorial to his pioneering efforts. His early health was poor so that he could not complete his course in law. Some years later he graduated from the Andover Theological Semi-

[1] A rather extensive history of the deaf is to be found in M.E. Frampton and H.G. Rowell, *Education of the Handicapped*, Vol. I., *History*, pp. 45-86.

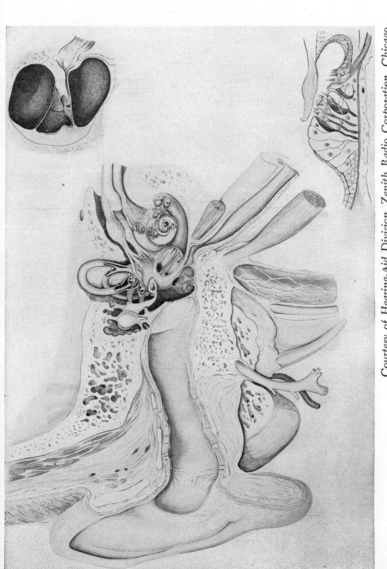

The human ear.

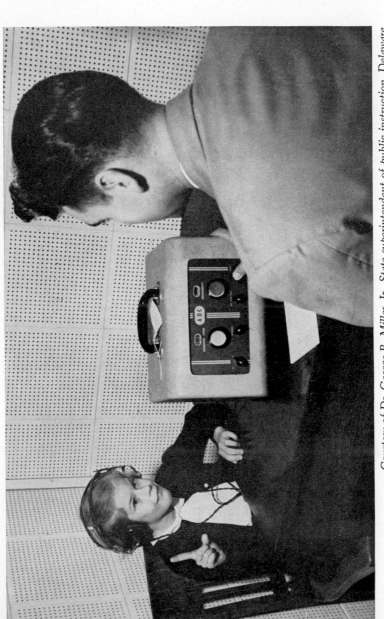

*Courtesy of Dr. George R. Miller, Jr., State superintendent of public instruction, Delaware.*

Testing for possible hearing loss.

nary, although he was not in good enough health to preach regularly. He became interested in trying to teach the small deaf daughter of Dr. Mason Cogswell according to the methods of Sicard. From private contributions he was sent to Europe to study methods of teaching the deaf. At first he was discouraged by the extreme reticence of the Braidwoods in England, but Sicard gave him a hearty invitation to France when he chanced to meet him while Sicard was lecturing in London. After a few months he returned to America and brought with him Laurent Clerc as a teacher for the deaf. The first school for the deaf was opened by Gallaudet at Hartford Conn., April 15, 1817.

In 1819 Massachusetts voted to send its deaf pupils to Hartford. Its action was followed by several other states as far away as Georgia. Gallaudet and Clerc were unusually successful salesmen in the extension of schools and financial support for the deaf. In 1818 Clerc persuaded Congress to allot 23,000 acres of wild land which were later sold for $300,000. These two men also began traveling from state to state in getting legislatures to establish schools for the deaf. They always had well-planned drives supported by the press and by many influential groups, so that the authorization was usually passed in a great emotional scene after a demonstration by deaf pupils from other state schools.

In discussing the history of the deaf the work of Dr. Alexander Graham Bell, inventor of the telephone, should be emphasized. Dr. Bell combined various motivations in his phenomenal success in teaching speech to the deaf. These factors included: knowledge of phonetics from a book entitled *Visible Speech* written by Bell's father; success in using this knowledge in teaching the deaf Mabel Hubbard to speak, a lady he later married; returns from his telephone inventions which enabled him to build the Volta Bureau Building in Washington. This building became the headquarters for the American Association to Promote the Teaching of Speech to the Deaf. Although his early efforts to interest schools for the deaf in possibilities of speech were largely ignored as impossible and not worth the tremendous effort, he eventually became a real leader in this modern field.

*Methods of instruction.* It was almost exactly two centuries ago that a controversy arose over two different methods of instruction. De l'Épée founded a school for the deaf in Paris and used the "signs" method of instruction. Contemporary with him was Heinicke's first public school for the deaf in Germany which practiced oral instruction. A bitter argument and controversy arose between these two methods which lasted for many years and was carried over into the establishment of schools in America. When the state legislature of Michigan authorized the establishment of a School for the Deaf in the Detroit Public Schools at the beginning of the present century, there was written into the code that the oral method of instruction must be used. In most of the residential state schools there was general use of the manual or sign method, but current practice is largely in the oral method in these schools as well. The change was gradual and came to pass because the oral method offered more opportunities for communication with the hearing as well as with the deaf or a few interested members of the family.

The manual or sign method was more than a literal learning of symbols standing for each letter of the alphabet which would have to be spelled out laboriously, a letter at a time. It was actually a sign language in which certain signs stood for whole expressions, and mingled with it were various bodily movements, raising of eyebrows, and other facial expressions which are used effectively by hearing persons either consciously or unconsciously with surprising effectiveness in their customary oral conversation. In its simpler forms the mentally backward deaf could understand signs because they were definite, specific, and visible. The oral method is rather difficult to learn because it involves many elements such as keen ability in visual observation and interpretation of the lips and speech processes of many persons, each of whom has his own unique mannerisms in speaking. The spoken language itself is made up of about forty phonetic elements with varying degrees of visibility. Only about one-third of these elements are clearly visible and hence the "listener" must fill in large portions by inference from the locale and from the other expressive looks of the speaker. The "listener" may utilize his own motor aptitudes by repeating to himself the observed speech movements and by repeating them he recognizes what was said. This brief and oversimplified statement should not give the impression that the oral method of speech reading is an easy method. It yields rich return in the social communication which it makes possible with the nonhandicapped as well as with the deaf.

The great majority of deaf children in all types of schools are being taught primarily by the oral method. The nonoral method is used in about eleven hundred cases. Various combinations of methods are used on about one-fourth of them.

## Current Educational Methods

Because of their characteristics, as noted in an earlier section, the education of the deaf should begin at the earliest possible age. If not, the young deaf child may lose interest in learning and settle into a state of complete dependency. In addition to parental care and training, nursery and preschool training should be provided. Patten[1] reports that such programs have been started by the Division of Maternal and Child Health of the Massachusetts Department of Public Health through money from Federal grants. The groups are using the facilities of public libraries, civic clubs, and public schools. There are usually two sessions weekly, one of which is financed through local funds. The staff usually consists of a trained nursery school teacher and a trained teacher of the deaf. The children are referred after diagnosis and recommendation by the medical staffs of nearby hospitals. Many of the schools for the deaf initiate their programs at the preschool level.

One of the main objectives is to develop a social sense which is basic to the needs of all children and in this regard deaf children are no exception. Unless a positive and happy emotional tone can be developed, the unusually extreme patience needed to break the communication barriers may easily go for naught. Obviously teachers of the deaf must be very talented in their love and friendliness for these little children.

*Speech reading.* The teacher may start playing with the young

[1] H.T. Patten, "Preschool Conservation of Health Program," *American Annals of the Deaf*, 1955, 100, pp. 319-320.

child in something as simple but interesting as a ball which they throw. At the same time she pronounces ball and has the child observe her lips and her facial expression. It does not take long for the child to catch on that the particular kind of facial expression means *ball*. A few other familiar objects are gradually introduced and shortly the deaf child can recognize the different objects which continue to be part of the game. Thus lip reading, which is now more commonly known as speech reading is under way. This method of learning is more than mere observation of the lips. It uses total facial expression and many other finer gestures of communication. After a few nouns have been learned, it is possible to introduce verbs of action and many other words, which begin to fill in as a workable language.

*The development of speech.* The pupil's observation of the teacher's speech movements begins to give clues as to how he may imitate her. Although the pupil may not hear any sound he imitates her actions and thus is taking his first step toward the development of speech. Eventually he realizes that whatever he does in this way pleases the teacher. He notices that she may respond when she is not looking at him, which means that some other mysterious system of communication must be in effect. He may not even try to understand what it is, but since it works it must be good. The teacher begins to follow up this new interest and now becomes a skilled teacher of speech. She must have complete knowledge of the mechanisms of speech and know how to apply these mechanisms to her pupil. One of the pioneers in this new method was Sophie Alcorn, a teacher and later the principal of the Detroit Day School for the Deaf. She patiently practiced it on a boy named Tad, and a girl named Oma, and today it is known as the Tadoma method. The pupil is encouraged to use the sense of sight as well as the sense of touch. He feels the face and throat of the teacher and then imitates her tensions and movements as she speaks. This basic method with many extensions and elaborations is being used possibly under different names in many schools for the deaf. Many hundreds of totally deaf children, young people, and adults use speech reading to understand speech and in turn through the development of their own speech they are able to converse in normal speaking voices themselves.

Through these modern methods they have made a permanent and effective bypass around what is otherwise a severe handicap to communication.

Through the use of modern electrical audiometers it has been learned that very few deaf persons are totally deaf, for in certain ranges of pitch and for certain intensities there is some response. Hearing aids are procured for them and even within a very narrow band they get enough of an idea of speech and of sound that it advances their learning of speech reading and of the development of speech at a much faster rate.

After communication has been established there comes the long process of teaching the deaf to read, write, and master the other processes of education. Subject matter looms large as an objective with other aims and goals to a satisfactory and well-rounded education.

### Multiple Handicaps

A principal purpose of this chapter has been to isolate deafness in the individual so that a better understanding of his characteristics and his problems may be gained. Actually it is not that simple. Even within the individual himself, there are known to be many factors and variables which affect him in overcoming the handicap of deafness. Any deaf individual finds others who share with him the common disability of deafness, but in addition they differ from him in other traits and qualities. The whole range of individual differences in many characteristics exist. Any one of such characteristics profoundly influences the success in dealing with the deaf.

The degree of intellectual brightness or dullness in the deaf is illustrative. What has just been described as speech reading and the development of speech appear to be easy, but any "ease" may be attributed in part to intellectual brightness. Actually for the intellectually bright who are deaf, there is no such thing as "easy" in their learning. The expression is only relative when used in contrast to the problems of the deaf who are mentally retarded.

*Deaf and mentally handicapped.* In the *Annals of the Deaf* three classes are listed for the deaf and mentally handicapped. They are in California, Colorado, and Minnesota and have a total enrollment of twenty boys and ten girls. It is common knowledge that there are many more than this number of the deaf and mentally retarded. Many of them are in residential and day schools for the mentally retarded.

MacPherson[1] made an extensive investigation of the status of the deaf and hard-of-hearing mentally deficient in the United States. His survey reported 1,593 such pupils in these schools and classes, although the division of numbers between the deaf and the hard-of-hearing was not stated. He recommended that national organizations in each of these fields form a joint committee to study the needs of these doubly handicapped children.

At this point the reader should review the chapter on the mentally retarded for a reorientation of their characteristics and general possibilities in learning. Among other deficiencies the mentally retarded have particular deficiencies in the development of language. A good background of language is essential to the teaching and training of the deaf. The gross difficulty of teaching the deaf and mentally retarded becomes more and more evident. There is a tendency in the mentally retarded toward social isolation and toward introversion into their own personal lives which does not lend itself readily to the communication goals set in the education of the deaf. At best, the greater the handicap, the greater the challenge.

*Other double handicaps.* Before discussing the deaf-blind a few other types of double handicaps are briefly considered. They include the deaf and crippled; and the deaf and cerebral palsied; and various emotional and behavior disorders. For each type it is necessary to think concurrently about the problems of the deaf and of the second handicap. Other chapters dealing with these handicaps should be reviewed.

*The deaf-blind.* There is just one internationally known and internationally traveled deaf-blind woman of great distinction who is deaf-blind—none other than Helen Keller. Born both deaf and blind

---

[1] J.R. MacPherson, "The Status of the Deaf and/or Hard of Hearing Mentally Deficient in the United States," *American Annals of the Deaf*, 1952, 97, pp. 375-386, 448-449, and 452-469.

she has risen above both handicaps to give lasting hope for those born in the dark silence. She has had recognition bestowed by kings, by presidents, and by others in many walks of life. Her own story of her travels after reaching the age of seventy years is reported in various numbers of the *New Outlook for the Blind* covers trips to Latin America, Africa, and around the globe and is always filled with hope and cheer. Upon the occasion of her seventy-fifth anniversary congratulations and felicitations from twenty-six famous people appeared in the June, 1955, *New Outlook for the Blind*.

While the total number of deaf-blind children is probably small their needs are so great that exceptionally well-planned training courses and facilities are needed. A joint committee was appointed by the Conference of Executives of American Schools for the Deaf and the American Association of Instructors for the Blind. A meeting was held at the Perkins Institution for the Blind at Watertown, Mass., in April, 1953, sponsored by the Perkins Institution and the American Foundation for the Blind. Shortly afterward these committees were united as the "National Study Committee on Education of Deaf Blind Children." The committee recommends national centers for research, regional schools, and other facilities unique to the needs of the deaf-blind.

### Educational Facilities for the Deaf

Approximately three deaf children out of every four are educated in residential schools rather than in day schools or classes. There is a practical and realistic reason for the greater number being in residential schools because of the comparatively few deaf children except in large population centers. It is needless to argue the advantages and disadvantages of the residential versus the day school. Being away from home is always a problem and the sheltered atmosphere of the residential school is recognized as somewhat of a liability. There is a growing practice of the residential schools to send their high school students out to the regular high schools in nearby communities for general community orientation.

*Teacher training.* Whether the teacher of the deaf is located in the residential or the day school the needs of training are equivalent. Enough has been said about the characteristics of deaf children and of instructional methods to indicate that there is need for specialization in speech reading, in the development of speech, in anatomy and physiology of the ear and of the organs of speech, as well as mastery of the fields of subject matter. These teachers must be endowed with unusual patience, yet have warmth and enthusiasm so as to inspire their pupils to overcome the barriers to social communication. Thirty-eight centers for teacher training are listed in the *American Annals of the Deaf*,[1] which includes ten offering training for teaching the deaf-blind. Approximately thirty hours of graduate work are required.

*Equipment and Supplies.* The problems of instruction for the deaf are such that the best of facilities should be available. The rooms and general atmosphere must be cheerful and have plenty of illumination so that the speech reading and other visual needs shall be well provided. Physical equipment such as audiometers of all kinds, hearing aids, and similar materials should be at hand. Opportunities for motor expression should be liberally supplied, with gymnasiums and opportunities for such physical activities as dancing and games. The feeling of rhythm from music give a great stimulation. Naturally the costs of such education are much greater than for the normal-hearing pupils. Liberal use of visual aids of all kinds supplements the program in many helpful ways. The costs are greater since many teachers get an additional salary differential which they justly deserve, classes are much smaller, and there is much individual instruction, and the other materials mount the financial needs. Many states allow liberal subsidies to local school systems for the additional expense. Additional costs include the auxiliary staffs of nurses, medical specialists, psychologists, and audiologists.

*The role of parents.* There is need for a very workable understanding with parents. Since much deafness is congenital parents are faced with it from early infancy. It is their problem to cooperate with the pediatrician and the medical specialists of the deaf long before the child is ready to enter nursery or preschool. Being able to *accept* the condition is the greatest problem of all. Interpretation

[1] *American Annals of the Deaf*, 1957, 102, pp. 180-185.

to parents, teachers, and to the general public has been extended very effectively in recent years by the addresses given by Mrs. Spencer Tracy who operates the John Tracy Clinic, established as a result of efforts to teach her own deaf son. Many children and their parents also receive special training when enrolled for the training course at that clinic.

*Rehabilitation.* After formal education has neared its end the facilities of Federal rehabilitation are available. Their local units operated by the states with matched funds reach into remote areas and provide their services. There are many occupations in which the deaf are very successful. At an early date Henry Ford employed a large number in his factories where the noise of heavy machinery did not prove a handicap to them. There is very little unemployment among those who have minimal education and who are willing to work. The deaf are a proud group who do not want charity, and when an additional personal income tax exemption such as is given to the blind was proposed in Congress they opposed it so violently that the idea was quickly dropped.

### Organizations and Periodicals

There are several long-established and highly respected organizations interested in the education and welfare of the deaf. One of these is The Conference of Executives of American Schools for the Deaf established in 1868, which publishes the *American Annals of the Deaf* whose first issue appeared on October 1, 1847. It is the official organ of the Convention and of the Conference. It is published at Gallaudet College in Washington, D.C. The *Annals* is also the official publication of the Convention of American Instructors of the Deaf, founded in 1850, and now in its second century. Another organization of long standing is the American Association to Promote the Teaching of Speech to the Deaf which was incorporated in 1890. The moving spirit back of this organization was Alexander Graham Bell whose invention of the telephone and other resources enabled him to build the Volta Bureau Building at 1537 35th St., N.W., Washington 7, D.C. and establish an Association *Review* whose name was changed to the *Volta Review* in 1910. This magazine appears in ten numbers each year and publishes a wide variety of articles in the interest of the deaf and the hard-of-hearing.

The American Hearing Society with headquarters at 817 14th St., N.W., Washington 5, D.C., has changed its name several times. It has chapters in many local communities and its information centers, employment bureaus, and social clubs of the impaired-hearing provide a very helpful service. It publishes several numbers of the *Hearing News* annually. There is a department of the National Educational Association on lip or speech reading, and the Council for Exceptional Children always has sectional programs in the field of impaired hearing and frequent articles in *Exceptional Children*. The resources of these organizations are very potent in the interests of the deaf.

The American Association to Promote the Teaching of Speech to the Deaf changed its name to the Volta Speech Association for the Deaf and on June 5, 1953, the name was changed to The Alexander Graham Bell Association for the Deaf, Inc., in honor of its founder.

## Questions and Topics for Discussion

1. Discuss orally or in writing any firsthand experiences which you may have had with any deaf persons and interpret them in the light of problems discussed in this chapter.
2. Discuss the distinction in definition between the totally deaf and the hard-of-hearing.
3. Make a detailed drawing of the ear and describe its various parts and their functions.
4. Report in more detail about the history of the education of the deaf as described in Vol. 1 of Frampton and Rowell's *Education of the Handicapped*.
5. Discuss some famous contemporary deaf persons and their contributions to modern society.
6. Read and report on *The Life of Helen Keller*.
7. Conduct an experiment in lip reading from a soundproof room and note the impressions and difficulties which are encountered.
8. With various members of the class, demonstrate the use of the manual alphabet, noting the individual differences among them in making the various letters accurately and rapidly.

9. Visit a school for the deaf and observe the various phases of the total program.
10. Make contacts with the local luncheon clubs to learn what they are doing for the deaf and report it to the class.
11. Visit the clinic of a local ear specialist and, if possible, have a demonstration of the various types of apparatus which he uses.
12. Make a list of bulletins and pamphlets which have been produced by various organizations interested in teaching the deaf.

## A. Organizations

1. The Conference of Executives of American Schools for the Deaf, Gallaudet College, Washington 2, D.C.
2. The Convention of American Instructors of the Deaf, Gallaudet College, Washington 2, D.C.
3. American Association to Promote the Teaching of Speech to the Deaf, 1537 35th St., N.W., Washington 7, D.C.
4. The American Hearing Society, 817 14th St., N.W., Washington, D.C.
5. The American Speech and Hearing Association, Wayne State University, Detroit 2.
6. The National Association of the Deaf, 2495 Shattuck Ave., Berkeley 4, Calif.
7. Alexander Graham Bell Association for the Deaf, 1537 35th St., N.W., Washington 7, D.C.

## B. Periodicals

1. *American Annals of the Deaf* (bimonthly), Gallaudet College, Washington 2, D.C.
2. *The Volta Review* (monthly except July and August), The Volta Bureau, 1537 35th St., N.W., Washington 7, D.C.
3. *Hearing News* (bimonthly), official organ of the American Hearing Society, 1800 H Street, N.W., Washington 6, D.C.
4. *Journal of Speech and Hearing Disorders* (quarterly), American Speech and Hearing Association, Detroit 2.

## C. Books

1. Best, H.A., *Deafness and the Deaf in the United States*, The Macmillan Co., New York, 1943, 675 pp.
2. Browd, V.L., *The New Way to Better Hearing*, Crown Publishers, New York, 1951, 226 pp.
3. Davis, H. (ed.), *Hearing and Deafness, A Guide for Laymen*, Rinehart Books, Inc., New York, 1947, 496 pp.

4. Gallaudet, E.M., *Life of Thomas Hopkins Gallaudet*, Henry Holt and Co., Inc., New York, 1888, 339 pp.
5. Getz, S., *Environment and the Deaf Child*, Charles C Thomas, Publisher, Springfield, Ill., 1956, 188 pp.
6. Goldstein, M.A., *Problems of the Deaf*, Laryngoscope Press, St. Louis, Mo., 1933, 580 pp.
7. Hirsh, I.J., *The Measurement of Hearing*, McGraw-Hill Book Co., Inc., New York, 1952, 364 pp.
8. Hodgson, K.W., *The Deaf and Their Problems: A Study on Special Education*, Philosophical Library, New York, 1954, 364 pp.
9. Huffman, M.B., *Fun Comes First for Blind Slow-Learners*, Charles C Thomas, Publisher, Springfield, Ill., 1957, 157 pp.
10. Lack, A., *The Teaching of Language to Deaf Children*, Oxford University Press, London, 1955, 380 pp.
11. Levine, E.S., *Youth in a Soundless World*, New York University Press, New York, 1956, 217 pp.
12. Madden, R., *The School Status of the Hard-of-Hearing Child*, Teachers College Contributions to Education, No. 499, Columbia University Press, New York, 1931, 64 pp.
13. Mandl, M., *Hearing Aids*, The Macmillan Co., New York, 1953, 158 pp.
14. Myklebust, H.R., *Auditory Disorders in Children*, Grune and Stratton, Inc., New York, 1954, 367 pp.
15. ———, *Your Deaf Child*, A Guide for Parents, Charles C Thomas, Publisher, Springfield, Ill., 1950, 133 pp.
16. Rocheleau, C., and R. Mack, *Those in the Dark Silence*, The Volta Bureau, Washington, D.C., 1930, 169 pp.
17. Streng, A., et al., *Hearing Therapy for Children*, Grune and Stratton, Inc., New York, 1955, 368 pp.
18. Warfield, K., *Keep Listening*, The Viking Press, New York, 1957, 158 pp.
19. Watson, L.A., and T. Tolan, *Hearing Tests and Hearing Instruments*, Williams and Wilkins Co., Baltimore Md., 1949, 579 pp.
20. Wever, E.G., *Theory of Hearing*, John Wiley and Sons, Inc., New York, 1949, 484 pp.
21. ———, and M. Lawrence, *Physiological Acoustics*, Princeton University Press, Princeton, N.J., 1954, 454 pp.

## D. Films and Filmstrips

1. *Ears and Hearing*, 11 minutes, 16-mm. Describes the physiology and operation of the human ear by means of animated drawings and close-up photographs of the ear as it is functioning. Also related 70-frame

35-mm. filmstrip with same title. Encyclopaedia Britannica Films, Inc., 1150 Wilmette Ave., Wilmette, Ill.

2. *Your Children's Ears,* 15 minutes, 16-mm. Explains by animated diagrams the physiology of the ear, and shows the close relationship between the nose and throat. British Information Service, 30 Rockefeller Plaza, New York 20.

3. *Out from Silence,* three 35-mm. color filmstrips
    A. *Nature of Hearing Loss,* 48 frames;
    B. *Safeguarding Your Hearing,* 44 frames;
    C. *Rehabilitation of the Hard-of-Hearing,* 48 frames.
   Society for Visual Education, Inc., 1345 Diversey Parkway, Chicago 14.

4. *Fundamentals of Acoustics,* 11 minutes, 16-mm., sound, color. Effects of wall surfaces upon the reflection of sounds; mechanics of hearing process; dramatization of the range of the human voice; effects of eliminating certain vibrational frequencies. Encyclopaedia Britannica Films, Inc., 1150 Wilmette Ave., Wilmette, Ill.

5. *That the Deaf May Speak,* 12 minutes, 16-mm., color, sound. This film, taken at the Lexington School for the Deaf, New York City, shows modern methods of teaching the deaf child, suitable for all groups. Volta Bureau, 1537 35th St., N.W., Washington 7, D.C.

6. *Helen Keller in Her Story,* 45 minutes, 16-mm., sound. Louis De Rochemont Film Library, 13 E. 37th St., New York 16.

Note: For a more complete list of films and filmstrips pertaining to deafness see *The Volta Review,* 1956, 58, pp. 158-160.

# PART 7

## Physical Disorders
## and Defects

# CHAPTER 24

## The Anatomy
## and Physiology of Speech

THE HISTORY of speech and language is the history of civilization. Vision and hearing are natural gifts but speech and language have had to be learned through long experience and training. Through speech the habits and mores of early peoples were carried from generation to generation long before written history and before records were devised and perfected. Speech communicates not only thoughts and ideas but the manner of speaking interprets personality and character of the speaker as well. The emotional tone which accompanies the spoken word joins it in influencing the opinions and lives of listeners. Orators have changed the course of history with their powerful words and with their resounding emphasis on them.

### The Significance of Speech

The twentieth century has witnessed a much more universal utilization of speech than was ever possible before. The telephone, the talking movie, the radio, and the audio of television have brought speech into constant use and within uninterrupted reach of every man, woman, and child. Except for brief periods of quiet for study, classrooms are humming with speech from within the class or from lectures and talks brought in by radio or television. It is too early to evaluate the tremendous changes which are taking place in human affairs because of speech.

Since speech is universal every individual has a basic need to participate. In the preceding chapters on impaired hearing and deafness the underlying need was shown to be to hear speech and to be able to speak. Even the deaf are now able to participate through speech reading and through the development of their own speech which they are unable to hear. Individuals with other types of handicaps use speech to compensate for their deficiencies. The blind listen to speech with an enrichment of interpretation not usually enjoyed by those who see, and they cultivate a perfection of their own speech to offset negative impressions from their handicap. In like manner the crippled and many other handicapped find effective speech a compensation for their disability. On the negative side speech is also put to unfortunate use by delinquents and by those with evil motives.

Turning to speech itself there are many individuals with none of the handicaps noted above, who are handicapped because of their own defective speech. They cannot enjoy the normal use of speech in social communication because their voices are different, their words incoherent, or their speech fails. These experiences frustrate them with inner forces as potent as those felt by individuals with other handicaps. Their quandary may be even greater because they feel that by greater concentration and effort speech defects would be remedied. This is seldom the case. Because of these many factors speech and its defects and disorders are an integral part of programs for exceptional children.

The preceding six chapters discussed vision and hearing which are two important senses. Vision and hearing receive sensations which give impressions of the environment and provide receptions of social communication. Speech enters the framework of communication and becomes an integral part of it although it is not one of the five senses. Speech sends or transmits impressions to the hearing and in the case of speech reading the impressions are on the vision. The connections with the nervous system are primarily *efferent* whereas the optic and auditory nerves are primarily *afferent* in nature. Although speech is not a sensory function in the true sense of the term, nevertheless it plays an important role in sensory functioning. There are many types of speech defects and disorders which disrupt normal communication.

Any child with deviate speech has disruptions in normal social communication and hence comes under the general classification of exceptional children.

## The Mechanisms of Speech

The mechanisms of speech are not provided with separate organs such as is true of the eye or the ear. Speech makes use of other bodily organs with a few additional specializations for speech production. Nature has thus simplified and reduced, as far as possible, the number of body organs. In this simplification process the respiratory system is one of the principal contributors to speech mechanisms, and with it the initial portions of the alimentary tract are also brought into play. The respiratory system, from the nose to the lungs, channels air into the body so that oxygen is made available for life's processes. The exhalation of air through the respiratory system produces air waves which may easily be modified in many ways as it reaches the ear. Likewise the mouth with its lips, teeth, tongue and other portions which function primarily in digestion is also part of the respiratory system as it functions in speech mechanisms. In the production of speech the respiratory tract functions in part through the mouth and in part through the nose.

Two important ducts or tubes lead down through the throat and neck. The esophagus leads to the stomach and carries the food from the mouth. The trachea is the duct for the passage of air from the nose and mouth to the lungs. When speaking the trachea is open but when swallowing foods or liquids it is closed temporarily by the larynx at its upper end. At times its closing does not function automatically enough so that food or liquid starts into the trachea causing temporary choking, and with more or less discomfort. The larynx contains the two vocal folds which are popularly but erroneously known as the vocal cords, a term which gives a false impression of their nature. The opening between the vocal folds is known as the glottis. The epiglottis is a cartilaginous structure of the larynx above the glottis, which can open or close the glottis as a function of the larynx.

*The voice process.* It is a comparatively simple matter to produce some vocal sounds. Young infants start immediately after birth and in the year or so before speech begins to function they continue these sounds. The exhaled air from the lungs passes through the larynx where sound waves are set up by the complete or partial opening and closing of the glottis which is between the two vocal folds. These air vibrations are affected by the amount of breath pressure as well as by the volume of exhaled air. The volume of air depends upon many factors such as lung capacity, general strength, and vitality as well as upon the emotional tone at any given moment. The breathing may be abdominal or thoracic or combinations of them so that several variables are operative. Whatever characteristics these sound vibrations have they leave the glottis and the vocal folds to be forwarded to the mouth and to the nasal cavities. Sound vibrations of the air undergo further modifications depending upon the anatomy and formation of the lips, the position of the tongue, the size and condition of the teeth, the general size and shape of the mouth, as well as the size and shape of the nasal passages, known as the resonating system. What may have started as the simple cry of the new born infant gradually develops into speech and language through imitation, speech training, and various educational processes. What may seem to be simple in the mechanisms of speech actually becomes very complicated and involved in the possible modifications offered by the many variables which can affect speech.

## The Examination of Speech

Since it is common knowledge that many children and adults have some type of defective speech, examination and treatment are desirable. Parents should be aware of speech defects and disorders as soon as the preschool child has developed a small but workable vocabulary of spoken words, but often they do not notice any deviations to which they have become accustomed. The pediatrician or the family physician should call attention to these deficiencies and refer to the speech pathologist.

If they have not been corrected by the time of school entrance, teachers should be alert to speech defects. Such factors as delayed speech, stuttering, lisping, and deviations of pitch, intensity, and general quality should be noted. Physical abnormalities such as a cleft palate and maloccluded teeth are more obvious, but note should also be made of limited intelligence, aphasia, cerebral palsy, and lack of speech accompanying impaired hearing. Lists of such pupils should be prepared and more detailed examinations should be conducted by the speech correctionist. Johnson[1] and others describe details of many phases of such examinations.

The speech teacher or speech correctionist examines for the many specific defects in the speech itself and in this examination process she is immediately aware of any anatomical abnormalities from the type of speech disorder. She refers such anatomical abnormalities to the speech pathologist who may advise or perform corrective surgery where necessary.

Defective speech may not be based on anatomical deviations but may be of neurological pathology. Aphasia is caused by lesions or defects in the central nervous system which affect the speech centers. Other neurological diseases and disorders may affect speech and should be examined and diagnosed by the neurologist. In the event that the speech disorder appears to have no anatomical, physiological, or neurological basis but is characterized by emotional disturbance, the psychiatrist and the clinical psychologist also cooperate in the examination, diagnosis, and recommendation for the level of mental maturity and for any special intellectual abilities or disabilities which may affect speech development. The audiologist and otolaryngologist become members of the examining team since hearing disorders are often closely related to disorders of speech or to the development of speech. In addition to descriptive notes furnished by the classroom teacher, she may give further valuable clues in extended conferences where interpretive enquiries are directed toward her. The team approach is becoming an important method in many types of exceptional children.

### The Number of Speech-Handicapped

When considering the possible number of speech-handicapped some clues may be taken from the preceding sections on the mech-

[1] W. Johnson, F.L. Darly, and D.C. Spriesterbach, *Diagnostic Manual in Speech Correction*, Harper & Brothers, New York, 1952, 221 pp.

anisms of speech and from the examining and diagnostic specialists who have entered the field. Any one must conclude that the number of speech handicapped is large. While there are many types of exceptional children the total in all of these other areas is equalled by the number of speech handicapped alone.

The Sub-Committee on Special Classes of the White House Conference on Child Health and Protection in 1930[1] dealing with the speech-handicapped made a careful attempt to estimate the number of cases by two methods. They sent a questionnaire on speech handicaps to all cities with general populations of ten thousand or more. A very small per cent of them were returned by forty-eight cities of various sizes in many parts of the country. However, these returns were probably a representative sampling of the total situation. When they divided the total school population of these cities into the number of reported speech-handicapped 5 per cent were defective; on a countrywide scale this number would have amounted to 1,177,893 at that time. On the present-day population this number would now be well over one and one-half million. The median per cent by cities arranged in order of largest to smallest percentage was 6.9; as a result the committee decided that at that time one million speech handicapped would be a conservative estimate.

As a second check, the committee made a careful survey of the 10,033 children of Madison, Wis., and found 710 children whom they classified as speech-handicapped. This number is approximately 7 per cent, or about equal to the median method of computing by reports from the forty-eight cities. In consideration of the committee's size of three members only and its limitation of finance and time a very creditable and accurate survey was made.

Frampton and Rowell[2] state that there are 8 per cent of the children in New York City who need speech correction, or a total of 27,000. Mills and Streit[3] made a speech survey of the 4,685 public

---

[1] White House Conference on Child Health and Protection, *Special Education: The Handicapped and the Gifted*, D. Appleton-Century Co., New York, 1931, pp. 353-356.

[2] M.E. Frampton and H. G. Rowell, *Education of the Handicapped*, Vol. II, *Problems*, World Book Co., Yonkers, N.Y., 1940, pp. 238-239.

[3] A.W. Mills and H. Streit, "Report of a Speech Survey, Holyoke, Massachusetts," *Journal of Speech Disorders*, 1942, 7, pp. 161-167.

school pupils of Holyoke, Mass All of the pupils in grades 1, 2, and 3 were tested and in the more advanced grades pupils were referred by their teachers or discovered by the examiners. It was found that 10.1 per cent of all pupils had some speech handicap.

One of the most comprehensive speech surveys was conducted in New England and reported by Pronovost.[1] The survey was conducted by teachers, speech correctionists, nurses, doctors, and others on 87,288 children. Speech handicaps were found in 7.8 per cent of them.

Wendell Johnson[2] comments on the number of speech defectives:

There should be one speech correctionist to approximately every 4,000 pupils. Estimating *very conservatively* that only 5 per cent of the pupils will be found to have significant speech correction problems, there would be 200 children needing speech correction among every 4,000 pupils. Some of them, possibly half, can be handled by their regular classroom teachers, with consultation and supervision by the speech correctionist. The rate of improvement and dismissal will then tend to keep the load of individualized and small-group cases in an enrollment of 4,000 down to a number —75 to 100—that one speech correctionist can handle efficiently.

### Plans of Action

The number of speech handicapped is large. Parents and teachers are able to detect minor handicaps in speech much more easily than they may detect minor handicaps in vision and/or hearing. Major speech handicaps are immediately obvious. As in the case of other defects early detection, diagnosis, correction and remedial measures are important for speech defects as well. Such programs should be initiated long before time of school entrance and while speech is still in its principal formative years.

In the following chapter it will be noted that children with speech handicaps continue to be enrolled in regular classes but have special periods of help, usually twice per week, with the speech teacher who

[1] W. Pronovost, "A Survey of Services for the Speech and Hearing Handicapped in New England," *Journal of Speech Disorders*, 16, 1951, pp. 148-156.

[2] W. Johnson, "Speech Handicaps," National Society for the Study of Education, Forty-ninth Yearbook, Part II, *The Education of Exceptional Children*, University of Chicago Press, Chicago, Chapter X, pp. 185-186. Quoted by permission of the Society.

is also known as the speech correctionist. They are not segregated into special classes as is necessarily true of some types of handicapped and this condition is highly in their favor.

The speech correctionist has taken on an additional group of children who are deaf or hard-of-hearing, whom she may handle along with the speech-handicapped. Her methods of speech reading and speech development, which are becoming adapted for pupils with impaired hearing, apply in many respects to the speech-handicapped. The speech correctionist has a broader training because of her knowledge of hearing impairment, which she uses to good advantage in her program of speech correction.

### Questions and Topics for Discussion

1. If you are particularly interested in the structure and functions of the organs of speech, prepare a more detailed description than is given in the text.
2. Give a report on the speech examination program in your local community.
3. Arrange for a speech correctionist to give a demonstration of her program.
4. Make a detailed list of signs to observe for possible evidence of speech handicap.
5. Describe experiences you have had in dealing with children or adults with speech handicap.

Note: Consult reference material at the end of Chapter 25.

# CHAPTER 25

## *The Speech-Handicapped*

VARIOUS ORGANIZATIONS and associations presently affiliated with the Council for Exceptional Children once represented principally separate and distinct types. Today it is different. There are so many children with multiple handicaps that joint section meetings are common practice. Mental hygiene, mental health, and the total personality of the child regardless of handicap have become common denominators in unified thinking. Any need for classifying handicapped children as distinctly and uniquely physical, sensory, or emotional has largely disappeared. Such is the case for the handicapped in speech who represent physical, neurological, and emotional problems. The education of the hard-of-hearing and of the deaf is so intimately involved with speech development that discussions of hearing handicaps should logically be associated with speech handicap. In like manner the pathology of speech handicap is so often based on some physiological defect that discussion of the physically handicapped such as the orthopedically handicapped is closely related. Speech handicap is also related to brain damage as in cerebral palsy and hence that topic also has a logical sequence. All things considered this location is a logical place for presentation of speech and for the speech handicapped if there is need for any order of presentation.

### Definitions

Speech difficulties arise from so many sources, are of so many kinds and degrees, and have so many attendant by-products that

393

simple, concise definitions are difficult to formulate. Pintner, Eisenson, and Stanton[1] offer the following:

Speech may be considered defective when it is not easily audible and intelligible to the listener. Speech is defective if it is vocally or visibly unpleasant or labored in production. Finally, speech is defective if it is inappropriate to the individual in regard to his mental and chronological age, sex, and physical development.

In considering speech difficulties there is need to distinguish between disorders and defects of speech. West, Kennedy, and Carr[2] make the following distinction:

These terms *disorders* and *defects* should be differentiated. The former is the more comprehensive; it takes into consideration not only the atypical acoustic end result, but also the underlying condition causing it. The latter considers only the acoustic end result. Further, a distinction may be made between (1) those defects that are also classifiable as disorders and (2) those that are merely defects. If the cause is an abnormality, the defect is classifiable also as a disorder; but if no abnormality underlies the speech defect, the term *disorder* should not be used to describe it.

A very practical and workable definition for classroom purposes has been proposed by Johnson[3] and others:

A working definition of defective or impaired speech should be, for classroom purposes, neither too inclusive nor too exclusive. That is, as much harm is done by having speech standards that are too high as by having standards that are too low. A teacher's ears, so to speak, can be too long or too short. She can pay too much attention to a child's speech or too little. A good general rule to follow is that a difference to be a difference has to make a difference. The main purposes of speech are satisfying self-expression and effective communication. If a child is achieving these purposes passably well, his speech does not present a problem in any very important sense, regardless of how he speaks. On the other hand, if he could plainly achieve these purposes more fully with improved speech, then, even though his speech may seem to be reasonably normal, there is something to be gained by him through speech correction.

[1] R. Pintner, J. Eisenson, and M. Stanton, *The Psychology of the Physically Handicapped*, F.S. Crofts Co., New York, 1940, p. 320.

[2] R. West, L. Kennedy, and A. Carr, *The Rehabilitation of Speech* (rev. ed.), Harper & Brothers, New York, 1947, p. 7.

[3] W. Johnson, S.F. Brown, J.F. Curtis, C.W. Edney, and J. Keaster, *Speech Handicapped School Children* (rev. ed.), Harper & Brothers, New York, 1956, p. 5.

## The Development of Speech

There are four phases in the normal development of speech. West[1] and others list them as follows: (1) phonatory, or voice; (2) articulatory, or modification of voice by various organs to produce speech; (3) linguistic, or a code of meaning; and (4) auditory, or learning the process of speech by listening and by watching others speak. The totally deaf can watch others speak and through speech reading may understand what is said. They learn to speak by imitation but with physical help and direction from the speech correctionist.

Speech defects and disorders may have several causes, each of which may lead to several kinds of difficulties. Some causes are physiogenic, or resulting from some anatomical abnormality such as cleft palate. Another group of causes is from neurological impairment which may result in cerebral palsy; a third group is psychogenic and sometimes results in stuttering; a fourth social cause may result in baby talk and delayed speech development. Each of these types of causes has several subtypes and may produce many kinds of speech impairments. Disorders may be classified as *organic* or as *functional* depending upon the nature of the condition intermediary between the cause and the defect. A cause such as inability to make certain speech sounds because of poorly spaced and malformed teeth is organic but it becomes functional if the defect continues after dental correction. There are no clear-cut lines between some causes and some effects and hence descriptions of relationships are not as definite as in some other fields that are primarily physiogenic in origin. With these limitations in mind some causes and some resulting speech impairments will be discussed.

### Causes of Defective Speech

Four major areas of causes have just been mentioned. All of them are important in causations of speech impairment.

*Physiogenic causes.* The capacity and general conditions of the lungs and abdominal muscles affect the general nature and vitality

[1] R.L. West, L. Kennedy, and A. Carr, *The Rehabilitation of Speech* (rev. ed.), Harper & Brothers, New York, 1947, p. 44.

of breathing although there is no proven correspondence between such volume and the power of the voice. Defects and deformities of the larynx and of the vocal folds affect the quality of the voice such as in hoarseness. Incomplete development of the skull and head with failure of the two halves to unite produces cleft palate and cleft lip, also known as harelip. This defect may also include the nose. Marked abnormalities may occur in the teeth, lips, tongue, jaw, and the general shape of the mouth and nasal passages. All of these and abnormalities of the tonsils and adenoids produce a great array of voice and articulatory variations beyond the range of normal speech. Deafness and impaired hearing prevent accurate imitation of speech sounds which is the principal avenue in learning to talk. Some of these defects may be remedied by surgery, by plastic surgery, by dental straightening or by dentures, but all such operations should be only upon the advice and utilizations of competent medical or dental specialists.

*Neurological causes.* In an earlier chapter neurological disorders and defects were discussed. There are twelve pairs of nerves which lead out of the base of the cranium to the various areas of speech and hearing processes. Several of them are known by number such as the eighth pair, which leads to the ear. Other nerves lead to the pharynx and to the muscles of inhalation and exhalation. When any or all of these nerves and their attendant areas of the central nervous system are impaired, some type of speech defect or disorder logically follows. Aphasia, or lack of articulation, or dysphasia, or disorder of articulation, come under this causative classification. Complete lack or disorder may also be present in anarthria and dysarthria which denote the area of articulation. Cerebral palsy is caused by nerve impairment arising in the central nervous system.

*Psychogenic causes.* Psychogenic causes are those which arise in the conscious mind or in the subconscious mind. Some types of stuttering are psychogenic in origin. Certain types of articulatory defects may arise from the memory of ridicule and each time the particular word or sound element is called into play a blocking occurs. The general self-consciousness which may accompany any speech defect tends to perpetuate and to intensify the impairment for many who have such impediments. After a physiogenic defect has been remedied the motivation to overcome the attendant speech disorder must often be of psychogenic origin. The phrase "mind over matter" is clearly illustrated in speech handicap.

*Sociological causes.* When parents do not follow the line of good sense but let their young children continue baby talk they impose a heavy burden upon them. There is not only the ridicule from merciless playmates and classmates, but the great difficulty of breaking well-established habits and substituting correct speech for them. Inarticulate speech and too rapid or too slow speech may be learned in the home. When families move into other sections of the country they bring with them a characteristic vernacular which is hard for their new associates to understand, or, in turn, it is difficult for them to understand the speech of their new neighborhood and community. Conditions in this direction are more extreme when they come with a foreign language. If they are completely ignorant of the new language they may be accepted with more grace than if they have made substantial progress in it but have a few speech errors which persistently recur. The speech impairments from social causes may seem of relatively less significance and consequence than from the other causes. However, if they take on psychogenic aspects their presence may be much more ominous.

## The Kinds of Speech Handicaps

*Stuttering.* Stuttering is often called stammering but in the field of speech impairment stuttering is the more commonly accepted term although they may be used synonymously. Stammering is the preferred word in England and in most other English speaking areas of the world outside of the United States. It is hesitation in speech due to an inability to enunciate speech sounds and syllables without repeated efforts. Johnson[1] and his associates propose what they believe to be an adequate definition:

Stuttering is an anticipatory, apprehensive, hypertonic avoidance reaction.

[1] W. Johnson et al., *Speech Handicapped School Children* (rev. ed.), Harper & Brothers, New York, 1956, pp. 216-217.

They explain further that stuttering is what a speaker does trying not to stutter again and hence "anticipatory," "apprehensive," and "hypertonic avoidance" are well chosen descriptive terms. The very fact of concentrating upon speech instead of letting it flow naturally is a common characteristic of stuttering. There are equivalent forms of blocking in actions not involving speech which follow the same pattern. Bowlers who consistently start their approach to the foul line with the same foot suddenly can't remember and throw themselves out of balance by a wrong start. Stopping to remember is the stumbling block. While there is some evidence that stuttering runs in families the fundamental cause may not be hereditary but due to constant imitation of the stuttering parent. Stutterers can usually speak normally about 90 per cent of the time, but in the remaining 10 per cent various crises arise such as trying to buy a railroad ticket just as the train is about to depart. The times when he speaks without stuttering his speech may be entirely free of any other speech handicaps such as disorders of articulation or voice.

*Articulatory disorders.* In this handicap children cannot produce all the speech sounds in the usual acceptable manner. There may be omissions of letters, syllables, or parts of words. Substitutions of sounds such as "v" for "th" are frequent and in distortions there are many ways in which the letter "s" is mispronounced. The causes of articulatory disorders are in many areas. Physiogenic malformations of such organs as lips, teeth, palate, and others throw the articulation out of line. Worry and emotional upset from overemphasis by parents or teachers on correcting speech brings frustration and is psychogenic in nature. Faulty learning at home, on the playground, and in the classroom accounts for many errors which might otherwise have been avoided. Since there are many speech sounds and many shades or degrees of error, the total possible number of articulatory disorders can be very great.

*Voice disorders.* In the preceding chapter there was some description of the anatomy of the many organs used in speech. Various defects and disorders of these organs may affect the general character of the voice. There may also be voice disorders of psychogenic origin and social causes from copying incorrect speech of family members and associates which contribute their quota of voice handicaps. The pitch level may be either too high or too low for comfortable listening. Any marked deviation in either direction attracts attention. Although there may be no relationship between an effeminate character in a man and a high pitched voice nevertheless this impression is very common. Abnormally high or low pitch of voice in a girl is considered a liability because the low pitch is incorrectly supposed to be related to masculinity. The actual cause may be in the anatomical structure of the vocal folds.

West[1] and others give interesting and simple instructions on how to discover the natural pitch of the voice. Pitch is important in the singing voice. Children who seem to have little or no feeling for pitch are called monotones. They are not welcome in music classes and the feeling is mutual on their part as well. Failure in being unable to sing a simple *do te do* gives a clue to difficulties in pitch discrimination.

A voice that is too loud often startles the listener and suggests anger or displeasure although this may not be the case. However, the listener may be unable to resist the temptation to shout and become tense in reply. Many children are afraid of parents or teachers whose voices are too loud. In clinical cases children sometimes develop pathological fears and regress into unacceptable behavior. The low or soft spoken voice is difficult to hear and puts the listener and the speaker at a social disadvantage. The listener may guess incorrectly at what has been said rather than question the speaker too often. The speaking voice should be pleasant and with some variety rather than seeming to be ground out with machine-like precision.

*Other speech impairments.* There are many other speech impairments which makes impaired speech one of the most complex of all types of handicaps. For example, the impaired speech of the cerebral palsied child often parallels his general muscular disability. His slow and labored speech accompanied by unpredictable jerks does not encourage regular teachers to wait patiently while the rest of the class can go rapidly. Impaired hearing generates speech problems. In severe hearing impairment the child cannot hear and judge his own voice

[1] R. West et al., *The Rehabilitation of Speech* (rev. ed.), Harper & Brothers, New York, 1947, pp. 543-545.

unless a trained speech correctionist provides the necessary training. He also misses the finer characteristics of voices when he listens and develops inaccurate patterns of speech from what he hears in part. Finally the cleft palate case should be helped by surgery as early as possible in the child's life. When unrepaired the voice has heavy nasality from the opened passages between nose and mouth. Sometimes appliances called obturators serve as a false palate but at best they cannot give the pliability to the voice as do the normal organs of the speech mechanism.

### Remedial and Preventive Measures

The discussion of speech in the preceding chapter, the description of causes, and the various speech impairments cited in this chapter have indicated and suggested many remedial and preventive measures. On the one hand the impairments sometimes seem to be a hopeless task with their many intermingling factors of multiple causes and effects. On the other hand there are so many different services presently available with each specializing in particular areas that there is a much brighter picture in prospect.

*Physiogenic areas.* There is a limited number of children with cleft palate, sometimes extending to cleft lip, which can be repaired by surgery. Deformities of the mouth, extremely enlarged tonsils and adenoids, and dental irregularities are further examples of possible anatomical corrections. While such corrections may seem spectacular because of their visible evidences they are only a small portion of the remedial program.

*Neurogenic areas.* Neurological impairments probably occur more frequently than those of physiogenic origin but, unfortunately, they are less susceptible to treatment. Conditions that affect the Broca area, the association areas of motor and kinesthetic activation, and the several nerve tracts leading to the organs of speech should be given the greatest possible therapeutic treatments. An improved general health helps to keep the nerve tonus on the positive side. Modern medication of nerve tissue is a rapidly expanding area of investigation which might hopefully approximate what uninformed but overzealous enthusiasts ascribe to it. In some cases of brain injury, tumors, and

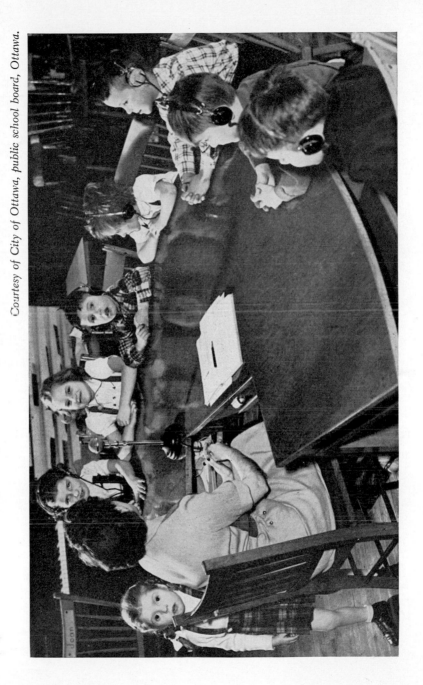

Lip-reading class, Cambridge Street School, Ottawa, Ontario.

*Courtesy of City of Ottawa, public school board, Ottawa.*

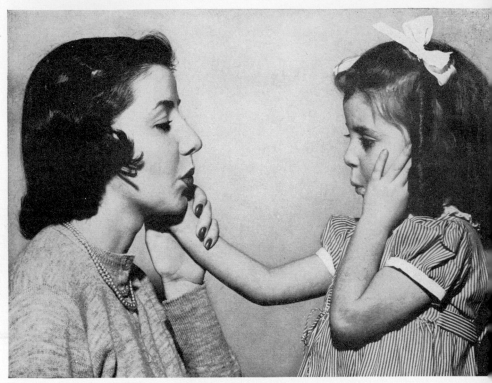

*Courtesy of Department of Special Education, Eastern Michigan College.*

Instruction of a deaf pupil by the Tadoma method,
Eastern Michigan College, Ypsilanti.

other trauma, surgery is the chief remedy. Whenever the neurological constitution is weak or below desired standard a reduced schedule of school work with rest, better nourishment, and a quiet home life minus tensions are positive prescriptions.

*Psychogenic areas.* The power of the mind is the most potent of all factors in remedial speech impairment. It can overcome many of the lesser speech handicaps and go surprisingly far in restoration and improvement of cases with primary physiogenic and neurogenic impairments. The power of mind operates concurrently with the actual improvement of speech to transform a person who has felt inferior, rejected, and socially isolated into a happy and self-confident individual able to face the world on an equal basis.

*Sociological areas.* Mention has been made of certain sociological causes of speech impairment. The child with the language or vernacular alien to his community deserves the best that speech correction has to offer. Classes under special teachers for the foreign born yield a high return in perfecting the prevailing language. Adult education classes for better speech in the home would indirectly benefit many children even though no foreign tongue is heard.

### The Remedial Speech Program

Many activities have been described which lead up to the remedial speech program. The job of the speech correctionist is not simple. The personality of the speech-handicapped child is one of the major factors to be taken into account at all times. A balance must be struck between too much and too little urging, with the emphasis shifted from time to time as conditions change. The child must have a real desire to improve which should be fortified with maximum cooperation of his parents.

One of the most common articulatory defects is the *s* sound. In making this sound which is produced by a single, strong stream of expired breath the proper adjustments of several articulators are necessary. The lips are drawn back slightly so that the breath stream may strike against the front teeth, and the tongue is elevated and spread with a V-shaped dip at the tip through which the air is forced. The velum or soft palate and the wall of the pharynx are placed so as to close off the air from passing through the nose. In cases of no speech handicap these processes function coordinately and without attention. This illustration is only one of the many which the speech correctionist must train and direct in remedial work.

Each cause of indistinct speech must be carefully analyzed. In cases of mental retardation the speech improvement must advance slowly and within the child's limited vocabulary. The child who stutters must be handled with special care so that his mental blockings are minimized. Frequently there are topics of conversation in which he does not stutter. Certain occasions such as birthday celebrations when he does not stutter should be utilized for reorientation whenever possible. Other deformities such as nasal or mouth impairments and cleft palate yield wholly or in part to corrective treatments. Detailed discussions of diagnosis and remedial treatment are given by West[1] and his collaborators and by Johnson[2] and his collaborators.

## The Number of Speech-Handicapped

Some general figures in the preceding chapter cite from 5 to 10 per cent with speech handicaps. As the many kinds of causes and types of resulting handicaps have been outlined it would not be surprising if the frequencies were higher. West reports that of the speech-handicapped approximately one-half had oral inactivity; 10 per cent each in articulatory structural; in stuttering, in sound substitution, and in functional vocal; and the remaining 10 per cent falling in a miscellaneous group. In most areas boys outnumber girls in the ratio of three to two. Attention is called again to the fact that the number of speech-handicapped equals the sum total of all other types of handicapped.

## History of the Speech-Handicapped

There was never any overwhelming sentiment for the speech-handicapped such as often attended the blind and to some extent the

[1] R. West et al., *The Rehabilitation of Speech* (rev. ed.), Harper & Brothers, New York, 1947, 650 pp.

[2] W. Johnson et al., *Diagnostic Manual in Speech Correction*, Harper & Brothers, New York, 1952, 221 pp.

crippled. In early historical times the speech-handicapped were often subject to taunt and ridicule. Since they managed to get along somehow in school and society, their plight did not become very apparent until the beginning of the twentieth century.

*Famous individuals.* As in the case of other handicaps, there were many famous men who had speech handicaps. Among them was the Greek orator, Demosthenes, who is said to have learned to orate clearly with pebbles in his mouth so that he would have a reserve power of clarity; he talked beside the ocean surf until he could be heard above its din and roar. There have been various stories to the effect that he could not pronounce *s* but produced *f* instead, that he could not pronounce *r*, and that he lisped and stuttered.

Moses tried to beg off as law-giver, describing himself as "slow of speech and of slow tongue" (Exodus IV: 10). Aristotle, Virgil, Charles Lamb, Erasmus, and other famous learned men were reputed to have had speech handicaps. This was also true of Napoleon and probably to a slight degree of George Washington. As in the case of other handicaps, speech disability frequently impelled men to great achievement. Their deeds often serve as guides and incentives to the handicapped today.

*Methods of diagnosis.* Although little was done about defects of speech from an educational point of view in early times, there were various theories about causes and for medical treatment. About 400 B.C., Hippocrates was probably the earliest physician to mention that stammerers with voluble tongues were full of black bile. In the fourteenth century a French physician, Guy de Chaulliac, shared the beliefs of others that there was too much heat in the body and particularly in the tongue. Since some speech-handicapped have emotional disturbances accompanied by blushing and by bodily agitation such conditions might have easily been attributed to mysterious fluids supposed to be in the human body.

From 1500 to 1800 certain authorities considered some speech handicaps to be psychological in nature. Advances were also made in knowledge of the physiology of speech handicaps. Johann Friedrich Dieffenbach (1792-1847) attempted an erroneous procedure of some muscular surgery on the speech-handicapped, but this was a forerunner of later and more successful surgery. Pierre Paul Broca (1824-1880) claimed to have localized an area of the brain as the seat of articulated language, and this was later known as Broca's area. In America, Alexander Melville Bell, and later, his son, Alexander Graham Bell, made progress in using Visible Speech symbols to teach speech, particularly to the hard-of-hearing and the deaf. Great advances have been made in recent years with newer techniques of voice reproduction and in allied areas.

*Establishment of classes.* Classes for the speech-handicapped are of comparatively recent origin. Moore and Kester[1] summarize these early American efforts. The superintendent of the New York City schools in 1909 requested an investigation of the needs for speech training, but it was not until June, 1916, that Dr. Frederick Martin became the first director of speech improvement. A 1910 survey showed 1,287 pupils with speech handicaps in the Chicago public schools, which resulted in the employment of ten teachers who had specialized in speech and oral expression at the rate of $65 per month. There had been some earlier attempts with one class reported in Potsdam, Germany, in 1887, and one in New York City in 1908. A few cities got their programs into operation by 1920.

*Professional organizations.* As early as 1891 the association known as Public Readers and Teachers of Elocution was organized, but before it dissolved in 1915 its name had been changed to National Speech Arts Association. In 1911 the English teachers in the National Education Association formed the National Council of Teachers of English, but by 1915 the speech correction teachers of this organization organized their own National Association of Academic Teachers of Public Speaking. This organization had so many interests that by 1925 a further interest in the speech handicapped resulted in the organization of the American Academy of Speech Correction. In 1927 its name was changed to The American Society for the Study of Disorders of Speech and in 1936 it became the American Speech Correction Association. With the interest in developing speech for the deaf

---

[1] P. Moore and D.G. Kester, "Historical Notes on Speech Correction in the Pre-Association Era," *The Journal of Speech and Hearing Disorders*, 1953, 18, pp. 48-53.

the activities of this association were expanded so that in 1948 it adopted its present title, American Speech and Hearing Association. These various titles and affiliations reflect the trend of progress in speech correction.

## Characteristics of the Speech-Handicapped

Lack of normal social communication is the key to some personality characteristics and to reactions of the speech-handicapped. They differ from the deaf who may regress unless training is early and communication is established. For the speech-handicapped a considerable amount of communication is possible, but the very process of communication is faulty. These imperfect avenues of communication set up frustrations which trigger personality deviations at some or all the time. These personality problems reflect back to accentuate the speech handicap itself and thus completes a vicious circle which is hard to break.

It would certainly be unjust to generalize very far on personality disorders attendant upon speech handicaps. When a child with a speech handicap presents personality problems it is easy to conclude that they are uniquely related but at the same time it is known that many other speech-handicapped children do not have such personality deviations. Likewise there are children with personality deviations who have no speech handicap. It is only to the extent that social frustration is a common denominator among the speech-handicapped that any generalization is acceptable. The real task of the speech correctionist is to adopt and practice the best principles of mental hygiene and apply them toward the mental health of the child.

## Training of the Speech Correctionist

There are many fields of training for the speech correctionist. They include anatomy and physiology of the organs and bodily areas adapted for use in speech. Since the speech correctionist is currently engaged in speech reading and in speech development for the hard-of-hearing and the deaf, her study must enter these areas as well. She must familiarize herself with many diagnostic procedures and with the liberal amount of remedial material which is becoming available. The many types of defects and disorders which have been listed in preceding sections give a further field of coverage with which she must be thoroughly familiar and in which she is able to function. One year or more of graduate study is scarcely sufficient to cover these many fields.

## The Program of the Speech Correctionist

The speech correctionist does not have just one class of pupils, but she must meet with many small groups one or more times weekly. Such groupings may have smaller sized but specially equipped rooms. These rooms need ample storage and file space for many diagnostic correction materials. Some type of recording instrument should be provided which can play back the child's speech. A mirror wide enough for the pupil and teacher to see themselves side by side, so that the child may imitate the speech sounds should also be provided.

The speech teacher or correctionist usually has one or more schools in which she works four days weekly. The fifth day is used for coordination; for this she can confer with the pupil's regular teacher and also observe her pupils in action within their own classes. She may also give many valuable hints for improving speech which the regular teacher can adapt and use to good advantage on all her pupils.

The speech correctionist has increased the sphere of her activities to three groups of pupils: (1) those with some type of speech handicap only; (2) those with a combination of speech and impaired hearing; and (3) those with impaired hearing only. While many school systems carry a larger case load, Johnson recommends a maximum of 75 to 100 pupils. Many states are now providing full subsidies to local systems for speech correctionists, which is encouraging a rapid expansion of the program. The chief limitation is in the number of teacher candidates to specialize in speech correction.

### Questions and Topics for Discussion

1. Describe any speech-handicap conditions of your acquaintances.
2. Visit and have a demonstration of a speech correction class.

3. Report on the number of speech phonetic sounds and how some of them are made.
4. Report on a more inclusive list of famous individuals who had speech defects.
5. Draw a detailed diagram of the body organs serving the production of speech.
6. Report on how your local community is providing for the education of its speech handicapped children.

## A. Organizations

1. American Speech and Hearing Association, 1001 Connecticut Ave., Washington 10, D.C.
2. American Speech Association, Office of the Secretary.
3. American Speech Correction Association, Box 3066, Ohio State University, Columbus, Ohio.
4. Speech Association of America, Department of Speech, University of Illinois, Urbana, Ill.
5. Volta Speech Association for the Deaf, 1537 35th St., N.W., Washington 7, D.C.

## B. Periodicals

1. *The Journal of Speech* (quarterly), American Speech Association
2. *The Journal of Speech and Hearing Disorders* (quarterly), American Speech and Hearing Association
3. *The Journal of Speech and Hearing Research* (initiated January 1, 1958), American Speech and Hearing Association
4. *Speech Teacher* (quarterly), American Speech Association

## C. Books

1. Backus, O.L., and J. Beasley, *Speech Therapy with Children*, Houghton Mifflin Co., Boston, 1950, 441 pp.
2. Berry, M.F., and J. Eisenson, *The Defective in Speech*, D. Appleton-Century Co., New York, 1942, 426 pp.
3. Bluemel, C.S., *Stammering and Allied Disorders*, The Macmillan Co., New York, 1935, 182 pp.
4. Brodnitz, F.S., *Keep Your Voice Healthy*, Harper & Brothers, New York, 1953, 234 pp.
5. Gottlober, W.G., *Understanding Stuttering*, Grune and Stratton, Inc., New York, 1953, 274 pp.

6. Hejna, R.F., *Your Child's Speech, A Handbook for Parents*, College Typing Co., Madison, Wis., 1955, 46 pp.
7. Heltman, H.J., *First Aid for Stutterers*, The Expression Co., Boston, 1950, 276 pp.
8. ———, *Handbook for Remedial Speech*, The Expression Co., Boston, 1948, 202 pp.
9. Johnson, W., *Because I Stutter*, D. Appleton-Century Co., New York, 1930, 127 pp.
10. ———, S.F. Brown, J.F. Curtis, C.W. Edney, and J. Keaster, *Speech Handicapped School Children* (rev. ed.), Harper & Brothers, New York, 1956, 575 pp.
11. ——— (ed.), *Stuttering in Children and Adults, Thirty Years of Research at the University of Iowa*, University of Minnesota Press, Minneapolis, Minn., 1955, 472 pp.
12. ———, *Your Most Enchanted Listener*, Harper & Brothers, New York, 1956, 215 pp.
13. Jones, M.V., *Speech Correction at Home*, Charles C Thomas Publisher, Springfield, Ill., 1957, 136 pp.
14. Mulgrave, D., *Speech for the Classroom Teacher*, Prentice-Hall, Inc., Englewood Cliffs, N.J., 1955, 450 pp.
15. Schreiber, F.R., *Your Child's Speech*, G.P. Putnam's Sons, New York, 1956, 256 pp.
16. Templin, M.C., *Certain Language Skills in Children*, University of Minnesota Press, Minneapolis, Minn., 1957, 183 pp.
17. Thomas, C.K., *Handbook of Speech Improvement*, Ronald Press Co., New York, 1956, 135 pp.
18. Travis, L.E. (ed.), *Handbook of Speech Pathology*, Appleton-Century-Crofts, Inc., New York, 1957, 1088 pp.
19. Van Riper, C., *Speech Correction: Principles and Methods* (rev. ed.), Prentice-Hall, Inc., Englewood Cliffs, N.J., 1947, 470 pp.
20. ———, and L. Gruber, *A Casebook in Stuttering*, Harper & Brothers, New York, 1957, 146 pp.
21. West, R., M. Ansberry, and A. Carr, *The Rehabilitation of Speech* (rev. ed.), Harper & Brothers, New York, 1957, 688 pp.
22. Young, E.H., and S.S. Hawk, *Moto-Kinesthetic Speech Training*, Stanford University Press, Stanford University, Calif., 1955, 176 pp.

## D. Films and Filmstrips

1. *Speech Defects*, three 35-mm. color filmstrips:
   A. *Nature of Speech Defects*, 55 frames;
   B. *How Speech Defects Develop*, 49 frames;

C. *What Speech Clinics Are Doing,* 48 frames.
Society for Visual Education, Inc., 1345 Diversey Parkway, Chicago 14.

2. *The Wisconsin Cleft Palate Story,* 36 minutes, 16-mm., sound, color. Bureau of Visual Instruction, University of Wisconsin Extension Division, 1328 W. Johnson St., Madison, Wis.

3. *Articulatory Movements in the Production of English Speech Sounds:*
   Part  I. *Consonants,* 16-mm. color, 25 minutes, illustrated with animated drawings and direct photography of movements of various speech organs.
   Part II. *Vowels and Glides,* 16 mm. color, 26 minutes. Live-action photography of movements with loss of facial tissue. United States Veterans Administration, Central Film Library, Washington 25, D.C.

# CHAPTER 26

## *The Orthopedically Handicapped*

THE TERM "CRIPPLED" persists as the popular conception of the ortho-pedically handicapped. A day seldom passes in which "crippled" children or adults are not likely to be seen since there are so many of them. There are many kinds of orthopedic handicaps, some easily recognizable, others not so noticeable, but nevertheless crippled in the full meaning of the term. Some are minus a hand or an arm, some have deformities of the hips or trunk, some walk with one or two canes or crutches, and some get about in wheel chairs. Another large group does not appear on the street because their orthopedic handicaps are so extreme; others are bedridden. Although modern society tries to care for them, a few crippled adults with a minimum of self-pride beg on street corners; in many other countries begging is a wide-spread practice. The few in America who beg reflect historical practices. The plight of this small minority is in sharp contrast to the generally enlightened treatment given to the orthopedically handi-capped today.

### Definitions

In a field as large as orthopedic handicaps it is difficult to formulate simple definitions which are broad enough to cover the various sub-classifications and narrow enough to have any specific meaning. At the White House Conference on Child Health and Protection[1] in 1930 two committees with different orientations offered somewhat

[1] White House Conference on Child Health and Protection, *Special Education: The Handicapped and the Gifted*, D. Appleton-Century Co., New York, 1931, pp. 23-24.

different definitions. The subcommittee on special classes proposed a short definition as follows:

The crippled child, in the orthopedic sense, is a child that has a defect which causes a deformity or an interference with normal function of the bones, muscles, or joints. His condition may be congenital or it may be due to disease or accident. It may be aggravated by disease, by neglect, or by ignorance. (Orthopedic, throughout this report, is used as meaning *to straighten the child.*)

The Committee on the Handicapped Child[1] defined as follows:

A crippled child is one, under twenty-one years of age, who by reason of congenital or acquired defects of development, disease or wound, is, or may be reasonably expected to become, deficient in the use of his body or limbs (an orthopedic cripple) including hare lip, cleft palate, and some other handicaps yielding to plastic surgery, and excluding physical difficulties wholly of sight, hearing, or speech, and those affecting the heart primarily, and also excluding serious mental or moral abnormalities unless found in conjunction with orthopedic defects.

The former definition contains sociological implications of neglect or ignorance while the latter definition specifically rules out certain other handicaps such as vision or hearing with no specific orthopedic handicap present, but it does include such handicaps as cleft palate.

There are a few marginal diseases or conditions which are not presently accepted under the classification of orthopedic, although the distinction is not very clear for some of them. A case in point is cerebral palsy which is caused principally by neurological impairment and more properly comes under that general classification and has been discussed in an earlier chapter. However, many cerebral palsy victims are quite handicapped in locomotion and for practical convenience are provided special transportation to orthopedic schools. Currently approximately one-third of children in orthopedic schools are the cerebral palsied. Cases of severe cardiac conditions who have no visible signs of physical handicap are sometimes transported to orthopedic schools where they may be housed in separate classrooms. By stretching a point it is possible to bring them under a subclass of orthopedic

[1] White House Conference on Child Health and Protection, *The Handicapped Child*, D. Appleton-Century Co., New York, 1933, p. 119.

since the heart muscles are affected, but they more properly belong
to a classification of handicaps known as lowered vitality or health
conservation. Muscular dystrophy cases fall into the same category
as the cardiac-handicapped except that their deficiency is in general
strength and vitality.

### Orthopedic Classifications

Crippling from infections. The best known of the orthopedic handicaps is poliomyelitis, more commonly called infantile paralysis. For
many years it had been such a mad killer that the genius of Dr.
Jonas Salk has risen in this emergency with a vaccine which holds
great promise. This disease is caused by a virus which is contagious
and has often reached epidemic proportions in late, dry summers in
the northern part of the country. The virus may be transmitted directly
from person to person and sometimes by carriers who do not have
the disease themselves. In its early stages it is characterized by upper
respiratory and gastrointestinal symptoms. Some cases progress to
involvement of the central nervous system with nonparalytic or paralytic effects. The paralytic form produces an acute inflammation of
the gray matter of the spinal cord and results in paralysis of one or
more portions of the body. The muscles whose actions are controlled
by the affected nerves atrophy and crippling takes over. After several
months of careful experimentation with the Salk vaccine matched
with a control group using a placebo consisting of some harmless
powders, the 1955 announcement was made that an effective vaccine
had been found. Since that time inoculations have been extended to
three per person and further refinements have been made in the
vaccine itself. While there has been a small number of cases in which
complete success has not been achieved, poliomyelitis is joining smallpox, diphtheria, and others in the list of controlled contagious diseases.
In The Crippled Child of June, 1955, Lawrence Linck,[1] executive
director of the National Society for Crippled Children and Adults
has written a stirring report of this milestone in preventive medicine.
    Another crippling infectious disease is osteomyelitis which produces

[1] L.J. Linck, "A Battle Won," The Crippled Child, June, 1955, pp. 4-6.

an inflammation of the marrow of the bones. The infection may be carried through the blood and results in destruction of the bone. It can attack any bone but quite frequently bones of the leg in the vicinity of the knee are affected. Tuberculosis may strike bones or joints. Growing portions of the bones are frequently attacked by this germ infection. Syphilis and rheumatoid arthritis are additional infections which may produce crippling conditions.

*Congenital anomalies.* Children may be born with congenital anomalies. The absence of one or more limbs and congenital dislocation of joints sometimes occur. Cleft lip, cleft palate, clubfoot, and clubhand are part of this group. Torticollis or wry neck is one twisted from its usual position causing the head to lean toward the shoulder on the affected side with the chin turned to the opposite side. Spina bifida is a congenital defect in which a portion of the spinal column is left open. A hernial sac is formed which contains cerebrospinal fluid and sometimes nervous tissue.

*Traumatic crippling.* Amputation of one or more limbs from accidents, injuries, or from infections is sometimes necessary. With the increase of traffic accidents traumatic crippling seems to be on the increase. Serious degree burns often result in great impairment of physical motion as well as the social rejection which ensues from any unfortunate appearance. Sprains from falls or from abnormal postures in play or in lifting may force various joints such as shoulders, elbows, wrists, hips, knees, and ankles out of normal positions. These contractures sometimes do not heal completely without permanent stiffness. In this subclassification crippling due to birth injuries may be included. Erb's palsy is caused by unusual strains and pressures usually on upper portions of the body in difficult birth delivery so that nerves are permanently injured. Paralysis of hands, arms, and other muscles of the chest may result. Fragile bones may be broken and dislocations of joints may occur in these difficult deliveries. Modern methods of X-ray pictures and measurements of mother's pelvic dimensions with Caesarian section if necessary should reduce the number of such crippling handicaps.

*Tumors.* Tumors are abnormal masses with no physiological function which produce excessive swelling and disruption of the normal life process. Tumors may develop in bones as well as in other organs or body systems. Cysts are collections of morbid matter which gather in various natural cavities including those in bones. Sometimes these various infectious growths develop into malignancy.

*Other types.* There are many other types and causes of crippling handicaps. Coxa plana is the technical term for atrophy or wasting away of the femur or principal thigh bone. When such wasting occurs in childhood the femur develops into an abnormally shortened and thickened state so that walking and other bodily movements cannot follow the normal pattern. Spinal osteochondritis is an inflammation of both bone and cartilage affecting the normal growth of the spine. Spinal curvature and hunchback are among a total of over seventy different causes of orthopedic impairment found in John Lee's[1] investigations.

### Remedial and Preventive Measures

The various causes and the resulting handicaps of the preceding section should have suggested remedial and preventive measures. The discovery and widespread use of Salk vaccine should reduce the number of polio victims to a near zero point. As in the case of diphtheria the inoculations should continue to be effective and not as in the case of stronger DDT needed for a tougher generation of flies. For several years to come the present generation of afflicted children will continue to need special physiotherapy and allied care such as is offered in modern schools for crippled children.

Knowledge of rapidly developing infections from injuries to bones leading to osteomyelitis indicates that even slight injuries may have serious results if the course of infection is not watched closely. Many such cases which developed in young men in military service are often traced back to seemingly incidental injuries to the same bodily members in childhood. Operative procedures are often successful on congenital anomalies and dislocations. Safer highways and compulsory driver training for young drivers should reduce this area of accidents

[1] J.J. Lee, "A Study of Certain Individual Differences Found among Crippled Children and of Certain Problems Involved in Their Education and Training," Doctor's dissertation, Ohio State University, Columbus, Ohio, 1942, pp. 205-224.

with attendant injuries. Periodic and complete physical examinations of all children and adolescents should detect many causes of infection in otherwise seemingly healthy bodies. All of these remedial and preventive measures require close cooperative teamwork between the regular school, schools for the orthopedically handicapped, nurses, physiotherapists, orthopedic surgeons, hospitals, and parents.

### Characteristics

There are so many kinds and causes of orthopedic handicaps that assessment of personality or other unique characteristics would be very difficult. Congenital handicaps with which a child has lived from earliest infancy may be accepted as a matter of course since he has never experienced anything different, although he may have some degree of awareness. An acquired handicap of marked degree which comes after several years of normal physical activity creates acute frustration which may lead to serious changes in personality and character. With these illustrations in mind some further interpretations and theories will be considered.

One of the comparatively recent exponents of relationship between bodily defects and behavior was the late Alfred Adler. He proposed as a driving force in human nature the need to excel and to overcome any handicaps. Orthopedic handicaps fitted nicely into his theory and in some instances the relationships were considerably overemphasized. Minor or major evidences of antisocial behavior were interpreted by this formula, although many other potent causative factors were known to exist. Since Adler was looking for causes, his contemporaries were stimulated to do likewise and hence a new and more promising era of personality study began.

Restriction of physical activity and blocking of normal channels of childhood play cannot help but have deep and far-reaching effects upon the natural tendencies of children. Many emotional problems and frustrations are dissipated in the vigorous play of nonhandicapped children, which is denied to some orthopedically handicapped children. Seeking such outlets through introspective rationalization from a wheel chair is a poor substitute for the exhilaration of a fast-moving game of baseball. In prevention and remediation the social worker has a virtually unexplored field of mental health as developed through mental hygiene.

A very interesting and enlightening investigation of the attitudes of crippled children toward their culture was made by Cruickshank.[1] The technique of sentence completion was utilized on a series of sentences which gave opportunity for expression of attitudes. Comparisons were made on 264 orthopedically handicapped pupils in junior and senior high schools in six cities with more than 400 who were not handicapped. The responses of one typical seventeen-year-old crippled girl showed much personal concern and introspection, whereas the nonhandicapped girl treated the same sentences in an offhand, superficial manner which indicated that she had not experienced the same degree of personal concern. Cruickshank summarizes:

> Throughout the entire series of sentences, several factors stood out which merit comment. Almost universally the physically normal children expressed either a positive or a negative feeling in completing the sentences, that is, they actually completed the sentence in some fashion meaningful to them. On the other hand, the physically handicapped children, likewise in almost every sentence, produced a statistically significant number of neutral, ambivalent or nonsensical responses, or entirely omitted responses. The latter almost never occurred in the responses of the normal children. This is interpreted as indicating the generally unsatisfactory situation in which physically handicapped children find themselves. The physically normal children, having had a continuous and varied series of contacts with many different aspects of society and involving numerous persons and situations, are able to evaluate and are able to react to social situations.

Further comparisons are made in relationships to peers, to fear and to guilt feelings, and in personal aspiration. Parents, teachers, and others who associate with the physically handicapped should face the realistic issues discovered in Cruickshank's study.

*Intelligence.* Arlitt and Fernald[2] tested 194 crippled children in Cincinnati and on the first test found a mean intelligence quotient

[1] W.M. Cruickshank, *Psychology of Exceptional Children and Youth*, Prentice-Hall, Inc., Englewood Cliffs, N.J., 1955, pp. 284-344.
[2] A.H. Arlitt and M.R. Fernald, "A Psychological Study of a Group of Crippled Children of Various Types," *School and Society*, 1935, 23, pp. 449-452.

of 82, and a correlation with a second test of .90. M.V. Lee found a mean intelligence quotient of 86.8 for 148 crippled children in Seattle; John J. Lee found a mean intelligence quotient of 89 on 619 crippled children in the Oakman School in Detroit; Witty and Smith summarized results on 1,480 crippled in several cities with a mean intelligence quotient of 84.5. All of these results are in fairly close agreement, and have a wide distribution of intelligence quotients from these means.

*Other characteristics.* John Lee's studies of 835 crippled children in the Oakman School on home and family status showed 28.2 per cent had broken homes; 19.6 per cent of the homes were lacking in motivation or were unwholesome; and that there was considerable moving about. His studies also showed that in addition to crippling conditions many other physical and sensory defects were present with an average of two per child. The multiple nature of handicaps in the case of the orthopedically handicapped is fairly illustrative of what is also true of many other types of handicapped children, and it demonstrates the need for consideration of all factors in addition to the principal defect.

### History of the Orthopedic

Through the centuries of history the crippled have had very checkered and generally unfortunate careers. Since their handicap was usually very obvious they were subjected to more scorn, contempt, and punishment than the deaf or those suffering from other less noticeable handicaps. Many of them were either put to death as part of religious rites or they were subjected to extreme cruelty and persecution. Although there are some instances here and there of protection, it was not until the eighteenth century that a more enlightened point of view began to develop.

During the nineteenth century the emphasis was chiefly upon physical care and surgery for crippled children. Probably the first orthopedic hospital in America was founded in 1854 in Brooklyn by Louis Bauer and Richard Barthelmess. The first professor of orthopedic surgery was Lewis A. Sayre at Bellevue Medical College in New York in 1861.

He became president of the American Medical Association and was the first president of the American Surgical Association. Minnesota established the first state hospital for crippled children in 1897, and since 1922 the Shriners have established fifteen hospitals in the United States and Canada. Chicago opened the first public school class for cripples in 1899 and many other large cities soon followed its example.

There have been many famous personalities who were crippled. Lord Byron's clubfoot drove him to such desperation that he became an expert swimmer, able to negotiate the Hellespont. Immanual Kant had a sunken chest which drove him into seclusion where he wrote his famous philosophical works. Beethoven was afflicted with asthma, was practically deaf, had a pockmarked and snub-nosed face, yet was a great musician and composer. Charles Steinmetz was born a cripple but sought the quiet of a laboratory and became one of the greatest students of electricity. The crippled condition of the late President Franklin D. Roosevelt in 1921 has been well known, along with his uphill fight to reach the highest office in the land where his influence in the interests of the crippled as well as in other areas of the handicapped gave the entire movement a great impetus.

Particular individuals stand out as pioneers in promoting the welfare and advancement of handicapped and exceptional children. Some of these have been physicians, some educators, and others public-spirited citizens. On Memorial Day in 1907 a crushing wreck of interurban trolley cars at Elyria, Ohio, killed sixteen and permanently maimed sixty-eight individuals who were the large majority of Elyria's high school senior class. Edgar "Daddy" F. Allen, in memory of his son and his classmates devoted the remainder of his life to promoting care for crippled children and adults. From his efforts there was born the National Society for Crippled Children and Adults which is the Easter Seal Society.

Another important source of lay effort has been the activities of the service clubs which have promoted educational programs and financial aid for crippled children. International Rotary has been a leader since its establishment in 1905. Kiwanis service clubs, established in 1915 along with several others have promoted further aid in this area. Allied organizations such as the American Legion, the

Junior League, the Elks, and the Shriners have participated while the Lions have specialized in aid to the blind.

Beginning in 1935 the Children's Bureau of the Department of Labor has had appropriations with a matching by all of the forty-eight states for crippled children's programs. Supported by the March of Dimes, the National Foundation for Infantile Paralysis, Inc., was started in 1938 through the efforts of the late President Franklin D. Roosevelt. Many millions of dollars are contributed annually to this program. The United Cerebral Palsy Association was established in 1950.

## The Number of Crippled

Since the orthopedically handicapped have had more servicing by hospitals and private physicians than by educators, there were fewer surveys made than in the case of other handicaps. One of the early attempts at a survey was made by the New York State Commission which sent out survey blanks on the basis of 2.5 per 1,000 of the children under eighteen years of age. This estimate was too conservative since the number was 3.4 excluding large cities and 4.90 when they were included. By December 31, 1946, the Crippled Children's Services of the United States Children's Bureau had listed 449,545 crippled children under twenty-one years of age in the United States and its territories.

There are periodic surveys of educational facilities for all types of exceptional children conducted by the United States Office of Education. The report for 1952-1953 listed only 17,813 crippled children in such schools or classes. Since this number is obviously only a small number of the total crippled children, it may be concluded that these are the ones living in or near fairly large cities. In the large cities there is a tendency to send the mildly crippled to the regular neighborhood schools and to transport only those who cannot readily travel to their neighborhood school. The extremely crippled are not in school except where large school systems may provide home teachers for them. Many others are confined in hospitals where schooling may be provided by the public educational systems. Surveys in various cities show that approximately 80 per cent of crippled children were congenital cases or had acquired their crippling handicap by the age of six or seven years. Although the educational facilities are not provided adequately, the combination of some education and much emphasis upon physical care is accomplishing much good for the large majority of the orthopedically handicapped.

### School Facilities

Where special schools have been provided they include many features especially fitted to the needs of the handicapped children. These orthopedic schools usually have one-story with loading and unloading platforms from buses so arranged that stairs are not necessary. The rooms have ample space and movable desks so that the pupils may move about freely. Toilet facilities should be readily accessible. Classrooms should be decorated in cheerful colors.

The physiotherapy programs are very important features of the crippled schools. All kinds of light and heat treatment are available, and liberal amounts of treatment are carried on by trained physiotherapists. Many children with little handicap of locomotion attend the special school to receive the benefits of physiotherapy which could not be available in their regular schools. Rest periods with suitable cots are part of the standard features of the program. Schools for the crippled coordinate the total activities with their time and effort divided appropriately between education and physiotherapy.

### Training of Personnel

The teachers of the orthopedic must have training usually required for all teachers and in addition have taken specialized courses in the anatomy and physiology of the human body. They must be aware of what each individual child may be able to do. Cooperation is always necessary with the physiotherapist, the orthopedic specialist, and the family. The teachers must cultivate pleasing personalities so that the happy atmosphere of the orthopedic school far excels that in most regular schools. The physiotherapists must have specialized training for their activities and endeavor to carry out the recommendations of the examining orthopedic specialist, as well as keeping in constant touch with the children's parents.

## Costs

The cost of education and treatment of the orthopedically handicapped is must greater than for regular pupils. The special schools have smaller classes and the many additional features of physiotherapy easily multiply the cost. Transportation by special bus is an added expense. In case home teaching is necessary only a small number can be serviced per teacher. Many other additional expenses involve some hospitalization which may be financed by Shriners and by service organizations. The rehabilitation services provided by federal and state grants contribute to the cost when these pupils are nearing or completing their education.

There is an intangible item of expense not measured in dollars, but which consists of the wholesome and effective cooperation of parent, doctor, teacher, physiotherapist, and the lay individuals who help foot the bills so that crippled children receive the education and care they deserve.

### Questions and Topics for Discussion

1. Prepare a report on the facilities for the orthopedically handicapped in your local city or community.
2. Visit a school for crippled children and note all features, both for educational and physical rehabilitation.
3. Discuss reasons why the percentage of different causes varies in different portions of the country.
4. Report on the financial aid provisions for education and rehabilitation.
5. Report on a more inclusive list of famous personalities who were crippled and state some of their accomplishments.
6. Report on the latest developments and results of the Salk vaccine.

### A. Organizations

1. Association for the Aid of Crippled Children, Inc., 345 E. 42nd St., New York 17.

2. International Society for the Welfare of Cripples, 127 E. 52nd St. New York 22.
3. Muscular Dystrophy Association of America, Inc., 1790 Broadway, New York 19.
4. National Foundation for Infantile Paralysis, Inc., 120 Broadway, New York 5.
5. National Society for Crippled Children and Adults, Inc., 11 S. La Salle St., Chicago 3.
6. United Cerebral Palsy Association, Inc., 369 Lexington Ave., New York.

Note: Several have state and local organizations.

## B. Periodicals

1. *The Crippled Child* (bimonthly), National Society for Crippled Children and Adults, Inc., 11 S. LaSalle St., Chicago 3 (discontinued August, 1958).

## C. Books

1. Association for the Aid of Crippled Children, *Prematurity, Congenital Malformation and Birth Injury*, The Association, New York, 1952, 255 pp.
2. Cardwell, V.E. (comp.), *The Cerebral Palsied Child and His Care in the Home*, Association for the Aid of Crippled Children, New York, 1947, 196 pp.
3. De Palma, A.F., *Clinical Orthopedics*, J.B. Lippincott Co., Philadelphia, 1954, 240 pp.
4. Egel, P.F., *Technique for the Treatment for the Cerebral Palsy Child*, C.V. Mosby, Co., St. Louis, Mo., 1948, 203 pp.
5. Hobart, L., *Laurie, Physical Therapist*, Julian Messner, Inc., New York, 1957, 192 pp.
6. Kitay, W., *Overcome Arthritis*, Prentice-Hall, Inc., Englewood Cliffs, N.J., 1957, 256 pp.
7. Mackie, R.P., *Crippled Children in American Education*, 1939-1942, Teachers' College Contribution to Education, No. 913, Columbia University Press, New York, 1946, 144 pp.
8. McBride, E.D., *Crippled Children*, C.V. Mosby Co., St. Louis, Mo., 1931, 280 pp.
9. National Society for Crippled Children and Adults, *Publications List*, 200 titles on all phases of the physically handicapped, the National Society for Crippled Children and Adults.

10. Shands, A.R., Jr., and R.B. Raney, *Handbook of Orthopedic Surgery*, C. V. Mosby Co., St. Louis, Mo., 1952, 644 pp.
11. Stern, E.M., and E. Castendyck, *The Handicapped Child: A Guide for Parents*, A.A. Wyn, New York, 1950, 179 pp.

## D. Films and Filmstrips

1. *First As A Child*, 22 minutes, 16-mm. Case history of a crippled child from the public health nurse's first visit to his home through diagnosis, treatment and after-care. Points out the necessary consideration given to the child's emotional troubles. International Film Bureau, 57 E. Jackson Blvd., Chicago 4.
2. The Irving Geist International Film Library with *Foreign Films* available, 127 E. 52nd St., New York.
3. Parent Education Visual Aid Series of filmstrips and slides:
   A. *What Parents Should Know About Cerebral Palsy;*
   B. *Living Is Learning;*
   C. *Up to His Feet;*
   D. *Fingers, Families, and Fun;*
   E. *The Teen-Ager's Gateway to Independence.*
   Available through The National Society for Crippled Children and Adults, 11 S. LaSalle St., Chicago 3.

# CHAPTER 27

## Lowered Vitality

AMONG THE LESS obviously handicapped children are several types which may be conveniently grouped under a general category of lowered vitality. Some of these are often classified as orthopedic and are found enrolled in orthopedic schools and classes. Such arrangements are mainly due to the need for special transportation and for a schedule of reduced physical activities. Although few of them seem to have any external physical handicaps their handicaps are real and merit suitable treatment by various services, including special education. The four principal causes are: (1) muscular dystrophy; (2) heart conditions; (3) tuberculosis; and (4) malnourishment.

### Muscular Dystrophy

Muscular dystrophy is a disease of peculiar origin. Childhood cases are not very common, although there are many more adults who are afflicted. It is characterized by a chronic degeneration of the muscular system, which becomes progressively worse and results in death in the case of children before reaching adulthood. Muscular dystrophy in young children usually begins in the muscles of the calves of the legs with the spread of the disease always being symmetrical. It is a disease of the muscles themselves and is not derived from any degenerative condition of the nerves.

*Causes.* The cause of muscular dystrophy is obscure. A small number of cases have unknown causes but the great majority have a hereditary factor. It is a sex-linked disease which appears in the male but is transmitted through the female in the pseudohypertrophic type which appears earlier in childhood. The inheritance appears to be Mendelian recessive in character. A second type, known as the facioscapulohumeral, affects both sexes in about equal numbers as a simple dominant hereditary factor. The upper portion of the body is usually affected first, particularly the arms and head. There is a gradual weakness in the muscles of the lips and eyelids, but serious incapacity does not usually occur until later in life. Two other types which are distributed about equally in males and females are of rare occurrence and are known as progressive dystrophic ophthalmoplegia and dystrophia myotonia. They usually occur in the third or fourth decade of life but may also be found in early childhood.

*Diagnosis.* Diagnosis is made by medical specialists. An important step in the diagnosis is the excretion in the urine of an unusually large amount of creatine and a smaller amount of creatinine than in the nonhandicapped. Creatine is an acetic acid ordinarily present in muscle tissue and has creatinine as its product. In muscular dystrophy cases abnormal amounts of creatinine are excreted. Because of muscle weakness the muscular dystrophy child cannot move about or manipulate various portions of his body in normal ways. For example, if he has been lying on his back and wishes to rise he must turn over, gradually raise himself on his four extremities, and then slowly "walk" his hands up his legs until he is upright. He waddles when he walks, with his feet far apart, and certain muscles seem hard and swollen. Fatty tissue fills in where the muscles have shrunk, and the general shape and appearance of the body have changed from normal status.

*Characteristics.* Some of the characteristics have already been mentioned. Children afflicted with muscular dystrophy are unable to live physically active lives. As their activities become more and more restricted the natural optimism of their childhood gradually wanes. Becoming bedridden is delayed as long as possible since conditions deteriorate more rapidly with complete restriction of exercise. Parents must play an important role which tends to go through a state of early prodding for what seems to be laziness; alarm at the truth when diagnosis has been confirmed; and acceptance of an early fatal outcome or a lasting crippled state. Many cases have chronic respiratory conditions which are especially dangerous and require costly medical care. Because of these many precautions the home life for all family members is usually restricted and lacking in normal social contacts.

*Education.* There is a gradually decreasing scale of normal educational placement and treatment. Many of these children may spend one or more years in regular classes until the conditions have declined to such a degree that some type of special education is necessary. Some of them are enrolled in schools or classes for crippled children where physiotherapy under medical advice arrests the rate of deterioration. They are among the few wheel-chair pupils in these schools. Sooner or later they cannot be transported to any school and home-bound teaching begins. Loss of contacts with other physically handicapped children and omission of physiotherapy subtract from the effectiveness of the educational process. Some of them who are hospitalized continue to receive more benefits than the home-bound, but they lose the parental contacts which may have become very close because of their relatively helpless state.

*Other factors.* Muscular dystrophy must have been a very baffling disease for both lay and medical groups. It was first described as a condition apart from the orthopedically handicapped and from the undiagnosed by Aran in 1850. The number of those afflicted with muscular dystrophy is unknown. Wallace[1] reports an estimate of 200,000 with the disease in the United States. The number of children is apparently much less than adults with New York City finding approximately twenty new cases under twenty-one years of age annually. In the same publication Morrow and Cohen reported on an investigation of twenty-nine patients with similar results on forty cases reported by Shank, Gilder, and Hoagland.[2] Although the numbers of children are comparatively few the gravity of muscular dystrophy has stimulated public attention and support. The Muscular Dystrophy Associations of America are pressing for research and for better facilities. An annual drive for funds through a house-to-house canvas is becoming

---

[1] H.M. Wallace, in *Special Education for the Exceptional,* Vol. II, Frampton and Gall, eds., Porter Sargent Publisher, Boston, 1955, p. 565.

[2] R.E. Shank, H. Gilder, and G. Hoagland, "Studies on Diseases of Muscle, 1. Progressive Muscular Dystrophy: A Clinical Review of Forty Cases," *Archives of Neurology and Psychiatry,* 1944, 52, pp. 431-442.

quite successful. There is always hope that the present grim outlook for children will be changed for the better.

## Cardiac Disorders and Diseases

Whereas the general public is relatively uninformed about such conditions as muscular dystrophy the opposite is true of the heart. An alarming number of adults suddenly become victims of heart attacks. Every adult knows of one or more heart victims among relatives or close associates. Panic and neuroses in the afflicted and in their families make the problem unnecessarily worse. There is ample cause for widespread concern since heart conditions and disease have risen from fourth to first place as the cause of death since 1900.

*The heart.* Since the heart is the center and key of the circulatory system its functioning must be continuous and its activity controlled involuntarily although various emotional disturbances can modify its normal functioning to some degree. The heart is truly a wonderful mechanism with its two atriums and its two ventricles, which are cavities or compartments into which the blood is received and forwarded by a system of valves which open and close in a coordinated movement. In its simplest form the venous blood, returning with waste products from all portions of the body, passes through the atrium and ventricle from which it is forced into the blood vessels which lead to the lungs. After the oxygen of the air in the lungs has replaced the carbons and other waste materials the blood returns to the left side of the heart where it is forced into the circulatory system of the body through the arteries. The energy of this continuous process in a normal life time would be sufficient to lift a weight of ten tons to a height of ten miles.

*Cardiac impairments.* Regular physical examinations by the pediatrician and by the family doctor should have noted the heart condition before the age of school entrance. Listening with a stethoscope gives some indication of the principal condition of the heart in regard to steadiness and force of the heart beat. A simple pressure test discloses the blood pressure which may register at an average point; above it in high blood pressure; and below it in low pressure. A sample of blood may be taken to give clues about its general condition and how it may be affecting the heart. The most thorough method of heart examination is by the cardiograph which records the electrical energy generated by the heart and which reveals its strength, the conditions of the valves, and other characteristics.

Some of the external signs of possible heart conditions which may be noted by teachers and parents are more than average breathlessness after vigorous exercise, flushed or slightly bluish color to the cheeks, to the lips, or to the fingertips, easy fatigue, and chest pains. Some of these symptoms may indicate other bodily impairments, but it is desirable to have medical examinations in such cases.

*Classification of heart diseases.* The American Heart Association adopted the following plan for the classification of Cardiopathic and Circulatory Disturbances.

*Organic Heart Disease:*

Class I: Patients with *organic disease,* but *able to carry on ordinary physical activity.*

Class II: Patients with *organic disease,* but *unable to carry on physical activity* (cardiac insufficiency).

    A. Activity slightly limited.

    B. Activity greatly limited.

Class III: Patients with *organic disease,* but *unable to carry on any physical activity,* i.e., who must remain in bed or in a chair (cardiac insufficiency).

*Possible and Potential Heart Disease:*

Class E: Patients with *possible heart disease,* not believed to be due to organic heart disease.

Class F: Patients with *potential heart disease.* Patients without circulatory disease whom it is advisable to follow because of the presence of history of an etiological factor which might cause diseases.

Classes I, E, and F of the above classifications may usually attend regular schools. Class IIA, and some of IIB are selected for special classes. Class IIB of the more severe type and Class III of less severe type may have home teaching. Class III of the more severe type should probably receive no instruction because of too severe illness.

*Causes of heart impairments.* There are four main causes of heart disease divided roughly according to age: congenital forms in infancy and in early childhood; rheumatic infections in the next age period; syphilitic infection in middle age; and arteriosclerotic changes in later life. Rheumatic fever is an acute or chronic inflammatory process disseminated in the connective tissues of many organs including the heart. The cause of the fever is unknown. It usually follows respiratory infections and is accompanied by loss of weight, nosebleeds, continued fever, and pain in joints. Rheumatic fever seldom starts before six years of age, but on or before the age of ten years. It seems to be associated with cold, damp weather, poverty, and poor housing. A period of quiet rest in bed under medical care and recommendation is imperative. The great majority recover and during the period of convalescence home teaching may be instituted after the more extreme phases have passed.

Some children have congenital heart disease or conditions which restrict their activities as noted in the five classifications which have just been cited. Any high fever over an extended period of time reduces the amount of oxygen which reaches the blood stream so that the life processes are affected. Excessive and prolonged strenuous play or exertion may weaken the heart or it may become enlarged from overwork. Infections from any portions of the body may be carried to the heart by the blood stream and spread to that organ. Badly infected tonsils, adenoids, liver, and other digestive organs may furnish such infections and should be treated or removed upon a physician's recommendation.

In addition to diseases and disorders of the heart the blood also has certain divergent characteristics which play an important role in health. Anemia is a condition affecting the red corpuscles of the blood and impairs the blood's ability to carry oxygen to the various bodily tissues. In one type of anemia the red cells are abnormally large and carry an abnormally large amount of hemoglobin which results in pernicious anemia. This disease is much more common in adults than in children. The second type has small red cells or cells lacking in hemoglobin. There is a deficiency in blood-building substances, such as iron, which is characterized as nutritional anemia and is common in children. Examination of the blood from a specimen is necessary to determine the kind of anemia and therapeutic prescriptions. Leukemia is a disease in which the white cells of the blood grow so abnormally that they crowd out or otherwise destroy the red cells. Leukemia exists in childhood and is presently the second cause of death in children. Little is known about the cause of leukemia, but it is to be hoped that some discovery as remarkable as the Salk vaccine for infantile paralysis may make an early appearance.

Hemophilia is a condition of the blood which prevents the usual process of coagulation or clotting. Whenever such a person has an injury which bleeds, it is very difficult if not impossible to stop bleeding. Operations of any sort are practically out of the question. It is a condition affecting only males but is transmitted through females. These "bleeders" must always be careful of health, exercise, and dangers of injury.

Some persons, mainly adults, firmly believe that they have heart disease, and although no organic basis is discovered, they remain convinced and seek different hospitals and doctors to prove their contention. They furnish the best illustration of what a fertile imagination can do.

*Remedial and preventive measures.* There is enough evidence to indicate that heart examinations should be made at regular intervals. Many adults die every day from heart conditions about which they were not informed. In the case of children, exercise and living routines should be gauged according to the cardiac status. School placement varies according to the conditions. Many cardiac cases continue in regular classes with possible reduction in physical exercise. A second group may attend classes for those with lowered vitality known under various titles such as health conservation, open window, rest classes, etc. It is also a common practice to transport them to schools for the crippled where they may be segregated within their own group. Some cardiac patients attend regular classes on half-day schedules upon physician's recommendation. More extreme cases have the benefit of teachers for the home-bound. Some school systems have tried telephone communication to regular classrooms on homebound children. Finally a small number whose days are already numbered are entertained at home by television, radio, and other projects by sympathetic parents.

### Tuberculosis

In a certain sense tuberculosis is not always characterized by lowered vitality, since some of its forms are acquired through contagion by persons whose physical health may have been perfect before the infection. However, certain other chronic forms keep the vitality at a low ebb and recuperation from extremely insidious tuberculous attacks keeps the person in a very weakened condition for a long time. Tuberculosis has been a great ravager and, although under much better control in the more enlightened countries today, in other areas it continues in unabated fury. It affects all ages and strikes in many different parts of the body.

*Definitions.* There are two principal types of tuberculosis. The primary infection was formerly known as childhood tuberculosis. It results from exposure to the tubercle bacillus, which occurs in a large majority of the population at some time in their lives. Most persons are unaware that they have been exposed, that some infection has occurred, or that the infection has become dormant or permanently healed. Some cases develop an active condition at the primary infection. The second type is reinfection tuberculosis which results from a second infection. It is more commonly found in adults than in children. The primary infection may run a dormant course unless discovered by chest X-ray or by serum tests. General lassitude and later discovery of poorly healed lesions of the lungs are typical characteristics.

*Classifications.* Bovine tuberculosis contagion has been largely eradicated in this country by slaughtering infected cows, although it is very common in other parts of the world. It settles in the bones and joints to such an extent that crippling makes it necessary for children to be enrolled in orthopedic schools. Meningitic tuberculosis attacks the membranes covering the brain. When discovered in its early stages it yields quite well to antimicrobial treatments which have been developed in very recent years. Its symptoms in infants include high fever and diarrhea, while headaches are more character-istic of affected adults. A third class is miliary tuberculosis which spreads throughout the entire body through the blood stream and unless quickly checked with drugs it may be fatal very shortly.

The most common form is chronic pulmonary or lung tuberculosis. There are several symptoms, such as hemorrhages of the lungs, short-ness of breath, chest sounds, upsets of digestion, and coughs with chronic hoarseness. This form of tuberculosis was popularly known as "consumption" and the term still persists even though the cause of tuberculosis has become known. Observations of symptoms are not enough and fortunately more positive methods are now avail-able.

*Diagnosis.* Tuberculosis is as old as mankind and existed even before his recorded history. Recently discovered Egyptian mummies had it and the early Greek physician, Hippocrates, gave detailed descriptions. As late as 1882 Robert Koch discovered the tubercle bacillus and started a whole new approach in this field. Tubercle bacillus is now cultivated as a filtered and sterilized fluid medium and is either applied by a patch or given as an injection known as the Mantoux test, a name which is also applied to other types of tuber-culous injections. When infection, swelling, and redness have occurred from the injection or patch within two days the condition is known as positive reaction. If none occurs it is a so-called nonreaction. In case of a positive reaction X-ray examination must be taken to determine if the infection is active or inactive. If it is inactive the person may live a normally active life, but periodic retests and examinations should be made.

*Remedies.* Once the causative factor in any condition or disease has been discovered the next problem is to discover and apply antidotes. Although the tubercle bacillus was discovered nearly a century ago it is only recently that discovery of modern wonder drugs holds hope in the case of tuberculosis. One of the projects is the development of bacillus Calmette-Guérin, or BCG vaccination, discovered by two French scientists, Calmette and Guérin. This vaccine is strong enough to heighten resistance to tuberculosis but not strong enough to cause active tuberculosis. Combinations of various drugs, including

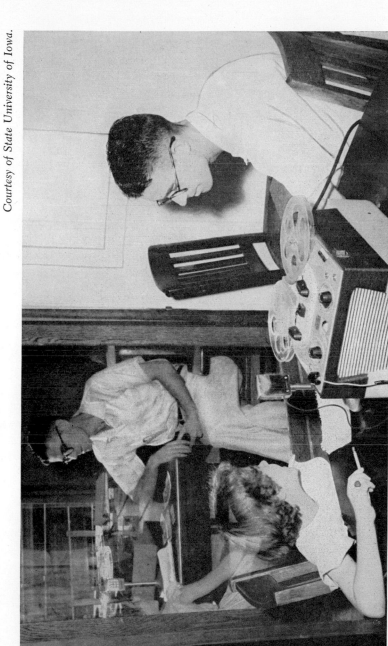

Speech correction activity, State University of Iowa, Iowa City, Iowa.

*Courtesy of State University of Iowa.*

*Courtesy of school district of Winnipeg.*

Physically handicapped pupils, Montrose school, Winnipeg, Manitoba.

streptomycin, paraaminosalicylic acid, cycloserine, and isoniazid, are yielding hopeful results.

In the active cases bed rest is highly recommended. While some of the critical cases are hospitalized it has been found that if rest routines and drug therapy are programmed encouraging progress is made at home. Surgery has been found effective in removing certain affected portions of the lungs and collapsing the lung for various periods permits quicker discovery. Much of the dread and fear which went with "consumption" and its fatalistic philosophy has disappeared. The writer recalls during his high school days in a small village his frequent visits to a younger neighbor boy camped in a tent under a shade tree waiting for the inevitable end. The death rate from tuberculosis has fallen rapidly since 1900 when it was the first in the causes of death. The rate of 202 deaths per 100,000 has now been reduced to 10 and it is tenth or less in the causes of death. However, in many backward countries it is still very high.

In the treatment of tuberculosis before the present era many experiments were tried. Although the lungs were congested and affected, cold and damp air was provided which probably aggravated rather than alleviated an infection now known to be from tubercle bacillus. The first open-air school was started in Charlottenburg, Germany, in 1904. For some kinds of ailments there was improvement. The open-air school movement spread to America with Providence, R. I., having its first in January, 1908. One of the unsuccessful experiments was the isolation of several cases in some stone cabins about five miles underground in Mammoth Cave, Ky., where dampness and coolness with uniform temperatures in the fifties were hoped to be beneficial, but proved otherwise.

*Characteristics.* The age of children and adults afflicted with tuberculosis shows that death rates were lower for children five to fourteen years of age than for those from one to four and from fifteen to nineteen. Primary infection is becoming more common in adults over forty years of age.

There is no particular reason to expect that individuals suddenly afflicted with tuberculosis were different in personality, character, and intelligence from other segments of the population. However, when the disease is found to exist in virulent form the person may go through a state of panic until becoming acquainted with the possibilities of recovery. The restoration of confidence may cause a considerable reaction of elation which should be helpful in recovery if wisely guided and controlled. Some children who must accept periods of reduced activities, bed rest, or possibly hospitalization find the change difficult to accept. Some of them feel that the sickness is punishment for some bad behavior about which they had often been scolded. The team of workers, including parents, should be aware of and know how to meet and treat such unfavorable impressions and attitudes.

*Educational adjustments.* There is the usual variety of educational adjustments possible to parallel the degrees and types of tuberculosis. As a general rule when the active stage of contagion has passed and the child's health is reasonably normal he should be enrolled in his regular classes. During his hospitalization, and if his health permits, special teachers of the home-bound should take over when he is confined at home. In some cities there are classes for lowered vitality in which the convalescing child may be placed to help restore him to full schedules in regular classes. In all of these situations the child's health should come first and education should be second.

*Organizational activities.* For many years tuberculosis has been a gripping challenge to the medical profession. The National Association for Study and Prevention of Tuberculosis was founded in 1904 with Dr. Edward L. Trudeau as its first president. It changed its name in 1918 to the National Tuberculosis Association. Shortly after the first organization was founded the American Sanatorium Association was founded on December 1, 1905, comprised, as the title suggests, mainly of physicians attached to sanatoriums. Their activities gradually spread beyond the field of tuberculosis to the more general area of cardiopulmonary physiology, cancer, and thoracic diseases, but in honor of Dr. Trudeau the name of this association was changed to the American Trudeau Society in 1939. The American Trudeau Society is the medical section of the National Tuberculosis Association and publishes as its official journal *The American Review of Tuberculosis and Pulmonary Diseases.* There is under consideration a further change of name to describe more nearly the comprehensive nature of the Society's activities.

## Malnourishment

In addition to the first three topics of this chapter another cause of lowered vitality is malnourishment. Malnourishment is not classified as a disease but when it exists the effects may be as great. There are many digestive organs and digestive secretions which assimilate the nutritive elements from a great variety of foods. In view of all factors it may be easily seen that there is a great range of nourishment and malnourishment. Although food seems plentiful in prosperous countries such as America, in the White House Conference of 1930 it was estimated that there were six million malnourished children. More than one-half of the world's population does not have sufficient food so that famine and starvation is a modern plague which staggers the imagination.

*The gastrointestinal system.* In the process of chewing, saliva moistens the food and also contains a small amount of ptyalin which exercises a digestive effect upon starch by transforming it into a reducing sugar. The food passes into the stomach where the various gastric juices breaks the food down into finer components. Hydrochloric acid in the gastric juice converts cane sugar into glucose and fructose. Pepsin in the gastric juice breaks the foods down into a fluid form so that fats may float on the surface. The fifteen-to-twenty-second recurring contraction waves of the stomach muscles also help to break the food up and force it into the duodenum which is the next unit in the gastrointestinal system.

At least two important processes take place in the duodenum: (1) it receives bile from the liver which absorbs the fats and then stores any excess bile in the gall bladder; (2) it receives pancreatic juice from the pancreas which assists in the digestion of fats, proteins, and carbohydrates. The next unit is the small intestine which is about twenty to twenty-five feet in length. It has a peristaltic action which moves the food along and a rotary action which allows the blood vessels located in the walls to absorb the food and transmit it to all portions of the body. At the end of the system is the large intestine which acts as a storage for the waste products which are ejected through the rectum.

There are many points at which disorders may occur and the nature of the food itself may produce disturbed conditions. The first difficulty comes in hasty and incomplete chewing which does not give sufficient time for the ptyalin of the saliva to transform the starch into a reducing sugar. Hasty eating throws an additional burden on the stomach to break up the food which the mouth did not complete as far as it should. The gall bladder becomes infected from too much bile stored too long and gall stones form. When conditions become aggravated the gall bladder must be removed by surgery which leaves no storage place for bile so that the bile functions are disrupted. Sometimes the walls of the intestine become attached to the walls of the abdomen so that the peristaltic action is hindered. A diverticulum, which is an enlarged sac in the intestine, may develop, blocking the passage of food, and become infected. The appendix is a vestigial sac which may become infected and then must be removed surgically. All four of these infections or conditions are sometimes removed in a single operation. Finally, constipation may develop and the elimination process deteriorates into a chronic condition. While many of these conditions more commonly affect adults, some children are afflicted as well.

In the process of digestion there are other waste products from the metabolic process. The carbon dioxide is discharged through the lungs while the skin may excrete excess heat from oxidation of fats. There are other wastes which are soluble in water and which are excreted as urine. The organs of this transformation are the kidneys which are equipped to carry a load many times larger than normal, thus insuring that poisoning will not occur from considerable reduction of process. Any excess of certain substances in the blood plasma appears in the urine such as additional sugar in the case of diabetes. The excretion of urine in young babies and in early childhood is involuntary but can usually be brought under voluntary control around the age of two or three years. Forced toilet training or other tense family situations may delay the process much beyond the usual age and sometimes it persists throughout adulthood.

*The characteristics of foods.* The human race has a range of foods as wide as where man lives. The tropics provide mainly abundant fruit but fish and animal meats are also sought. The Eskimos survive on the whale and the walrus, while inhabitants of the temperate zone enjoy a greater variety; but within this group some persons are strictly vegetarian and others eat mainly meats of many kinds. By means of modern refrigeration and air transportation the food products of any portion of the world can be delivered fresh within a matter of hours and may shortly change the food habits of the entire world.

Some foods are rich in certain types of constituents and a whole new classification is possible in terms of their values. These elements are described in a rapidly expanding list of vitamins each of which exists in minute quantities of natural foodstuffs and which are vital for life. Vitamin A is now manufactured synthetically but was originally found in cod-liver oil. It acts as a stimulant to visual acuity and to the maintenance of mucous membranes. There are several subclasses in vitamin B such as $B_{12}$ which tends to arrest the course of pernicious anemia. Vitamin C or ascorbic acid is abundant in citrus fruits, in tomatoes, and in some vegetables and acts as a preventive of scurvy. Rickets may occur when there is a lack of vitamin D from egg yolk and cod-liver oil. At present practically all letters of the alphabet designate certain vitamins with subclasses particularly under vitamin B. It is evident that the presence or absence of various vitamins has profound effects upon digestion and the various bodily organs which are involved.

*Metabolism.* Metabolism is the final or end process of digestion. It has the two phases of building up to restore the tissues of the body and of tearing down in the use of energy for activity. The former process is known as assimilation which is synonymous with anabolism or constructive metabolism. The functioning of the endocrine gland system seems to be a governing force in how well assimilation operates. The latter process is catabolism, which releases energy and sets up certain excretion products. There is a complex relationship between the amount and the kind of food and the resulting condition of bodily growth, gain or loss in weight, and the amount of energy expended in daily activities. The great varieties of food and their vitamin contents have just been noted. The twofold metabolic process is influenced by many variables which are dependent upon the chemistry of the body. One person may eat very large quantities of rich food without being able to add a single ounce to his light weight, whereas another person adds pounds to his heavy weight condition with a very light diet of relatively unnutritive foods. Loss or gain of weight has an enigmatic relationship to the amount of work, vigorous exercise, or children's play. Endocrinologists have been able to narrow down to some extent the unknown or unsolved areas of metabolic processes, and nutritionists have added a whole new field in their area of specialization.

*Symptoms of disorder.* There are many symptoms of digestive disorder. Wheatley and Hallock[1] list such symptoms as halitosis, belching, vomiting, loss of appetite, constipation, and diarrhea. These authors list three intestinal parasites which interfere with the digestive processes and cause much discomfort. *Pinworms* are tiny, white, threadlike intestinal worms which infect the rectal area as well as the vaginal areas of girls. Good sanitary practices may quickly eliminate this parasitic problem. One of the most common causes of malnutrition is *hookworm*. It is a parasitic disease which is especially prevalent in tropical and southern countries where there is heavy rainfall. The International Health Board made a survey in Alabama in 1925 and found hookworm among children of school age ranging from less than 5 per cent in larger towns to 95 per cent in some of the heavily infested rural communities. Children were the group most commonly infected. The hookworm enters the body in larvae form through the bare feet and eventually reaches the intestines where it lays its eggs and worms are produced. Severe cases with more than five hundred worms become undernourished, suffer from headaches, and are underweight. Negroes have much less infection than whites in the South. *Roundworms* (*Ascariasis*) are a large type of worm which infests the intestines and have their origins in unsanitary living conditions. They produce nervous and restless conditions which may result in colicky pain and diarrhea. Good medical treatment and a

[1] G.M. Wheatley and G.T. Hallock, *Health Observation of School Children* (2nd ed.), McGraw-Hill Book Co., Inc., New York, 1956, pp. 257-264.

strict code of sanitation are necessary to completely eliminate ascariasis.

In addition to the types of foods and the variations of the digestive process psychological and emotional factors are important influences. Difficulties may arise in babyhood if there is strict regimentation of amounts and times of breast or bottle feeding. Tiny babies are soon conditioned to the emotional and disciplinary attitudes of their mothers who should always strive to keep feeding upon a happy and pleasant basis. Throughout childhood and adolescence the same rules should apply but unfortunately they may not. Scenes may be made over foods which children do not like or disciplinary action may be unwisely taken by denial of food. The entire digestive process is very susceptible to many psychological factors. Sociological conditions affect the preparation of food and mealtimes. In broken homes or where both parents work irregular hours, too much responsibility for meals may be thrown upon young children who rely on cold foods hastily eaten whenever they are hungry.

*Educational provisions.* Observant teachers may note many symptoms of food and digestive irregularity in children. School systems have a system of milk and crackers in the middle of morning session for children who are known or found to be under par in conditions of nourishment. In more extreme cases some type of health class may be necessary where rest and nutrition take precedence over the usual school subjects. Half-day attendance to regular school may be recommended by the family physician. If all the facts were known many of the minor episodes and interruptions of regular classrooms stem from nutritional deficiencies rather than deliberate disciplinary infractions to which they are so commonly ascribed. Food, eating, and digestion are not always simple, automatic processes. The teacher should know more about the food, eating habits, and home atmosphere of every pupil.

## Questions and Topics for Discussion

1. What provisions do your local school systems make for the four types of diseases and defects discussed in this chapter?

2. Report on any case of muscular dystrophy you have known, describing physical characteristics and time of affliction.
3. Make a detailed drawing of the heart with labels for all its parts.
4. Describe the immediate steps in treating a case of sudden collapse from heart attack.
5. Describe some adult who has been afflicted with tuberculosis but has made a satisfactory recovery.
6. Outline the steps necessary if tuberculosis is to be eradicated.
7. Recall your early childhood experiences with regard to food and resulting status of nourishment.
8. Discuss the various theories in vogue for reducing.

## A. *Organizations*

1. Muscular Dystrophy Association of America, Inc., 1790 Broadway, New York 19.
2. American Heart Association, 44 E. 23rd St., New York 10.
3. National Tuberculosis Association, 1790 Broadway, New York 19.
4. American Trudeau Society, Medical Section of the National Tuberculosis Association.
5. American Medical Association, 535 N. Dearborn St., Chicago 10.

## B. *Periodicals*

1. Reprints and Articles on *Muscular Dystrophy*, Muscular Dystrophy Association of America, Inc., 1790 Broadway, New York 19.
2. *The American Heart Journal*, C.V. Mosby Co., 3207 Washington Ave., St. Louis 3, Mo.
3. *The American Review of Tuberculosis and Pulmonary Diseases*, National Tuberculosis Association, 1790 Broadway, New York 19.
4. *Diseases of Children*, American Medical Association, 535 N. Dearborn St., Chicago 10.

## C. *Books*

1. Kiefer, N.C., *Present Concepts of Rehabilitation in Tuberculosis: A Review of Literature, 1938-1947*, American Tuberculosis Association, New York, 1948, 398 pp.
2. Marvin, H.M., et al., *You and Your Heart: A Clinic for Laymen on the Heart and Circulation*, New American Library of World Literature, Inc., New York, 1953, 192 pp.
3. McMullin, N.D., *How to Help the Shut-In Child*, E.P. Dutton and Co., Inc., New York, 1954, 192 pp.

4. Medlar, E.M., *The Behavior of Pulmonary Tuberculosis Lesions*, The American Review of Tuberculosis and Pulmonary Diseases, New York, 1957, 240 pp.
5. Myers, J.S., *The Child and the Tuberculosis Problem*, Charles C Thomas Publisher, Springfield, Ill., 1932, 246 pp.
6. National Tuberculosis Association, *Diagnostic Standards and the Classification of Tuberculosis*, National Tuberculosis Association, New York, 1950.
7. Opie, E.L., H.R.M. Landis, F.M. McFredran, and H.W. Hetherington, *Tuberculosis in Public School Children*, Henry Phipps Foundation, University of Pennsylvania, Philadelphia, 1929, 636 pp.
8. Parker, C.S., *Your Child Can Be Happy in Bed; Over 200 Ways Children Can Entertain Themselves*, Thomas Y. Crowell Co., New York, 1952, 275 pp.
9. Rogers, J.F., *Schools and Classes for Delicate Children*, Government Printing Office, Washington, D. C., 1930, 65 pp.
10. Sadler, S.S., *Rheumatic Fever: Nursing Care in Pictures*, J.B. Lippincott Co., Philadelphia, 1949, 151 pp.
11. Sparer, P.J., *Personality, Stress, and Tuberculosis*, International Universities Press, New York, 1956, 629 pp.
12. White, P.D., *Heart Disease*, The Macmillan Co., New York, 1950, 1015 pp.

## D. Films and Filmstrips

1. *Progressive Muscular Atrophies, Dystrophies, and Allied Conditions*, 27 minutes, 16-mm., silent. Illustrative cases are given for each of the above groups. Distinctive diagnostic features are pointed out. Distribution limited to professional groups. New York University Film Library, New York.
2. *Care of the Cardiac Patient*, 33 minutes, 16-mm. Nursing care given a cardiac patient, including comfort, rest, sleep, diet, feeding, elimination, cleanliness, and diversional and occupational therapy. Supplementary film strip, 77 frames, United World Films, 1445 Park Ave., New York 29.
3. *Guard Your Heart*, 27 minutes, 16-mm. How the heart works and what changes take place in major heart diseases. Animation and live-action photography. Produced in cooperation with the American Heart Association. Bray Studios, Inc., 729 Seventh Ave., New York 19.
4. *Stop Rheumatic Fever*, 12 minutes, 16-mm. Emphasizes that rheumatic fever can be prevented by prompt treatment of its forerunners,

streptococcal infections. American Heart Association, 44 E. 23rd St., New York 10.

5. *TB-Everybody's Problem,* 48 frames, 35-mm., color. Pictorial explanation of tuberculosis, its cause, spread, treatment, control, and prevention. National Tuberculosis Association, 1790 Broadway, New York 19.

6. *Tuberculosis,* 11 minutes, 16-mm. Nature, transmission, diagnosis, and treatment of pulmonary tuberculosis. Encyclopedia Britannica Films, 1150 Wilmette Ave., Wilmette, Ill.

7. *Digestion of Foods,* 11 minutes, 16-mm. Digestive process in the mouth, stomach, and small intestine; secretions, enzymes, and relation of circulatory and nervous systems to digestive process; supplementary filmstrip, 86 frames. Encyclopedia Britannica Films, 1150 Wilmette Ave., Wilmette, Ill.

8. *Human Digestion,* 10 minutes, 16-mm. Principal steps of the digestive process. Athena Films, 165 W. 46th St., New York 19.

# CHAPTER 28

## Bodily Growth and Stature

THE MOST OBVIOUS illustration of individual differences is the bodily growth and stature of children. As any class of children enters its classroom, almost without exception one or two children are fully a head or more taller than most of the class, while a little less noticeable is one who is much shorter and smaller than the others. Sometimes the larger child is older and the smaller child is younger, but quite often they are the same age as all the others. Various factors unique to the particular child cause these growth differences. Some factors are from natural hereditary traits in parents who were taller or shorter, but others are conditions within the child such as endocrine disturbances or metabolic deviations allied to endocrine disturbances.

### Psychological Characteristics

While children are growing the differences in size becomes more of a problem than after they have attained their adult stature and have gradually become adjusted to it. Some unusually large or unusually small adults may continue to feel certain frustrations throughout life if they have been teased about their size through childhood or if they are very sensitive to it as adults.

*Effects of being tall.* The person who is slightly taller than average, probably enjoys a certain feeling of physical superiority with a slight advantage in his favor. When an individual is extremely tall he may have feelings of inferiority because he does not belong to the normal, average group. If he makes an awkward move, it seems twice as awkward because he is twice as large. He finds low doorways a constant source of danger, and dancing with a very short girl is a social embarrassment. On the other hand, if he is strong and well proportioned, he is a great asset on athletic teams at his high school and university. He may qualify for some unique position in life where tallness is a definite requirement, and under such favorable circumstances tallness is a psychological asset rather than a liability. Extreme tallness in girls offers similar problems with probably fewer opportunities to capitalize on it in athletics and in other positions. As an antidote for possible social maladjustment, many college students have formed Tip-Toppers Clubs in which the men must be well over six feet in height and the women over five feet, ten inches to qualify for admission. By these means some compensations are possible, although the total number belonging to such organizations is relatively small.

One of the most common characteristics of the tall and oversized child is that he is judged by his size rather than by his age. More maturity is often expected of him than he is able to give. In case he is mentally advanced also, he can often live up to expectation for his unusual size. Hence no problem is evident. However, if he is mentally slow for his age and very slow for his size, his emotional and social problems are greatly aggravated. The constant expectation and strain under which he lives are likely to make him nervous and give him a vague feeling of injustice. Something is wrong which he cannot understand.

*Effects of being short.* Being short tends to bring social isolation and feelings of inferiority. There are fewer opportunities to compensate by athletic prowess as in the case of tallness. Inferiority in physical stature is often erroneously assumed to be paralleled by shortcomings in desirable traits of personality and character. Therefore, the short person has to make unusual effort to show superiority in some areas if possible.

The short child is often assumed to be much younger than he actually is and hence not as much is expected of him as he may be capable of giving. He senses a compromising attitude upon the part of older children and adults which is very disturbing and difficult to neutralize. If he is mentally slow and socially immature he assumes the role of a younger and a less mature child. If he is very alert mentally, he rises to the occasion and often makes a successful bid for recognition in spite of being small.

*Social effects of overweight and underweight.* The overweight child is frequently clumsy and physically inactive. Many of them fall into characteristic personality patterns because of endocrine disturbances. They are teased by being called "Fatty" and they are often miserable in many ways. "Skinny" is a favorite nickname for the underweight child. His general lack of weight and underdevelopment open many avenues of social ostracism. In some of his investigations the author found a fairly close relationship between deviations in size and stature and unwholesome parental and sibling attitudes toward such children.

### Growth Standards and Individual Differences

Many factors must be taken into account in evaluating the height and weight of growing children. The status of growth, not only at any particular year, but growth over a period of years should be recorded. Growth proceeds at irregular rates, with plateaus followed by sudden, sharp rises. There is some evidence that intellectual and personality development parallels these physical-growth irregularities. This knowledge throws light on some periods in which there seems to be no progress in education, accompanied by a feeling of general discouragement. Suddenly life takes a new start and everything seems right with the world. In independent, but somewhat similar studies, S.A. Courtis and Willard C. Olsen of the University of Michigan have made extensive studies in these fields.

One of the most illuminating examples of individual differences in standards of growth was made by Stuart and Meredith[1] on basic measurements of children attending the University of Iowa experi-

[1] H.C. Stuart and H.V. Meredith, "Use of Body Measurements in the School Health Program," *American Journal of Public Health*, 1946, 36, No. 12.

mental schools in a fifteen-year period. The five measurements included weight, height, hip width, chest circumference, and leg girth with separate data for boys and girls. The age range by half-year intervals is from five to eighteen years. It is reported at the 10th, 25th, 50th, 75th, and 90th percentiles. The greatest range of variability between the 10th and 90th percentiles was an average of approximately 33 per cent in weight; 20 per cent in leg girth; 16 per cent in hip width; 15 per cent in chest circumference; and 12 per cent in height. Their results at the 50th percentile exceeded Olsen's tables by about one to two inches in height and by five pounds in weight. As a group American children are gradually showing higher standards of height and weight. It is important to compare a child with his relative standing in his own age group as well as with the standards of the group itself.

Norman C. Wetzel has prepared a very useful grid upon which to plot the height and weight throughout childhood and adolescence. There are three principal channels for obese, medium, and thin types with three subdivisions in each. Since there is a tendency for a child to move in a particular channel, if he deviates from it there is evidence of a change in nutritional or health status. The Wetzel Grid is published by the N.E.A. Service.

Sheldon[1] and his collaborators have developed a system of physical measurements, known as somatotyping. Seventeen measurements are selected from five different regions of the body and a tri-polar set of dimensional components was developed. The first component was endomorphy, or the relative preponderance of bodily structure in digestive and assimilative areas; the second component was mesomorphy or emphasis on bone, muscle, and connective tissue; the third component was characterized by dominance of the skin and its appendages, including the nervous system. Each of these three components is rated on a seven-point scale with "one" being a marked deficiency and "seven" a preponderance of the component. While the majority of individuals tend to be rated near average, there are extremes. Quite often an individual has preponderance in two of the three areas and a relative deficiency in the third component. The authors have noted a general

[1] W.H. Sheldon, S.S. Stevens, and W.B. Tucker, *The Varieties of Human Physique*, Harper & Brothers, New York, 1940, 347 pp.

correspondence of three components of human temperament to the physical components as described in an earlier chapter of this book. The relationship gives some interesting clues to the understanding of human temperament.

There have been many investigations and studies of size and growth. Scammon[1] and others mention four kinds of growth: general or skeletal, neural, lymphoid, and genital. Family influences on growth and development was studied by Palmer[2] who prepared data on 193 pairs of brothers and 154 pairs of sisters during the age period from seven to twelve years at times when they reached the same chronological age, since there were no twins in the study. The correlation between heights for both sexes was .44, and .33 for weight. These correlations do not show a very marked correspondence, with less for weight than for height. Brothers are more nearly alike than sisters, but both sexes tend to decrease in family correlation as they grow older. Any one who has observed family group pictures of grown children usually notes great difference in height and weight among them. It would appear that each individual tends to grow at a rate only slightly related to the other members. It is interesting to note that when a child who has very large parents is only of average size little comment is made about it, but when a child of that family is very large also the family heredity is offered as explanation. Other studies note racial and nationality differences in size and that some years seem to be better "growing" years than others for large segments of the population.

## Causes of Variations

As noted in the preceding paragraphs, many of the deviations in growth are from natural causes such as individual differences; some are racial; and others from variations in food assimilation and the amount of food consumed. Among the causes of disorders and deviations in growth are the malfunctioning of the endocrine glands. This

[1] J.A. Harris, C.M. Jackson, D.G. Patterson, and R.E. Scammon, *The Measurement of Man*, University of Minnesota Press, Minneapolis, Minn., 1930, 215 pp.

[2] C.E. Palmer, "Age Changes in the Physical Resemblances of Siblings," *Child Development*, 1934, 5, pp. 351-360.

topic has captured the popular imagination in the past few years, entirely out of proportion to the frequency of actual glandular disturbances or to the possibilities of treatment. Endocrinologists have found it difficult to exercise the necessary caution in the face of overzealous and misinformed enthusiasts.

*Overweight and oversize.* One of the common misconceptions centers in the idea that obese children have some glandular disorder. A truly obese child is overgrown, ruddy, and has skin stretched tightly over his adipose deposits. Wilkins[1] comments that the hypothyroid child is usually overweight because of myxedema with loose, subcutaneous tissue. He classifies obesity under three causes: (1) excessive food intake with excessive appetite; (2) decreased expenditure of energy with sedentary habits or with poor health; and (3) altered fat metabolism which causes fat to be stored although the caloric intake is very much below normal requirements. It is evident that in obese children better regulated habits of eating and of exercise are important remedies.

Unusual tallness and very rapid growth may have their causes in endocrine disorders. In certain cases a lack of thyroid secretion before adolescence causes tallness for age along with long extremities and slender body proportions. This condition is known as the *Forme Fruste* type and is characterized by excessive fatigue and results in much restlessness, accompanied by poor behavior. Prescribed rest, additional feeding, and medication may arrest the rate of growth before it reaches undue proportions. A second condition of oversize is known as *gigantism*. It is caused by excessive secretion from the anterior lobe of the pituitary gland. Often parents realize too late that this rate of growth was not merely a fine endorsement of their care and good ancestry. Some medication of a compensatory type to other endocrine glands is helpful if the unusual growth has not progressed very far.

*Underweight and undersize.* In addition to previously noted causes, endocrine disorders produce some conditions of underweight and undersize. In one form of thyroid deficiency there develops a bodily type which is short, with short arms and legs, short, stubby fingers, and

---

[1] L. Wilkins, *The Diagnosis and Treatment of Endocrine Disorders in Childhood and Adolescence* (2nd ed.), Charles C Thomas Publisher, Springfield, Ill., 1957, pp. 473-482.

square body proportions. This conditions is known as cretinoid thyroid deficiency and is characterized by mental slowness and by generally slow and sluggish behavior. Early detection and medication are the factors favorable for prevention and remediation. Dwarfism may have several types of causes in addition to the cretinoid type. Sexual precocity produces an abnormally rapid rate of growth which encounters compensations and halts growth before full maturity is reached. Some rather rare types are due to pituitary deficiency when the true nature of such cases is not disclosed until adulthood is reached.

Two additional types of drawfism have no evidence of endocrine deficiency and their bodily processes are normal. The pygmies in remote parts of the world have genetically determined causes of dwarfism. The "midget" is a second type with no evidence of abnormality except smallness of stature. Midgets are few in number and several families usually travel together as features of circuses. They always excite great interest. The mock weddings staged by normal young children resemble the midget activities as well as does the modern dress of young, normal boys and girls which is more closely patterned after adult fashions than was true some years ago.

There is no known cause for a rare variant type which becomes prematurely aged in appearance in early childhood. The features become sunken and drawn and are accompanied by wrinkled skin and baldness. Another rare type seems somewhat more normal up to early childhood after which growth ceases and the features become peaked and bird-like in appearance. For them, death occurs in early adulthood.

*Disproportions in size.* Some dwarfism cases become disproportionate in size. Another type is known as *acromegaly* and is caused by hyperpituitarism after adolescence. Physical growth starts again after adult maturity has been reached. It affects the hands, feet, and portions of the face, with painful results. The nose becomes larger, the tongue grows out of proportion and the teeth become more widely spaced with growth of the jaws. The condition needs whatever help the endocrinologist is able to give. In Morquio's disease there is shortening of the chest but with less shortening of the limbs so that a crouching position results. In achondroplasia the body is much longer in proportion to the legs. In Hurler's syndrome the head seems to be set flat onto the body with a very short neck. Many of these various types are mentally retarded and so physically incapacitated that they are institutionalized for permanent care or are excused from attending school if remaining in the community. There are also some children whose heads are abnormally large, and such hydrocephalism is caused by excess cranial fluid which distends the skull bones. Microcephalism is an opposite condition, which results from a too early closing of the sutures of the skull. Both types are usually mentally retarded and are easily identified in institutions for permanent care.

*The endocrine system.* In the preceding paragraphs there has been some mention of endocrine glands which cause disorders of growth. Attention will now be directed toward them as specific parts of the endocrine system. The first of these is the thyroid gland which is a small body located at the base of the neck and usually weighs less than an ounce in the normal adult. The thyroid hormone is a major factor in body metabolism and hence its function is closely related to growth. Both hyperthyroid and hypothyroid disorders have been discussed. In exophthalmic goiter there is a great increase in nervous tension, extreme restlessness, and a distension of the eyeballs. The parathyroids are four tiny bodies embedded in the thyroid tissue. Their functioning seems to be related to the general control of the nervous system. Great care must be exercised in thyroid operations so that the parathyroids are not removed or injured and muscle contractions and convulsions do not thus occur.

The pituitary gland must be very important in the total bodily system, since it is the most hidden and the best protected with its location in a small, bony socket in the center of the skull. Its malfunctioning produces various deviations of growth and is related to retarded sexual development with a pattern known as Froelich's syndrome. The thymus gland is located in the upper chest region. It reaches its maximum growth at about two years of age, but by adolescence it has atrophied or practically disappeared. Its function is to act as a check upon sexual development until the human body has more nearly reached its full physical development, which is a relatively long period. Cases of premature sexual development are usually associated with thymus atrophy. The pineal gland, a small body located near the pituitary gland, may have been the vestige of some important organ of the body in early evolutionary days. It appears to be related to the functioning of the thymus gland in the regulation of sexual development. The suprarenal or adrenal gland which is located immediately above the kindneys causes malfunctioning of the heart and fluctuations of blood pressure. The sexual hormones control the normal functioning of the sexual processes. Whenever there are deviations either in positive or negative directions there may be corresponding changes in bodily growth and development as well as distinctive alterations in personality and character.

*Educational adjustments.* There is no special type of class or school for cases afflicted with growth deviations or disorders of glandular functions. Undoubtedly such cases would be much happier and more at ease if they were segregated with similar types. As it is, they learn to adjust as best they may with classmates in regular grades. Few of them or their parents receive much helpful interpretation on how to make social adaptations. Thus far the chief interest has been centered in dietary and endocrinological programs which may alleviate the physiological conditions but not the educational and sociological phases of their problems.

## Questions and Topics for Discussion

1. If you had to choose, would you prefer being very tall or very short? Give your reasons.
2. Describe a person you have known who was extremely tall. What inconveniences did he experience?
3. Explain the difference between mass or composite standards and individual or longitudinal standards, with advantages and disadvantages of each.
4. Make a list of physical characteristics of the races.
5. Visit an endocrine clinic and have a demonstration of cases with explanation of treatment and of diagnostic procedures.
6. Review in more detail some unusual gland conditions reported in Wilkins' *The Diagnosis and Treatment of Endocrine Disorders in Childhood and Adolescence.*
7. Report on the use of Wetzel's grid.

## A. Organizations

1. American Medical Association, 535 N. Dearborn St., Chicago 10.
2. American Public Health Association, 1790 Broadway, New York 19.
3. National Health Council, 1790 Broadway, New York 19.

## B. Periodicals

1. *American Journal of Diseases of Children*, American Medical Association, 535 N. Dearborn St., Chicago 10.
2. *American Journal of Orthopsychiatry*, American Orthopsychiatric Association, 1790 Broadway, New York 19.
3. *The Journal of Pediatrics*, C.V. Mosby Co., St. Louis, Mo.

## C. Books

1. Ausubel, D.P., *Theory and Problems of Child Development*, Grune and Stratton, Inc., New York, 1958, 650 pp.
2. Harris, J.A., C.M. Jackson, D.G. Patterson, and R.E. Scammon, *The Measurement of Man*, University of Minnesota Press, Minneapolis, Minn., 1930, 215 pp.
3. Sheldon, W.H., S.S. Stevens, and W.B. Tucker, *The Varieties of Human Physique*, Harper & Brothers, New York, 1940, 347 pp.
4. Wheatley, G.M., and G.T. Hallock, *Health Observation of School Children*, McGraw-Hill Book Co., Inc., New York, 1956, 488 pp.
5. Wilkins, L., *The Diagnosis and Treatment of Endocrine Disorders in Childhood and Adolescence* (2nd ed.), Charles C Thomas Publisher, Springfield, Ill., 1957, 526 pp.
6. Williams, R.H., *Textbooks of Endocrinology*, W.B. Saunders Co., Philadelphia, 1950, 793 pp.

## D. Films and Filmstrips

1. *Principles of Development*, 17 minutes, 16-mm. Outlines the fundamental of child growth with variables. McGraw-Hill Book Co., Inc., Text-Film Dept., 330 W. 42nd St., New York 36.
2. *Child Care and Development*, 17 minutes, 16-mm. Covers good habits of daily living, (also filmstrip). McGraw-Hill Book Co., Inc., 330 W. 42nd St., New York 36.
3. *Somatic Endocrine Types*, 26 minutes, 16-mm., silent. Illustrates various types, Mongolism, cretinism, etc. Distribution limited to professional groups. New York University Film Library, 26 Washington Pl., New York 3.

# CHAPTER 29

*Miscellaneous Physical*

*Conditions*

IN ADDITION TO the several physical conditions described in the preceding chapters there are many others which occur with variable frequency. Some conditions are chronic, and while they are not as obviously handicapping as blindness or deafness, nevertheless they are a source of constant inconvenience. Many children who are afflicted but have no obvious physical symptoms are often restless and unable to concentrate on schoolwork. They are incorrectly judged to be misbehavior or mentally retarded cases. Accurate diagnosis and remedial measures often turn the tide toward a better understanding.

### Allergies

An allergy is an altered reaction to some specific substance, such as a particular food, article of clothing, household object, or something else in the immediate environment. Indigestion and abnormal reaction of the various digestive processes may occur shortly after eating. Since there is usually a variety of foods in a meal the real cause of the allergy may be difficult to isolate. Spots may break out on the face or over portions of the body. In case of food allergy once the particular food has been identified prevention automatically occurs with avoidance of that food. One method of detection is to make tiny scratches in the skin with needles containing samples of many foods or substances so that the particular allergy or allergies may be discovered. Newer methods of allergy detection are being continually developed. Some persons have reactions to penicillin and allied drugs to such a degree that antidotes must be used. Certain fabrics may not touch the skin, and occasionally some very unsuspected article of furniture or other items in the surroundings are causes. Unless allergies are understood, children who are subject to them are often punished and berated for disobedience, adding insult to injury. Some adults with allergies continue to endure them in the thought that there must be a certain amount of suffering and discomfort as their lot. Parents should realize that some foods and articles which do not produce allergy in them may be doing so in their children. With the new advances of knowledge in food chemistry and in other substances, coupled with improved knowledge of body chemistry the number and frequency of allergic conditions should be greatly reduced. Histamine and its antidotes are helpful in certain allergies.

### Diabetes

There are several types and forms of diabetes which are centered principally in the functioning of the kidneys and in the amount and characteristics of urine. While diabetes is more commonly a condition occuring in middle age or later, it is being recognized much more frequently in children than formerly. The most common type is *diabetes mellitus*, an inherited, constitutional disease. Its cause is unknown, but it is characterized by inability of the body to oxidize certain carbohydrates which accumulate as sugar in the blood and in the urine where its presence may be detected by analysis. Contrary to the usual trend of sex differences, girls outnumber boys in diabetic conditions by about two to one. Early in the 1920's Sir Frederick Banting was able to produce insulin from the pancreas of animals, and since then the death rate from diabetes in children and youth has been reduced by about 75 per cent.

Parents of diabetic children must cooperate closely with the family physician in the control of diabetes which centers around proper diet, insulin treatment, and exercise. In the early acute stage the child may have to take a prolonged bed rest. There is danger in mild fevers and other conditions which may upset the digestive processes. When sugar is not being burned in sufficient quantity, poisons from acids may bring on a *diabetic coma* which is a sign of immediate danger. The amount of insulin intake must be carefully regulated so that there is not too much nor too little. If there are bodily reactions of sweating, nausea, nervousness, etc., the diabetic child who is being treated with insulin should carry two lumps of sugar to use immediately when insulin reaction develops. With these precautions the health of the diabetic child can be greatly improved.

A second form is *diabetes insipidus* which results from injury or infection of the hypothalamus. There is intense thirst and dehydration along with production of large quantities of urine of low specific gravity. It is relieved by extracts of the posterior pituitary lobe. There are several other forms, such as *amino diabetes*, characterized by excessive quantities of amino acids, glucose, and phosphate in the urine. In any suspected conditions of diabetes medical diagnosis and prescription should be available.

### Asthma

Asthma is classified as a respiratory allergy. There are various mucous membranes of the body which are easily affected and are known as shock tissue. The mucous membrane of the bronchial tissues is affected in asthma. The bronchial tubes become highly irritated and cause coughing spasms which are very difficult to control. At times they run along a severe course during which time the child develops great fears that it will never cease. Parents are extremely concerned and become oversolicitous, which in turn generates greater anxiety in the child himself. It is a difficult question to decide whether the asthma has caused the disturbed personality or whether a disturbed personality causes and aggravates the asthmatic condition. There is some evidence from examination by use of the Rorschach test that asthmatic patients had personality disorders before the onset of asthma. Alleviation of anxiety in both parents and child tends to lessen the frequency and acuteness of onsets.

## Hay Fever

In many cases asthma has its beginnings in milder forms of allergy, particularly in hay fever. Hay fever is a pollen allergy with ragweed leading the list of pollen producers. This allergy affects the mucous membranes of the nose, the roof of the mouth, and in the more severe forms, it reaches the lungs and tends to cause asthmatic reactions. Adults recognize the affliction in themselves but frequently believe that children's hay fever is only a chronic cold which continues for many weeks or months and is accompanied with suffering and inconvenience. While there is no known cure except to go to cooler environments where the pollen does not exist, few people can make such arrangements. Air conditioning also relieves hay fever victims because it filters the air. In the meantime some of the new antihistamine drugs provide relief but should be taken under doctor's prescriptions.

## Albinism

At some time or other most people have see individuals with striking-looking white hair, a pale or pink skin, and squinting and unusual appearing eyes. They are known as albinos. It was probably easy to pass them by, believing that it would be hard to cultivate them as intimate friends because of their unusual characteristics. Some of the qualities will be discussed.

Scheidemann[1] offers the following definition:

For practical purposes an albino may be defined as an individual having skin of milky whiteness or of characteristic pallor, white hair, possibly tinged with yellow or straw, eyes with pink or red pupils and pink, red, violet, very pale blue or blue-gray irises, and the usual accompaniments of nystagmus, photophobia, and defective vision.

This definition indicates that lack of skin pigmentation may be partial or complete. Cases of very mild albinism deviate from the normal so slightly that they are accepted as being in the normal range but have enough variation to have a certain unique attractiveness.

[1] N.V. Scheidemann, *Psychology of Exceptional Children*, Vol II, Houghton Mifflin Co., Boston, 1937, 460 pp.

The typical albino has a skin of a dull pallor, often with a character-istic tinge, because of the blood showing under its thin and delicate surface. A soft, white down often covers the body, giving the general impression that albinos have a soft and delicate bodily structure. This impression of delicateness is also carried out in the hair, which is fine, silky, and usually white. Some special types of albinos with red hair are known as rufous albinos.

*Causes.* The specific or topographical cause of albinism is unknown. On the etiological side it is hereditary as a recessive rather than as a dominant trait. It occurs only when both parents are "carriers" and may be dormant in both families for one or more generations. It tends to exist more frequently in districts in which there are many con-sanguineous marriages. Nearly seven hundred families[1] have been studied in which albinism has existed and which serve as the basis of the knowledge about hereditary causes. Albinos have been found in every race and in all parts of the world. Albinism has been known throughout the ages, but in the early days was mentioned chiefly by writers of the classics rather than by physicians or other scientists.

*Number.* The number of albinos is comparatively few. Various estimates in different countries, based upon inadequate surveys, show one case in approximately every twenty thousand of the population. In Glasgow there were seven or eight albinos among approximately one hundred thousand school age children. As in the case of other defects, there are probably many more partial cases who do not show the extreme or pure characteristics usually associated with the albino.

*School placement.* Because of their oversensitiveness to light, albinos must exercise great caution and care in the use of their eyes. Wherever facilities are available they are enrolled in classes for the partially-seeing so that particular attention may be given to their needs. Scheidemann noted that albinos in the Los Angeles schools were characterized by above average intelligence and eyes with black pupils, which indicated that they were not true albino types. It is

[1] K. Pearson, E. Nettleship, and C.H. Usher, A *Monograph on Albinism in Man,* Draper's Company Research Memoirs, Dulau and Company, London, 1911, 4 vols.

believed that their conditions become less extreme in adulthood and they gradually learn how to adjust their eyes to light.

## The Teeth of Children

Although no types of special classes or schools are established for children with defective teeth, there is much pain, infection, indigestion, loss of school time, and many other attendant ills arising from this source. Since a toothache or the loss of a tooth is not considered as serious as an eye injury or as deafness, there is probably more neglect of teeth than of any other defect or handicap. There continues to be much lack of information and misinformation about the care of the teeth which confuses the issues and slows progress in care and treatment of the teeth.

*Causes of dental defects.* There are many causes of dental defects. Some of them are accidental or incidental. Children fall on their faces, are hit in play, or run into objects which break their teeth. They lose teeth in automobile accidents. They crack the enamel in biting on hard substances and suffer from other dental situations which are not limited to children only. Although these various causes take a sizable toll the principal cause of teeth decay is caries. This disease was discovered by W. E. Miller, an American dentist, in 1882. The hard enamel coating of the teeth, which seems to be sufficient protection from the hardest usage, actually is very vulnerable to decalcification. Certain bacteria in the saliva produce acids which tend to dissolve the enamel. This condition is intensified in the fermentation of carbohydrates which is generated in the overabundance of candies and sweets in modern rich diets. These acids adhere so firmly to the teeth that even vigorous brushing does not remove all of them, particularly from those portions embedded along the edges of the gums. Wheatley and Hallock[1] comment:

The old admonitions regarding toothbrushing ran something like this: Brush your teeth after each meal, if possible, or at least twice a day—in the morning and before going to bed. However, the usual 30-second brush-

[1] G.M. Wheatley and G.T. Hallock, *Health Observation of School Children,* McGraw-Hill Book Co., Inc., New York, 1956, p. 283.

offs the first thing in the morning and the last thing at night accomplish little except to make the mouth and teeth feel pleasantly clean.

Irregularities in the teeth are frequent with various causes such as extra teeth, teeth out of alignment in the jaw, and teeth spaced too widely so that some speech sounds are difficult to make. There is increased use of dental braces to correct these irregularities to improve personal appearance as well as insure better preservation of teeth. Gingivitis is an infection of the mucous membrane of the gums which spreads to the roots of the teeth and results in decay. Pyorrhea may arise from gingivitis and is a purulent discharge which sets up infections with decay and loss of teeth. Many of these infectious conditions and diseases spread into the blood stream where they are carried to the heart and to other portions of the body. In turn, they affect the heart and set up a chain of other bodily infections. Tartar is an incrustation which forms around the portions of the teeth just above and below the gums. Full knowledge of resultant damages is lacking, but undoubtedly the general life of the gums and the teeth is affected.

*Preventions.* In view of the fundamental cause of dental caries, it is obvious that less emphasis upon consumption of candies and other sweets would be of considerable benefit, although not all children who indulge in them are badly affected. Careful brushing after each meal, snack, or candy bar is a little too difficult and time-consuming. It has been discovered the fluoride in the drinking water prevents a great amount of dental caries. Artificial fluoridation of city water systems is getting to be a more commonly accepted practice since the amount is so small that it does not modify the taste of the water. Controlled experiments with fluoride as compared to none in some New York cities showed an average of two less decayed teeth per child when the fluoride had been used. Since the number of decayed teeth reaches astronomical figures any helpful preventive such as fluoridation will ultimately be of great benefit.

While preventive dental measures of general benefit to all children are possible, the principal responsibility lies with parents. The teacher and school nurse may cooperate with them in pointing out the needs, but they cannot carry out the programs of remedies and preventions. A visit to the dentist's office when the child is very young and when there is little likelihood of pain sets the stage for better cooperation than when the visits are under emotional and physical stress. A "Gallup" type of survey would probably show that many adults today dread such visits from their own initial experiences or from "bear" stories about them. The dental profession has recognized the psychological implications of satisfactory relationships to children as well as to adults.

### Laterality

As the term implies, in laterality the organs on one side of the body take the more dominant role. The eye, hand, foot, probably the ear, and general bodily status may be included. In many respects, laterality opposite to that which is characteristic of most persons, is not necessarily a handicap nor does it make the child exceptional. However, there are some features of laterality which need interpretation. Handedness is the most common and most obvious of the laterality activities.

*Psychological characteristics.* The condition of laterality itself is much less of a problem than are certain emotional upsets and frustrations resulting from treatments for it. A small percentage of parents forcibly try to change handedness to the right side rather than to the left. The various episodes in this situation have results quite similar to disagreements over foods, clothes, or going to bed. Eventually the emotion becomes so involved that cause and effect can scarcely be distinguished.

*Causes.* The causes of laterality continue to be puzzling. Many authorities believe that heredity plays the significant role. Right laterality is believed to be the dominant, and left laterality the recessive, Mendelian trait. However, in some families, the left laterality appears to be dominant. According to Mendelian laws, one-fourth of the population would have left laterality whereas only about 6 per cent are obviously so characterized. This discrepancy of 19 per cent is sometimes explained by noting that training in right laterality may account for the difference. Chamberlain[1] reports that in fifty-five families in which the mother was left-handed, 13.77 per cent of the children were left-handed; in eighty-two families in which the father was left-handed, 9.7 per cent were left-handed; while in thirty-three families in which both parents were left-handed, 46 per cent were left-handed.

Causes of laterality are also believed to exist within the constitutional make-up of the individual body. In the evolutionary process of embryonic development one side of the body may progress more rapidly and with more vitality than the other which might produce a dominant condition. Within the brain there is an area in the third frontal convolution claimed by Broca to be the speech center. In case of right laterality the Broca area is supposedly in the right hemisphere and opposite the motor area which has crossed over from the opposite side. In the left laterality these conditions may be reversed. There is probably no complete division of this type since the various processes of the brain are know to be somewhat scattered and diverse. In one school of thought some cases of speech disturbance have been noted when there has been forced change of handedness. It has not been clearly demonstrated whether such relationship exists on a physiological basis or whether the psychological and emotional effects of forcing by parents have produced the speech disturbance.

*Disadvantages in left laterality.* There are a few disadvantages and inconveniences for left-handed persons in a predominantly right-handed world. Many tools and gadgets are made for the right-handed, although in some instances manufacturers have accommodated them, such as with left-handed golf clubs. The left-handed person generally accommodates himself to shaking hands with his right hand. There is a subtle psychological problem in distinguishing when the transfer of operation is necessary. When instructed to make a right turn in traffic the left-handed driver must sometimes concentrate carefully in actually making the right turn, rather than the left turn since he projects his handedness into the situation. Desks in lecture halls seldom have writing spaces on the left side. Left-handed people

[1] H.D. Chamberlain, "The Inheritance of Left-Handedness," *Journal of Heredity*, 1938, 19, pp. 557-559.

eating in the traditionally crowded boarding house lack sufficient elbow room. Pushbutton gearshifts are eliminating the inconvenience of shift levers on the wrong side.

*Advantages in left laterality.* The most obvious advantage of left-handedness seems to be in baseball. Left-handed pitchers have certain advantages over the right-handed batters who are in the majority, and the substitution of a new pitcher to face one batter only is becoming a common practice. The left-handed batter has the slight advantage of a shorter distance to first base. Ambidextrous batters are very valuable to ball teams. Any possible stigma of left-handedness has been quite well neutralized by baseball.

*Methods of diagnosis.* One of the most obvious evidences of laterality is the use of the preferred hand, foot, or eye, but there are some left-handed children who have been trained to do most things right-handed and vice versa. Mere use is not always the test of true laterality. For young children various investigators have devised tests noting which hand was used in cutting with scissors, winding a string around a pencil, throwing, reaching, and other simple tasks. Ojemann[1] notes that the hand farthest from the "business" end of the shovel or broom is the dominant hand with the right-handed person shoveling toward the left with his hand nearest the shovel. In an interesting discussion of directional confusion Bernice Leland[2] notes that before children are ready to read but are attempting to print their names, many of them proceed from right to left. By careful and patient teaching this error can usually be corrected before bad writing habits become established. After the correction has been established young children are much more likely to begin from left to right in reading. Leland advises that kindergarten and first-grade teachers observe any pupils who have these tendencies in various actions and change them if possible before they have progressed very far and before reading is begun.

*Educational problems.* The principal difficulty with school subjects

[1] R.H. Ojemann, "Studies in Handedness: II Testing Bimanual Handedness," *Journal of Educational Psychology*, 1930, 21, pp. 695-702.
[2] B. Leland, "Symptoms of Directional Confusion among Children Who Cannot Read," *Childhood Education*, 1938, 14, pp. 406-410.

has usually been in handwriting. The left-handed child naturally wishes to write from right to left which would result in what is known as mirror-writing. Since this style of writing is not ordinarily legible to others, the left-handed child resorts to awkward and inefficient methods of writing with his left hand. In modern teaching the left-handed child holds his paper in a position so that the line of writing is at right angles to his writing arm and hand. He holds his pen or pencil far enough below the line so that he can see the letters or words he has written. As a result the writing may proceed normally and meet the general standards for all children.

Many modern schoolrooms use tables with enough space for comfortable working conditions with either hand. The traditional type of desk also served the left-handed pupil fairly well. In all of these situations both at school and at home matters should proceed in a quiet manner so that there is no emotional strain or feelings of frustration.

## Questions and Topics for Discussion

1. Describe your own condition in regard to allergies to types of food, articles, etc.
2. Describe modern methods of allergy examination.
3. Discuss the various types of diabetes and cite examples.
4. What are some homemade remedies for relief of asthma? How effective are they?
5. What measures do you or your friends take in attacks of hay fever?
6. Are there any albinos in your school system and if so what educational provisions are made for them?
7. Relate your own experiences with your teeth in regard to extractions, fillings, early care, etc.
8. Does your community provide for fluoridation of water?
9. Discuss some adaptations which you or your friends make in case of left-handedness.

## A. Organizations

1. American Diabetic Association, 1 E. 45th St., New York 17.
2. American Dental Association, 222 E. Superior St., Chicago 11.
3. American Medical Association, 535 N. Dearborn St., Chicago 10.
4. American Public Health Association, 1790 Broadway, New York 19.

## B. Periodicals

1. *American Journal of Diseases of Children,* American Medical Association, 535 N. Dearborn St., Chicago 10.
2. *American Journal of Orthopsychiatry,* American Orthopsychiatric Association, 1790 Broadway, New York 19.
3. *The Journal of Pediatrics,* C.V. Mosby Co., St. Louis, Mo.

## C. Books

1. Haefner, R., *The Educational Significance of Left-Handedness,* Teachers College Contribution to Education, No. 360, Columbia University Press, New York, 1929, 84 pp.
2. Parsons, B.S., *Left-Handedness,* The Macmillan Co., New York, 1924, 185 pp.
3. Starling, E.H. (ed.), *Principles of Human Physiology,* (9th ed.), Lea and Febiger, Philadelphia, 1945, 1155 pp.
4. Weiss, E., and O.S. English, *Psychosomatic Medicine,* W.B. Saunders Co., Philadelphia, 1943, 687 pp.
5. Wheatley, G.M., and G.T. Hallock, *Health Observation of School Children,* McGraw-Hill Book Co., Inc., New York, 1956, 488 pp.

## D. Films and Filmstrips

1. *Getting Ready for the Dentist,* 11 minutes, 16-mm. Home preparation for dental visit. New York University Film Library, 26 Washington Pl., New York 3.
2. *Save Those Teeth,* 11 minutes, 16-mm. Care of teeth and reasons for tooth decay. Encyclopedia Britannica Films, 1150 Wilmette Ave., Wilmette, Ill.

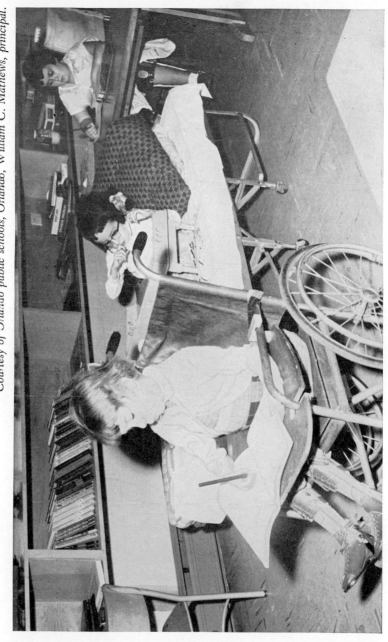

Orthopedic pupils, Forest Park school, Orlando, Florida.

*Courtesy of Orlando public schools, Orlando, William C. Mathews, principal.*

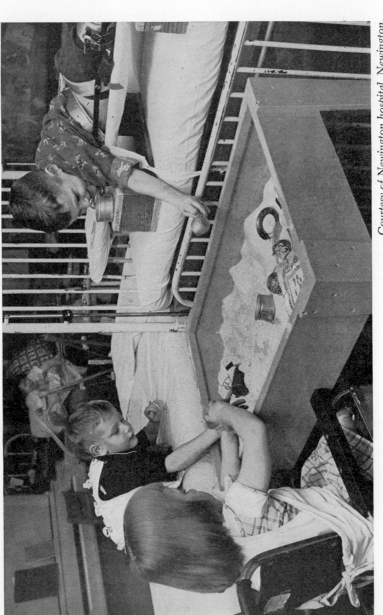

Courtesy of Newington hospital, Newington.

Crippled children, Newington hospital, Newington, Conn.

# PART 8

*Sociological and
Community Responsibility*

# CHAPTER 30

### Family and Social
### Problems

THROUGHOUT MOST of the preceding chapters the emphasis has been on specific physical and sensory handicaps, disorders, and diseases. In this chapter discussion is directed to family and social problems which generate unusual adjustments for children. They include bilingual children, indigent families, homes with parents mentally ill or in prisons, and multiple-birth children.

## Bilingual Children

As the term implies, there are children who hear or speak two languages at home. In the early days of American life, English was the chief language used in America with the exception of a little French and Dutch. In the past hundred years there has been a large immigration, first from northern Europe and more recently from southern Europe, involving languages other than English. Aside from the inconvenience of a second language many other problems have accompanied these immigrants to our shores. While America has openly welcomed the newcomers there have been many complicating attendant problems. In 1930, 28 per cent of the American population was foreign born. In some large cities it runs well over 50 per cent.

*The problem of language.* At first thought it might be concluded that learning two languages is no problem and that children are at a great advantage in knowing more than one language. There is confusion for young children in learning two languages, particularly if both languages are spoken to them by the same individuals such as parents and siblings. Better results are obtained when different individuals speak a particular language to a child, so that he associates one language with one individual, according to Smith.[1] In some respects learning one language is a difficult task for a young child and therefore two languages at an early age is a double burden. Some words of any two languages are very similar, but others are very different. In most all languages the idioms and sentence structure are unique to that particular language so that the general pattern of thought formulation must be different. The practice of generally delaying the study of foreign languages until high school or college is mute evidence of the implied difficulty of mastering two languages.

*Intelligence and bilingualism.* Many studies of the intelligence of different nationalities represented in American schools show median scores below the average American standard. When these scores are equated with native born children of the same socio-economic status the differences disappear, even in the case of verbal material, according to findings by Pintner and Arsenian.[2] Other investigators have obtained similar results. There is much less difference between results, either with verbal or non-verbal test material than has been assumed from earlier investigations. The real difference does not lie in the language but in the lower social and economic status of the majority of immigrants with a non-English language background.

There is a second confusing element in that individuals with dull or defective intelligence have much greater difficulty with bilingual situations than do children of average or superior intelligence. Whenever a child shows considerable confusion and slowness in English, and has heard a second language spoken in his home from early childhood,

---

[1] M.E. Smith, "Some Light on the Problems of Bilingualism as Found from a Study of the Progress in Mastery of English among Pre-School Children of Non-American Ancestry in Hawaii," *Genetic Psychology Monographs*, 1939, 21, pp. 121-184.
[2] R. Pintner and S. Arsenian, "The Relation of Bilingualism to Verbal Intelligence and School Adjustment," *Journal of Educational Research*, 1937, 31, pp. 255-263.

there is a strong tendency to account for his English backwardness by bilingualism. It is a fact, likely to be overlooked, that one of his brothers and sisters who has lived in the same bilingual home speaks English fluently as well as the second language. Obviously the real difference must lie in the native brightness since the language experiences were the same. If hearing a second language were a universal handicap, bright children as well as slow-learning would have equal difficulty, but this is not the case. Whenever a child continues to be backward in English after several years experience at home, in school, or at play, it is quite certain that mental slowness of some degree is the real difficulty.

*Social customs.* In addition to language difficulty there are more serious problems arising out of different social customs. The American way of life is different. Homesick parents cling to their early customs and language. They expect their children to continue with them as well, but their children are in closer touch with American ways and wish to adopt them fully. They resist their parents and sometimes become ashamed of them. Fathers take an unusually harsh and dominating attitude in matters of discipline, similar to that of their own early childhood, but out of line with current American methods. Children try to escape from these restrictions by joining gangs whose similar feelings create close bonds. There is developed a vicious circle of causes and effects, leading to delinquency. In the larger cities the delinquency centers are located in the midst of immigrant groups, the second generation being the most fruitful source of trouble. In his studies of delinquency, Shaw[1] showed that the rates of delinquency remain practically unchanged in certain areas although one immigrant language group after another lives in them.

Unless very definite measures are taken on a comprehensive scale the behavior difficulties of these groups run true to form regardless of the particular foreign language spoken in the home. There needs to be a better assimilation by parents of the customs of their adopted land and greater tolerance on their part for their children who are trying to fit into the American pattern. The parents themselves become

[1] C.R. Shaw, *Delinquency Areas*, University of Chicago Press, Chicago, 1929, 214 pp.

very discouraged since they do not achieve all of the glorious results which some of their more successful peers have been able to do in this land of opportunity. America has paid a high price in delinquency and crime for many of its more recent immigrants. Some of this price could have been lowered if the true nature of the pattern had been known and community efforts had been made to meet it. The schools should assume their share of this program and interpret problems to the parents in such neighborhoods.

### Problems of Indigency

Children from indigent families create problems for the schools, a few of which will be discussed briefly. Schools are democratic agencies and must attempt to treat all children as nearly alike as possible. Many critical problems are encountered. In neighborhoods where there are mixtures of indigent and well-to-do families, the children themselves often draw sharp lines which are very difficult for the teaching staffs to minimize. In preparing for pageants and special occasions, care must be taken not to make demands for costumes or other materials which cannot be met by a limited family budget.

Children often feel particularly apologetic about their clothes and develop feelings of inferiority which carry over into their general attitude toward school. They give false reasons for not wishing to do some particular task because the class will focus its attention upon them. Some school systems in large metropolitan areas require uniform clothes for all children within each of the two sex groups so that financial differences are better concealed.

With the more universal use of free or partially free lunches for indigent children various plans are in operation by which their special credit cards are not too obvious. Schools may also find ways in which indigent children may receive special praise and recognition for achievements in their chosen fields which is an excellent device in good mental hygiene. Any school which has many of these problems may do well to have an administrative and teacher committee on strategy to plan ways and means of meeting the problems which constantly arise in indigency.

There is need for close cooperation and understanding between the schools and the relief or welfare agencies in the interests of indigent children. A small percentage of indigent families disclose entirely different attitudes toward the schools than to the relief agencies. To the former they may show a type of rebellion about their condition and vent their feelings upon the schools with supercritical attitudes, whereas to the latter they present a most favorable picture of their children's success in school, and cordial cooperation with the teachers. A comparison of these divergent attitudes and a more comprehensive plan of cooperation is very helpful since children are easily disturbed by such discrepancies.

The problem of finances is a relative matter at all levels and is not confined to indigency. Children at all economic levels reflect minor differences. Among the well-to-do, merciless comparisons are often made between the qualities of fur coats which children wear to school or whether a chauffeur calls for the child in the family limousine. Children tend to make comparisons about the most trivial things, such as the quality of their lead pencils, with a view to building up their own personal vanity on the discomfort and embarrassment of their associates. Problems at the level of indigency are not particularly different than at other levels so far as social and psychological effects are concerned. They are worse only in absolute degree.

In teaching regular-grade children, there is a vast difference in the general attitudes toward the school between the higher and the lower economic levels. At first thought one might prefer to teach in a well-to-do neighborhood where the families and the general cultural status are above the general community standard. Experience has shown that in such areas the schools find it difficult to compete with homes of children in culture and information. No matter how proud a school may be of its encyclopedia some children explain with a disdainful air how much more elaborate and costly is the one at home. In like manner, any report of the teacher's summer vacation trip to a far-away land is more than matched by several pupils both as to distance and elegance of travel. It is difficult for the school to assume any position of leadership in communities of this kind, and teachers are continually challenged with comparisons unfavorable to themselves.

By contrast, the school in a neighborhood of poor economic and social status is the chief source of culture and inspiration, supplemented by the activities of the churches. There are very few other community agencies, no one travels far, there are very few books or magazines in the home, and the school is the highest standard known. The school library is patronized, the school building becomes a community center for evening meetings of adults, and the school principal is constantly consulted by parents about community problems not directly concerned with children. Although the children may be more backward socially and mentally, as a group, than those in the schools in the better economic areas, teaching staffs often derive more satisfaction from their work. Whereas the schools of a large system may be standardized in construction and equipment of buildings and the training and personnel of administration and teachers, they serve entirely different functions depending upon the type of community in which they are located.

Indigency is not a problem distinct from other economic levels but is only one step in the ladder. There are problems of equal importance throughout the entire scale of financial conditions. The conditions are somewhat more exaggerated at the lowest economic levels since there is no lower group upon which to compensate for inadequacies. By bringing out the best abilities and by giving recognition to good individual performance, the economic obstacles may be largely overcome.

### Other Social Conditions

In Chapter 11 there was a discussion of the number of individuals ill with mental diseases and it was estimated that 5 per cent either are actively ill or will be at some time or other. Many of these unfortunate people have children in school and their condition are sometimes unknown to teachers. Needless to say there is much confusion and emotional unrest in their homes which is not conducive to quiet study and application to school tasks. Some of these children serve as guards for the safety of such parents until late evenings, on week ends, and when other members of the family must be absent at work. The strain and responsibility as well as actual physical danger in certain cases place a burden upon immature children far out of proportion to what they should logically be expected to stand. The irrational demands made upon them are most disconcerting including extreme obedience, absolute quiet, and sudden changes in mood which are quite outside of the realm of reasonable expectation. These conditions usually come on gradually so that the extreme gravity of the problem is not recognized even by other adults in the family.

If the parent is eventually sent to a mental hospital there may be relief from that immediate problem, but the responsibilities of the household may continue to fall more completely upon the children. Furthermore, they sometimes become alarmed over the possibilities of a hereditary condition coming upon themselves. They also feel the stigma of neighborhood knowledge about the condition which has developed in their home. Sometimes mentally ill parents have made extremely unreasonable demands upon the school, thus further embarrassing their children. In other instances, the children share a wild delight in the orgy of threats of violence uttered at home against the school. Any schools or pupils that have escaped such experiences may indeed be considered fortunate. The small army of children who live in such conditions need a type of service for themselves and for their parents which the schools are usually unable to provide. Often there is little provision through other community sources.

If a community is able to develop a comprehensive social point of view, misunderstanding and lack of information about home conditions between the home and the school should be reduced. Otherwise, children are the victims of predicaments such as have just been described. Their schoolwork is always certain to suffer and with it the chances of successful preparation for an occupation worthy of their abilities.

Another group of children have one or both parents serving sentences in prison. About three hundred thousand new adults are imprisoned each year. Many parents of children in school, and in a ten-year period this amounts to three million individuals. Sometimes the schools are not aware of it, but neighbors usually are, and gossip eventually brings it to school in a distorted form. The child himself often knows all the details and has been forced to become a silent partner in the offenses. Whenever such children have previously held very high ideals about their parents, such an experience has lasting effects. Occasionally children are asked in school to give as a project oral or written reports about their homes and parents. Ordinarily it is motivated by interesting, intimate details, but in such cases it becomes very embarrassing.

A situation which offers special consequences for children occurs when both parents work and the children are left to look out for themselves. When the mother is at home she is very busy with her double duties and has little time for children. In cases in which one parent is dead and the other parent works full time, the situation is much the same. Many such children become very lonesome and hungry for affection. In school they cling to their teachers and crave personal attention which is not very practical for the school to give, except in incidental ways.

To all of these irregular conditions—bilingual children, indigent children, differences in general culture, parents who are mentally ill, parents in prison, parents who work all the time—may be added various other types of conditions. In many respects these children are fully as handicapped as those with vision defects who are placed in sightsaving classes, yet their handicaps are not so obvious and seldom is there much understanding or special provision made for them.

It is not the purpose of this chapter to paint a dark and discouraging picture about the army of children who suffer from these general social conditions. However, if the schools are to reach their maximum efficiency and to realize the general goals and aims of education, there must be cooperation and understanding between the school and community in the improvement of conditions for children.

### Multiple-Birth Children

Plural or "multiple-birth" children is a term applied to all births of more than one child at a time. They include twins, triplets, quadruplets, quintuplets, and any theoretically higher number. Any multiple-birth group attracts attention and great interest has been focused on it since 1934 with the birth of the Dionne quintuplets at Callendar, Ontario. Several full-length motion pictures of them have been very popular, while a nation-wide series of radio talks by their physician, the late Dr. Dafoe, as well as numerous articles in popular and scientific magazines attest to the interest which was aroused. Since there are over a million multiple-birth people in this country, their problems are worthy of discussion.

A few facts about the number of multiple births are of interest. One birth in every eighty-eight is twins, which would be 1.1 per cent of the births. Since two children in every eighty-nine are twins they constitute 2.2 per cent of all births. The birth ratio for triplets is one to the square of eighty-eight, or one in every 7744 births. By the same logic of ratios, quadruplets occur once in about every seven hundred thousand births, and quintuplets once in every five billion which makes this last group a very rare occurrence. Just why these ratios should occur is a puzzle to everyone, including those who discovered that they exist.

In multiple births there are two types of pre-natal development, one called identical in which all members develop from one egg or ovum, the other fraternal in which each has a separate egg or ovum. In one set of quadruplets reported by Newman[1] two of the four were identical, but each of the other two were separate, or a total of three eggs. The Dionnes are all identical. One-fourth of all twin births are identical and the remainder fraternal, which would indicate that fraternal births among twins is a dominant hereditary trait and identical is recessive. Identical twins are much more alike than fraternal, and are always of the same sex. Before the days of modern research on twins, Sir Francis Galton shrewdly guessed that twins were of the fraternal and identical types. Heredity plays a very important part in determining the probability of twins. The term "Siamese" twins arose from a famous pair of twins born in Siam in 1811, known

[1] H.H. Newman, "Aspects of Twin Research," *The Scientific Monthly*, 1941, 52, pp. 99-112.

as Chang and Eng, who were identical twins joined together in portions of their bodies until their death at the age of sixty-three years.

*Characteristics.* It is not necessary to enlarge upon the generally accepted practices in the care and training of twins. As a group they are usually the objects of more indulgence than single-birth children. They become the center of greater interest and hence may be more likely to become spoiled. Since they are often mistaken for each other, they have to resist more temptation to masquerade as the other member, although such deception may be of a trivial nature.

The chief psychological problem centers around the basic question of whether multiple-birth children should be encouraged to merge their activities, interests, and emotional lives into one closely knit unit or whether they should be encouraged to adopt a more individualistic point of view similar to those of single-birth children. There is a strong tendency for many parents to encourage the former point of view by dressing them alike, expecting them to do the same things at the same time, and generally to live a communal rather than an individual life. Each member of multiple-birth groups is not encouraged to act or think without reference to the other. If one member falls into a mudhole and soils his clothes, which is an individual matter, the other must also change his clothes, too, which is a communal matter. A few parents practice these uniformities on children of different ages, making them the equivalent of a multiple-birth group. In all such cases the issue should revolve about the best adjustments of children rather than the fancies and personal desires of parents.

In early childhood attempts at communal uniformity are not so serious as in adolescence or as in adulthood when each individual naturally becomes much more individualistic about many important decisions. One pair of rather successful twin brothers recently stated that it was still difficult at the age of twenty years to make an individual decision without each first consulting the other.

There is some evidence that twins tend to lead very self-sufficient lives as a sort of subfamily unit by themselves. Therefore, they feel much less need for parental guidance or for the company of other children. They are likely to develop ideas and attitudes of an immature and childish nature similar to what would probably happen if children were allowed to grow up without any parental or other associates. This same phenomenon of a subfamily within a family is likely to occur when two children are nearly of the same age, or it may even happen less commonly when they are of quite different ages but with similar interests and psychological constitutions.

The other siblings of twins often live a somewhat unusual life because of extreme jealousy over the attention which their twin siblings receive at home and elsewhere. These feelings and practices are likely to be much more intense than in the case of one favored child in the family. In focusing attention upon the twins, parents are likely to be less aware than usual of the problems of their other children.

Identical twins tend to be very much alike in most respects and some who have been separated from infancy have been rejoined by the chance meeting with some person who knew one and recognized the other. Fraternal twins have no particular biological reasons for being any more similar than other members of the same family, except that they are born at the same time, pass through babyhood together, and have other associations of a very coincidental nature on account of like ages. There is a larger percentage of left-handedness among one of a pair of twins than among the remainder of the population with approximately 15% as compared to 6% for the total population. It is not known whether this phenomenon is due to heredity, or whether it comes from the position which one of them must assume *in utero* during the prenatal period.

Howard[1] gathered data by means of questionnaires and other methods for 229 sets of triplets. A sampling of preschool and school-age triplets on tests of general ability, language, and nonlanguage, showed them to be somewhat inferior to average single children of their age, but with the school-age group being nearer to the average standard. In tests of masculinity and femininity, they had interests and attitudes normal for their sex. Allowance was made for rural areas and lower socio-economic levels.

[1] R.W. Howard, "Intellectual and Personality Traits of a Group of Triplets," *Journal of Psychology*, 1946, 21, pp. 25-36.

*Studies of heredity and environment.* One of the most fundamental problems of education is the improvement of the human race either through heredity or environment or both. It is as yet largely an open question what phases of human nature are susceptible to change through either heredity or environment and how these may be brought about if such changes are believed desirable. The study of twins offers one of the most profitable avenues for the study of these problems.

There are several combinations which it is possible to study for these influences. Whenever identical twins are brought up together and fraternal twins are likewise treated, it is possible to study the influence of the greater hereditary resemblance of the identical group over the fraternal group. This is also true of the environmental influences. Freeman[1] studied nineteen sets of identical twins, reared apart, and contrasted with them identical twins raised together, as well as fraternal twins. He found one extreme case in which there was a difference of twenty-four points in I.Q. in favor of the girl brought up in the more favorable environment which is a very hopeful sign for the environmentalists. However, he does not report about the intelligence of these two girls at birth. There is a strong possibility of cerebral anoxia at birth upon the part of the one placed in the less favorable environment. He notes that due to the environment there seem to be greater differences in personality development than in intelligence or in physical factors. These findings correspond to the writer's results that personality factors are among the most pliable in a background as noted in Chapter 6.

Freeman's investigations were conducted very carefully and in the light of all information that was available. It should be possible to coordinate studies of this type with the program of child-placing agencies so that by comparing siblings, fraternal twins, and identical twins of matched abilities in different environments, further information would be gained on this most vital problem of human interest. It is not the purpose to remove the glamor which goes with multiple

[1] F.N. Freeman, "Heredity and Environment in the Light of the Study of Twins," *The Scientific Monthly*, 1937, 44, pp. 13-19.

births, but the welfare of children rather than the entertainment of parents should always be the guiding principle.

## Questions and Topics for Discussion

1. Describe any experience which you may have had with a case of bilingualism and interpret it.
2. Consult various sources of statistical data about the number of people from the various nationality groups in America.
3. Illustrate some comparisons which children make with each other at many different economic levels.
4. Consult prison and mental hospital statistics for the numbers and ages of their inmates' and patients' children.
5. Visit some home or neighborhood where any of these conditions are frequent and gain firsthand information about the effects upon children without creating unfavorable impressions by your visit.
6. Make a more complete report on the Dionne quintuplets.
7. Cite your own observations about the behavior and development of a pair of twins with which you are familiar.
8. Make a further report on the heredity of multiple births.

Note: Consult reference material at the end of Chapter 32.

# CHAPTER 31

## Cooperation in Problems
## of Exceptional Children

IT IS NO easy task to conduct a comprehensive program for handicapped and exceptional children. Within the school system the special teacher, the special supervisor and administrator of the program, the principals of schools, and the school superintendent are all concerned beyond the needs and problems of regular class pupils. The board of education must have a general comprehensive philosophy for special educational as well as for regular educational programs. There must be effective cooperation with the many agencies and organizations listed below if the program is to be effective.

### Regular Teachers and Pupils

Special education for handicapped and exceptional children cannot be considered as something apart, distinct, and unrelated to the program for all children. Teachers of regular classes should be encouraged to accept exceptional children as an integral part of the school. These pupils have needs which cannot otherwise be met and are serviced by those who are specially trained and in rooms specially equipped. They should welcome the help of services which they themselves are unable to provide. They have a further opportunity not only to accept such a philosophy but to impart it to their own pupils as well. All negative references should be avoided and the worth of the individual pupil should be respected.

Many handicapped children are enrolled in regular classes and report to the special teacher for the unique services which she is able to provide. The number of pupils served by this general plan is increasing with the use of the itinerant teacher in several fields. Such programs for the partially-seeing are moving in this direction rather than to full-time enrollment with the special teacher. Participation in discussions in regular classes is recognized as a highly acceptable social goal in the education of exceptional children. Any program of special education, either within a large school building or in an entire school system, may rise or fall by the attitudes of the regular teachers. It reflects the leadership attitudes of the immediate administrator. An introductory course in the survey of exceptional children should be a required rather than an elective course in teacher preparation so that a better appreciation may be developed.

There should also be a realistic attitude upon the part of regular pupils. As a matter of fact many of them have members of their own families or their close friends among the handicapped. They should willingly lend a helping hand to the blind, and a word of positive encouragement to the antisocial and the delinquent. They should be alerted about what to do for the epileptic in his *grand mal* attack, and accept their opportunities to be of service in the same spirit as that in saving anyone from drowning or from a burning building. These attitudes cannot be developed into full-blown acceptance in a single day but much more should be accomplished in the long-time program. There should be a fine balance maintained between discussing enough of the nature of handicaps to give appreciation of the individual's needs without invading the secrets of his private life. Progress in pupils' attitudes will eventually be reflected in their understanding and treatment of the adult handicapped or of deficiencies in their own children.

### Cooperation with Parents

The cooperation with parents is the most difficult of all the contacts which need to be made since it is on a very personal and emotional basis. Children are the reflection of parents in many respects and hence what affects the child affects the parents as well. Many handicapped and exceptional children have prolonged and unusually difficult periods of babyhood which unduly increases parental apprehension as well as greater attachment and love. Some parents are too close to the problems and too involved to look at the needs of their children objectively although they are certain that no one else can possibly understand their children as well as they do.

There are as many possible parental attitudes toward children as there are children and their many handicaps. In the more severe physical and sensory handicaps such as blindness, deafness, and severe orthopedic disabilities parents generally recognize the serious import of such conditions. Whatever the school is able to do is gratefully accepted and duly credited. There is less acceptance of other conditions such as extreme mental retardation and mild forms of cerebral palsy. In the milder forms of mental retardation and in certain types of speech impairment conditions may be discounted by parents who vainly hope that better mental effort and concentration are all that are necessary.

Whatever the condition there will be little progress in satisfactory parental relationships unless they *accept* the condition in a realistic manner. Acceptance of extreme mental retardation is apparently the most difficult of all. The Association of Parents of Retarded Children on a national, state, and local basis has recognized *acceptance* as their principal problem. The opposite attitude makes for very poor relationships between parents and school with the former demanding actual school enrollment with results as good as for average children. The schools should always realize that when any child fails to come up to hopeful expectation parents are potentially threatened. One dissatisfied parent who "broadcasts" freely about school inefficiency may do untold damage which cannot be neutralized by the unheralded success of hundreds of others. Schools must always weigh parents' general attitudes and deal quietly in accordance with the status of such cases.

Parents of mentally accelerated pupils also need interpretation of their children. Many characteristics of gifted and mentally accelerated children were discussed in Chapter 14. A significant problem for parents is the independence and self-assurance of such children. They do not want to be babied and pampered from the days of early childhood and they wish to proceed about their own affairs without parental interference. Naturally, parents cannot give them complete freedom. However, the limits of such freedom should be interpreted on a much more liberal basis than for average children. What should be very friendly and satisfactory relationships between parent and child often deteriorate into unfortunate battles for control. Parents need interpretation along the same lines which teachers have found necessary for most effective relationships with these pupils in the classroom. The National Congress of Parents and Teachers with its local chapters in thousands of schools offers invaluable aid in closer relation between the home and the school.

## Cooperation with Physicians and Health Services

Many handicapped and exceptional children have been under special medical care since birth. Their physical or sensory impairments put specified limitations upon their activities both in school and at home. Careful records of medical recommendations should be thoroughly familiar to the school staffs and faithfully observed at all times. Unless medical recommendations generally conform to what the schools are able to practice, the pupil may have to be excused from school attendance.

The medical recommendation is oriented toward the physical welfare of the individual pupil. While the school respects this orientation it has an obligation for educational progress within reasonable limits. Frequent personal conferences between school and medical personnel are necessary to keep a good balance and to promote mutual understanding. Parents may cause some misunderstanding by encouraging physicians to recommend that children be continued in school when the school personnel knows that it is not practical. Nevertheless the physician's recommendation may carry undue weight beyond what he has actually intended and hence conferences are necessary.

Parents and schools should realize that the physician is often a specialist and has been requested to consider only some particular type of disability. He may not have examined all areas, yet it is assumed that such examinations have been done. When he reports that conditions are satisfactory all parties may assume that everything is in good order. Teachers would have a better appreciation of the physician's difficult position if they recall that it is almost impossible in their own profession to be expertly prepared and immediately ready to teach any and all subjects of the school curriculum from kindergarten through high school. The medical profession has as many specializations as teaching and hence the situation is similar to that of the teaching profession.

The teacher's opinion of physical conditions is usually regarded highly by the medical specialist since her period of continued observation is much longer than he is usually able to give. The eye specialist appreciates what she observes about continued eye strain, or the hearing specialist is helped by knowing how much and under what conditions the hard-of-hearing pupil is able to hear. The psychiatrist does not often see a pupil in a state of deviant behavior or of personality impairments performing in the same way in the quiet of his office. Hence he should evaluate what the teacher reports as well as his own observations.

Among all groups outside of teachers the physicians get more information about schools from pupils and their parents. These observations are too often colored by the biased evaluations of the pupils by themselves and as interpreted by parents in remote control. It is unfortunate if physicians become unduly influenced in their judgments about education because they should be one of the most influential groups in behalf of education. The teaching profession should be aware of such dangers and cooperate closely in a bona fide interpretation of education.

### Cooperation in General Welfare

Modern society has developed a great number of specialized services for children and their families under the classification of general welfare. The schools should take advantage of these opportunities to improve the conditions of families so that pupils may be happy and well adjusted outside of school.

*Family services.* It would be highly unrealistic for schools to assume that family conditions are generally ideal for all of their pupils. Unfortunately such is not the case. Domestic discord, alcoholism, separation, unemployment, extended illness, and many other factors disrupt normal home life. There are agencies which deal with these problems, although too often they are not brought in for the service. Families do not always continue with it once they have started. The schools can perform an important supporting or cooperating function by urging parents to utilize the help which is available. The school's reasons for continuing service are the predicaments in which they see their pupils, with their worries, with their unhappy state of mind, and their inability to concentrate on school studies. It has been noted in earlier chapters that girls of all ages suffer more than boys from many unfavorable conditions since they are closer to it. Although they may tolerate these troubles by silence at school when they are young, many of them become highly disorganized in adolescence. In many localities family social services serve all religious groups, but there are also available Catholic, Lutheran, and Jewish agencies which parents may prefer to patronize.

*Child placement.* There are literally thousands of children who are denied the right of a regular home of their own. Parents are separated, deserted, or dead. Unless close relatives take care of them, they become wards of the state assigned to child-care and to placement agencies. Many handicapped children have this additional burden. Although adoptive practices are well planned, and boarding homes are under licensing with inspection regulations the schools should take special interest in the general welfare of such children. The children's aid societies should be adequately staffed and trained to keep in close touch with their wards which should include frequent school conferences. The pupils themselves do not want to be objects of too great pity or sympathy. Some of them develop remarkable strengths of character from the rigors of their experience.

*Court contacts.* Many older pupils have a different side of their life than the orderly routines of school. In their community activities their various acts of violence have brought them into the hands of the police. They have been in court, placed on probation, or have served time in detention homes or in various types of reform schools. Probation officers usually call for periodic reports about their school adjustment which is easier to evaluate than their out-of-school behavior. These contacts should be private enough in nature that the pupil is not embarrassed nor his problem widely advertised to his classmates.

### Recreation Programs

Life outside of school has its pleasant aspects and among them are many types of recreational programs. They offer in an organized way opportunities for children who otherwise would find much idle time on their hands. Schools should cooperate as completely as possible with these facilities although not all of them are able to accommodate handicapped children.

*Group recreational projects.* There are private and public recreational centers in most of the larger cities. They may be operated by departments of recreation, by churches, and by such agencies as the Y.M.C.A. As a member of the First Kiwanis Club, located in Detroit, the author is concerned with the cooperation of the schools in the selection of children transported at Kiwanis expense after school to facilities in the downtown Y.M.C.A. building as well as with financing the activities. In addition to regular recreational staff members students from Wayne State Unversity provide volunteer service in completing a one-hundred-hour requirement for each in such activities, in order to qualify for admission as students in the college of education. This project is typical of hundreds to be found in some form, financed, and given cooperative support by many types of civic organizations. Schools enjoy opportunities for close cooperation and integration of efforts with these community projects.

*Scouting.* The Boy Scout movement is a twentieth century development which has its female counter part in Girl Scouts and Camp Fire Girls. The emphasis is upon character and dependability as well as the orderly activities prescribed in the various manuals and activities. Many teachers are scout leaders and were scouts themselves. Various civic leaders sponsor scouting and meetings are held in school buildings, recreation centers, and churches. The Cub Scout units start with the younger boys and eventually a few older boys advance through all stages to become Explorer Scouts. Such character building activities supplement whatever efforts schools are able to make in these important areas of human development.

*Summer Camps.* Many of the agencies noted above provide summer camp programs either free or on a limited cost basis. In many instances the summer camp provides the first opportunity for children to spend time away from parents and to enjoy the pleasures of outdoor activities close to nature. More camps for handicapped children are being provided. Schools are asked to nominate candidates for various types of camps and the beneficial effects of camping are reflected throughout the school year. The great majority of summer camps are manned by school teachers or by college students for whom summer employment is necessary and whose experiences in living close to the lives of children supplement their regular activities in most helpful ways.

## Vocational Rehabilitation

Teachers of handicapped children now enjoy sharing opportunities for participating with vocational rehabilitation programs. After World War I vocational rehabilitation for disabled veterans was established at the national level. It was soon expanded to include civilians and was organized by states to match federal funds. In the early days of the program, service was limited to the physically handicapped. Services were financed which would rehabilitate the handicapped individual so that he could become gainfully employed. These services took a great variety of forms.

In recent years service has been expanded to all types of handicaps and to pupils as early as twelve or thirteen years of age in the belief that vocational preparation must be a long-time process started much before the day the pupil leaves school. These programs coordinate closely with hospitals in certain physical restorations, with such private agencies as the League for the Handicapped and the disabled employees of the Goodwill Industries. The rehabilitation staffs have close contacts with industries and businesses in seeking opportunities for job placements.

As their programs expand the services for handicapped children and for adolescents, the rehabilitation organizations are most helpful in assuring brighter futures for the handicapped. School personnel should become acquainted with the local staffs of rehabilitation services which have branches in larger cities and widely scattered field representatives. Teachers should also be alerted to utilization of this service by parents whose children inform the schools of parental handicaps.

### The Significance of Cooperation

The several types of cooperating agencies and services listed above do not by any means exhaust all that are available. Many of them provide some outlets for the handicapped as well as for regular pupils. Full knowledge of such opportunities provides a rich field for cooperative activities between schools and the functional life of neighborhoods and communities. Schools cannot exist apart from the community, and the activities with handicapped children make such cooperation imperative and results pleasurable. In turn, the cooperating agencies take new and understanding interest in schools and what they are attempting to do for children.

### Questions and Topics for Discussion

1. Describe the extent of cooperation with nonschool agencies and programs in your school system.
2. What special medical services and nurses are provided for your school system?
3. How are the general recreation programs related to the schools? What are the advantages and disadvantages?
4. What rehabilitation services are available? What uses are made of them?
5. How active are the parent-teacher associations in your school system? What are their principal activities?

Note: Consult the reference material at the end of Chapter 32.

# CHAPTER 32

## Desirable Attitudes
## Toward the Exceptional

IN THIS FINAL CHAPTER there is little need for summarizing what has already been said about each type of exceptional child. It is more fitting to turn attention to the attitudes which should be developed upon the part of those who deal intimately with such children. These include the school administrator, the regular and the special teacher, the children, and finally the general public whose children are the subject of study.

### The School Administration

Adequate educational programs for exceptional children are the responsibility of the school administration. The chief responsibility in this area lies with the superintendent. Under his general policies, determined by boards of education from facts and recommendations presented to them by the superintendent, it is his duty to administer the program of special education along with his other administrative problems. The success of the program is dependent mainly upon his enthusiasm, interest, and sponsorship. If he has the sympathetic support of the community and the board of education, the program will overcome many obstacles and be a success.

In large school systems the details of the program are delegated by him to administrative aids, to principals of buildings, and to supervisors of the various fields. His personal interest and enthusiasm must continue to function through these channels or there will not be the complete success which should otherwise be realized. In employing or promoting administrative staffs, school systems should carefully choose candidates who have had training or experience with exceptional children. Unless some firsthand experience or training has been gained, the program of special education offers enough problems so that there is a temptation to neglect this field in favor of more familiar territory. It should be remembered that the more time and effort that is put into a project, the more is likely to result from it, and special education is no exception.

## The Special Supervisor

The special supervisor or administrator of classes for the exceptional has a very important role. His duties include not only the administration of the program but many phases which are closely related to other fields. It is necessary to keep abreast of texts and subject-matter presentations in all fields of instruction and adapt them to use in special types. For example, the acquisition of instructional material for Braille classes is a constant challenge. Likewise all of the special equipment and apparatus become his responsibility.

Suitable health programs as outlined by competent medical authorities are to be integrated into the school program and into the all-year program for children both in- and out-of-school hours. Arrangements for transporting handicapped children to central buildings, lunches for them, and problems of finance and special state aid are included among their duties. In large cities these duties involve full-time work and include the nomination and selection of teachers, offering courses in special education in teacher-training centers, and many similar projects.

## The Special Teacher

The special teacher is an important key person in the program of special education. She should be well trained and familiar with her own particular field and the other types of exceptional children as well. It is assumed that all of the highly desirable attributes of good teachers should be highly exemplified in her attitudes toward her particular assignment. She must be proud of her class and impart a feeling of its importance to the regular teachers. If she lives in an apologetic frame of mind with regard to her work and her class, her fellow teachers in the same building or among her acquaintances are likely to despise both her and her class.

There should be a free and easy transition of exceptional children from the regular grades to the special classes, and vice versa. In most types of special classes there is opportunity for children to mingle with those in regular grades for certain subjects and activities. Unless the relationships between the special teacher and the regular teachers are most cordial and satisfactory, this kind of program will not function properly.

The special-class teacher must have unusual patience and understanding of children. As noted many times, most exceptional children have a combination of defects and often they have been subjected to ridicule by a world which is harsh and in which competition is ruthless. It requires an unusual amount of enthusiasm and encouragement to neutralize these negative influences and to build a positive psychology for such children.

The problems of the special teacher are influenced by the attitudes of the school administration and the general attitudes which have been developed by tradition in the community. If one or more teachers who previously held these positions have been unsuccessful or have engendered undesirable attitudes, the task of the new teacher is doubly difficult. When the teacher is a pioneer in her community or school in the establishment of a special class she has many problems to face and the success or failure of special education in that school lies with her for many years after her initial years. Any special teacher who operates alone in a building in which there are many regular teachers encounters more problems than if she were one of a staff of several in a special school, such as a centralized school for crippled children. The teacher who prepares for the teaching of exceptional children must expect to face many of these problems and to take them in stride.

### The Regular Teacher

As noted in the preceding chapter, all teachers should have at least one introductory course in exceptional children in order to recognize potential cases among her pupils and to have a sympathetic understanding of the program of special education. Much of the success or failure of the special program centers around the attitudes which regular teachers assume toward the exceptional. It is important that teachers appreciate the fact that special education offers opportunities for exceptional children which cannot be realized as completely in the regular grades. If children and parents may be prepared in advance to feel that the special class is an opportunity, the actual transfer into such a class upon the recommendation of the authorized diagnostic agency will be greatly facilitated.

It may be difficult for teachers to realize that children have failed in regular classes because of some handicap of which the regular teacher may have not been aware. Such results are more likely in the case of comparatively mild defects and also in case of mental, neurological, and related causes whose exterior symptoms are not so obvious as poor vision or an orthopedic condition. Children who show behavior symptoms because school work is difficult for them due to subtle eye strain or slightly impaired hearing, are not always viewed with the patience and understanding which are expected in case of nonbehavior problems. However, the special classes or programs for them are just as opportune as any other type of case. In any event threats of special class transfers as a means of punishment are among the most undesirable practices and, fortunately, are limited to a very small minority of teachers. Whenever a teacher is fortunate enough to have a system of special classes available for her candidates, she should realize that her own success is increased if the potential failures have been removed from her group. The attitude of the regular teacher is highly important to the success of special education.

### The Exceptional Child

The exceptional child himself offers problems which have been the central theme throughout this book. He is not only a child with a speech defect or with a cardiac condition, but he is the product of many problems which result from his handicap. He not only has to overcome his speech defect but also must overcome the ridicule and ostracism which may have been his lot because of that defect. If he is a behavior case, he must not only seek to overcome his present behavior trends but also live an exemplary life for a long time so that the finger of suspicion will no longer be pointed at him.

If his defects are very severe, such as total deafness, blindness, or orthopedic disability, he must learn to face a stern reality. In the face of such an outlook he must try to master an education suited to his handicap and seek to become a self-supporting citizen. Mere idle words about his problems as outlined here are nothing as compared to the realities which lie ahead for him.

The proof of success lies in the records of thousands who have benefited by special education and who in adult occupations and in the course of living have met the test. It is sometimes a matter of speculation what changes would occur in the world of today if the non-handicapped as a group had put as much time and effort accordingly into their education and vocation as the exceptional have been forced to do.

### The Public's Attitude

Finally, the attitude of the public is most important if there is to be an adequate program of special education in every community, large or small, rich or poor. This attitude covers a great many kinds of people and affects the handicapped children in many ways. A few of these will be noted.

The parents of exceptional children often need to be educated to the importance of the program for their own children. In the days when they themselves were in school there were few provisions for exceptional children, and hence this is a new and unfamiliar experience to them. Instead of recognizing the program of special education as an opportunity, they occasionally resist and believe that their children have been selected for special punishment because of school failure and antisocial behavior. The great majority of them accept the special program in the spirit in which it is intended. Any school system which maintains a program of special education has a minimum number of such problems. As the benefits of all types of special classes become evident objections gradually disappear.

The citizen who has no children in special education or no children at all must be helped to realize the significance of such a program. He should accept the principle that all children are entitled to the best education of which they are capable. If some kind of education costs more than others, it should still be provided at public expense, and the additional cost, if pro rated among all children, does not perceptibly raise the average educational cost for all children. In many states this additional cost is assumed for some types of the exceptional by state subsidies so that the local communities do not feel it at all. America is the richest nation of the world and can afford to provide the best possible education for all children, including the exceptional.

In the past two or three decades the interest among the recently established service and luncheon clubs in the interests of exceptional children has been a most hopeful sign. In many instances the projects by these groups have been directed toward the physical health and general social welfare of exceptional children with the assumption that their educational programs are already adequate. In view of the fact that not more than 10 per cent of the exceptional have special educational provisions the moral support and persuasion of these influential adults for local and state educational support would be welcome also.

The parent-teacher associations and similar groups have also been influential in bringing organized support to the program of education for all children. The movement toward more universal education and better education for all has focused attention upon the needs of the exceptional as well. Living in the present-day world is a complicated task and educational requirements are being raised higher and higher each year. Service in the armed forces makes much greater requirements of the average soldier than was formerly true since warfare has become one of the most highly technical projects of history.

## The Outlook

In this book an attempt has been made to introduce and outline a few of the main problems of exceptional children. It is obvious that there have been many pioneers and champions of their cause. These founders have struggled not only with the defects themselves but with methods of education which needed to be adjusted to the particular defects. Many organizations have been founded—local, national, and international—to aid the program for furtherance of the exceptional and most of them have achieved their primary goals.

It is time to consolidate efforts for all types of exceptional children. Support for the crippled is a worthy cause, but it is no more worthy than for the child with a reading disability, with a feeble mind, or with an emotional problem. All efforts must be directed toward unification of a program for all of the exceptional, no matter what their afflictions may be. There is progress when one city has provided for one type of handicapped children and a second city for a second type. The program has passed through its most difficult stages; effort must always be maintained if the maximum is to be realized for exceptional children.

In the introductory chapter four aims of education were listed as self-realization, human relationships, economic efficiency, and civic responsibility. These aims are as worthy for exceptional children as for normal, average children. For both groups it is not a question of worthiness but of an effective program to realize these aims. Self-realization cannot be achieved for the exceptional unless defects are remedied and educational programs suitable to their abilities are made available. Human relationships for the exceptional do not work out satisfactorily unless they are understood at home, in school, and in the community. Many investigations have been cited with regard to deviations of character and personality, particularly in cases where no special educational programs have been offered. The improvement of human relationships is very imperative for exceptional children.

The aims of economic efficiency and civic responsibility likewise will not be realized unless optimum programs both educationally and vocationally are available. Wherever such programs have been established, the exceptional have shown surprisingly good results in attaining these two important goals. The test of any set of aims and objectives does not lie in how well they are formulated but how well they are put into effect. Such is the challenge of exceptional children.

## Questions and Topics for Discussion

1. What does your own community do for its exceptional children? What should you do about it?
2. What is the attitude of the school administration and the teaching staff toward these children?
3. What factors are favorable to further progress in special education? What factors are unfavorable?

## A. Organizations

1. National Congress of Parents and Teachers, 700 N. Rush St. Chicago 11.
2. Parents' Institute, Bergenfield, N.J.

Note: See also educational organizations at end of Chapter 1.

## B. Periodicals

1. *National Parent-Teacher* (monthly), National Congress of Parents and Teachers, Chicago.
2. *Parents' and Family Home Guide Magazine,* Parents' Institute, Bergenfield, N.J.

Note: See also educational periodicals at the end of Chapter 1.

## C. Books

1. Anderson, V., and D.R. Davies, *Patterns of Educational Leadership,* Prentice-Hall, Inc., Englewood Cliffs, N.J., 1956, 248 pp.
2. Brownell, C.L., L. Gans, and T.Z. Maroon, *Public Relations in Education,* McGraw-Hill Book Co., Inc., New York, 1955, 249 pp.
3. Bruce, W., and A.J. Holden, *The Teacher's Personal Development,* Henry Holt and Co., Inc., New York, 1957, 346 pp.
4. Fine, B., *Educational Publicity* (rev. ed.), Harper & Brothers, New York, 1951, 561 pp.

5. Grinell, J.E., and R.J. Young, *The School and the Community*, Ronald Press Co., New York, 1955, 444 pp.

6. Griswold, G., and D. Griswold (eds.), *Your Public Relations*, Funk and Wagnalls Co., New York, 1948, 634 pp.

7. Harlow, R.F., and M.M. Black, *Practical Public Relations*, Harper & Brothers, New York, 1947, 442 pp.

8. Kindred, L.W., *School Public Relations*, Prentice-Hall, Inc., Englewood Cliffs, N.J., 1957, 454 pp.

9. Lundborg, L.B., *Public Relations in the Local Community*, Harper & Brothers, New York, 1950, 228 pp.

10. Olsen, E.G., *School and Community Problems*, Prentice-Hall, Inc., Englewood Cliffs, N.J., 1949, 510 pp.

11. Reeder, W.G., *An Introduction to Public-School Relations* (rev. ed.), The Macmillan Co., New York, 1953, 284 pp.

12. Yauch, W.A., *How Good is Your School?* Harper & Brothers, New York, 1951, 213 pp.

13. Yeager, W.A., *School-Community Relations*, The Dryden Press, New York, 1951, 464 pp.

## D. Films and Filmstrips

1. *American Teacher*, 15 minutes. Discusses responsibility of a citizen for the quality of the education in his community. McGraw-Hill Text-Film Department.

2. *Design of American Public Education*, 16 minutes. Responsible citizens in a democratic society. McGraw-Hill Text-Film Department.

3. *Lessons in Living*, 20 minutes, sound. Revitalization of a community through a school improvement project. National Film Board of Canada.

4. *Planning for Personal and Professional Growth*, 18 minutes. Four teacher cases show importance of planning. McGraw-Hill Text-Film Department.

5. *Practicing Democracy in the Classroom*, 20 minutes, sound. Democratic methods compared with laissez-faire and authoritarian procedures. Encyclopedia Britannica Films.

6. *Preparation of Teachers*, 20 minutes, sound. Experiences of two student teachers in trying to understand children's behavior. United World Films, New York.

7. *Role-Playing in Human Relations*, 25 minutes, sound. Technique for training leaders. National Training Laboratory in Group Development.

8. *School and the Community*, 14 minutes, sound. School and com-

munity working together to produce an educational process geared to learners' needs. McGraw-Hill Text-Film Department.

9. *School: The Child's Community*, 16 minutes, sound. Pupil participation in the "community" activities of an elementary school develops personal responsibility. Wayne State University, Detroit.

10. *Social Class in America*, 16 minutes. Contrasts three boys from lower, middle, and upper social classes and beginning of increasingly different lives. McGraw-Hill Text-Film Department.

11. *Who Will Teach Your Child?* 24 minutes. How to attract better teachers. McGraw-Hill Text-Film Department.

# Appendix

In CHAPTER 14 reference was made to an Appendix in which the details of a plan for the selection of major-work pupils was to be presented. In the Detroit experiment in 1939 all pupils in four elementary schools were rated by this plan and the ratings proved valuable in a better understanding of all children.

## General Direction

A 3 x 5-inch card was made for each pupil with ten headings as follows:

Name _____ Grade _____

|  | Value |
|---|---|
| I. General behavior | _____ |
| II. Effort as related to ability | _____ |
| III. Rating for group intelligence | _____ |
| IV. Rating for age, birthday____age____ | _____ |
| V. Rating for height, height____age____ratio____ | _____ |
| VI. Rating for weight, weight____age____ratio____ | _____ |
| VII. Reading comprehension, grade level____ | _____ |
| VIII. Latest scholarship, E____S____U____Total____ | _____ |
| IX. Number of permanent teeth, number____age____ratio____ | _____ |
| X. Rating for special activities | _____ |
| Total | _____ |

The detailed information is given below.

## I. General Behavior

Have the teacher rate each pupil on general behavior. Use five ratings as follows:

| Rating | Value | Suggested Per Cent |
|---|---|---|
| Excellent | 5 | 10 |
| Good | 4 | 15 |
| Average | 3 | 50 |
| Poor | 2 | 15 |
| Very Poor | 1 | 10 |

The following suggestions are offered in evaluating behavior:

| Value | Description |
|---|---|
| 5 | Very model behavior, composed, has self-respect, commands respect, considered a worthy leader in school citizenship. |
| 4 | Above average, usually quite stable, may have one minor defect, such as unable to control giggling. |
| 3 | Average behavior, minor mischief at occasional times, attitudes only fair. |
| 2 | Either shy, timid, retiring, weeps readily, nervous or apt to join those with poor behavior, suggestible, will play for attention, even with poor behavior. |
| 1 | Chronic troublemaker, not accepted by the class, has one or two friends of very doubtful behavior. |

The suggested per cent is very optional; a teacher might have no "very poor." It is recommended to select first the excellent, second the good, third the very poor, fourth the poor, fifth the average.

After the ratings have been completed, have the teacher enter the score values, such as 5, or 4, and so on, after item I for general behavior.

## II. Effort as Related to Ability

Rate each pupil on effort as related to ability.

Use the same terminology and plan as for rating for general behavior. See suggestions below.

Enter these score values, 5, or 4, and so on, after item II.

### Suggested Scale Values

5—Has a fine attitude toward study, works up to capacity, generally good in all subjects.

4—Means to do well and generally above average, inclined to rely upon great effort and long hours, rather than general resourcefulness.

3—Average effort, some pupils are variable as to school subjects, tries hard in some, poor in others.

2—Average pupil does fair for grade, but not very good when compared to pupils of same age.

1—Inattentive, discouraged, expects teacher and others to help him. Merely idles time away.

### III. Rating for Group Intelligence

Have the latest group mental ratings translated into the following values:

| Rating | Value |
|--------|-------|
| A | 5 |
| B | 4 |
| C+, C, C− | 3 |
| D | 2 |
| E | 1 |

Enter these values on line III.

## Recording Age, Height, and Weight

From permanent record enter the *month* and *year* of birth, such as 10-28, on the blanks on line IV just after "age." On line V record the latest height, and on line VI the latest weight.

## IV. Rating for Age

Convert the month and year of birth from line IV into age in years and month from Table XIII, such as 10-11, on line IV, just *after* the birth date.

At this point, put all the records of any half-grade, such as 3B, from different sections or rooms together.

Sort all the papers of any half-grade into piles according to the age in years and months. Sort first by years and then by months within each year. Arrange in order from *youngest* to *oldest* for all pupils in a half-grade.

Arrange into five piles according to the following per cents:

| | Per cent | Rating |
|--|----------|--------|
| Youngest | 10 | 5 |
| Next youngest | 15 | 4 |
| Middle | 50 | 3 |
| Next oldest | 15 | 2 |
| Oldest | 10 | 1 |

In Table XIV the number of cases is shown which should fall into the various percentage groups. For example, if 40 cases are in a group, 4 is 10 per cent, 6 is 15 per cent, 20 is 50 per cent, and so on.

After the youngest 10 per cent of the entire half-grade has been determined, put a rating of "5" on their records on line number IV. In like manner rate the next 15 per cent "4" and record the 4's. Complete the next 50 per cent with ratings of "3," the next 15 per cent with 2's and the oldest 10 per cent with 1's.

## V and VI. Rating for Height and Weight

At this point separate the records of boys and girls. Take the boys' records and use Tables XV and XVI. Convert the height on line V from the body of Table XV by reading height years at the top and months at the left, and record it on line number V immediately to the right of the height. (See explanation at top of Table XV.)

Consult Table XVI for weight in like manner and record on line VI. Be sure to use correct table, column, and line.

In like manner compute the age, height, and weight for girls, using Tables XVII and XVIII.

These ages for height and weight must next be interpreted with respect to each pupil's life age or chronological age as recorded on line number IV.

Use the Inglis' I.Q. book to compute the height and weight ratios by reading the chronological age at the left, while the mental age at the top should be read, first as height age, and then as weight age. Record these ratios, such as a chronological age of 10-0 and a height age of 11-0, as a ratio number of 110 after "ratio" at the right end of line number V. For weight, record the similar ratio at the right end of line number VI.

Reassemble the boys' and girls' records together, then arrange them in order from highest to lowest height ratio from line number V. Divide them into five groups as follows:

|  | Per cent | Rating |
|---|---|---|
| Largest ratios | 10 | 5 |
| Next largest ratios | 15 | 4 |
| Middle ratios | 50 | 3 |
| Next smallest ratios | 15 | 2 |
| Smallest ratios | 10 | 1 |

Record the ratings 5, 4, and so on, at the end of line number V.

In like manner, rank all the pupils in order of weight ratio from highest to lowest as per line number VI, determine the ratings 5, 4, and so on, and record on line number VI.

## VII. Reading Comprehension

After "grade level" on line VII record the latest grade level of reading comprehension, such as 5B. Arrange the pupils in order of grade levels from highest to lowest. Rate as follows:

|  | Per cent | Rating |
|---|---|---|
| Highest | 10 | 5 |
| Next highest | 15 | 4 |
| Middle | 50 | 3 |
| Next lowest | 15 | 2 |
| Lowest | 10 | 1 |

Record the ratings on line VII.

## VIII. *Latest Scholarship*

On line VIII record the last scholarship marks. Record as follows: 2 E's, 6 S's, 1 U, and compute the scholarship rating. Multiply the number of E's by 3, the S's by 2, and the U's by 1; add the products and record the sum after "total" on line VIII.

Arrange the pupils' records from highest to lowest in terms of scholarship total, using the 10 per cent largest number as 5, the next 15 per cent as 4 as in earlier sections, record the 5's, 4's on line VIII.

## IX. *Number of Permanent Teeth*

Record the number of permanent teeth on line IX.

Consult Table XIX for dental ages and record in years and months. Either sort separately for boys and girls or exercise great care in using the proper columns from Table XIX.

Use the I.Q. book and proceed as in getting height or weight ratios. Record these ratios on line number IX. Rank them from highest to lowest, divide into the 5 per cent, group with 5's for the highest 10 per cent, and so on. Record these ratings on line IX.

## X. *Rating for Special Activities*

Give a rating for special activities, both from school and home as leader in community activities as per the following suggestions. Use your best judgment in placing pupils who engage in special activities not specifically mentioned below. Rate as 5, 4, etc., on line X.

### *Suggestions for Rating*

5—The Safety Patrol captain, or a leading role in school plays, and one or more others such as unusual in auditorium, member of Safety Patrol.

4—Runner-up to captain, also outstanding in one or more other special activities, unusual in art, writing.

3—In two or more special activities, and considered above average in at least one of them.

2—In one special activity, such as orchestra, special music lesson, Safety Patrol.

1—Not unusual in any fields nor participating in any.

These descriptions apply more specifically to upper grade pupils, but if teachers of lower grades study the general plan noted above, they should be able to make a plan or rating which is similar.

### Final Selection

Total the ratings on lines I through X, or on as many lines as are filled out for each pupil. Try to have the same number of lines filled out on all the pupils of a given half-grade.

After the totals have been completed, rank the pupils within each half-grade from highest to lowest in total. Select the highest 5 per cent as being the most gifted within any half-grade as follows:

|  | *Select* |
|---|---|
| Groups of 29 or less | 1 |
| Groups from 30 to 49 | 2 |
| Groups from 50 to 69 | 3 |
| Groups from 70 to 89 | 4 |
| Groups from 90 to 109 | 5 |

Use your judgment about including one more in the smaller groups and two or three more in the larger enrollments, taking the next ones on the total score.

TABLE XIII

## CHRONOLOGICAL AGES AS OF SEPTEMBER, 1939

(For a birth date of 10–28 read down the 1928 column to the tenth month; the age at the intersection is 10–11).

| Month of Birth | 1921 | 1922 | 1923 | 1924 | 1925 | 1926 | 1927 | 1928 | 1929 | 1930 | 1931 | 1932 | 1933 | 1934 | 1935 |
|---|---|---|---|---|---|---|---|---|---|---|---|---|---|---|---|
| 1 | 18-8 | 17-8 | 16-8 | 15-8 | 14-8 | 13-8 | 12-8 | 11-8 | 10-8 | 9-8 | 8-8 | 7-8 | 6-8 | 5-8 | 4-8 |
| 2 | 18-7 | 17-7 | 16-7 | 15-7 | 14-7 | 13-7 | 12-7 | 11-7 | 10-7 | 9-7 | 8-7 | 7-7 | 6-7 | 5-7 | 4-7 |
| 3 | 18-6 | 17-6 | 16-6 | 15-6 | 14-6 | 13-6 | 12-6 | 11-6 | 10-6 | 9-6 | 8-6 | 7-6 | 6-6 | 5-6 | 4-6 |
| 4 | 18-5 | 17-5 | 16-5 | 15-5 | 14-5 | 13-5 | 12-5 | 11-5 | 10-5 | 9-5 | 8-5 | 7-5 | 6-5 | 5-5 | 4-5 |
| 5 | 18-4 | 17-4 | 16-4 | 15-4 | 14-4 | 13-4 | 12-4 | 11-4 | 10-4 | 9-4 | 8-4 | 7-4 | 6-4 | 5-4 | 4-4 |
| 6 | 18-3 | 17-3 | 16-3 | 15-3 | 14-3 | 13-3 | 12-3 | 11-3 | 10-3 | 9-3 | 8-3 | 7-3 | 6-3 | 5-3 | 4-3 |
| 7 | 18-2 | 17-2 | 16-2 | 15-2 | 14-2 | 13-2 | 12-2 | 11-2 | 10-2 | 9-2 | 8-2 | 7-2 | 6-2 | 5-2 | 4-2 |
| 8 | 18-1 | 17-1 | 16-1 | 15-1 | 14-1 | 13-1 | 12-1 | 11-1 | 10-1 | 9-1 | 8-1 | 7-1 | 6-1 | 5-1 | 4-1 |
| 9 | 18-0 | 17-0 | 16-0 | 15-0 | 14-0 | 13-0 | 12-0 | 11-0 | 10-0 | 9-0 | 8-0 | 7-0 | 6-0 | 5-0 | 4-0 |
| 10 | 17-11 | 16-11 | 15-11 | 14-11 | 13-11 | 12-11 | 11-11 | 10-11 | 9-11 | 8-11 | 7-11 | 6-11 | 5-11 | 4-11 | 3-11 |
| 11 | 17-10 | 16-10 | 15-10 | 14-10 | 13-10 | 12-10 | 11-10 | 10-10 | 9-10 | 8-10 | 7-10 | 6-10 | 5-10 | 4-10 | 3-10 |
| 12 | 17-9 | 16-9 | 15-9 | 14-9 | 13-9 | 12-9 | 11-9 | 10-9 | 9-9 | 8-9 | 7-9 | 6-9 | 5-9 | 4-9 | 3-9 |

TABLE XIV

## NUMBERS FOR PER CENTS AT VARIOUS TOTAL NUMBERS

| No. Cases | 10% | 15% | 50% | 15% | 10% | No. Cases | 10% | 15% | 50% | 15% | 10% |
|---|---|---|---|---|---|---|---|---|---|---|---|
| 11 | 1 | 2 | 5 | 2 | 1 | 56 | 5 | 8 | 28 | 9 | 6 |
| 12 | 1 | 2 | 6 | 2 | 1 | 57 | 6 | 8 | 28 | 9 | 6 |
| 13 | 1 | 2 | 7 | 2 | 1 | 58 | 6 | 9 | 29 | 9 | 6 |
| 14 | 1 | 2 | 7 | 3 | 1 | 59 | 6 | 9 | 29 | 9 | 6 |
| 15 | 2 | 2 | 7 | 3 | 1 | 60 | 6 | 9 | 30 | 9 | 6 |
| 16 | 2 | 2 | 8 | 3 | 1 | 61 | 6 | 9 | 30 | 10 | 6 |
| 17 | 2 | 2 | 8 | 3 | 2 | 62 | 6 | 9 | 31 | 10 | 6 |
| 18 | 2 | 2 | 9 | 3 | 2 | 63 | 6 | 9 | 31 | 10 | 7 |
| 19 | 2 | 3 | 9 | 3 | 2 | 64 | 6 | 9 | 32 | 10 | 7 |
| 20 | 2 | 3 | 10 | 3 | 2 | 65 | 6 | 10 | 32 | 10 | 7 |
| 21 | 2 | 3 | 10 | 4 | 2 | 66 | 6 | 10 | 33 | 10 | 7 |
| 22 | 2 | 3 | 11 | 4 | 2 | 67 | 7 | 10 | 33 | 10 | 7 |
| 23 | 2 | 4 | 11 | 4 | 2 | 68 | 7 | 10 | 34 | 10 | 7 |
| 24 | 2 | 4 | 12 | 4 | 2 | 69 | 7 | 10 | 34 | 11 | 7 |
| 25 | 2 | 4 | 12 | 4 | 3 | 70 | 7 | 10 | 35 | 11 | 7 |
| 26 | 2 | 4 | 13 | 4 | 3 | 71 | 7 | 11 | 35 | 11 | 7 |
| 27 | 3 | 4 | 13 | 4 | 3 | 72 | 7 | 11 | 36 | 11 | 7 |
| 28 | 3 | 4 | 14 | 4 | 3 | 73 | 7 | 11 | 36 | 12 | 7 |
| 29 | 3 | 4 | 14 | 5 | 3 | 74 | 7 | 11 | 37 | 12 | 7 |
| 30 | 3 | 4 | 15 | 5 | 3 | 75 | 7 | 11 | 37 | 12 | 8 |
| 31 | 3 | 5 | 15 | 5 | 3 | 76 | 7 | 11 | 38 | 12 | 8 |
| 32 | 3 | 5 | 16 | 5 | 3 | 77 | 8 | 11 | 38 | 12 | 8 |
| 33 | 3 | 5 | 16 | 5 | 4 | 78 | 8 | 11 | 39 | 12 | 8 |
| 34 | 3 | 5 | 17 | 5 | 4 | 79 | 8 | 12 | 39 | 12 | 8 |
| 35 | 4 | 5 | 17 | 5 | 4 | 80 | 8 | 12 | 40 | 12 | 8 |
| 36 | 4 | 5 | 18 | 5 | 4 | 81 | 8 | 12 | 40 | 13 | 8 |
| 37 | 4 | 5 | 18 | 6 | 4 | 82 | 8 | 12 | 41 | 13 | 8 |
| 38 | 4 | 5 | 19 | 6 | 4 | 83 | 8 | 12 | 41 | 13 | 9 |
| 39 | 4 | 6 | 19 | 6 | 4 | 84 | 8 | 12 | 42 | 13 | 9 |
| 40 | 4 | 6 | 20 | 6 | 4 | 85 | 8 | 13 | 42 | 13 | 9 |
| 41 | 4 | 6 | 20 | 7 | 4 | 86 | 8 | 13 | 43 | 13 | 9 |
| 42 | 4 | 6 | 21 | 7 | 4 | 87 | 9 | 13 | 43 | 13 | 9 |
| 43 | 4 | 6 | 21 | 7 | 5 | 88 | 9 | 13 | 44 | 13 | 9 |
| 44 | 4 | 6 | 22 | 7 | 5 | 89 | 9 | 13 | 44 | 14 | 9 |
| 45 | 5 | 6 | 22 | 7 | 5 | 90 | 9 | 13 | 45 | 14 | 9 |
| 46 | 5 | 7 | 23 | 7 | 5 | 91 | 9 | 14 | 45 | 14 | 9 |
| 47 | 5 | 7 | 23 | 7 | 5 | 92 | 9 | 14 | 46 | 14 | 9 |
| 48 | 5 | 7 | 24 | 7 | 5 | 93 | 9 | 14 | 46 | 14 | 10 |
| 49 | 5 | 7 | 24 | 8 | 5 | 94 | 9 | 14 | 47 | 14 | 10 |
| 50 | 5 | 7 | 25 | 8 | 5 | 95 | 10 | 14 | 47 | 14 | 10 |
| 51 | 5 | 8 | 25 | 8 | 5 | 96 | 10 | 14 | 48 | 14 | 10 |
| 52 | 5 | 8 | 26 | 8 | 5 | 97 | 10 | 14 | 48 | 15 | 10 |
| 53 | 5 | 8 | 26 | 8 | 6 | 98 | 10 | 14 | 49 | 15 | 10 |
| 54 | 5 | 8 | 27 | 8 | 6 | 99 | 10 | 15 | 49 | 15 | 10 |
| 55 | 5 | 8 | 27 | 9 | 6 | 100 | 10 | 15 | 50 | 15 | 10 |

## TABLE XV

### HEIGHT AGES FOR BOYS
### (After Olson)

(If a boy is 40.5 inches tall, his height of 40.5 is found in the body of the table; years at the top and months at the side; the age if 4 years 5 months, written 4–5.)

| Months | Years | | | | | | | | | | | | | | |
|---|---|---|---|---|---|---|---|---|---|---|---|---|---|---|---|
| | 2 | 3 | 4 | 5 | 6 | 7 | 8 | 9 | 10 | 11 | 12 | 13 | 14 | 15 | 16 |
| 0 | 33.8 | 36.9 | 39.3 | 42.0 | 45.4 | 47.9 | 49.7 | 51.3 | 53.5 | 55.2 | 57.0 | 59.6 | 61.9 | 64.3 | 66.8 |
| 1 | 34.1 | 37.2 | 39.5 | 42.1 | 45.6 | 48.0 | 49.8 | 51.4 | 53.6 | 55.3 | 57.2 | 59.8 | 62.1 | 64.5 | 66.9 |
| 2 | 34.4 | 37.4 | 39.8 | 42.1 | 45.8 | 48.2 | 49.9 | 51.6 | 53.8 | 55.4 | 57.4 | 60.0 | 62.3 | 64.7 | 67.0 |
| 3 | 34.6 | 37.6 | 40.1 | 42.2 | 46.0 | 48.3 | 50.1 | 51.8 | 53.9 | 55.6 | 57.6 | 60.1 | 62.5 | 64.9 | 67.1 |
| 4 | 34.8 | 37.9 | 40.3 | 42.6 | 46.2 | 48.5 | 50.2 | 52.0 | 54.1 | 55.7 | 57.8 | 60.3 | 62.7 | 65.1 | 67.2 |
| 5 | 35.0 | 38.2 | 40.5 | 43.0 | 46.4 | 48.6 | 50.3 | 52.2 | 54.2 | 55.9 | 58.0 | 60.5 | 62.9 | 65.3 | 67.3 |
| 6 | 35.2 | 38.4 | 40.7 | 43.3 | 46.6 | 48.8 | 50.5 | 52.4 | 54.3 | 56.1 | 58.3 | 60.7 | 63.1 | 65.5 | 67.4 |
| 7 | 35.5 | 38.6 | 41.0 | 43.5 | 46.8 | 48.9 | 50.6 | 52.6 | 54.4 | 56.3 | 58.5 | 60.9 | 63.5 | 65.7 | 67.5 |
| 8 | 35.9 | 38.9 | 41.3 | 43.7 | 47.0 | 49.1 | 50.7 | 52.8 | 54.5 | 56.4 | 58.7 | 61.1 | 63.7 | 65.9 | 67.6 |
| 9 | 36.2 | 39.1 | 41.6 | 44.0 | 47.2 | 49.2 | 50.9 | 52.9 | 54.7 | 56.5 | 58.9 | 61.3 | 63.9 | 66.1 | 67.7 |
| 10 | 36.4 | 39.2 | 41.7 | 44.5 | 47.4 | 49.4 | 51.0 | 53.1 | 54.8 | 56.6 | 59.2 | 61.5 | 64.1 | 66.3 | 67.8 |
| 11 | 36.6 | 39.2 | 41.8 | 45.0 | 47.6 | 49.5 | 51.2 | 53.3 | 55.0 | 56.8 | 59.4 | 61.7 | 64.2 | 66.5 | 67.9 |

## TABLE XVI

### WEIGHT AGE FOR BOYS
### (After Olson)

| Months | Years | | | | | | | | | | | | | | |
|---|---|---|---|---|---|---|---|---|---|---|---|---|---|---|---|
| | 2 | 3 | 4 | 5 | 6 | 7 | 8 | 9 | 10 | 11 | 12 | 13 | 14 | 15 | 16 |
| 0 | 26.3 | 30.8 | 34.9 | 37.9 | 42.9 | 50.4 | 54.4 | 60.6 | 65.9 | 71.9 | 78.3 | 88.3 | 98.1 | 110.0 | 121.2 |
| 1 | 26.6 | 31.1 | 35.0 | 38.0 | 43.5 | 50.8 | 54.9 | 61.0 | 66.4 | 72.5 | 79.1 | 89.1 | 99.0 | 111.0 | 122.0 |
| 2 | 26.9 | 31.4 | 35.1 | 38.2 | 44.1 | 51.1 | 55.4 | 61.5 | 66.9 | 73.0 | 80.0 | 89.9 | 100.0 | 112.0 | 122.8 |
| 3 | 27.2 | 31.6 | 35.2 | 38.4 | 44.8 | 51.4 | 55.9 | 62.0 | 67.3 | 73.5 | 80.8 | 90.7 | 101.0 | 112.8 | 123.6 |
| 4 | 27.6 | 32.0 | 35.4 | 38.8 | 45.5 | 51.7 | 56.5 | 62.4 | 67.8 | 74.0 | 81.7 | 91.5 | 102.0 | 113.6 | 124.4 |
| 5 | 28.0 | 32.4 | 35.6 | 39.5 | 46.1 | 52.1 | 57.0 | 62.8 | 68.3 | 74.6 | 82.5 | 92.3 | 103.0 | 114.4 | 125.2 |
| 6 | 28.4 | 32.9 | 35.8 | 40.2 | 46.7 | 52.4 | 57.5 | 63.3 | 68.8 | 75.1 | 83.3 | 93.1 | 104.0 | 115.2 | 126.0 |
| 7 | 28.8 | 33.2 | 36.2 | 40.5 | 47.3 | 52.7 | 58.0 | 63.8 | 69.3 | 75.6 | 84.1 | 94.0 | 105.0 | 116.2 | 126.8 |
| 8 | 29.2 | 33.6 | 36.7 | 40.7 | 48.0 | 53.0 | 58.5 | 64.2 | 69.8 | 76.1 | 84.9 | 94.8 | 106.0 | 117.2 | 127.6 |
| 9 | 29.6 | 34.0 | 37.1 | 41.0 | 48.6 | 53.4 | 59.0 | 64.6 | 70.3 | 76.7 | 85.8 | 95.6 | 107.0 | 118.2 | 128.4 |
| 10 | 30.0 | 34.3 | 37.4 | 41.6 | 49.2 | 53.7 | 59.5 | 65.0 | 70.8 | 77.3 | 86.6 | 96.4 | 108.0 | 119.2 | 129.2 |
| 11 | 30.4 | 34.6 | 37.7 | 42.3 | 49.8 | 54.1 | 60.0 | 65.4 | 71.4 | 77.8 | 87.5 | 97.2 | 109.0 | 120.2 | 130.0 |

## TABLE XVII

### HEIGHT AGES FOR GIRLS
#### (After Olson)

| Months | \  Years 2 | 3 | 4 | 5 | 6 | 7 | 8 | 9 | 10 | 11 | 12 | 13 | 14 | 15 | 16 |
|---|---|---|---|---|---|---|---|---|---|---|---|---|---|---|---|
| 0 | 33.0 | 36.4 | 39.3 | 41.7 | 43.7 | 47.4 | 49.1 | 51.0 | 53.6 | 55.5 | 57.5 | 59.8 | 61.8 | 63.1 | 63.7 |
| 1 | 33.3 | 36.7 | 39.5 | 41.9 | 43.9 | 47.6 | 49.2 | 51.3 | 53.8 | 55.6 | 57.6 | 60.0 | 61.9 | | |
| 2 | 33.7 | 36.9 | 39.6 | 42.0 | 44.1 | 47.7 | 49.4 | 51.5 | 53.9 | 55.8 | 57.8 | 60.1 | 62.0 | | |
| 3 | 34.1 | 37.1 | 39.8 | 42.2 | 44.3 | 47.9 | 49.5 | 51.7 | 54.1 | 56.0 | 58.0 | 60.3 | 62.1 | 63.3 | |
| 4 | 34.4 | 37.3 | 40.0 | 42.3 | 44.6 | 48.0 | 49.7 | 51.9 | 54.2 | 56.1 | 58.2 | 60.4 | 62.3 | | |
| 5 | 34.6 | 37.5 | 40.2 | 42.3 | 44.9 | 48.2 | 49.8 | 52.1 | 54.3 | 56.3 | 58.4 | 60.6 | 62.4 | | |
| 6 | 34.9 | 37.8 | 40.4 | 42.4 | 45.3 | 48.3 | 50.0 | 52.3 | 54.5 | 56.4 | 58.6 | 60.7 | 62.5 | 63.4 | 63.8 |
| 7 | 35.2 | 38.0 | 40.7 | 42.6 | 45.7 | 48.5 | 50.1 | 52.5 | 54.7 | 56.5 | 58.8 | 60.9 | 62.6 | | |
| 8 | 35.5 | 38.3 | 41.0 | 42.8 | 46.0 | 48.6 | 50.3 | 52.7 | 54.9 | 56.8 | 59.0 | 61.0 | 62.7 | | |
| 9 | 35.7 | 38.5 | 41.2 | 42.9 | 46.4 | 48.7 | 50.5 | 52.9 | 55.0 | 57.0 | 59.2 | 61.2 | 62.8 | 63.6 | |
| 10 | 35.9 | 38.7 | 41.3 | 43.2 | 46.7 | 48.8 | 50.6 | 53.1 | 55.2 | 57.2 | 59.4 | 61.4 | 62.9 | | |
| 11 | 36.2 | 39.0 | 41.5 | 43.4 | 47.0 | 49.0 | 50.8 | 53.3 | 55.3 | 57.3 | 59.6 | 61.6 | 63.0 | | |

## TABLE XVIII

### WEIGHT AGE FOR GIRLS
#### (After Olson)

| Months | \  Years 2 | 3 | 4 | 5 | 6 | 7 | 8 | 9 | 10 | 11 | 12 | 13 | 14 | 15 | 16 |
|---|---|---|---|---|---|---|---|---|---|---|---|---|---|---|---|
| 0 | 24.6 | 28.8 | 32.2 | 36.1 | 40.3 | 50.2 | 53.8 | 61.2 | 69.2 | 75.8 | 83.7 | 96.3 | 106.0 | 118.0 | 123.0 |
| 1 | 25.0 | 29.3 | 32.6 | 36.3 | 41.2 | 50.5 | 54.5 | 61.8 | 69.7 | 76.3 | 84.7 | 97.1 | 107.0 | 118.5 | 123.1 |
| 2 | 25.4 | 29.7 | 33.1 | 36.6 | 42.0 | 50.8 | 55.1 | 62.5 | 70.3 | 77.1 | 85.8 | 97.9 | 108.0 | 119.0 | 123.2 |
| 3 | 25.8 | 30.2 | 33.6 | 36.8 | 42.8 | 51.1 | 55.7 | 63.1 | 70.8 | 77.8 | 86.8 | 98.7 | 109.0 | 119.5 | 123.3 |
| 4 | 26.1 | 30.5 | 33.7 | 37.1 | 43.6 | 51.4 | 56.3 | 63.8 | 71.4 | 78.4 | 87.9 | 99.5 | 110.0 | 120.0 | 123.4 |
| 5 | 26.5 | 30.8 | 33.9 | 37.3 | 44.5 | 51.7 | 56.9 | 64.4 | 71.9 | 79.0 | 88.9 | 100.3 | 111.0 | 120.5 | 123.5 |
| 6 | 26.9 | 31.0 | 34.0 | 37.6 | 45.3 | 52.0 | 57.6 | 65.1 | 72.5 | 79.6 | 90.0 | 101.1 | 112.0 | 121.0 | 123.6 |
| 7 | 27.2 | 31.2 | 34.5 | 38.0 | 46.1 | 52.3 | 58.2 | 65.7 | 73.0 | 80.3 | 91.0 | 101.9 | 113.0 | 121.3 | 123.7 |
| 8 | 27.6 | 31.3 | 35.0 | 38.5 | 46.9 | 52.6 | 58.8 | 66.4 | 73.6 | 81.0 | 92.1 | 102.7 | 114.0 | 121.7 | 123.8 |
| 9 | 27.9 | 31.5 | 35.4 | 38.9 | 47.7 | 52.9 | 59.4 | 67.1 | 74.1 | 81.7 | 93.1 | 103.5 | 115.0 | 122.0 | 123.9 |
| 10 | 28.2 | 31.7 | 35.6 | 39.4 | 47.5 | 53.2 | 60.0 | 67.8 | 74.7 | 82.4 | 94.2 | 104.3 | 116.0 | 122.3 | 124.0 |
| 11 | 28.5 | 32.0 | 35.8 | 39.8 | 49.3 | 53.5 | 60.6 | 68.5 | 75.2 | 83.0 | 95.2 | 105.1 | 117.0 | 122.7 | 124.0 |

# TABLE XIX

## DENTAL AGE EQUIVALENTS FOR THE ERUPTION OF PERMANENT TEETH

| No. of Teeth | Boys Dental Age | Girls Dental Age |
|:---:|:---:|:---:|
| 1 | 5–10 | 5–9 |
| 2 | 6–1 | 5–11 |
| 3 | 6–4 | 6–1 |
| 4 | 6–6 | 6–2 |
| 5 | 6–9 | 6–5 |
| 6 | 6–11 | 6–8 |
| 7 | 7–1 | 6–11 |
| 8 | 7–4 | 7–2 |
| 9 | 7–8 | 7–5 |
| 10 | 8–0 | 7–8 |
| 11 | 8–5 | 8–1 |
| 12 | 8–11 | 8–7 |
| 13 | 9–5 | 9–0 |
| 14 | 9–10 | 9–4 |
| 15 | 10–2 | 9–8 |
| 16 | 10–5 | 9–10 |
| 17 | 10–7 | 10–1 |
| 18 | 10–11 | 10–3 |
| 19 | 11–2 | 10–6 |
| 20 | 11–4 | 10–8 |
| 21 | 11–6 | 10–10 |
| 22 | 11–7 | 11–1 |
| 23 | 11–9 | 11–4 |
| 24 | 11–11 | 11–6 |
| 25 | 12–2 | 11–9 |
| 26 | 12–6 | 12–1 |
| 27 | 13–0 | 12–8 |
| 28 | 13–3 | 12–9 |

# Author Index

References to bibliographies have been set in italics.

# Subject Index

517